Federalist Papers 10,51
Constitution
Bill of Rights
Decloration of
Ch 2,3   Independence

AMERICAN
GOVERNMENT

Houghton Mifflin Company ★ Boston

Dallas   Geneva, Illinois   Palo Alto   Princeton, New Jersey

AMERICAN GOVERNMENT

Alan R. Gitelson
Loyola University of Chicago

Robert L. Dudley
George Mason University

Melvin J. Dubnick
University of Kansas

To Idy, Laura, and Rachel, and to my parents, Esther and Alfred Gitelson—as always for their love and understanding.

A.R.G.

To the memory of Phebe M. Dudley in the hope that she would have been proud.

R.L.D.

To Randi, Heather, and Philip.

M.J.D.

Library of Congress Catalog Card Number 87-80372

ISBN: 0-395-35878-7

BCDEFGHIJ-DOH-9543210-898

Illustration Credits

Illustrations by Boston Graphics, Inc.
Cover photograph COMSTOCK, Inc./Michael Stuckey

Chapter 1: **Opener, page xx,** © Michael J. Pettypool/Uniphoto; **3,** © Gabor Demjen/Stock, Boston; **4,** Michael Weisbrot and Family/Stock, Boston; **7,** Charles Steiner/Sygma; **11,** *"Parson Weems' Fable,"* by Grant Wood, 1939, courtesy Amon Carter Museum, Fort Worth, Texas.
Chapter 2: **Opener, page 14,** Photo Researchers, Inc.; **18,** © Michael Evans/Sygma; **25,** Photo Researchers, Inc.; **27,** Sygma; **32,** UPI/Bettmann Newsphotos; **34,** The Granger Collection; **38,** AP/Wide World Photos.

Copyright page continues on page A-63

Contents

Preface

In writing *American Government*, we kept two specific goals in mind. First and foremost, we present students with a concise yet comprehensive picture of American government and politics. Through a traditional organization of fifteen brief chapters, the text covers all of the basic information essential for understanding today's political affairs.

Our second goal is closely tied to the first. We believe that a textbook should help students to think critically about politics, and in so doing to confront certain myths that they or other Americans may hold about government. Thus each chapter begins with a brief exposition of one or two preconceptions or misconceptions found in discussions of politics. A myth—as defined in Chapter 1—is a partial truth, a shorthand way of thinking, or an oversimplification about the role and activities of government and the people who run it. Examples of typical myths include the myth of the omnipotent president, the myth of the courts above politics, and the myth of the manipulative media. Myths pervade the American political system and represent much of the misunderstanding among ordinary citizens about what government does and how politics works.

Naturally, students may not subscribe to all of the myths introduced in the book, so we present evidence—frequently supported by public opinion polls—that many people do hold such beliefs. Indeed the role of myth in American political life did not escape the notice of President John F. Kennedy when he addressed a college commencement audience with the perceptive warning that "the great enemy of the truth is very often not the lie—deliberate, contrived, and dishonest—but the myth—persistent, persuasive, and unrealistic." It is our hope that through understanding the myths of American politics and how they evolved, students will be able to think more critically and systematically about our complex political system.

FEATURES OF AMERICAN GOVERNMENT

Each of the fifteen chapters in the text is concise and to the point, covering every important topic essential to an introductory textbook on American government and politics. To ensure proper scope, we have included separate chapters on public opinion, the mass media, interest groups, bureaucracy, domestic policy, and foreign policy. To help students understand the various topics, we have included several features in each chapter. **Preview outlines** open and point-by-point **summaries** follow each chapter. The **conclusion** of each chapter provides a retrospective glance at the myths in light of the whole chapter discussion. Brief **background boxes** placed strategically within chapters give students additional details on topics related to the text. For example, in Chapter 7 on campaigns and elections, the box elaborates on some of the reasons why more Americans do not register to vote. **"Myth and reality" boxes** appear at key points in most chapters to explore additional myths relevant to the chapter. For instance, in Chapter 9 on the media, the box contrasts the hard news that the media claim to report with an audio-visual transcript of actual television coverage of a presidential campaign. Each chapter includes a handful of **suggested readings** as well as a **list of important terms.** All important terms are given brief definitions in a **glossary** at the end of the book. An **appendix** contains important documents, such as the Declaration of Independence, the Constitution, and *Federalist Papers* Nos. 10 and 51.

THE TEACHING PACKAGE

American Government offers an extensive package of supplementary materials, for both the instructor and the student:

- The *Instructor's Manual,* written by the authors, includes learning objectives, a chapter overview, a discussion of the use of myths in the classroom, lecture outlines, and questions and exercises for class discussion.

- A *Test Item Bank,* prepared by Jonathan Webster of Walla Walla Community College, provides essay questions for each chapter and approximately 50 multiple-choice items per chapter.

- *MicroTest,* a computerized test-generation program, is available for IBM, Apple II, and Macintosh computers. This program enables instructors to prepare custom examinations using the test items in the printed test bank as well as test items they have produced themselves.

- Two-color *Transparencies* of important charts and graphs from the text are assembled in a separate package.

- *Lecture Bank,* available for IBM and Apple II computers, is a computer-based file of detailed ideas for lecture topics that can be edited and printed out, using any standard word processor.

- *GPA: Grade Performance Analyzer* is a microcomputerized "grade book" that keeps course records, creates class rosters, analyzes scores, computes averages, and converts scores to letter grades.

- The *Study Guide,* also written by Jonathan Webster, is keyed closely to the text and features many exercises with write-in blanks for the student. An introductory section focuses on study skills, such as outlining, reviewing, and analyzing charts, graphs, and tables.

- *Microstudy Plus,* also available in IBM and Apple II formats, is a computerized study guide that enables students to respond to multiple-choice and true/false questions reproduced from the printed study guide. This program gives students immediate feedback on both correct and incorrect responses and provides page references that link the questions directly to the text.

ACKNOWLEDGMENTS

Many people contribute to the success of a textbook and such is the case with *American Government.* We happily acknowledge the many helpful comments of the following reviewers. A great deal of the credit for whatever merit this work may have can be attributed to their suggestions:

Hugh M. Arnold, Clayton State College
Theodore S. Arrington, University of North Carolina at Charlotte
C. C. Bailey, Cabrillo College
John T. Barnard, Green River Community College
J. Vincent Buck, California State University, Fullerton
Allan J. Cigler, University of Kansas
Kristina K. Cline, Riverside City College
Thom M. Hendrickson, Cerritos College
Katherine A. Hinckley, University of Akron
Doris R. Knight, Holyoke Community College
Dale A. Krane, North Texas State University
Michael A. Maggiotto, University of South Carolina
Thomas R. Marshall, University of Texas at Arlington
Lawrence W. Miller, Collin County Community College, Texas
Betty Jane Moore, Prince George's Community College
William J. Murin, University of Wisconsin—Parkside
Bruce I. Oppenheimer, University of Houston
Elliot E. Slotnick, Ohio State University

Barbara S. Stone, California State University, Fullerton
Richard J. Tobin, State University of New York at Buffalo
Janice Tulloss, Northeastern University
Jonathan Webster, Walla Walla Community College

We would like to thank Jonathan Webster for his tireless efforts in writing a first-rate *Study Guide* and *Test Item Bank.* Able research assistance provided by Julie Soboleski is also much appreciated.

In an undertaking of this magnitude, authors realize early on that the success of a textbook is closely tied to the editors associated with the project. Fortunately for us, we were blessed with a staff at Houghton Mifflin of creative, dedicated, and sensitive people. We are much indebted to their intelligence and commitment.

We want to give unqualified thanks, filled with love, to Idy, Laura, and Rachel Gitelson; Judy, Pat, and Michael Dudley; and Randi, Heather, and P. D. Dubnick, who tolerated our absence on more evenings and weekends than we would like to remember as we labored on this book.

Finally, we would like to emphasize the equal role played by all three authors in the writing of this textbook. There was no junior partner in this project. Gitelson's name appears first on the cover because he administered the project. A flip of a coin determined the order of names for Dudley and Dubnick.

A. R. G.
R. L. D.
M. J. D.

AMERICAN GOVERNMENT

1

CHAPTER

Myth and Reality in American Politics

WHAT GOVERNMENTS DO

WHAT GOVERNMENT IS

FUNDAMENTAL ISSUES OF GOVERNMENT AND POLITICS

Who Should Rule? *Representative democracy*

How Much Should Government Be Doing? *Liberal and conservative perspectives*

Where Should Government Power Be Located? *Local, state, and national government*

MYTH AND REALITY IN AMERICAN GOVERNMENT AND POLITICS

OVERVIEW OF THIS BOOK

1

The discussion in the introductory class on American government starts off on a mild note. The professor asks two questions: "What is government? For that matter, what is politics?" Students in the class think for a few moments about the answer. Finally, one student speaks up. "Government," he says, "is a necessary evil that we need for our nation to function, and politics is the game some people play in order to benefit from that evil." Many of his classmates agree with this rather cynical response.

The reaction is not surprising, for it is easy to be skeptical about the role of government and the motives of politicians. Much of that skepticism stems from the quality of information Americans receive about government and politics. Negative stories and editorials about public officials and politicians fill the mass media—television, radio, newspapers, and magazines. Conversations with friends and neighbors often reinforce these negative perspectives. Little wonder then that we have so little faith in government and those who run it.

The student's answer, however, reflects more than skepticism. It also shows limited understanding of what government does and how politics works. Like many Americans, the student may have a general sense of the impact of government and politics but is unaware of the specific ways in which the public sector affects our lives.

Consider the price of a new car or the interest you might pay on a college loan. Would it surprise you to learn that the cost of both is greatly influenced by government? After all, the government requires that all car manufacturers meet specific pollution emission and safety standards, and the expense of doing so affects the price of cars. Similarly, the interest rate charged by your local bank or credit union reflects a number of requirements that government imposes on financial institutions.

Or consider the price of the clothes you wear, the condition of the roads you use, the availability of over-the-counter drugs, and the cost of hospital care. Think about the quality of the water you drink, the content of the textbooks used in high school science classes, the cost of gasoline, the cleanliness of your streets, and so on. These are just a few of the areas in which government and politics have an impact on your life and the lives of those around you.

Why then are Americans so doubtful about the value of government? We argue in this textbook that many of the opinions Americans hold about politicians and government are steeped in myths—partial truths and over-simplifications about the role and activities of government and the people that run it. Myths pervade the American political system and cause a great deal of misunderstanding about what government does and how politics works. One of our objectives in this book is to make you aware of such myths. Another is to inform you about the complex realities that the myths

Government is where we least expect it Even college students relaxing at the beach must obey the powerful, if little-noticed voice of government authority and regulation.

sometimes hide. We believe that separating myths from reality will help you to start thinking critically about American government and politics. First, however, let us consider the meaning and importance of some key terms.

★ ★ ★
WHAT GOVERNMENTS DO

Has government always been important in the lives of most Americans? The answer is yes. Government has always affected economic and social life, but in the past its impact had not been as widespread as it is today.

Early in the nation's history, citizens expected government to perform such traditional functions as providing for law and order and resisting aggression by foreign nations. But government often did more.

From the time when the first European settlers established their communities, colonial governments played a major role in developing and regulating local economies. Colonial (and later state) governments helped to finance new enterprises, build ports, construct turnpikes and canals, and even control wages and prices in local markets. The Northwest Ordinances, laws passed in the 1780s, established the rules for selling land and organizing local governments in the large territory stretching from the Ohio River to the Mississippi River and north to the Great Lakes. Land was even reserved to support public schools. One of the earliest examples of the national government's role as "an active promoter of the economy" was its 1803 purchase of the Louisiana Territory. This vast territory was vital to the prosperity of farmers working the lands along the entire length of the Mississippi River.[1]

The role of government continued to grow throughout the 1800s and early 1900s. Attempts to solve the economic and social problems of the Great Depression of the 1930s led to an explosion of new programs. Soon an army of bureaucrats was managing the economy, promoting stable economic growth by helping find jobs for the unemployed, and enforcing price controls designed to hold down the prices of goods and services.

As the United States became a mobile society, Americans demanded that the national government pay more attention to problems once solved by families and communities—problems of the poor, the handicapped, the elderly, and others. Between 1932 and the present, literally millions of Americans have been touched directly or indirectly by programs covering everything from early childhood nutrition, health care, and unemployment benefits to food stamps and social security for the elderly.

The government, however, did not limit its interest just to the economy and social welfare programs. As destruction threatened the vast American

A social safety net A product of the expansion of social services in the 1960s, food stamps are a kind of grocery store currency that can be redeemed for food. Despite this and other innovative government programs, poverty remains a pressing problem in the United States.

forests and pollution tainted air and water, Americans turned to government for environmental management, ranging from conservation programs to regulations affecting many polluting industries. In support of such goals as preventing environmental damage and securing a steady supply of energy, government has lowered speed limits on highways, pushed for the development of nuclear energy, and implemented a variety of other policies. In short, government has grown more important than ever, entering more and more areas of our lives.

★ ★ ★
WHAT GOVERNMENT IS

Who or what is government and how does it accomplish its varied responsibilities? In brief, **government** comprises those institutions and officials who execute and enforce public programs. Government is the presidents, judges, bureaucrats, legislators, and other elected and appointed officials who work in the institutions that make up the executive, legislative, and judicial branches of federal, state, and local governmental systems. The power to enact and enforce laws is crucial to the functioning of government. If citizens did not accept the power of government, its decisions would have no meaning.

The work of government involves politics. In its most general sense, **politics** is the act of influencing or controlling government for the purposes of formulating or guiding public policy. We will be discussing the politics of running for or being appointed to office, choosing policy alternatives, and bargaining, negotiating, and compromising to get the policies enacted and executed. The politics of student loans, for example, involves presidents and legislators negotiating such issues as who receives loan benefits and who pays the bills. And these presidents and legislators are influenced in their decisions by students, parents, bankers, and college administrators.

★ ★ ★
FUNDAMENTAL ISSUES OF GOVERNMENT AND POLITICS

By now government must strike you as much more than the necessary evil cited by the skeptical student at the beginning of this chapter. Clearly, modern societies need governments to solve a complex array of problems. But how much government is enough and how should it be organized? Who should rule? How much should government be doing? Where should government power be located?

Who Should Rule?

The question of who should rule has been answered in a variety of ways throughout the ages. The ancient Greek philosopher Aristotle believed governments could be classified into three general types: government by the one, by the few, and by the many. For each type, he believed, there is a good, or "right," form and a bad, or "wrong," form. A right form of government is one that serves the common interests of the people. A wrong form of government serves the personal interests of the ruler.

When discussing government by the many that serves the common interests of the people, Aristotle used the term *polity.* He used the term *democracy* to refer to a government of the many that serves their personal interests. Aristotle and many other political thinkers through the ages have feared democracy, believing that self-interest would rule if government was turned over to the "rabble in the streets." In fact, his other term for democracy was "mobocracy," or rule by the mob.

Aristotle's views on democracy would not be popular today. Most Americans believe that democracy is the most appropriate type of government for the United States. What do they mean by **democracy**? Their idea can best be described as a belief in government based on the consent and will of the majority. Asked "who should rule?" a vast majority of Americans would state that the people—the many—should govern.

However, American belief in democracy does not mean a commitment to direct rule by the majority. As we will see, the framers of the Constitution, as well as many other Americans, did not believe that government should be directly in the hands of the people. The United States is a **republic,** or **representative democracy,** in which decisions are made by elected or appointed officials. In effect, the people govern indirectly through their presidents, members of Congress, governors, mayors, state legislators, and other elected officials.

How Much Should Government Be Doing?

What should be the scope of government activity? This has been a critical question for Americans for more than two centuries. Some people believe that government is unnecessary and that all the problems now solved by government can be left to other social institutions, such as the family or private organizations. This set of beliefs, called **anarchism,** has very few followers in the United States. Another group of people wants government to do no more than what is minimally necessary to maintain law and order, protect basic individual rights, and provide for national defense. This extremely individualistic view has been associated with the **libertarian** movement in recent years.

A conservative rides here The cluster of beliefs that we have labeled conservative are well represented by these bumper stickers, which call for—among other changes—reversal of the Supreme Court's decisions on abortion and school prayer.

The majority of citizens subscribe to conservative or liberal views closer to the center of the political spectrum. It is important to note, though, that few Americans can be labeled as strict conservatives or liberals. In fact, many people display both conservative and liberal tendencies.

Conservatism is a set of beliefs tending to favor individual liberty and resistance to government activity. Conservatives prefer private initiative over public intervention on most economic and social issues. They tend, however, to strongly support government activity in the maintenance of social order. Thus, many conservatives support strong government intervention on such issues as punishment of criminals and the banning of pornography.

Liberalism is a set of beliefs holding that government must ensure individual liberty but at the same time promote equality. Thus, liberals tend strongly to support traditional personal rights of freedom of speech, but also tend to favor strong government intervention to provide for equal opportunity, social welfare, and job programs, and to promote school busing plans as a means toward integration and affirmative action programs for women and minorities.

Democratic socialism advocates more substantial governmental intervention in the economic system than does liberalism. Placing a high priority on government solutions to problems whenever they arise, it also argues for limits on private ownership of the means of producing goods and services. One of its major goals is organizing workers into an articulate voice in government. These changes, according to socialists, can be brought about through democratic institutions.

By contrast, **communism** advocates a centrally directed economic and political system. Communism is based on the view that it is necessary to abolish the institution of private property and that this action involves an inevitable struggle between the workers and upper classes. Many communists assert that change can only come about by revolutionary means. Other communists, however, particularly those in many Western European nations, argue that change can be introduced through representative institutions.

Extremely individualistic or revolutionary views have never gained much support in the United States. This nation has generally taken paths advocated by conservatism and liberalism. Both approaches have influenced government in the years since World War II. And both have played a major role in determining how Americans answer questions about what the scope of government should be.

Where Should Government Power Be Located?

Should government power be located in local communities, in governments close to the people? Or should the power to take action be located in the political center of the nation, Washington, D.C.? Or, for that matter, should it be located in the fifty state capitals—in Albany, Springfield, Austin, Sacramento, and Topeka? Answers to these questions are complex because the range of government activities is so broad.

Would it make sense, for example, for the national government to run your town's fire department? Would it be efficient for you to call the FBI when someone tried to steal your car? Most Americans believe in local self-government because they feel that many problems can best be solved there. Many citizens also argue that local officials are more democratic and open to the public's view than is state or national government.

Although problem solving by local government is often humane and efficient, there is no way that towns and cities or even states can deal effectively with foreign policy, national defense, regional unemployment, and other major economic and social issues. Consequently, most Americans also believe that only the national government, with its vast economic resources and national perspective, can tackle such issues. Many people also argue that such policies reflect the will of the American people, and that federal-level policies are less likely to discriminate against racial, religious, and political minorities than local policies.

Most complex modern societies have found that to ensure effective governance intermediate levels of government are needed as well. Different nations have solved this problem in different ways. The United States has developed a unique solution that allows national, state, and local governments

BACKGROUND 1.1

Myth and Reality in Contemporary Politics

In the final minutes of the 1950 movie *The Jackie Robinson Story*, the narrator boldly declares that America is a land "where every child has the opportunity to become president or play baseball for the Brooklyn Dodgers." In many respects the quote best reflects our meaning of the word *myth*—a partial truth that is a distortion of reality. Everyone knows, of course, that no one can grow up to play baseball for the Brooklyn Dodgers anymore. He or she also knows that not everyone can grow up to become president of the United States. Blacks, women, and Jews, for example, still find this achievement unattainable. Yet for many Americans the myth that anyone can be president persists.

Myths are a basic part of the American experience. Americans are raised on myths. Stories about George Washington admitting that he cut down his father's cherry tree and Abraham Lincoln reading by the light of a flickering fire are perhaps the first history we learn. Although the tale of patriotic, honest George contains strong elements of truth, according to observers of the time, Washington could sometimes be an "impossible prig." And while Lincoln did indeed rise from humble beginnings, the trials of his youth are probably greatly exaggerated, as are his patience, tolerance, and wisdom.

The sources of cherished myths are not easy to trace. Such myths come from novels, movies, television, and even textbooks. For the most part, these myths are useful; they provide Americans with heroes and a sense of national identity. In fact, the Washington and Lincoln myths speak well for the nation, reflecting as they do respect for the qualities attached to the memories of these great men.

However, myths can also blind people to reality, and as such they can be dangerous. President John F. Kennedy, speaking at the Yale University commencement in 1962, suggested that myth is a distraction everywhere—in government as in business, in politics as in economics, in foreign affairs as in domestic affairs. "The great enemy of truth," he suggested, "is very often not the lie—deliberate, contrived, and dishonest—but the myth—persistent, persuasive, and unrealistic." Thus the myth in the 1960s and early 1970s that we were winning the war in Vietnam contributed heavily to our continued fighting in that country long after it was apparent to many observers that the war was lost.

In the following pages you will encounter many myths—great and small—that give an incomplete view of the record of American government and politics. Many have served the nation well and given the American people a sense of pride in their institutions and in themselves as a people. Other myths have served the country poorly and have led to the kind of skepticism about government expressed by the student in the very opening paragraphs of this chapter.

Will the contrast between myth and reality simply add to that skepticism? We think not. Although the truth is often hard to find, we argue that in the reality of American government and politics there is much cause for pride. Even difficult realities are worth your attention because there lie both the possibility for a better understanding of the strengths and weaknesses of the American political system and the light for constructive political change.

to share power. We will discuss the struggles over the location of power in greater detail in Chapter 3, on federalism.

★ ★ ★

MYTH AND REALITY IN AMERICAN GOVERNMENT AND POLITICS

As must be clear by now, government plays an important role in the lives of most Americans. Does it matter that many citizens are skeptical or harbor misconceptions about its value? We argue that it does—that government in a democracy depends on its citizens developing a reasonable understanding of what is happening in their communities, states, and nation. Ill-informed citizens are often indifferent to politics. Yet participation has always been a basic principle of the American system.

Becoming an informed citizen takes time and effort. Government is complicated, and understanding it does not come easily. To be informed, you need to read newspapers or news magazines regularly, listen to television and radio reports, talk about politics with family and friends, and take advantage of civics, history, and government courses.

Even informed citizens use mental short cuts to help them through the maze of government. No one, no matter how conscientious, can possibly have an informed position on every important issue. For instance, do you think it serves the country's best interests to send troops to Central America or believe that prayer should be permitted in the public schools? These questions are so complex that some people base their answers on **ideology,** a set of strongly held beliefs about social processes and institutions. Taking a conservative or liberal position on foreign or economic policy sometimes helps to reduce the complexities of these issues to manageable size.

As we will see throughout this textbook, in analyzing political problems and in making political decisions, we use other short cuts—for example, identification with political parties. The problem, of course, is that short cuts may give an incomplete view of the scenery. Some conservatives argue that the United States should intervene in Central American nations such as Nicaragua and El Salvador—that these countries are vital to our national security because of their proximity to the United States. These conservatives assert that the Soviet Union is responsible for unrest in the region. Liberals often respond that the unrest stems from local poverty and the oppression of previous regimes and that the United States should let the countries manage their own internal affairs. An appropriate policy may fall somewhere between these two positions.

Myths are another kind of short cut. They are oversimplifications that misrepresent political reality. To state it formally, **myths,** as we use them in

The cherry tree myth In this painting, titled *Parson Weems's Fable,* Grant Wood makes fun of the patriotic myth. Note that the artist has given Washington an adult face based on the famous Gilbert Stuart portrait. Its point is to emphasize the myth-making of the adoring parson, who invented the story.

this book, are widely held, popular attitudes about politics and government that give a distorted view of reality. They are not necessarily falsehoods, but rather misconceptions and oversimplifications that contain nuggets of truth. Thus, for example, it is a myth to say that all Democrats are liberals and all Republicans are conservatives. Such a statement misrepresents reality. Some Republicans are quite liberal, just as some Democrats are quite conservative. Liberal Republican Senator Lowell Weicker of Connecticut and conservative Democratic Senator Howell Heflin of Alabama are just two examples.

Myths can spring up because individuals have inadequate information. For example, an incomplete knowledge of history has given rise to the myth that the founding fathers were homespun freedom fighters who grabbed their rifles off the wall and rushed out to ambush the British. It is a good story, and certainly some of the founding fathers conformed to this mythic image. But many more were businessmen, bankers, merchants, and aristocratic farmers who used sophisticated arguments to persuade their fellow colonists, as well as foreign governments, to support the Revolution and who developed brilliant guerrilla tactics to outwit the better-trained, better-equipped British army.

Myths also develop because people find them more fitting than an often uninspiring reality. The myth that anyone can grow up to be president is a good example. As you will see in Chapter 7, on elections, women, blacks, Jews, and other ethnic and religious minorities are not likely to occupy the White House in the near future.

Perhaps you do not subscribe to many of the myths that we will discuss in this text. However, we will offer you evidence that many people hold such beliefs. You will find in our analysis some useful tools for thinking critically about America's complex political system.

★ ★ ★
OVERVIEW OF THIS BOOK

The first step in developing a realistic view of American politics is to become informed about the major institutions and processes of government. Providing you with that information is the main purpose of this book. As you learn, for example, what bureaucrats do and how the agencies of the executive branch interact with Congress and the public, you will get a sense of the reality behind the myth that bureaucrats are lazy and incompetent.

We begin with an overview of the background to American politics: the historical and constitutional basis for the organization and functioning of the system. Chapter 2 deals with the Constitution—its creation and its principal features. In Chapter 3, on federalism, we consider the relationship among the various levels of government. Chapter 4 looks at some limits on government power: the civil liberties protected by the Constitution and civil rights guaranteed to citizens by the Constitution and by law.

We then turn to a discussion of the activities and institutions that link citizens to their government. In Chapter 5, we discuss the opinions people have about government and how these opinions affect their participation in politics. The role of political parties is the subject of Chapter 6. Chapter 7 considers the most widespread form of participation: nominations, campaigns, and elections. This discussion is followed by an analysis of two important institutions that influence the political system: interest groups and the media (chapters 8 and 9). The media have an enormous impact on the way people perceive politics. Interest groups also shape politics by making it possible for people with similar goals to band together to influence public policy.

Chapters 10, 11, 12, and 13 discuss the four central institutions of government: Congress, the presidency, the bureaucracy, and the courts. We begin with Congress because for the Founders it was the first branch of government—in fact, it had been the only branch during the earliest days of the union, prior to the adoption of the Constitution. Finally, in Chapters 14 and 15, we examine the nature of domestic and foreign policy.

In each chapter, we will point out one or more myths that are associated with each topic. For example, in Chapter 6, on political parties, we will tell you about Tweedledum and Tweedledee, the identical twins from Lewis Carroll's *Through the Looking-Glass.* Then we will ask whether, in the wonderland of American politics, the Republicans and Democrats are as alike as Tweedledum and Tweedledee. As we consider this and other myths, we will show you the nuggets of truth that have given rise to them, as well as the ways in which they distort reality.

We hope that you will find this approach interesting and that it will stimulate discussion and debate regarding some of your basic assumptions about government and politics. Like the classic tales of the Greek gods, the myths of American politics reflect the rich imagination and the anxieties of those who created them.

★ ★ ★

KEY TERMS

government
politics
democracy
republic
representative democracy
anarchism
libertarian

conservatism
liberalism
democratic socialism
communism
ideology
myths

★ ★ ★

SUGGESTED READING

- Robertson, James Oliver. *American Myth, American Reality.* New York: Hill and Wang, 1980. A survey of the various myths used by Americans, especially those myths related to government. The author not only highlights different myths but shows the important role played by myth in shaping both the American past and present.

CHAPTER 2

Constitutional Foundations

They began arriving in Philadelphia in May 1787. Most of their names are unfamiliar to us, but collectively we honor them as this nation's founders. There were fifty-five of them. That summer they took part in a rare moment of "decisive political creation": they applied their knowledge and experience of government to the creation of a new constitution.[1] They represented some of the best political minds the young nation had to offer. Among their number were merchants, physicians, bankers, planters, and soldiers. Over half of them were trained in the law, and more than two-thirds had served in the Continental Congress, which governed the new nation during the Revolutionary War.

The meeting in Philadelphia came about because many of the country's political leaders felt that the national government under the **Articles of Confederation** was not strong enough to cope with the young republic's problems. Ratified in 1781 as America's first constitution, the Articles had established a loose union of states and a congress with few powers. By 1787 it was clear that the government under the Articles could not conduct an effective foreign policy or settle disputes that developed between the states.

The worst failure of congress under the Articles was its inability to deal with the nation's financial problems. Congress had no power to tax, and its requests for funds from the states were largely ignored. The country's public debt remained unpaid, and there were no funds to cover the interest. When some states began to print tons of worthless paper money to pay off their debts, spiraling inflation hit the economy.

Within the states, many small farmers faced bankruptcy and the loss of their farms. In western Massachusetts, where the situation was particularly bad, a group of farmers led by Daniel Shays disrupted court foreclosure proceedings and tried to seize a government arsenal. This incident became known as **Shays' Rebellion.** It convinced many of the nation's leaders that major changes had to be made in the American constitutional system.[2]

And so the delegates gathered in Philadelphia to do something about the Articles of Confederation. According to observers at the time, the delegates were a group of rather distinct personalities.[3] Gouverneur Morris, a delegate from New York, was described as possessing "one of the best organized heads on the continent, but without manners, and, if his enemies are to be believed, without principles. . . ." Hugh Williamson, a North Carolina physician and astronomer, was regarded as "Extremely bizarre, loving to hold forth, but speaking with spirit." And Nicholas Gilman, a delegate from New Hampshire, was characterized as a "pretentious young man; little loved by his colleagues. . . ."

No women took part in the Constitutional Convention, nor did members of any racial minority. Mostly well educated and wealthy, the delegates included at least two men of international reputation: George Washington and Benjamin Franklin. Washington, an imposing figure, was unanimously elected to chair the meeting. A tight-lipped person, he contributed little to the convention's debates but could enforce its strict rules because the delegates feared his anger.

Benjamin Franklin was eighty-two at the time and other delegates constantly sought his opinions. They listened to his every word, and his support helped in the eventual passage of the document. During the hours of debate, Franklin often gazed at a picture of the sun just above the horizon, which decorated the back of Washington's chair. He often wondered if the picture represented sunrise or sunset. As the delegates finally signed the Constitution, Franklin told those around him that he no longer doubted "it is a rising, and not a setting sun."[4]

To a great many Americans, the image of the U.S. Constitution as a rising sun seems appropriate, since the document heralded a new day in the history of political systems. For two centuries the Constitution has stood as a symbol of the American nation and its people—an impressive accomplishment in several respects.

In seven clearly written Articles and twenty-six Amendments, the Constitution establishes the fundamental institutions and rules that today govern a nation of more than 242 million people. Furthermore, the provisions of the Constitution have proved extremely adaptable. During the past two centuries American society has undergone changes in size and character that the Founders could not have imagined. Yet the government they established remains strong.

Most striking of all is the degree of respect the Constitution receives from the American people. In public opinion polls and in other forums, Americans express their overwhelming pride in the constitutional system, and few want changes in the structure of government established by the Constitution.[5] For most, in fact, the document represents the American people as a nation.[6] The reason for this view, according to the late Theodore H. White, is that the American nation is tied together by a commonly accepted idea rather than by geography—an idea about government embodied in the United States constitutional system.[7]

The constitutional idea has endured for the last two hundred years because of the spirit and resourcefulness of the American people, the vast natural resources of this continent, and the economic prosperity of the nation throughout most of its history. What has greatly helped to keep it strong, however, is the myth of the timeless and perfect Constitution.

According to this myth, the U.S. Constitution is more than a legal document. It is a blueprint for a timeless and nearly flawless "machine that would go of itself"—a device so perfectly crafted by the founders that it has needed only a bit of adjustment and repair during its 200 years of constant operation. There have been attempts to tinker with the constitutional framework, and twenty-six times the blueprint has been modified through the

A not-so-perfect Constitution Like the children shown here, most people feel awe in the presence of the actual Constitution. Nevertheless, many blacks are questioning the myth of the timeless and perfect Constitution. As federal Judge Leon Higgenbotham recently said, "Under the original document blacks were not people. . . . [They were] viewed as property, as subhumans."

formal amendment process. But to those who adhere to the myth of the timeless and perfect Constitution, the machinery designed by the framers remains intact and operates as efficiently as ever.[8]

If this is a myth, what is the reality? We will show you in this chapter that there is more to the Constitution than the words written on the parchment enshrined in the National Archives. The Constitution is a creation of the late 1700s that has been constantly reinterpreted and adapted to grapple with modern problems. You will see that the Constitution's meaning is bound by time rather than timeless. The framers' genius lay in their ability to structure a governmental system that combines long-term stability and a flexible capacity to change (see Myth and Reality 2.1).

The impact of the Constitution on the way government works will be evident in many chapters of this book. It is appropriate therefore to begin our story of American government by exploring the provisions and principles that make up the American constitutional system.

★ ★ ★
THE GOALS OF THE CONSTITUTION

The framers of the Constitution had several goals. To shape a viable national government, they needed to establish its authority and work out its basic structures. Consequently, they created the three branches of government and defined and limited their powers. They also worked out the procedures by which the Constitution itself could be changed.

Establishing Authority

Governments are worthless unless they can effectively exercise political power. How many Americans would file their federal income taxes with the Internal Revenue Service by April 15 each year if they felt that the government could not collect those revenues? How many car manufacturers would include pollution-reducing devices in their vehicles if they believed the government could not enforce its environmental protection laws? The power of any government is enhanced by the willingness of its citizens to obey government officials. A government is most effective when its citizens believe that those officials have a legitimate right to pass and enforce laws. That is why the establishment of government authority is so important.

The authority of the U.S. government is rooted in the Preamble to the Constitution. In a few words, the framers make clear the source of authority for the republic. "We the People . . ." begins the Preamble. The choice of words was important. The Articles of Confederation were regarded as an agreement among the states. The Constitution leaves no doubt that the national government's right to exercise authority comes directly from the people and not from the states.

Structuring Authority

The Constitution establishes the core institutions responsible for governing the nation. It does so in the first three Articles, which define the primary structures of government and outline the roles, powers, and responsibilities of the public officials who occupy those offices.

The basic structure emerged from a series of compromises reached among the delegates to the Constitutional Convention. When the convention opened,

MYTH AND REALITY 2.1

The Apolitical Constitution

A widely held belief among Americans is that questions about what the Constitution says and what its framers intended when they wrote the document are apolitical, that is, above politics. According to this myth, constitutional issues are the domain of legal scholars, and the courts make decisions without regard to social conditions or political circumstances. In fact, the Constitution is more than simply a legal document and is often at the center of some very political controversies.

In 1985 the American public was treated to a rare public debate among key members of the legal community about how the Constitution was to be interpreted. Attorney General Edwin Meese, head of the Justice Department and a close friend of President Reagan, spoke out against rulings by federal court judges that he believed violated the original intentions of the framers. Meese, a conservative, felt that the federal judiciary, led by the justices of the Supreme Court, had abandoned the historical intentions of the Constitution's framers and had inappropriately changed the document's meaning to fit their own ideological views of the law. "Those who framed the

Constitution," Meese argues, "chose their words carefully; they debated at great length the most minute points. The language they chose meant something. It is incumbent upon the court to determine what that meaning was."

Meese's comments drew responses from two members of the Supeme Court. Justices John Paul Stevens and William J. Brennan defended themselves and the rest of the judiciary by noting that the courts must always interpret the Constitution in light of the political, social, and economic issues as they see them. "I still work hard to interpret the Constitution as I believe it must be read," stated Justice Brennan.

The quotations above are from Edwin Meese III, "The Attorney General's View of the Supreme Court: Toward a Jurisprudence of Original Intention," *Public Administration Review*, 45 special issue (November 1985), 704; and (Brennan quote) Jeffrey T. Leeds, "A Life on the Court," *The New York Times Magazine*, October 5, 1986, p. 77. See also Richard Claude, "The Supreme Court Nine: Judicial Responsibility and Responsiveness," in Leroy N. Rieselbach, ed., *People vs. Government: The Responsiveness of American Institutions* (Bloomington, Ind.: Indiana University Press, 1975), pp. 119–150.

the delegation from Virginia offered a series of resolutions for the meeting to consider. Under the **Virginia Plan,** there would be a unicameral (one-house) congress in which each state's representation would be based on its population relative to other states. Under the Articles of Confederation, a state could send several representatives to congress, but each state had only a single vote. And although the Articles did not provide for separate executive or judicial branches of government at the national level, the Virginia Plan called for both.

Delegates from states with larger populations welcomed the Virginia Plan's provisions. But the smaller states felt it necessary to offer a counterproposal. Known as the **New Jersey Plan,** it called for strengthening the existing Articles by adding executive and judicial offices. The powers of congress would also be increased, especially its ability to force reluctant states to cooperate with the national government. The delegates, however, voted to reject the New Jersey Plan. They disagreed on a number of issues, particularly the question of representation.

To avoid a stalemate, the delegates adopted the **Connecticut Compromise,** which led to the acceptance of the structure of American national government as we know it today. It called for the establishment of a Congress of the United States consisting of two bodies, the House of Representatives and the Senate. Article I of the Constitution outlines the composition of this bicameral (two-house) legislature and describes the rules and restrictions that apply to members of the legislative branch.

The Connecticut Compromise also included provisions for executive and judicial branches of government. Article II establishes the executive offices of president and vice president. The article also specifies their qualifications for office and the method of election (which has since been changed). Later sections describe the president's general responsibilities and provide guidelines for relations with Congress. Article III creates a judicial branch of government that is composed of "one supreme Court, and . . . such inferior Courts as the Congress may from time to time ordain and establish."

The Connecticut Compromise was just one of a number of solutions to problems plaguing the delegates. The economic and political crises that had brought the framers to Philadelphia were due in part to conflicts between the states and the national government. The convention concluded that a **federal system** would answer the problem. In Article IV, the framers defined a system in which some powers of government were to be exercised at the national level, other powers were reserved to the states, and still others would be shared between the two.

Distributing and Describing Government Powers

A series of compromises helped define the powers of the three branches of government. The right to make laws rests in the hands of Congress, the authority to execute and enforce laws belongs to the presidency, and the power to hear and judge disputes arising from the law lies in the courts.

Of all the powers set out in the Constitution, those given to Congress in Article I are primary. Among them are a detailed list of responsibilities including the authority to tax, borrow money, regulate commerce, coin money, declare war, and raise and support an army and navy. These and most of the other powers named in Section 8 of Article I are the **delegated powers** of American national government.

The same section of Article I provides Congress with the authority "To make all Laws which shall be necessary and proper for carrying into Execution the foregoing Powers, and all other Powers vested by this Constitution in the Government of the United States. . . ." This "necessary and proper" clause establishes **implied powers** for Congress that go explicitly beyond those listed elsewhere in the Constitution.

For example, the Constitution does not expressly grant Congress the power to establish a national bank or to regulate the American banking system. Nevertheless, after considerable debate, the First Congress chartered a national Bank of the United States in 1791 as a means of implementing its power to coin and regulate the value of money. That Bank survived until President Andrew Jackson's opposition caused it to expire in the 1830s. In 1913 Congress once again set up a system for managing the banking system. That agency, the Federal Reserve System, still regulates our nation's major banks. Congress's right to set up such banks is implied in the "necessary and proper clause."

The Constitution does not list the powers of the states. Instead, the Tenth Amendment makes clear that all powers not expressly given to the national government or denied to the states belong to the states. These **reserved powers** include such responsibilities as providing for public education, building local roads and highways, and regulating trade within a state's borders.

Limiting Governmental Powers

The Constitution also sets limits on both the national and the state governments. For example, Section 9 of Article I forbids Congress to suspend the privilege of a writ of habeas corpus except in time of rebellion or invasion. A *writ of habeas corpus* protects people against arbitrary arrest and detention. Another provision prohibits the national government from passing a bill of attainder or an ex post facto law. A *bill of attainder* declares a person guilty of a crime and sets punishment without the benefit of a formal trial. An *ex post facto law* makes an action criminal even though it was legal when it was performed.

Perhaps the best known limits on the powers of the national government are the first ten Amendments to the Constitution, popularly known as the **Bill of Rights.** These Amendments guarantee the fundamental liberties of citizens. They were added to the Constitution to satisfy the demands of critics who complained that the original document did not adequately protect individual rights.

The First Amendment protects freedom of expression—speech, press, assembly, and religion. Other amendments prohibit national officials from infringing on the right to bear arms (Second), from arbitrarily ordering families to quarter soldiers (Third), from conducting unreasonable searches and seizures (Fourth), from forcing any person to testify against himself or herself in a criminal trial (Fifth), and from requiring excessive bail or inflicting "cruel or unusual punishment" (Eighth).

The Fifth Amendment also forbids the national government to take any action that might deprive a person "of life, liberty, or property" without "due process of law" or "just compensation." The Sixth ensures a "speedy trial, by an impartial jury" in criminal cases, and the Seventh extends the right of jury trial to civil cases.

The Constitution places limits on the powers and actions of the states as well. Section 10 of Article I, for instance, contains a list of powers denied to the states. Other sections set limits on the power of the states in relation to each other and to the national government. Article IV requires that each state give full faith and credit to the "Acts, Records, and judicial Proceedings of every other state." It also mandates that the "Citizens of each State shall be entitled to all Privileges and Immunities of Citizens in the Several States." The latter provisions were the source of considerable debate and compromise at the convention as the framers sought to create a strong national government while maintaining state autonomy.

How could they ensure that laws of the national government would take priority over the laws of the states? One proposal called for giving Congress the power to declare state laws illegal if they interfered with congressional policies. Another asked for a constitutional provision allowing national officials to use armed force if necessary to obtain state compliance. In the end, the delegates settled for the statement found in Article VI. It declares that the Constitution and all laws and treaties "made in Pursuance thereof" would be considered "the supreme Law of the Land. . . ." Commonly referred to as the supremacy clause, this provision was to be enforced through both national and state courts.

Changing the Constitution

Finally, like all constitutions, the American document also describes the way it can be changed. The framers did not make amendment easy. The procedures require action at both the state and the national level (see Figure 2.1). Amendments can be proposed in either of two ways: by a two-thirds vote of both houses of Congress or by a national convention called by Congress at the request of two-thirds of the states. Congress then decides how the Amendment will be ratified: by three-fourths of the legislatures or by ratifying conventions in three-fourths of the states. The method used for all but one of the twenty-six Amendments has involved a proposal by Congress and ratification by state legislatures.

The sixteen Amendments to the Constitution passed since the Bill of

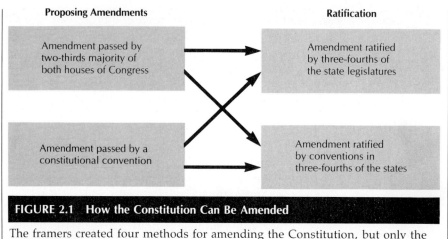

FIGURE 2.1   How the Constitution Can Be Amended

The framers created four methods for amending the Constitution, but only the Congress/state legislature route (at top) has so far been used.

Rights have covered a wide range of topics. Five of those Amendments have extended voting rights:

Right to vote for all men, regardless of race (Fifteenth)

Right to vote for women (Nineteenth)

Right to vote in presidential elections for citizens of Washington, D.C. (Twenty-third)

Elimination of the poll tax (Twenty-fourth)

Right to vote for all citizens eighteen years of age or older (Twenty-sixth)

Another group of Amendments changed some of the rules for electing officials, as well as the period of time they serve in office. The Twelfth Amendment spells out the process for electing the president and vice president. The Seventeenth Amendment calls for the direct election of senators; before its adoption, senators were elected by state legislatures. The Twentieth Amendment changes the dates for the inauguration of the president and the convening of Congress, while the Twenty-fifth clarifies the procedures for presidential succession in cases of disability, death, or resignation. The Twenty-second Amendment limits the tenure of elected presidents to two full four-year terms.

Still other Amendments made changes in the constitutional powers of government institutions. For example, the Eleventh Amendment limited the power of federal courts to hear cases involving the states, and the Sixteenth Amendment gave Congress the power to establish a national income tax.

The Thirteenth and Fourteenth Amendments dealt with the rights of citizens. The former ended slavery. The latter forbids states to deny individuals

Marching for constitutional change Women achieved the right to vote in 1920 only after years of petitioning and protest, including this 1916 parade in New York City.

Carrie Chapman Cott, who coordinated plans for the Twenty-sixth Amendment, recruited President Woodrow Wilson to the cause, which gave it a significant boost.

the rights guaranteed under the Constitution; these rights include due process and equal protection of the laws for all. Interestingly, only two Amendments have actually addressed policy questions. In 1919 the states formally ratified the Eighteenth Amendment, which prohibited the manufacture, sale, or transportation of alcoholic beverages in the United States. After more than a decade of Prohibition, however, this Amendment was repealed by adoption of the Twenty-first Amendment in 1933.

Despite two hundred years of growth and change, the Constitution has been amended only twenty-six times. There have been many more attempts to amend it, however. Congress has considered at least six thousand proposals since it first convened in 1789, but Americans seem reluctant to modify this crucial document. In part that reluctance stems from the myth that the Constitution is timeless and perfect.

To sum up, the U.S. Constitution plays at least five pivotal roles in American government.

It establishes the authority of the national government.

It describes the basic institutional structures of American government.

It defines the formal powers of those institutions.

It places formal limits on those powers.

It specifies the procedures that can be used to make formal changes.

★ ★ ★

ROOTS OF THE CONSTITUTION

Many Americans believe that the Constitution reflects extraordinary wisdom on the part of its authors. The framers' achievement, however, did not come by accident, for the roots of the Constitution run deep. To understand the unique circumstances that led to its creation, we must explore the traditions that guided its authors.

British Constitutional Heritage

With a few exceptions, the leaders of the American Revolution respected the British constitutional system from which they were attempting to free themselves. Indeed, many of them saw the Revolution as a fight to secure their rights as Englishmen.[9] Therefore, when the time came to devise their own system of government, the framers relied heavily on the British constitutional tradition.

What was that tradition? The question is not easy to answer. The British constitution was not then—and is not now—found in any single document. Rather the British constitution is composed of three British legal institutions with deep historical roots: charters, common law, and several major statutes.

Charters. During the Middle Ages, feudalism dominated European society. Feudalism involved social, political, and economic arrangements in which landless families secured farmland and protection in exchange for providing services and resources to the land's owner. These arrangements were often written down in formal agreements called **charters.** Charters described the rights and duties of both the landowner and those bound to him. They were usually drawn up to settle or avoid disputes in the feudal relationship.

In 1215 such a disagreement about the rights of those who served under the British Crown caused a major conflict between King John and the nobility. After losing on the battlefield, John signed the **Magna Carta,** a document that reaffirmed long-standing rights and duties of the English nobility and defined the limits placed on the king. The charter stands for the principle that everyone, including the king, must obey the law. Over the centuries it became an almost sacred guarantee of law and justice,[10] and as such it was the first prop on the stage of the American Revolution.

Common law. During medieval times monarchs, not legislatures, made laws. A king or queen would proclaim the law of the land, sometimes (but not always) after seeking the advice of a legislative body. Legislatures did not become a major source of laws in England until the 1600s. In the meantime, a large gap remained between the broad coverage of most royal proclamations and the details of legal disputes.

Into that legal breach stepped judges appointed by the British Crown to settle such disputes, and from their work came common law. **Common law,** also called judge-made law, represents the collection of legal doctrines that grew out of the many cases heard by those judges. Over an extended period of time, some of those doctrines developed into basic principles of law applied throughout England.

When the British Parliament eventually began to pass laws, conflicts arose between its statutes and the common law being applied by the British courts. These conflicts came to a head in 1610, when the English courts held that common law would be given priority over statutory law if the two disagreed.[11] The priority of common law remains fundamental to the British constitutional system; so does the independence of the judiciary, implied in

A moving tribute The symbols of two countries travel together across nineteen states in this celebration of the Constitution's bicentennial. The Magna Carta stands for law and justice in the eyes of the British people. The flag, representing the first thirteen states, and the strong, swift eagle have come to represent America to Americans.

the 1610 decision. Both principles were adopted in the American constitutional system.

Major statutes.   Despite that setback for legislative law, several major acts of Parliament helped shape the British constitutional tradition. The **British Bill of Rights** (1689), for instance, established some basic principles of constitutional government: Parliament's supremacy over the monarchy, guarantees of a jury trial, and prohibitions against excessive bail and cruel and unusual punishment. Other laws asserted the independence of the judicial branch from the monarchy (Act of Settlement, 1701) and the right of representation in determining taxes (Petition of Right, 1629)—an issue that would be central to the complaints of the North American colonists.

The American constitutional system owes a great deal to its British heritage. But the framers of the Constitution were also deeply influenced by the British treatment of the North American colonies.

The Colonial Heritage

Most British colonies were established under royal charters allowing settlers to govern themselves in most matters. In several colonies, the settlers modified or supplemented these agreements. The *Mayflower Compact,* written by the Pilgrims, set forth several major principles for the Plymouth Colony's government. That agreement became part of the colonial heritage that helped shape the Constitution.[12]

When thinking about colonial rule, Americans often picture whole populations being crushed by oppressors. People rarely see colonial government as a breeding ground for self-government and openness. Yet, from the 1620s until the American Revolution, England let its North American colonies govern themselves. It made no attempt to establish a central administration to rule them.

Each of the colonies remained primarily a self-governing entity, and by the early 1700s most had developed similar governmental structures. A typical colony had three branches of government: a governor appointed by the king, a legislature, and a relatively independent judiciary. Local government consisted of self-governing townships and counties. As participants in these institutions, the leaders of the American Revolution gained political experience and an understanding of how governments operate.[13]

Intellectual Roots

The intellectual atmosphere of the time also influenced the framers of the Constitution. Raised in a society that took its religion seriously, they grew up with such concepts as equality before God and the integrity of each human life—concepts rooted in their Judeo-Christian religion.[14] The idea of a covenant, or contract, between members of society developed from this tradition, as did the distrust of the monarchy and the need for a system of laws to protect individual rights.

The framers were also children of the Enlightenment. Usually dated from the 1600s to the 1800s, this period in European intellectual history was dominated by the idea that human reason, not religious tradition, was the primary source of knowledge and wisdom. One of the most influential authors of the period, Thomas Hobbes, argued that governments depend on the consent of the governed. His views helped to justify revolution in the North American colonies more than a century later.[15]

Another British political philosopher, John Locke, offered an explanation of political life and government that was quite popular among colonists. Locke asserted that people possess an inherent right to revolution. Therefore any government can continue to exist as long as it proves convenient to its citizens and does not interfere with their pursuit of the good life. But if the government violates this arrangement, then the citizens have a right to replace their government with another.

The work of a French aristocrat, Charles de Montesquieu, also found favor with those who wrote the Constitution. James Madison and others often cited his ideas and words. What struck them especially was Montesquieu's argument about the structure of government: it must be so designed that no person or group could oppress others. This end is best achieved, he wrote, by separating the legislative, executive, and judicial functions into three distinct branches of government.

Finally, just as the seeds of the American Revolution were being planted, a Swiss-born theorist named Jean-Jacques Rousseau published several works that argued for popular sovereignty. According to the concept of **popular sovereignty,** the best form of government is one that reflects the general will of the people, which is the sum total of those interests that all citizens have in common. Although Rousseau's major writings influenced the French Revolution much more than the American Revolution, he had his followers in the American colonies. Among them was Thomas Paine, a British-born American revolutionary whose pamphlets had a great influence during the American Revolution. His best-known work, *Common Sense,* is among the most often cited writings to come out of the American Revolution.

The Stirring of Revolution

In the 1760s the British for the first time intervened in the political life of the colonies. Given their legal, political, and intellectual heritage, it is not surprising that the colonists responded with a stirring of revolution. Britain needed men and resources to fight the French and so began to impose demands and commercial restrictions on the American colonists. In 1765 the British passed the **Stamp Act**—the first tax levied directly on the colonists by Parliament. Relying on the rights granted all British subjects under English law, the colonists protested against "taxation without representation." Even though the Stamp Act was repealed within a few months, other controversial issues arose. For instance, the British granted a monopoly over the sale of tea to a British firm, thus interfering with the interests of many colonial merchants. In 1773 a group of Boston citizens responded by raiding a ship loaded with tea and dumping its contents overboard. That incident, now known as the Boston Tea Party, caused the British to close Boston harbor and tighten control over the colonial government in Massachusetts. The events leading to rebellion soon escalated, and by 1774 even some of the moderate voices in colonial politics were calling for change.

These then were the circumstances in which representatives from the colonies gathered as the First Continental Congress in Philadelphia in September 1774. After passing resolutions protesting recent British actions, the delegates set a date for reconvening the next year and adjourned. By the time they reconvened as the Second Continental Congress in May 1775, colonists and British troops had exchanged gunfire at Concord and Lexington.

The Second Continental Congress took a number of steps that officially launched the American Revolution. It organized itself as a provisional government, and in June 1775 it created a continental army to be headed by George Washington. In May 1776 the Congress voted to take the final step of drawing up a statement declaring the colonies to be a free and independent nation. On July 2, 1776, it adopted the **Declaration of Independence.** Two days later independence was formally declared.

The Declaration of Independence accomplished several purposes. It accused the British of abusing the rights of the North American colonists— rights given them under the British constitution and long-standing traditions of self-government. It announced the intention of the colonial revolutionaries to sever their ties with England and explained the reasons for such drastic action. Most important, it articulated two fundamental principles under which the newly formed nation would be governed. First, the Declaration held that governments have one primary purpose: to secure the "unalienable rights" of their citizens, among which are "life, liberty, and the pursuit of happiness." Second, it stated that such governments derive their powers and authority from the "consent of the governed." Furthermore, it asserted that if any government violates the rights it was established to secure, "it is the Right of the People to alter or to abolish it" and to create a new government in its place.[16]

★ ★ ★

THE ENDURING PRINCIPLES

According to the myth of the timeless and perfect Constitution, what emerged from these roots was a government designed to serve the needs of Americans for generations to come. In one sense, those who believe in that myth are correct, for the Constitution has served American citizens very well for over two centuries. But it would be incorrect to think of the U.S. constitutional system as some well-designed and carefully maintained machine that has been efficiently operated for all this time. Instead, American citizens have benefited from a living constitution that has thrived on five enduring principles that have allowed our system of government to adapt to the changing conditions of the last 200 years. These principles —the rule of law, republicanism, the separation of power, checks and balances, and national supremacy—are at the heart of that living constitutional system.

The Rule of Law

Although the words *rule of law* are never mentioned in the Constitution, the idea is one of the most important legacies of the framers. **Rule of law** means that in American government the rulers, like those they rule, are answerable to the law. No individual stands above the law, no matter what his or her background or office. Just as there are laws that address the behavior of general citizens, so there are laws that focus on the behavior of public officials. Those laws generally set limits on the powers of the officials or prescribe the procedures they must use in carrying out their jobs. Under the rule-of-law principle, those limits and prescriptions must be adhered to if the American constitutional system is to function properly.

The framers of the Constitution helped establish the rule-of-law principle in the Constitution by limiting the power of government. As we have said, certain provisions of the Constitution describe specific (delegated) powers of the national government. Other provisions explicitly prohibit certain types of actions by national or state government officials—for example, ex post facto laws. The Bill of Rights and the Fourteenth Amendment place additional limits on both national and state governments.

The best evidence of the importance of this constitutional principle is its influence on the day-to-day operations of American government. Almost every action government agencies undertake, from the most routine to the most dramatic, is carefully designed to meet the requirements of due process of law and other constitutional standards. Any deviation from these standards is likely to draw unwelcome attention. In fact, both state and federal courts are constantly hearing criminal cases and lawsuits in which possible violations of the rule of law are at issue.

Even more crucial is the fact that no one is exempt from the rule of law. The most powerful political officials have had to bend to its force. In August 1974, for example, President Richard M. Nixon resigned in the face of charges that he took part in a governmental cover-up: the cover-up of a break-in, sponsored by the White House, into the Democratic party's national head-quarters at the Watergate office complex in Washington, D.C. Although

A last hurrah Richard Nixon leaves for the first leg of a flight to California after an emotional goodbye to members of his staff at the White House. His resignation in the aftermath of the Watergate scandal demonstrated that even presidents are not above the rule of law.

Nixon and many of his supporters perceived the Watergate cover-up as a relatively minor offense, the president's attempt to circumvent the law resulted in enough political pressure to bring about the first presidential resignation in American history (see Background 6.1 on page 141).

Republicanism

As we mentioned in Chapter 1, the framers of the Constitution had questions about the ability of the American people to rule themselves directly. By advocating **republicanism,** the framers were calling for a government in which decisions are made by elected or appointed officials who are ultimately answerable to the people. In this way, they hoped to avoid what they perceived as real dangers of a purely democratic government.

The framers opposed a direct democracy because they distrusted human nature and the capacity of ordinary citizens to govern themselves. We know something about their views thanks to documents like *The Federalist Papers*, a series of editorials that James Madison, Alexander Hamilton, and John Jay wrote in 1788 to support the ratification of the Constitution. In *The Federalist*, No. 10, Madison offers a clear summary of the basic ideas about political life and human nature underlying the republican principle.

Madison argued that the problems of government can be traced to the "mischiefs of faction." He defined a faction as a group that puts its shared interests ahead of the rights of others or the interests of the community as a whole. These self-serving factions can be small or large; they can even include a majority of the people.

According to Madison, all factions, great or small, pose a threat to the general well-being of society. Since the causes of faction are basic to human nature, eliminating them is impossible. Thus, if any government is to serve the general interest of the people, it must be designed so that the potentially destructive power of factions can be eliminated or controlled.

Madison and the framers favored a republican form of government in which the people had some voice—but a voice that was filtered through their representatives. The community was to be governed "by persons holding their offices . . . for a limited time or during good behavior." And although all officials would be answerable to the people, some would be more insulated from public pressure than others. Members of the House of Representatives were to have the most exposure: they alone would be elected directly by the American voters and have comparatively brief terms, two years.

Senators and the president were assigned longer terms, and under the original provisions of the Constitution, the people did not elect them directly. Instead, state legislators selected senators, and an Electoral College, with members selected by the states, chose the president. These methods were

James Madison: the father of the Constitution Widely read in philosophy, law, and history, Madison brought a wealth of scholarship to the convention debates. One of his major goals was to create a national government that would be a disinterested mediator in disputes between different groups.

later changed by amendment and by the action of state legislatures. Supreme Court judges received additional protection from the whims of constantly changing public opinion. They have lifetime appointments and can be removed only through the lengthy and difficult process called impeachment. But even though the framers felt impelled to take these precautions, they never lost sight of the basic principle of republicanism: that the ultimate responsibility of U.S. government officials is to the American public.

Separation of Powers

The principle of the **separation of powers** is also linked with the effort to control factions. By splitting power among several branches of government and giving each an area of primary responsibility, the framers sought to minimize the possibility that one faction could gain control. "The accumulation of all powers, legislative, executive, and judiciary, in the same hands," states

Madison, "may justly be pronounced the very definition of tyranny."[17] Thus, to help avoid tyranny, the power to make, execute, and judge the law was divided among the three branches: Congress, the presidency, and the courts.

The framers also understood the costs this principle might impose on the operations of American government. Therefore they created a system of checks and balances so that the three branches could work together and none would encroach on the others (see Figure 2.2).

Checks and Balances

The principle of **checks and balances** lets the executive and legislative branches share some responsibilities and gives each branch some control over the other's activities. The Constitution is not clear about the power of the judicial branch to review the actions of the other two branches. This power was established later through court cases.

The principle of checks and balances is strengthened by the different methods of selecting officials, which the framers believed would ensure that the different branches represented different public perspectives. Variations in terms of office were intended to add a further check. For example, senators, responding from the perspective of their six-year terms in office, were expected to act in a more measured and conservative way than their peers in the House, who had only two-year terms.

The major support for checks and balances comes from the distribution of powers. Each branch depends on the others to accomplish its objectives, but each acts as a counterpoint to the others as well. The legislative actions of Congress, for example, can be checked by the president's power to **veto,** or reject, legislation. The veto, in turn, can be overruled by a two-thirds vote of both chambers of Congress. However, in the past two hundred years, Congress has been able to override less than a hundred presidential vetoes out of a total of 2,400.

Congress can restrict presidential power in a variety of other ways. Under the general principle of rule of law, presidents must ask Congress for authority to undertake any course of action. Congress usually responds favorably, especially in the area of foreign policy (see Chapter 15, on foreign and defense policy). At times, however, Congress may pass laws that place narrow limits on presidential authority.

The Senate may also check the president's power by using its right to approve or reject presidential nominees for judicial and executive positions. Although the Senate rarely says no, many such nominations have been withdrawn because they were unlikely to get the necessary number of votes.

The control of the public sector's purse strings by Congress is also a powerful check on presidential power. Although the budget is the president's

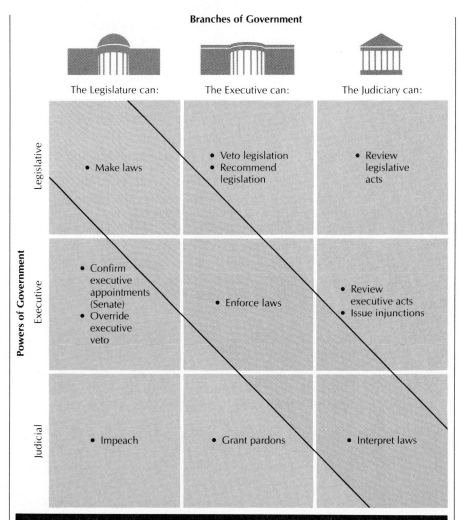

FIGURE 2.2 Separation of Powers and Checks and Balances

Separation of powers is the assignment of lawmaking, law-enforcing, and law-interpreting functions to separate legislative, executive, and judicial branches. This is illustrated by the colored portion of the figure. *Checks and balances* give each branch some power over the other branches. For example, the executive branch possesses some legislative power, and the legislative branch possesses some executive power. These checks and balances are illustrated within the columns and outside the colored section of the figure.

Source: K. Janda, J. M. Berry, and J. Goldman, *The Challenge of Democracy* (Boston: Houghton Mifflin, 1987), p. 86. Copyright © 1987 by Houghton Mifflin Company. Used by permission.

creation, the actual appropriation of funds is in the hands of the House and Senate.

The ultimate restraint on presidential authority, however, resides in the power of Congress to **impeach,** or remove a president from office for "high crimes and misdemeanors." Impeachment proceedings have been carried out against only one president, Andrew Johnson. In the 1868 trial, the Senate failed to convict Johnson by just one vote. More recently, a House committee vote in favor of impeachment precipitated President Nixon's resignation in 1974.

The courts are also involved in the system of checks and balances. Through the power of **judicial review,** the courts can declare the acts of Congress to be in conflict with the Constitution. Because they can hear lawsuits about the actions of public officials, courts also have an influence on the behavior of officials from the executive branch. At the same time, the president's power to appoint federal judges with the advice and consent of the Senate gives the White House some power over the courts. The powers of Congress over the courts derive in part from its constitutional authority to create or abolish any court other than the Supreme Court. And as with the presidency, Congress can impeach judges charged with a major crime.

In setting up the elaborate system of checks and balances, the framers pitted the three branches of government against one another. Not surprisingly, this has resulted in a slow and ponderous system that often frustrates the desire of some public officials to deal quickly with critical issues. Too rapid decision making is what the framers feared. The system works the way they planned it—deliberately and with care.

National Supremacy

Earlier we pointed out that the U.S. Constitution provides for a federal system in which national and state governments divide and share the authority of American government. Such a complex arrangement can work only if there is some principle that helps government officials settle fundamental disagreements between the different levels of government. If such a principle did not exist, then "the authority of the whole society" would be "everywhere subordinate to the authority of the parts." That, argued Madison, would have created a "monster" in which the head was under the control of its member parts.[18]

In the American constitutional system, this principle is **national suprem-acy.** As noted earlier in this chapter, the supremacy clause of Article VI of the Constitution makes the Constitution and those laws and treaties passed under it the "supreme Law of the Land." As we will see in Chapter 3, on federalism, this principle has been a central factor in the evolution of the

Support for national supremacy In a major application of the principle of national supremacy, President Dwight Eisenhower sent troops into Little Rock, Arkansas, in 1957 to enforce the Supreme Court's public school desegregation decision. Eisenhower was not a strong supporter of civil rights, but with the safety of these young women and others at stake, he joined the battle between the Court and those who resisted its authority.

American federal system. Starting as a highly legalistic concept, it now has a crucial function in implementing many social, economic, and environmental policies.

CONCLUSION: Timeless Words and Living Principles

At the beginning of the chapter, we learned about the great pride that most Americans take in their Constitution and the important role the document plays in defining our national identity. We also discussed the myth of the timeless and perfect Constitution usually associated with national pride. According to that myth, the American constitutional system has succeeded because of the commitment of generations to U.S. citizens to the governmental structures and governing instructions set forth by the Constitution's framers. By adhering to the words and wisdom of the founding fathers, the myth implies, we have firmly established one of the most effective and representative governments in history.

There are a number of problems with that myth, the most obvious being that a governmental constitution is more than words written on a piece of paper. Our written Constitution is a wonderfully crafted document that deserves all the accolades it receives from its many admirers here and abroad. Nevertheless, the written Constitution does not necessarily reflect the real operational constitution of the United States that is applied daily in this country. The way our government operates depends on the interpretation and reinterpretation of the Constitution's provisions and on the principles implicit in the document. As you will see in later chapters, government also depends on laws, policies, court decisions, political attitudes and behavior, customs, traditions, and even the myths that surround the exercise of public authority in America.

The words of the Constitution may not be timeless and perfect, but they do provide the foundation of the American constitutional system. It would be a mistake, however, to think one could appreciate the complexities of U.S. government by merely knowing the Constitution. Understanding comes from an examination of the behaviors, institutions, and policies that constitute American politics.

★ ★ ★
SUMMARY

1. The first goal of the framers of the Constitution was to establish the authority of the government of the United States, which comes directly from the people, and to create the institutions that would carry out that authority.

2. The framers considered the Virginia Plan, the New Jersey Plan, and the Connecticut Compromise—three solutions to the problem of how to divide authority. Their decision, laid out in Articles I, II, and III, established legislative, executive, and judicial branches of government.

3. The Constitution describes the specific, or delegated, powers of the three branches, and in its "necessary and proper" clause, it permits implied powers. It also sets limits on national and state power and specifies the rules for making amendments.

4. The roots of the Constitution can be found in the British legal tradition, including the principles that government officials, as well as ordinary citizens, must obey the law and that judge-made law has priority over laws made by legislatures. The colonial experience of self-government

and the political philosophy of Hobbes, Locke, and others also helped guide the Constitution's framers.

5. The framers established in the Constitution the following fundamental principles of American government: the rule of law, republicanism, separation of powers, the system of checks and balances, and national supremacy. These principles have provided our constitutional system with the flexibility that has made it work for over 200 years.

★ ★ ★

KEY TERMS

Articles of Confederation
Shays' Rebellion
Virginia Plan
New Jersey Plan
Connecticut Compromise
federal system
delegated powers
implied powers
reserved powers
Bill of Rights
charters
Magna Carta
common law

British Bill of Rights
popular sovereignty
Stamp Act
Declaration of Independence
rule of law
republicanism
separation of powers
checks and balances
veto
judicial review
impeach
national supremacy

★ ★ ★

SUGGESTED READINGS

- Diamond, Martin. *The Founding of the Democratic Republic*. Itasca, Ill.: F. E. Peacock 1981. This work provides a clear presentation of the issues and ideas that influenced the work of the framers at the Constitutional Convention.

- Herson, Lawrence J.R. *The Politics of Ideas: Political Theory and American Public Policy*. Homewood, Ill.: The Dorsey Press, 1984. A survey of American political theory focusing attention on the basic ideas implicit in the work of the framers.

- McDonald, Forrest. *Novus Ordo Seclorum: The Intellectual Origins of the Constitution*. Lawrence, Kans.: University Press of Kansas, 1985. An intellectual history of the ideas and concepts informing the work of the framers.

● Pritchett, C. Herman. *Constitutional Civil Liberties.* Englewood Cliffs, N.J.: Prentice-Hall, 1984.
———. *Constitutional Law of the Federal System.* Englewood Cliffs, N.J.: Prentice-Hall, 1984. Each volume provides a historical survey of the major issues and cases surrounding the Constitution for the past two centuries.
● Rossiter, Clinton, ed. *The Federalist Papers.* New York: Mentor Books, 1961. A collection of the key works that have played an important role in our understanding of what the framers meant when they wrote the Constitution.

3

CHAPTER

American Federalism

A mong all the institutions of American government created by the Constitution, none is more complex than the American federal system. It ties together the work of national, state, and local officials. Through the federal system, our national government conducts most of its business.

Yet some claim that the federal system is also the major obstacle to effective and efficient government policies. They argue that its complexities hamstring government officials in dealing directly with the problems plaguing the American people.

Consider, for example, the federal government's efforts to keep America's water resources clean and fit for human consumption. During the 1970s Congress passed legislation allowing federal officials at the U.S. Environmental Protection Agency (EPA) to ban the discharge of hazardous waste products into America's rivers and streams and to protect the drinking water supplies of America's communities.

In enforcing these laws, the EPA banned the discharge of gypsum into the nation's waterways. This action was taken because gypsum, a chalky white by-product in the manufacturing of chemical fertilizers, is marginally radioactive. Since the late 1970s, that ban has forced several Louisiana chemical companies to store millions of tons of gypsum wastes on land located along the Mississippi River between Baton Rouge and New Orleans. But this solution turned out to be a short-term one.

By the mid-1980s the EPA faced a dilemma. The hills of gypsum wastes along the banks of the Mississippi stood nearly fifty feet high, and those who lived and worked near them complained to both local and state officials about the potential health hazards to their communities. In addition, the instability of the land along the muddy river demanded quick action. EPA officials decided that the only viable solution was to permit discharge of some of the gypsum wastes into the river.

Although federal officials had the legal right to permit such discharges, they hesitated to do so since releasing the wastes would contaminate the water downstream, particularly in the city of New Orleans. Unable to handle such contamination of its drinking water supply, New Orleans would find itself in violation of federal laws regarding safe drinking water. Ironically, the EPA would have to enforce the safe drinking water standards in New Orleans.[1]

As this example illustrates, relations between national and state officials have become very complicated in recent years as governments at all levels have attempted to deal with an increasing number of social, economic, political, and ecological problems.

The relations of the national government to the states is at the heart of a major debate on the nature of American government. One side in the controversy believes that the national government has been too weak and that more power should be given to officials representing the interests of the whole nation. The other side maintains that state and local governments, which are closest to the people, best serve their needs.

This debate is not new. In the early 1800s Americans identified quite closely with their state and local governments. Alexis de Tocqueville, a French observer of American life during the period, commented on the individuality of these governments. "Every village," he wrote, "is a sort of republic accustomed to rule itself."[2] He saw state and local officials exerting control over policy while the national government grew weaker each day and its very existence was "in danger."[3]

More than 150 years later, the public's views are not quite as well defined. Contemporary Americans still tend to give their trust to the public officials closest to them. In one survey, 71 percent of those polled agreed that state and local government officials are "more sensitive" than national government officials to the needs of hungry and poor Americans. Two-thirds of those polled favored a proposal that would turn over food stamps and other welfare programs to state and local governments.[4]

Despite these and similar opinions, support for state and local government has faded somewhat in recent years. Instead, Americans have increasingly looked to Congress, the Supreme Court, and the Washington bureaucracy for solutions to their problems. By the 1980s the national government was engaged in a wide range of programs that had once been state and local responsibilities alone—for instance, health care for the elderly, education for the young, and the construction of roads and sewage treatment plants. According to Senator Terry Sanford of North Carolina, a former governor, the "people seem to conclude that the state vehicle is not so driveable as the federal vehicles."[5]

The growing power of the national government has led some observers to wonder whether state and local governments have become mere servants to Washington, dancing to the tune played in the nation's capital.[6] At the heart of this popular attitude is the myth of creeping centralization. According to this myth, the once highly decentralized constitutional system has slowly eroded. State and local governments have not disappeared, but their powers have steadily declined, and national officials now wield public authority. As a national newspaper noted, "One cannot conceive of an example of public policy making that the states can engage in . . . without fear of contradiction by the Federal Government."[7] State and local governments are being integrated into a single, national system of government in which public policies made in Washington, D.C., are carried out by state and local officials.

Since the national government has indeed taken a larger and more varied role in the nation's domestic affairs, it is easy to understand why the myth of creeping centralization has become so popular. In this chapter, we will look at the evolution of the federal system and how it functions. As we explore the activities of the many actors who play out the drama of American federalism, you will see that the myth of creeping centralization offers an incomplete and oversimplified picture of the federal system.

★ ★ ★
THE FEDERAL SYSTEM REVISITED

As you will recall from Chapter 2, on the Constitution, the American federal system was born out of compromises struck between supporters of a strong national government and those who wanted the states to retain a high degree of independence. The **federal system** allowed a division of government authority between the national government and the states: some powers of government would be exercised by the national government, some other powers would belong to the states, while still other powers would be shared.

Finding the Federal Solution

In designing a system to distribute authority among different levels of government, the framers of the Constitution rejected two models: a unitary system and a confederal system. A **unitary system** like Great Britain's places constitutional authority entirely in the hands of a national government. Under this model, political subdivisions created by the central government perform much of the day-to-day work of governing. In Britain, all constitutional authority formally rests with the Parliament and the Crown, but counties, boroughs, and other forms of local government carry out most of the work of government.

Of course, the framers could have retained the confederal system that was already in place under the Articles of Confederation. In a **confederal system,** the formal authority of government rests with political subdivisions, which join together in an agreement that permits some powers to be exercised at the national level. Each state formally retains its constitutional authority and can withdraw from the common agreement at any time.

The federal system that the framers designed borrows from both of these forms of government. Some governmental authority—for example, foreign policy—belongs exclusively to the national government (see Figure 3.1). State governments, on the other hand, have the sole right to exercise such powers as the regulation of commerce within state borders. Finally, the national and state governments share various kinds of authority—for example, establishing a system of lower courts to hear lawsuits and criminal cases. What makes the system work is the constitutional guarantee that each level of government—national and state—can exercise authority without interference from the other level.[8]

	Powers Granted to the States	Powers Denied to the States
Powers Granted to the National Government	to tax to borrow money to establish a court system to charter banks and corporations to pass laws	to tax imports and exports to coin money to make treaties to wage war
Powers Denied to the National Government	Explicit: 　to ratify and amend the 　　U.S. Constitution 　to choose U.S. senators 　to run elections Implicit: 　All are controversial, though 　　traditionally they have included 　　the following powers: 　to establish local governments 　to regulate public health and safety	to grant titles of nobility to tax interstate commerce

FIGURE 3.1　The Constitutional Basis of the Federal System

The box on the upper left lists powers shared by the two levels of government; the box on the lower right shows powers denied to both. Powers on the upper right belong to the national government exclusively, while those on the lower left are the states'.

★ ★ ★

THE EVOLUTION OF AMERICAN FEDERALISM

In theory, the federal system was supposed to achieve a balanced distribution of power between the national government and the thirteen states. In practice, however, the system has grown into an institutional framework through which a union of fifty states has met the complex challenges generated by a vast territory and a large and diverse population. The myth of creeping centralization pictures this evolution as a constant expansion in national power. A more realistic view shows a widening and increasingly complex set of relationships among the national, state, and local governments.

Regional diversity: northern farmer Nowhere is economic and geographic diversity more striking than in the contrast between rural and urban America. With the introduction of mechanization (here the mechanical harvester) small farms have been consolidated into large agribusinesses and the farm population has drastically declined.

Battles over Meaning (1790s–1860s)

The Constitution is not completely clear on the powers of the national government relative to those of the states. This lack of precision caused conflict in the early years of the republic. Was the national government primary or could states ignore the laws of Congress when they chose? Two competing answers emerged, one centered on the states and the other on the nation.[9]

Supporters of **state-centered federalism** took a narrow view of the powers of the national government. They argued that states could overrule national laws. This view was first expressed in the Virginia and Kentucky Resolutions of 1798. In those resolutions, coauthors Thomas Jefferson and James Madison called for the "nullification" of the unpopular Alien and Sedition Acts—laws that had led to the conviction of several newspaper editors critical of American

from interfering with the other's work. Thus the states could not interfere with the federal government's regulation of interstate trade, but the federal government could not interfere with the power of states to regulate the sale or manufacture of products or services within their own borders. For example, the national government could tell a New York clothing manufacturer what kind of material to use in making infant pajamas that would be shipped to Kansas. It could not tell either New York or Kansas, however, what qualifications to require in licensing morticians or barbers.

The theory of dual federalism first appeared in pre–Civil War court cases, but the Supreme Court did not apply it consistently until the late 1800s. In 1871 the Court held that within the borders of each state there are "two governments, restricted in their sphere of action, but independent of each other, and supreme within their respective spheres." Neither, it said, can intrude on or interfere with the other's action.[10] By 1918 the Court was declaring that those powers "not expressly delegated to the National Government are reserved" to the states.[11] This was dual federalism at its height.

Despite the Court's strict interpretation, the formal separation between the two levels of government was breaking down in the world of practical politics. The first step in this process was **grant-in-aid programs,** through which state policies and programs were funded or provided with other support. The Morrill Act (1862) gave federal land grants to states for the purpose of establishing agricultural colleges. Later on, cash grants helped states with experimental agricultural stations, textbook programs for the blind, marine schools, forestry programs, agricultural extension services, state soldiers' homes, vocational schools, road construction, and a variety of other projects. By 1927 these grant programs were bringing state governments $123 million in national funds annually.[12]

Toward Cooperation and Local Participation (1930s–1950s)

The Great Depression of the 1930s altered the relationship between Washington and the states. Demand for public services grew. At the same time, state and local governments faced tight finances because tax revenues had fallen in the declining economy. The national government was expected and willing to respond. There was an explosion of new and cooperative programs in which the national and state governments shared an increasing number of functions (see Background 3.1).

During this period of **cooperative federalism,** conflict between Washington and the states diminished. Public officials worried less about the level of government that performed certain functions and more about their specific program responsibilities. State and national officials began to see each other as "allies, not as enemies."[13]

Cities and other local governments also became participants in the federal system. Before the 1930s, American cities were regarded as merely subdivi-

━━━━━━━━━━ **BACKGROUND 3.1** ━━━━━━━━━━

The Menagerie of Federal Grants

At the heart of the system of intergovernmental relations that emerged during the 1930s was a variety of grant-in-aid programs, which financed highways, social and educational projects, and other programs. Many were *conditional grants-in-aid,* under which state governments received federal funding for specific purposes only if they met certain general requirements. For example, states were expected to operate in an efficient and business-like fashion, free of corruption and undue political influence. If states failed to meet federal standards, support was withdrawn. Thus during the Depression, Washington took charge of public assistance programs in six states where officials could not meet federal requirements. Public welfare programs in other states were closely watched to make sure that they were following federal rules.

Under another federal program, states received *formula grants* based on population, number of eligible persons, per capita income, and other factors. One of the largest of these grants,

the Hill-Burton progam, used a formula heavily weighted to favor states with substantial low-income populations. By 1986 over $3 billion of Hill-Burton funds had been used to construct and modernize health care facilities throughout the United States.

Project grants are awarded only after submission of a specific program or plan of action. The United States Housing Act of 1937 was one of the earliest and largest of such programs. Under provisions of that act, local governments could obtain funds to build public housing. By the 1960s there were more than 4,000 such projects with more than a half million dwelling units.

In many instances the national government required recipient governments to provide a certain percentage of the funds needed to implement the programs. Among these *matching grants* were a program that provided aid to dependent children under the Social Security Act of 1935 and one that gave states nine dollars for every one dollar spent to build interstate highways.

sions of the states. Grants or other forms of support came from state capitals, not from Washington. In 1932, for instance, only the nation's capital received aid from the federal government. By 1940, however, the situation had changed significantly. That year the federal government handed out $278 million in direct grants-in-aid to local governments for a variety of public housing and public works programs. In the 1950s the national government expanded support to include slum clearance, urban renewal, and airport construction. By the start of the 1960s local governments were receiving $592 million worth of direct grants.[14]

A new style of federalism had emerged that recognized the interdependence of Washington and state and local governments. Called **intergovernmental relations,** it is a system in which the various levels of government share functions, and each level is able to influence the others. The new system offered a variety of grant-in-aid programs covering a wide range of policy concerns. The number and size of these programs grew dramatically during this period, increasing from $1 billion in 1934 to $6.8 billion in 1959.

Cooperative federalism in action In the economic boom that followed World War II, millions of families could afford to flee the city for the suburbs. As cities began to decay in the wake of the exodus, urban officials turned to Washington for help. Here you see one of the first urban renewal projects, the James Weldon Johnson Houses, built in 1947 in New York City.

The Urban Focus (1960s–1970s)

The intergovernmental relations system continued to grow during the 1960s and 1970s, and by 1980 grant-in-aid programs to state and local governments had surpassed $85 billion. Starting in 1960, other notable changes took place.[15] For example, grant systems expanded into new policy areas. The percentage of funds devoted to highways and public assistance declined, and funding for programs in education, health care, environmental protection, manpower training, housing, and community development increased significantly.

In a shift in the flow of funds, a growing number of intergovernmental programs were targeted at local, rather than state, governments. President Lyndon B. Johnson's "Great Society" policies included dozens of new and innovative grant programs with an urban focus. For the first time, community-based programs for feeding the urban poor, training the unemployed, and educating the children of low-income families received support. One important initiative, the Model Cities program, helped cities develop projects addressing a variety of economic and social problems. In 1974 Model Cities and other programs were consolidated under the Community Development Block Grant Act. By 1985 the federal government was disbursing nearly $5 billion directly to local governments under the block grant program.

Until the early 1960s federal grants were used by policy makers as a method by which Washington could help states and localities perform their traditional government functions. State and local governments might be asked to modify their personnel policies or their methods of bidding for contracts, but rarely were they required to take on new policy responsibilities. In contrast, the grant programs of the 1960s and 1970s were designed to involve these governments in achieving national policy objectives.

States or localities that initiated new or special programs promoting national goals received substantial grants. The Model Cities program, for example, encouraged cities to institute programs for improving the quality of life for poor and low-income groups. In other instances, Washington threatened to reduce or cut off funding to governments that failed to change old policies or adopt new ones that complied with national standards. Thus, for example, by the 1980s the national government was using the threat of withholding highway funds to establish a nationwide minimum drinking age of twenty-one and to promote the adoption of mandatory seat belt laws.[16]

Reforming the Grants System (1970s–1980s)

Inevitably, the rapid spread of grant programs and their requirements led to problems. Local recipients criticized federal officials for administering programs without regard to the unique circumstances and dilemmas they were facing. During the 1950s and 1960s state officials complained that the national government ignored them in designing and implementing many new programs. Members of Congress reacted impatiently to the poor coordination and cooperation in the massive intergovernmental relations system. As a result, there was almost constant pressure to reform the grants system.

Responding to pressures for an increased role for state and local officials, Washington took a number of steps designed to loosen its control over grant programs and to enhance state and local authority. During the early 1970s, for instance, the federal government provided funds to support the formation of local and regional councils of governments. These associations of local governments helped their member governments contend with such common problems as coordinating local applications for federal grants. In addition, Presidents Johnson and Nixon reorganized grant system administration, increasing the power of federal field offices in order to ease the burdens of both state and local governments.

In two additional reform efforts, the government introduced new funding systems designed to further reduce the national government's control and make procedures more flexible. Most of the established programs were based on **categorical,** or **conditional, grants,** in which money given to the states and localities was to be used for limited purposes under specific rules. In the mid-1960s, however, Congress introduced **block grants.** Block grants were a way of consolidating categorical grants in a given area so that the recipients would have great freedom to spend funds and paperwork would be reduced. By 1974 seven major block grants covered such areas as health, education, and other social services. Nevertheless, in financial terms, they constitute only a small portion of the total amount of federal aid flowing to states and localities.

The other new form of federal aid was called **general revenue sharing** (GRS). This small but innovative grant-in-aid program had no significant conditions attached to it. State and local governments received funds according to a complex formula based on population and related factors. The GRS program was modified considerably and its funding was reduced late in the 1970s. By the mid-1980s it had all but disappeared from the intergovernmental system.

The Federal System in Transition

In 1981, President Ronald Reagan came to office committed to two goals: reducing the size of government in general and cutting back the role of the national government in particular. To achieve these objectives, the Reagan administration instituted reforms designed to reduce government spending on all levels and increase state and local control and responsibility.

At first, Reagan attempted a major overhaul of the intergovernmental system. He formally proposed to Congress that many governmental functions be turned back to the states in exchange for the federal assumption of most public welfare programs. When this strategy failed, Reagan administration officials tried to bring about changes by adjusting the way grant-in-aid programs were administered. These efforts at administrative reform had a major impact on the federal system. Between 1978 and 1983, for example, the national government's spending for grant-in-aid programs to state and local governments declined by more than 36 percent when adjusted for inflation.[17] The Reagan administration also increased the authority of states and localities over the grant money they did receive.

At the same time, Congress worked toward consolidating categorical programs into broad block grant programs. In 1982 alone, Congress converted seventy-six categorical programs into nine block grants.[18] Despite these efforts, in 1984 over four hundred categorical grant programs remained on the books, in addition to twelve major block grants and a small general revenue sharing program (see Figure 3.2). There is little dispute, however, that the Reagan administration had significantly changed the direction of intergovernmental relations, at least for the short term.

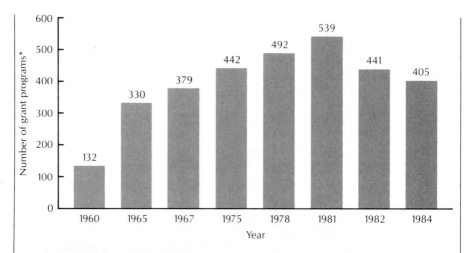

*Includes categorical grants, block grants, and revenue sharing programs.

FIGURE 3.2   The Rise and Fall of Categorical Grants

When Richard Nixon succeeded to the presidency in 1969, he had a deep commitment to slowing the growth of categorical grant programs, which had boomed during Lyndon Johnson's War on Poverty. As you can see, Nixon and his successors had limited success in this endeavor.

Source: Advisory Commission on Intergovernmental Relations, *Significant Features of Fiscal Federalism, 1985–86*, Washington, D.C.: ACIR, 1986), p. 19.

★ ★ ★

THE DRAMAS OF AMERICAN FEDERALISM

As this brief history indicates, there is some truth to the view that nation-state relations have become increasingly centralized over the past two centuries. At the same time, however, the American federal system has grown wider and deeper as interactions between the different levels of American government have increased and become more complex. Today the federal system involves a cast of hundreds of agencies, thousands of political and administrative personnel, and millions of citizens who depend on government for daily public services. Here we briefly describe the many actors who occupy the modern stage of American intergovernmental relations.

National Government Actors

In formal terms, only one national government exists in the American federal system. In practical terms, however, dozens of national-level actors play out daily dramas on the intergovernmental relations stage.

The Supreme Court. In the two centuries of American federalism, no national institution has been more important than the U.S. Supreme Court. We have already seen how in *McCulloch* v. *Maryland*, the Court helped establish the national government's dominant role and how the post–Civil War Court supported the notion of dual federalism.

In recent years the Court rulings, some observers believe, have all but eliminated the states as effective policy makers. They point to *Baker* v. *Carr* (1962), which forced the states to reapportion their legislative seats to guarantee equal representation for all their citizens. They also cite *Roe* v. *Wade*, a landmark 1973 decision in which the Court limited a state's authority to regulate abortion. Finally, in *Garcia* v. *San Antonio Metropolitan Transit Authority* (1985), the Court held that federal wage and hour laws apply to state and local governments.[19] Through these and other cases, the Court has given shape and direction to the American federal system.

Congress. Although presidents often receive credit for major policy innovations, Congress has always played a central role in the evolution of the federal system. This has been especially true in the past twenty years, during which Congress has rapidly increased its authorization of grant programs.

Chief Justice Marshall never dreamed of this Under the doctrine of implied powers, established by John Marshall in the case of *McCulloch* v. *Maryland*, the national gov- ernment gained powers necessary to act on enumerated powers. Without such power there would be neither a U.S. Naval Academy nor this ecstatic graduation ritual.

Some students of Congress point to strong incentives for members of the House and Senate to create and fund federal grant-in-aid programs for state and local governments.[20] These programs give almost every state and local government an opportunity to obtain federal funding. Therefore members of Congress can claim credit for passing and supporting their constituents' grant applications. As a result, even fiscally conservative members of Congress often find it hard to avoid supporting calls for new and larger intergovernmental grant programs. "Philosophically, I have not been one to jump rapidly to new programs," comments one Virginia representative. "But if programs are adopted, my district is entitled to its fair share. And I do everything I can to help—if they decide to apply for aid."[21]

The White House. American presidents have proposed new federal grant programs and worked to reform the intergovernmental system. Johnson's Great Society agenda, for example, emphasized the Model Cities and other new and innovative projects. The administrations of both Johnson and his successor, Richard M. Nixon, strove to improve the coordination of federal grant programs. President Jimmy Carter issued several executive orders aimed at simplifying the complex grant application and reporting procedures that had developed in recent decades.

Other White House initiatives sought to expand the role of state and local governments in the federal system. Johnson called for the establishment of a "creative federalism," involving a partnership of all levels of government, as well as community and private organizations. Nixon proposed a "new American Revolution," which would give "power to the people" by turning many national domestic programs back to state and local governments. Reagan announced a "new federalism," which would revamp the intergovernmental grant system over a ten-year period. Under this proposal, by 1991 the states would receive only 3 or 4 percent of their revenues through federal grants-in-aid compared with the nearly 24 percent they obtained in 1984. Some changes in the American federal system emerged from each of these presidential initiatives, but none has led to radical alterations in intergovernmental relationships.

The federal bureaucracy. Perhaps the greatest increase in the numbers of national-level actors on the intergovernmental stage has been in the bureaucracy, especially in such agencies as the Departments of Housing and Urban Development, Health and Human Services, Agriculture, Interior, Transportation, and Education. Some bureaucrats in these agencies determine the eligibility of state and local grant applicants and the appropriateness of their proposals. Others monitor the use of grant-in-aid funds and constantly consult with other actors in the intergovernmental system about the need to modify specific grant programs.

The emergence of these intergovernmental bureaucracies has added a new dimension to United States government. On the one hand, the bureaucrats of such agencies are expected to disburse funds and assist state and local government officials in making effective use of those resources. On the other hand, these federal administrators are expected to make certain that state and local programs meet federal standards and live up to federal requirements. In other words, the growing federal bureaucracy assigned to intergovernmental programs is supposed both to facilitate and regulate state and local grant recipients. These bureaucrats are actors on the intergovernmental stage with dual, and often contradictory, roles.

States in the Federal System

Though the myth of creeping centralization gives them a passive image, the states remain extremely active participants in the contemporary intergovernmental arena. States are responsible for the regulation of gambling and liquor, education, criminal justice, and public health. They also play a major role in enforcing statewide environmental, safety, and health regulations. For years they have been the chief regulators of public utilities and savings banks.

States empower and determine the organization of local governments. Local governments are created by the actions of state legislatures. Thus, theoretically, they can be legally terminated by state officials. In practice, however, states rarely use this life-and-death power, although they have on occasion eliminated entire city governments through legislative action. City governments cannot impose their own sales or income taxes unless state laws grant them that authority. If a state legislature concludes that local officials are corrupt or inefficient, the state may even take over their responsibilities. This happened in Kansas City, Missouri, when the state assumed control of that city's police force.[22]

The states have also made their mark in creative and innovative approaches to solving public problems. For example, Wisconsin regulated railroads and democratized the nomination process long before national adoption of such policies. Recently, California led the way in developing building construction standards to help reduce energy costs. Such state-initiated innovations are common in almost every major area of domestic policy.[23]

Most important, however, is the states' pivotal role as middlemen in the intergovernmental relations system. The national government uses state agencies to administer their grants in a wide variety of policy areas. In addition, local governments rely on state officials for technical assistance as well as financial aid. In short, state governments may be the *key* link—not the weak link—in the U.S. federal system.[24]

The role of states in the intergovernmental relations system is always changing. When their influence wanes, students of American government tend to pronounce their doom. According to one observer in the 1930s, the

"American state was finished. I do not predict that the states will go, but affirm that they have gone."[25] At other times the importance of the states has been such that one can hardly imagine how American government might operate without them.[26]

What accounts for these gains and losses in power? First, the states' authority changes dramatically as the Supreme Court shifts between strict and flexible interpretations of the Constitution. Second, the states' role depends on the actual political power they can mobilize. During certain periods of American history, state officials managed to exercise considerable influence in Washington through their representatives in the House and Senate. At other times, state governors and legislators have carried relatively little weight either in the White House or in the halls of Congress.

Public opinion also determines the extent of states' influence. Although state governments have always been important policy makers, the American public has not always looked to the states for solutions to their collective problems. At times the public has depended on local governments, and more recently it has expected Washington to help.

The question of public support for state government is complicated by the fact that citizens' attitudes toward their state governments tend to vary from place to place and across time. For example, a public opinion poll conducted in 1980 showed citizens of Connecticut and New Hampshire to be pleased with the job their state officials were doing. Residents of Alabama, Massachusetts, and New Jersey, on the other hand, were quite critical of their state governments.

Finally, the role of states in the federal system depends on their administrative capabilities. If states lack the administrative resources and managerial talent to deliver the goods and services demanded by the public, then they cannot play a major role for very long. Most observers believe that state administrative capabilities have improved markedly in recent years.[27] Ironically, much of that improvement has come as a result of pressures imposed by Washington over the past several decades—the pressures of requirements attached to the grant-in-aid programs.

Local Governments

When you think of local governments, you probably picture city halls and county courthouses occupied by small councils of elected officials and a few offices occupied by record-keeping clerks who collect taxes and issue dog tags and automobile licenses. American local governments are much more than that, however, and their role in the intergovernmental relations system is a major one.

As noted earlier, all local governments are creations of the individual states. Under the formal provisions of the federal system established in the Constitution, governmental powers are divided between the national gov-

MYTH AND REALITY 3.1

The Wonderful World of Reedy Creek

When asked to name the different types of local government in the United States, most Americans will immediately list cities, towns, villages, and counties. Few individuals are likely to name the most numerous type of local governmental unit, the *special district*. A significant share of government activity is carried out by special districts—including school, library, fire protection, mosquito abatement, drainage, and cemetery districts, to name a few. In fact, there are over 40,000 special district governments in the United States.

Among the unique local governments in the United States is a special district located in Orange County, Florida. Called the Reedy Creek Improvement District, it was created "to promote and create favorable conditions" for the principal property owner located within its border—the Disney World amusement complex.

As a government, Reedy Creek does a great many things that you would expect of any local government. It builds roads, offers fire prevention and paramedic services, operates its own waste-water treatment and solid-waste disposal facilities, and controls land-use in the 28,000 acres of land over which it has jurisdiction. Reedy Creek is governed by a board of supervisors composed of five of the district's citizens who are elected by the district's eligible voters.

Despite its lack of a great many permanent residents, the Reedy Creek Improvement District must contend with the nearly 20 million visitors who visit Disney World annually. To finance its operations and pay its 180 employees, Reedy Creek collects $16 million in property taxes from its local residents and area businesses. It just so happens that all 50 permanent residents are Disney World employees or their families, and that all the businesses within the district are owned by Disney World or its subsidiaries.

Being a duly constituted government chartered by the state of Florida, Reedy Creek is capable of borrowing money at extremely low interest rates. In fact, the district had debts amounting to nearly $350 million in 1986, all of it devoted to financing improvements to Disney World property. Under Florida law, all such debts must first be approved by the district's voters. During the last bond election, the vote was 29-0 in favor of issuing the necessary bonds.

ernment and the states. Local governments, in other words, have no constitutional standing. Their very existence and legal authority is derived from legal charters granted to them under state laws.

In practice, however, Americans have always treated local governments as if they had separate and legitimate standing in the federal system.[28] There are just under eighty thousand local governments in the United States. This figure includes county, municipal, township, and other general service governments that provide a range of public services to those who live within their borders. There are more than fifteen thousand school districts. In addition, nearly twenty-six thousand special district governments perform such single and distinctive government functions as public transportation or sewage treatment (see Myth and Reality 3.1). All of these local governments participate in some way in the intergovernmental relations system.

The problems of local governments are not all alike since those governments reflect a variety of physical, social, cultural, political, or economic conditions. Between the extremes of small, rural, lightly populated townships and huge, densely populated metropolitan areas are cities and towns and counties of every conceivable size and shape. To understanding the distinctive role played by local governments in the intergovernmental system, we need to perceive their differences.

Of particular importance are wide economic disparities among various local governments. These differences in wealth influence the way community leaders approach the intergovernmental system. The per capita income in Newark, New Jersey, for example, is just over $5,000, less than half the per capita income of Tulsa, Oklahoma. Newark's government wants more federal aid programs targeted for job training programs, public housing, public health facilities, and similar projects aimed at helping the urban poor. Tulsa's government will actively seek more federal funding for new highways, constructing new recreation facilities, and other amenities.

Besides the economic status of the citizenry, age and ethnic background also bear on local problems and needs. The interests and concerns of Hollywood, Florida, are unique compared with many other communities because more than a fourth of its residents are over sixty-five years old. In El Paso, Texas, a third of the population is eighteen years old or under. The people of Hollywood seek federal and state help in funding special programs for the elderly, while the citizens of El Paso are more interested in state and federal aid for elementary and secondary school programs. The fact that El Paso has a very large Hispanic community is relevant as well. The intergovernmental relations system, for instance, can offer El Paso's schools funds for bilingual education programs that might not be available if the schools had to depend on local resources.

These and other factors make it difficult to generalize about the roles played by local government actors on the intergovernmental relations stage. Nevertheless, there is no doubt that local officials have become major participants in the federal system during the post–World War II period and will remain important. Much of their influence is exercised through local members of Congress who are responsive to the needs of the folks back home. They also exert influence through membership in intergovernmental lobbying groups, which make up an increasingly important set of actors in the federal system.

The Intergovernmental Lobby

The **intergovernmental lobby** includes individuals and groups that have a special interest in the policies and programs implemented through the growing intergovernmental relations system. Some of these lobbyists represent private

Members of the inter-govenmental lobby
Mayors of big cities are important actors on the national stage. Here Boston Mayor Raymond Flynn (left) confers with Chicago Mayor Harold Washington.

interests that hope to benefit or expect to be harmed by some intergovern-mental program. For example, environmental lobbyists push for effective state and local enforcement of national air quality and water quality standards. Lobbyists for the poor or the disabled strive to ensure federal funding of social welfare and educational programs. Other intergovernmental lobbyists support social regulations to strengthen automobile safety, consumer protec-tion, or occupational health. Representatives of businesses seek to reduce these regulations and to weaken state and local enforcement.

In recent years a new kind of lobby has emerged: **public sector interest groups,** which represent the interests of elected officials and other major governmental actors involved in the intergovernmental relations system. For example, the National Governors Association and the U.S. Conference of Mayors are two of the most active groups in Washington that lobby on domestic policy issues. The American Society for Public Administration and the International City Management Association represent the interests of public administrators and other nonelected public sector workers. Still others—such as the National League of Cities, the National Association of Counties, and the Council of State Governments—lobby on behalf of their own government jurisdictions. The growth in the number of public sector interest groups, as well as their political influence, has paralleled the growth of the intergovernmental system itself.[29]

The Role of the Citizen

The largest group of actors on the intergovernmental stage are the citizens of the United States—the intended beneficiaries of all the policies and public services of American government. Hardly an area of American domestic policy remains untouched by the intergovernmental relations system; yet many Americans remain unaware of the role of intergovernmental relations. Every person who drives a car on the highways, attends public schools, uses city buses, or receives emergency care at the community hospital benefits from intergovernmental programs.

Of course, the American people are more than just the beneficiaries of the many goods and services provided through the intergovernmental system. As taxpayers, citizens also pay for those programs, often indirectly. Most intergovernmental programs are paid for with general tax revenues collected by the various levels of government. However, a portion of the money comes from special trust funds established for a particular program. For instance, each time you purchase a gallon of gasoline for your car, you pay a special federal tax. This tax is deposited in the Highway Trust Fund for the construction and maintenance of interstate highways and other roads.

Most important, the American people generate the demand for intergovernmental programs. The pressures that the public brings to bear on the system are most evident when popular grant programs are threatened with major cuts, or when a community faces a crisis that cannot be handled with local resources.

Consider, for example, social service programs for the elderly or handicapped. When members of the Reagan administration suggested cutbacks in Social Security in 1982, the public reacted so negatively that President Reagan felt compelled to promise never to cut those benefits. And when a crisis or tragedy strikes some community—when a tornado or flood devastates a small town or buried hazardous wastes contaminate a community's soil and water supply—the call for action goes out to Washington as well as the state capitol and city hall. These kinds of actions generate intergovernmental activity.

Many Actors on the Stage

Obviously, the intergovernmental stage would be an extremely crowded one if all the actors were involved at the same time. That rarely if ever happens, for few issues exist that interest everyone in the federal system. In fact, only twice in recent history did a great many actors stream onto the intergovernmental relations stage: when Presidents Nixon and Reagan suggested major reforms of the federal system itself.

More typically, the dramas of the federal system are played out on different parts of the stage by a relatively few actors. For example, before 1974, the money in the Highway Trust Fund—raised through federal taxes on gasoline purchases—was used exclusively to build and maintain interstate and other federal highways. For years, however, a coalition of environmentalists and local officials from major urban areas pushed Congress to divert some of those funds to building and maintaining urban mass transit systems. Though the political battle was not highly publicized, it was fiercely fought in a corner of the intergovernmental stage. Finally, Congress passed the National Mass Transportation Act of 1974, allowing state officials to spend some of the Highway Trust's funds on mass transit projects.

Similar instances of intergovernmental politics and policy making take place daily in Washington, in state capitols, in county courthouses, and in city halls. Who is involved in those dramas on the various sections of the intergovernmental stage depends to a great extent on what is at stake.

CONCLUSION: The Myth Versus the Dramas

The image of intergovernmental relations being played out on different parts of the intergovernmental stage poses a challenge to the widely held myth of creeping centralization. According to that myth, the American federal system has been evolving from a decentralized arrangement in which states were the dominant forces to a centralized system that threatens the very existence of the states as viable governments, which Americans can turn to in time of need.

At first reading, American constitutional history seems to support the myth of creeping centralization. There is no doubt that the national government is playing a greater role today than ever before, while the states often seem invisible on the domestic policy scene. On closer examination, however, we see the emergence of an intergovernmental relations system in which the role of all governments—national, state, and local—has increased considerably.

A useful approach is to picture the intergovernmental relations system as a stage upon which many governmental dramas are being played out by a variety of different casts. Because the actions are taking place on so many different parts of the stage, it is impossible to determine if any particular actor or set of actors is dominant. Federal government officials do play an important and often highly visible role in these plays, but so do state, local, and even private actors.

The American federal system today is too complex to be summarized in simple images. To say that there is a trend toward or away from centralization simply distorts an ever-changing reality. Rather, the American federal system is a flexible arrangement among different levels of government that adapts as problems and circumstances change. In that sense, American federalism is very much like the constitutional system from which it emerged.

★ ★ ★
SUMMARY

1. Relationships among national, state, and local officials are becoming increasingly complex. This growing complexity is central to the changing nature of the American federal system.

2. The American federal system emerged as a compromise among the Constitution's framers. American federalism represents a compromise between unitary and confederal forms of government and reflects the idea of national and state governments sharing formal authority.

3. The evolution of the American federal system has been shaped by the distinctive challenges that have faced the United States over the past two centuries. Out of that evolution has emerged a complex system of intergovernmental relations based on a variety of grant-in-aid programs. The intergovernmental relations system has been characterized by periods and episodes of conflict and cooperation.

4. The dynamics of American federalism are best understood as a number of dramas being played out on various parts of the intergovernmental stage by several groups of actors, including the courts, the Congress, the White House, the federal bureaucracy, local and state officials, intergovernmental lobbies, and the American people.

5. The complexities and dramas of American intergovernmental relations challenge the simplistic view that U.S. federalism is driven by a "creeping centralization."

★ ★ ★
KEY TERMS

federal system
unitary system
confederal system

state-centered federalism
nation-centered federalism
dual federalism

grant-in-aid programs
cooperative federalism
intergovernmental relations
categorical, or conditional, grants

block grants
general revenue sharing
intergovernmental lobby
public sector interest groups

SUGGESTED READINGS

- Bowman, Ann O'M., and Richard C. Kearney. *The Resurgence of the States.* Englewood Cliffs, N.J.: Prentice-Hall, 1986. A survey of the increasingly important role played by the states in the American federal system, with emphasis on the growing influence of governors, state legislatures, and other state institutions.

- Davis, S. Rufus. *The Federal Principle: A Journey Through Time in Quest of Meaning.* Berkeley, Calif.: University of California Press, 1978. A classic survey of the meaning of federalism as a constitutional and political concept in Western civilization. Focuses on the historical emergence of federalism in the United States.

- Sharkansky, Ira. *The Maligned States: Policy Accomplishments, Problems, and Opportunities.* New York: McGraw-Hill 1972. A defense of the importance of states in the U.S. political system, written at a time when states were held in low esteem.

- Walker, David B. *Toward a Functioning Federalism.* Cambridge, Mass.: Winthrop, 1981. An introduction to the growth and dynamics of the modern intergovernmental system.

- Wright, Deil S. *Understanding Intergovernmental Relations,* 2nd ed. Monterey, Calif.: Brooks/Cole, 1982. A comprehensive survey of the research in and issues of U.S. intergovernmental relations.

4

CHAPTER

The Heritage of Rights and Liberties

I n 1977 Frank Collin, a Chicago area leader of the American Nazi party, announced his intention to lead a parade through the streets of Skokie, Illinois. Seeking confrontation, the Nazis chose Skokie because of its large Jewish population, many of whom had survived the Holocaust. Skokie officials knew that the sight of the marchers would evoke pain and anger in many residents; besides, other groups had announced plans for counterdemonstrations. Citing these facts, the officials quickly requested a court order prohibiting the march.

Initially, an Illinois trial court issued an order barring the Nazis from parading in uniform, displaying the swastika, or distributing pamphlets. However, the Nazis, with the help of an attorney provided by the American Civil Liberties Union (ACLU), appealed the decision. Eventually, the United States Supreme Court overturned the trial court order, but the matter did not end there. While the request to ban the march was still in the courts, Skokie officials passed a series of laws that created a permit system for marches and required those desiring a permit to obtain $300,000 in liability insurance. The laws also barred marches by organizations distributing racist literature and forbade demonstrators to wear military-style uniforms.

Once again, the Nazis and their ACLU attorney took the issue to the courts. In October 1978 the Supreme Court cleared the way for the Nazis to demonstrate in Skokie by letting stand a lower court ruling that the local ordinances were unconstitutional denials of free speech. Meanwhile, Collin had called off the announced march in Skokie, holding it in a Chicago park instead. The community of Skokie was thus saved from the possibility of serious disruption, and the Nazis held a peaceful rally. But the ACLU, which in the cause of freedom of speech had agreed to represent the Nazis, found itself in turmoil. Disagreements over the decision to represent the Nazis led to resignations of members and a drop in contributions. The nation's oldest civil liberties organization found its membership badly split on just how far it should go in protecting freedom of speech.[1]

As the Skokie case shows, questions of civil liberties and rights affect people deeply. Much of the work of the Supreme Court, the institution that must decide most questions of civil liberties and rights, involves sorting out the very real human conflicts that emerge in the exercise of liberties and rights. Questions of freedom of speech, press, religion, and due process all present challenges to our understanding of civil liberties. **Civil liberties,** most of which are spelled out in the Bill of Rights, protect individuals from excessive or arbitrary government interference. **Civil rights** guarantee protection by the government against discrimination or unreasonable treatment by other individuals or groups.

As we all learned in grade school, the Declaration of Independence states that "all Men are created equal, that they are endowed by their Creator with certain unalienable Rights, that among these are Life, Liberty, and the Pursuit

No nukes is good news Or it would be to this environmental activist, arrested for blocking access to the Shoreham nuclear power plant in New York State. Such arrests underscore the unreality of the myth of absolute liberty. No one is free to break the law, no matter how just he or she believes the cause to be.

of Happiness." We remember these words because they express the American ideology—how we see our nation and ourselves.

Life, liberty, and the pursuit of happiness are certainly stirring words. But what do they mean? What is it that we so enthusiastically support? All too often these words seem to evoke a myth of absolute, or complete, liberty: the perception that since this is a free country we can do as we please. As we will see, liberty is not absolute, nor has it ever been considered so. More important, perhaps, few Americans really believe in absolute liberty when it applies to unpopular groups. When asked general questions about First Amendment liberties, Americans almost universally support them. But support for exercising these liberties drops significantly in regard to such groups as the Nazis. As you read this chapter, notice how our understanding of liberty has changed. It is not just a static concept enshrined in the Bill of Rights and other constitutional provisions, but one that has been and continues to be modified.

Public attitudes toward civil rights tend to reflect a second widely held myth, the myth of political and social equality. According to this myth participation in the political and social system is open equally to all. Yet discrimination still marks American society. Instead of guaranteeing individual civil rights, national, state, and local governments have often enforced discrimination. The rights of minorities have often been ignored in favor of the interests of the majority. Our understanding of civil rights—like our understanding of civil liberties—is constantly changing. Even as our nation struggles to live up to the promise of political equality for blacks and women, there are new demands for civil rights.

In this chapter, we will look at the way difficult choices are made regarding the rights and liberties protected by the Constitution. We will briefly explore the expansion of liberties as the courts have interpreted and reinterpreted the Bill of Rights. We will also look at the way the Supreme Court has treated minorities and claims for equality, noting particularly its interpretation of the Fourteenth Amendment as it affects the rights of blacks and women.

★ ★ ★

NATIONALIZING THE BILL OF RIGHTS

The original Constitution, unlike several state constitutions, made no mention of a bill of rights. Just why no protection of this kind was specified is unclear. Most historians argue that the framers simply felt that a listing of rights and liberties was unnecessary. The federal government was to have only the powers granted to it, and the Constitution did not give the new government any power to infringe on the people's liberties. Therefore many delegates reasoned that there would be no problem. No doubt they also assumed that the separation of powers and the system of checks and balances would thwart any movement to diminish individual liberties.

The failure to include a bill of rights in the Constitution caused clashes at the state ratifying conventions. State after state ratified the Constitution only with the understanding that the new Congress would strengthen the document with a guarantee of certain personal liberties. Consequently, the First Congress, meeting in September 1789, proposed twelve amendments to the Constitution. Ten of these amendments were ratified by the states within two years of proposal. These ten amendments, collectively referred to as the Bill of Rights (although only the first eight provide for individual freedoms), constitute a list of specific limits on the federal government.

Originally, the provisions of the Bill of Rights were understood to limit the actions of just the national government. States were restricted only by

BACKGROUND 4.1

Civil Liberties, Civil Rights, and the Supreme Court

The Supreme Court serves as the final arbiter for civil liberties and civil rights cases. To understand how the Court makes its decisions, you need to know some of its basic features. More information can be found in Chapter 13, on the Court, judges, and the law.

Originally numbering six justices, today the Supreme Court has eight associate justices and a chief justice, all nominated by the president and confirmed by the Senate for life terms. As one of the three branches of government, the Court has the power to influence public policy. When vacancies arise on the Court, presidents—obviously aware of this power—nominate candidates who share their own ideological, philosophical, and policy preferences.

President Ronald Reagan's 1986 nomination of Associate Justice William Rehnquist to fill the seat of retiring Chief Justice Warren Burger and Judge Antonin Scalia to take Rehnquist's place illustrates Supreme Court politics. Both men are strong conservatives whose views on civil liberties and civil rights issues reflect many of Reagan's own positions. Since justices serve life terms, appointments like these can extend the influence of a president well beyond the term of office.

A vast majority of the cases that the Supreme Court hears come to it on appeal from lower federal courts. Since the Court can review only about two hundred of the more than four thousand appeals made in every session, selection of the cases to be heard is an extremely important part of the judicial process. The justices make their decisions by majority vote. Although they do not always explain their ruling, they usually write an opinion outlining the logic of the decision. Judges who dissent from the majority often write a separate opinion reflecting their views.

As the final arbiter in civil liberties and civil rights cases, the Supreme Court exercises enormous power. Having the last word on the meaning of the Constitution makes the Court a central actor in the political and policy-making process.

the provisions of their individual constitutions. The Supreme Court decision in *Barron* v. *Baltimore* clarified this view (1833).[2] John Barron, the owner of a wharf in Baltimore, sued city officials who had redirected several streams that fed into the harbor where his wharf was located. By redirecting the streams, the city had caused large deposits of sand to build up around his wharf, making it inaccessible to ships. Because the city had destroyed his business, Barron claimed that officials were required by the Fifth Amendment to provide just compensation.

After reviewing the precise wording and the historical justification for adoption of the Bill of Rights, Chief Justice John Marshall, writing for a unanimous Court, ruled against Barron. According to Marshall, the Bill of Rights applied only to the national government. That is why, Marshall argued, the first word of the First Amendment is "Congress." This position remained unchallenged until the ratification of the Fourteenth Amendment in 1868.

Drafted chiefly to provide equality before the law to the recently emancipated slaves, the Fourteenth Amendment contains much broader language. Its very first paragraph contains this statement: "nor shall any State deprive any person of life, liberty, or property without due process of law." The statement is critically important for understanding the role of the Bill of Rights in modern society. To some, this "due process" clause clearly indicates that the framers of the Fourteenth Amendment intended to reverse the *Barron* v. *Baltimore* decision. For instance, throughout his long career, Supreme Court Justice Hugo Black steadfastly maintained that the Fourteenth Amendment **incorporated** (that is, made applicable to the states) the entire Bill of Rights.[3]

Although a majority of the Supreme Court has never accepted Black's sweeping interpretation of the Fourteenth Amendment, most provisions of the Bill of Rights have since been applied to the states. Beginning in 1925, the Supreme Court slowly increased the number of provisions applicable to the states. It did so by using an approach known as **selective incorporation** —the making applicable to the states of only those portions of the Bill of Rights that a majority of justices felt to be fundamental to a democratic society. The 1937 case of *Palko* v. *Connecticut* illustrates this approach.[4]

Frank Palko was found guilty of second-degree murder and sentenced to life in prison. The prosecutor, desiring a conviction for first-degree murder, successfully appealed the trial court's decision and retried him. This time Palko was found guilty of first-degree murder and sentenced to death. Palko then appealed his case to the Supreme Court, claiming that the second trial was unconstitutional because the due process clause protected an individual from being tried twice for the same crime. Writing for the Court, Justice Benjamin Cardozo acknowledged that the Bill of Rights contains guarantees so fundamental to liberty that they must be protected from state as well as national infringement. Among these guarantees, however, he did not include the protection against being tried twice for the same crime. Consequently, Frank Palko was executed.

In 1969 the *Palko* decision was overturned, and by the early 1970s the Supreme Court had managed to incorporate almost all provisions of the Bill of Rights. As Table 4.1 shows, only a handful of protections remain unincorporated, and these are likely to stay that way. It is doubtful, for instance, that the Court will ever require the states to provide jury trials in all suits involving amounts of more than twenty dollars. For all intents and purposes then, the Bill of Rights is now equally applicable to the states and the federal government.

Incorporating the Bill of Rights is one thing, but giving meaning to the words is another. We turn now to the Court's interpretation of the Bill of Rights, beginning, naturally enough, with the First Amendment.

TABLE 4.1 Selective Incorporation of the Bill of Rights

Although the Bill of Rights was designed to protect individual freedom, it was not immediately clear whether the protection extended to the states. In a series of decisions—mostly in the 1930s through the 1960s—the Supreme Court ruled that the states as well as the national government are barred from infringing on citizens' constitutional rights.

Amendment, Provision, and Year of Incorporation

First Amendment

Freedom of speech (1927), press (1931), religion (1934), assembly (1937), free exercise of religious belief (1940), separation of church and state (1947), association (1958)

Fourth Amendment

Prohibition against unreasonable searches and seizures (1949)

Fifth Amendment

Prohibition against being forced to testify against oneself (1964); prohibition against double jeopardy—being tried twice for the same offense (1969)

Sixth Amendment

Right to fair (1932), public (1948), and speedy (1967) trial; right to counsel in capital cases (1932), all felony cases (1963), all criminal cases entailing a jail term (1972); right to cross-examine witnesses (1965); right to jury trial in cases of serious crime (1968)

Eighth Amendment

Prohibition against cruel and unusual punishment

Provisions Not Incorporated

Second, Third, Seventh Amendments

All

Fifth Amendment

Right to indictment by grand jury

Eighth Amendment

Prohibition against excessive fines and bail

Source: Adapted and reprinted by permission from *Constitutional Interpretation: Cases—Essays—Materials,* 3rd ed. by Craig Ducat and Harold W. Chase, pp. 906–7; Copyright © 1983 by West Publishing Company. All rights reserved.

★ ★ ★

THE FIRST AMENDMENT

Since the First Amendment is written in absolute terms ("Congress shall make no law . . .") it is more subject to the myth of absolute liberty than the other Amendments. But as we will see, the exercise of First Amendment freedoms often conflicts with other highly desirable goals of society. Most justices have found it unworkable to protect all liberties without qualification. Instead, the issue has been one of balance. Sometimes the Court has interpreted the safeguards of the First Amendment strictly, giving maximum protection to individual liberties. At other times, it has allowed the government great latitude in pursuing its interests. Drawing the lines has never been easy, but it has always been necessary.

Free Speech

Freedom of speech is essential for a democracy. As the late Justice Black observed, "Freedom to speak and write about public questions is as important to the life of our government as is the heart to the body."[5] The First Amendment states that "Congress shall make no law . . . abridging the freedom of speech or of the press. . . ." Nevertheless, the freedom to speak has often been the target of government regulation. No matter how highly we value free speech, each of us is likely at some time or other to see its exercise as dangerous. This is simply a recognition that ideas have consequences—consequences that we may disapprove of or even fear.

Although the First Amendment is phrased in a manner that prohibits any limitations on speech, the Supreme Court has never viewed freedom of speech as immune from all governmental restriction. Justice Oliver Wendell Holmes once noted that freedom of speech does not protect someone who is "falsely shouting fire in a crowded theater." The Court has tried to define the circumstances under which the government may limit speech. To this end, it has employed a series of tests designed to strike a balance between the constitutional protection and the need for public order or security.

The first of these tests was developed by Justice Holmes in *Schenck* v. *United States* (1919).[6] Charles T. Schenck had been convicted under the Espionage Act of 1917 for distributing leaflets urging young men to resist the World War I draft. Writing for a unanimous Court, Justice Holmes rejected the proposition that speech was always protected from government restriction and instead expounded the **clear and present danger test.** The question, Holmes said, was whether speech would cause evils the government had a right to prevent. If the speech could be shown to present grave and immediate danger to its interests, the government had a right to punish it. The justice admitted that in ordinary times the defendant would have been within his constitutional rights, but these were not ordinary times. Urging young men to resist the draft during a war was, he said, a serious threat to the nation's safety.

Almost immediately after Holmes's decision, the majority of the Court began to substitute for clear and present danger the **bad tendency test.** This test allowed the government to punish speech that might cause people to engage in illegal action. Announced in *Gitlow* v. *New York* (1925), the bad tendency test removed the need to prove a close connection between speech and the prohibited evil. To justify a restriction of speech, the government needed only to demonstrate that the speech might, even at some distant time, present a danger to society. Thus Benjamin Gitlow, a member of the Socialist party, could be convicted under a criminal anarchy law that prohibited anyone from advocating the overthrow of the government, even though there was no evidence that his efforts had any effect.

During the 1960s questions of free speech became numerous as the civil rights movement and the movement against the Vietnam War generated a succession of mass protests. Sit-in demonstrations, protest marches, and draft card burnings raised new issues of free speech. The liberal Supreme Court of this era, led by Chief Justice Earl Warren, rejected the bad tendency test of the earlier period. It substituted the **preferred freedoms test,** which proposed that some freedoms—free speech among them—are so fundamental to a democracy that they merit special protection. The government can restrict these freedoms only if they present a grave and immediate danger to the larger society. Theoretically then, government may limit speech, but in practice it is difficult to design a law that passes the test. The preferred freedoms doctrine comes close to an absolute ban on all government restriction of speech.

Symbolic speech.   Not all speech is verbal. In fact, one may engage in what is called symbolic speech without uttering a word. Gestures and even the wearing of garish clothing may convey opinion, perhaps even more effectively than speech. Because symbolic speech is a form of communication, the Supreme Court has generally accorded it the protection of the First Amendment. During the 1960s and 1970s, for instance, the Court upheld the right of high school students to wear black arm bands as a sign of protest against the Vietnam War. The black arm bands were, the Court said, exercises in symbolic speech. The Court used similar logic to overturn the conviction of a young man who had attached a small American flag to the seat of his pants.[7]

Not all symbolic acts have been so protected, however. In 1968, for example, the Court ruled that burning a draft card was not a protected form of symbolic speech, despite the obvious political message conveyed by the

Drawing by D. Fradon; © 1987 The New Yorker Magazine, Inc.

act.[8] Similarly, the Court decided in 1984 that demonstrators attempting to dramatize the plight of the homeless by sleeping in the District of Columbia's Lafayette Park could be evicted, since they were not engaging in symbolic speech.[9] Sleeping may be a form of protest, but it is not currently protected by the First Amendment.

A Free Press

The same language protects the freedom of the press, which is closely linked with freedom of speech. Since the rights at stake are so similar, many of the interpretations applied to free speech cases also fit freedom of the press. As with free speech, however, the majority of justices who have served on the Supreme Court have rejected the proposition that freedom of the press is an absolute.

Prior restraint. Even though the Supreme Court has never accepted complete freedom of the press, it has repeatedly struck down laws imposing a prior restraint on newspapers. **Prior restraint** is the blocking of a publication before it can be made available to the public. The First Amendment has stood as a strong check against would-be censors. The first significant prior restraint case, *Near* v. *Minnesota* (1931), illustrates the point.[10]

At issue in *Near* v. *Minnesota* was a state statute that provided for the banning of "malicious, scandalous and defamatory" newspapers or periodicals. After he had printed a series of articles criticizing the local police department, Jay Near, the publisher of the Minneapolis-based *Saturday Press,* was ordered to cease publication of the weekly scandal sheet. Aggravating his attacks on city officials was a constant anti-Semitic, pro–Ku Klux Klan theme that appeared in each edition of the paper.

Clearly, the *Saturday Press* was malicious, scandalous, and defamatory. Yet the Supreme Court lifted the ban on publication, with Chief Justice Charles E. Hughes observing that prior restraint could be applied only in "exceptional cases." Hughes did admit that under some circumstances the government might prohibit the publishing of truly harmful information—for example, information about troop movements in war time. But in ordinary circumstances the presumption should be to favor publication.

A more serious challenge to freedom of the press arose in *New York Times* v. *United States* (1971), also known as the Pentagon Papers case.[11] Both the *New York Times* and the *Washington Post* published portions of a classified report on the history of American involvement in Vietnam. Citing a breach of national security, the government sought an order to prevent further publication of the materials by the two newspapers. A sharply divided Court (6 to 3) ruled that the newspapers could continue publishing the report because the government had not justified the need for prior restraint. Still, only Justices Black and William Douglas took the position that the government could never restrain a publication. The four others in the majority assumed that in extreme cases national security could justify an injunction, thus raising the possibility of a constitutional exercise of prior restraint.

The great leeway granted the press by the Court in questions of prior restraint does not mean that the press is free to do as it pleases without regard to consequences. The press can be punished after publication. Two forms of expression—libel and obscenity—are particularly open to punishment.

Libel. **Libel** is the use of print or picture to harm someone's reputation. **Slander** is injury by spoken word. Traditionally, these actions have been outside First Amendment protection; therefore, they have been punishable by criminal law and subject to civil prosecution for damages.

Until 1964 the only defense against a libel suit was proof that the statements in question were substantially true. But in 1964 the Court expanded press protection by requiring proof that statements against a public official were made with "actual malice."[12] In order to recover damages, the official must prove not only that the accusation is false, but also that the publisher acted "with knowledge that it was false or with reckless disregard of whether it was false or not." This "actual malice" standard was later extended to cover public figures—private citizens who because of their station in life or their activities are newsworthy. Because actual malice is very difficult to prove, the Court's decisions virtually immunized the press against libel suits.

More recently, the Court has reconsidered the application of this standard. Public officials and public figures must still prove actual malice, but the category of public figures has been narrowed. In *Time, Inc.* v. *Firestone* (1976),[13] the Court awarded damages against the news magazine *Time*. In an article about a divorce proceeding, *Time* referred to the divorcee as an adulteress, a finding not substantiated in the trial court's decree. Ruling against the magazine, the Court redefined a public figure as one who voluntarily enters "into the forefront of public controversies." Because parties to a divorce do not meet such a test, Mrs. Firestone did not need to prove actual malice, but only negligence—a lack of care in checking the facts. Obviously, negligence is much easier to prove than actual malice.

Obscenity. As we noted earlier, obscenity has never been considered deserving of First Amendment protection. Any work judged obscene may be banned. But what is obscene? Again and again the Court has confronted that question, and each time the justices have struggled to give meaning to the elusive concept. Indicative of the difficulty is Justice Potter Stewart's admission that he could not define hard-core pornography, but "I know it when I see it."

In the first of the modern obscenity cases, *Roth* v. *United States* (1957),[14] Justice William Brennan observed that sex and obscenity are not synonymous. Therefore Brennan attempted to formulate a legal test for obscenity that would protect the right to deal with sexual matters and yet reserve to the government the power to prohibit what was truly obscene. The test he proposed was "whether to the average person, applying contemporary community standards, the dominant theme of the material taken as a whole appeals to prurient interest." Later cases attempted to clarify the test by describing the community standards as national standards, not local ones, and requiring proof that the work was "utterly without redeeming social value."[15] This latter aspect of the test made it virtually impossible for prosecutors to obtain pornography convictions.

As a presidential candidate in 1968, Richard M. Nixon vigorously criticized the rulings on pornography as overly permissive. Thus, it came as no surprise that the Supreme Court led by Chief Justice Warren Burger, which included four Nixon appointees, moved to limit the spread of sexually explicit materials. In *Miller* v. *California* (1973)[16] the Court said that prosecutors no longer need demonstrate that the work was "utterly without redeeming social value."

From *Miller* on, prosecutors must prove only that the work "lacks serious literary, artistic, political, or scientific value."

In the *Miller* decision, the Court also rejected the previous rulings that community standards mean national standards. Arguing that it is unrealistic to require the same standard in Maine or Mississippi as in Las Vegas or New York, Chief Justice Burger expressed faith in the ability of jurors to draw on the standards of their local community. Nevertheless, the question of what constitutes obscenity remains a perplexing judicial and social question.

Religious Freedom

The freedom to worship was one of the dominant motives behind the founding of the American colonies. Yet surprisingly, the original Constitution makes only one mention of religion. Article VI states in part: "no religious test shall ever be required as a qualification to any office or public trust under the United States." Not till the First Amendment do we find guarantees of religious freedom. The Amendment begins: "Congress shall make no law respecting an establishment of religion, or prohibiting the free exercise thereof. . . ."

As we have seen, the myth of absolute freedom has seldom been upheld because First Amendment rights have often conflicted with other important social values. The problem is particularly acute in *the case of religious freedom.* The guarantee of the free exercise of religion clearly means that the state must avoid coercion with regard to religious beliefs. But what about social policies that offend particular religious beliefs? Does the state have the right to require school attendance and vaccinations of those whose religious beliefs forbid such practices? Of course, the easy answer is to make an exception, but exceptions run the risk of violating another First Amendment provision— the establishment clause—by showing favoritism to one religion.[17]

Establishment of religion. What does the establishment clause really mean? Years of debate over this question have produced two distinct bodies of opinion. One view holds that the clause was meant to be interpreted narrowly, merely barring Congress from establishing an official, publicly supported church like the Church of England. Those who favor this interpretation argue, however, that nothing in the establishment clause forbids state support of religion as long as all religions are treated equally.

Others see the establishment clause as a broad-based prohibition against any governmental support of religion. Accordingly, they read the First Amendment as banning government involvement in all religious affairs, even in a completely evenhanded way. Advocates of this view claim that the First Amendment requires a complete separation of the government and religion,

A chink in the wall of separation Although Thomas Jefferson argued for complete separation of church and state, succeeding presidents have taken a more flexible view. Religious leaders grace the platform at most public ceremonies, and presidents often speak at religious events like this prayer breakfast. Here President Kennedy (right) prays with evangelist Billy Graham (center).

or as Thomas Jefferson put it, a "wall of separation" between church and state.

The Supreme Court has consistently espoused the "wall of separation" view. Yet in many cases the Court's decisions appear contradictory. They indicate that the justices have not completely rejected the idea of government aid to religious institutions so long as the government does not favor one religion over others. Thus intense debate continues over the establishment clause. It usually focuses on two questions: aid to religious schools and prayer in public schools.

The question of government aid to church-supported educational institutions has long been a knotty problem for the Court. In 1947 the Court allowed to stand a New Jersey plan for providing free bus transportation for children attending parochial schools.[18] Justice Black, writing for the Court, reasoned that the plan was designed to aid the children and their families, and not the religious institutions. Using this so-called child benefit theory, the Court has sustained state programs providing parochial schools with textbooks on secular subjects, school lunches, and public health services normally available in public schools.

In *Lemon* v. *Kurtzman* (1971)[19], however, the Court declared unconstitutional those state programs that used public funds to supplement the salaries of parochial school teachers. Chief Justice Burger argued that supplementing teachers' salaries would require an "excessive entanglement" of government with religion.

Currently, the Court seems divided over establishment clause questions. Some members seek an accommodation of secular and religious practices, while others are intent on maintaining a high wall between church and state. A third group on the Court seeks to present a middle position. As a result, the Court has had difficulty drawing a clear line between permissible and impermissible aid programs.

The Court's decisions on prayer in public schools have created intense controversy. In 1962 public protests followed a ruling[20] that a twenty-two-word nondenominational prayer composed by the New York State Board of Regents for daily recitation by New York schoolchildren violated the establishment clause. One year later the Court added to the controversy by declaring unconstitutional a Pennsylvania law requiring public schools to begin each day with a short reading from the Bible.[21]

Despite the fierce opposition of many religious and political leaders, the Court has maintained its stance that government sponsored prayers in the classroom violate the First Amendment. The Court, however, has never prohibited prayer in public schools; rather it has forbidden government encouragement or involvement in prayer. Nevertheless, none of the frequent efforts to institute voluntary prayer in schools has met with the Court's approval.

We must stress, though, that the Court has not opposed all exercises of religion in public life. For example, the Court has sustained the practice of opening sessions of Congress and state legislatures with a prayer.[22] In 1984 it also ruled that the annual nativity scene erected by the government of Pawtucket, Rhode Island, was constitutional.[23]

Finally, it should be noted that many school districts have evaded or ignored the Court's rulings on prayer in public schools. Furthermore, opponents of these rulings are working to amend the Constitution to permit voluntary prayer in schools.

The free exercise of religion. The First Amendment also guarantees that Congress shall not prohibit the free exercise of religion. This straightforward command means that the practice of religious beliefs must be free of government censure. The Court has consistently refused to examine the content of religious beliefs. Thus we are free to adopt any set of beliefs and to call anything a religion.

Freedom to believe is not the same as freedom to act. You can believe in a religion that demands human sacrifice, but the state has a right to make such sacrifices a crime. Consequently, the Court upheld a law that made it a crime to have more than one husband or wife at the same time, despite objections from Mormons.[24] It has also sustained Sunday-closing laws that caused problems for Orthodox Jews[25] and laws that require children to be vaccinated despite the parents' religious objections.[26] On the other hand, the Court has sustained the right of members of the Native American Church to wear their hair longer than prison rules normally allow and the right of Amish children to leave school after the eighth grade.[27]

Freedom to Assemble

The First Amendment also prohibits any law abridging "the right of the people peaceably to assemble, and to petition the government for a redress of grievances." Although resembling those of free speech, the issues surrounding freedom of assembly involve some form of conduct, such as picketing or mass demonstration. Like freedom of speech, freedom of assembly has been subjected to limitations. As long ago as 1941, for example, the Court recognized that local communities may require groups planning a parade or demonstration to secure a permit beforehand, provided public authorities do not discriminate among those seeking approval on the basis of their beliefs. On the other hand, the Court has ruled that special-purpose facilities, such as prisons,[28] military installations,[29] and public schools[30] are improper forums for the exercise of free speech.

★ ★ ★
DUE PROCESS AND CRIME

Like the liberties discussed earlier, the rights of persons accused of crimes are rooted in the Bill of Rights, especially the Fifth Amendment's guarantee of "due process of law." These rights are meant to protect the individual from the arbitrary use of police power. When it comes to criminal suspects, however, there is little public support for the myth of absolute liberty. The Court has tried to balance the majority's demand for protection from the criminal against the suspect's need to be protected from excessive government power.

Right to Counsel

The Sixth Amendment to the Constitution guarantees the right to have a lawyer defend you. But for most of our history, this right did not extend to the states, even though most prosecutions occur in state courts. In 1932 the Supreme Court did allow a limited right to representation by counsel by declaring that in capital offenses—those carrying the death penalty—the state

Gays exercise right to assemble Because gay activists believe that their private rights have been restricted by society, they have increasingly claimed the public right to protest discriminatory treatment.

was obligated to provide a lawyer to those unable to afford one (*Powell* v. *Alabama*).[31] The occasion for this ruling was a famous trial known as the Scottsboro case. In this trial, lasting only one day, Ozie Powell and seven other young black men were charged with and convicted of raping two young white girls. Before the trial, the local magistrate appointed all members of the local bar to represent the defendants. Not surprisingly, no lawyer stepped forward to defend them, and they were sentenced to death without ever having had adequate time to secure effective counsel.

Not until 1963 did the Supreme Court extend this right to everyone charged with a felony (*Gideon* v. *Wainwright*).[32] Nine years later the Court broadened this guarantee to cover any penniless defendant being tried for an offense for which there is a jail term.[33]

Considerably more controversial, and some would say more effective, were the Court's decisions providing for the right to counsel before trial. Even the most gifted lawyer is unlikely to be of much help to a client who

The Scottsboro defendants The young men in this famous case of the 1930s were eventually represented by an out-of-state lawyer assisted by a local attorney. They underwent four trials, and the last of the group remained in jail until 1950.

has, during police questioning, given incriminating statements. In view of this fact and the likelihood that pretrial questioning plays upon the fear and ignorance of suspects, the Warren Court expanded the right to counsel to include the investigative stages preceding the trial. Justice Arthur Goldberg, speaking for the Court in *Escobedo* v. *Illinois* (1964),[34] announced that the right to counsel applied whenever the investigation turned from a general inquiry to a focus "on a particular suspect."

Two years later the Court bolstered the *Escobedo* decision by requiring that police officers inform suspects of their constitutional rights. In overturning the rape-kidnapping conviction of Ernesto Miranda, the Court, in *Miranda* v. *Arizona*,[35] created specific guidelines for police interrogations. Accordingly, suspects must be told that (1) they have the right to remain silent; (2) anything they say may be used against them in a court of law; and (3) they have the right to the presence of an attorney, and if they cannot afford an attorney, one can be appointed prior to any questioning.

Although police departments around the country reacted negatively to the *Miranda* decision, most departments comply with the decision. Each officer is given a wallet-sized card (referred to as a Miranda card) listing the rights that are to be read to suspects. Often the list is in both English and Spanish. Nevertheless, the *Miranda* decision continues to be one of the most controversial Supreme Court decisions.

Recently, the Court has been willing to allow some exceptions to *Miranda*. For instance, it let stand the rape conviction of Benjamin Quarles. Prior to having been read his Miranda rights, Quarles, at the request of the police, implicated himself in the crime by pointing to the place where the weapon could be found. In upholding Quarles's conviction, the Court argued that considerations of public safety may outweigh the need to strictly adhere to the *Miranda* decision.[36]

Searches and Seizures

The Fourth Amendment states that "the right of the people to be secure in their persons, houses, papers, and effects, against unreasonable searches and seizures, shall not be violated. . . ." Notice that only unreasonable searches are prohibited. Unfortunately, the Amendment does not tell us what is reasonable, making an absolute application of the Amendment impossible.

As a general rule, a search may be conducted after a **search warrant,** which grants written permission, is issued by a neutral magistrate. The authorities must fill out an application that describes what they expect to find and where they expect to find it. In addition, the officers must set out facts that enable the magistrate to conclude that there is "probable cause" to justify issuing the warrant. Over the years, however, the Court has recognized certain exceptions to the warrant rule.

If a suspect consents, a warrantless search is legal, even if the suspect was unaware of the right to refuse.[37] Recognizing that cars are mobile and relatively public places, the Court has allowed them to be searched without a warrant, if the officer has "probable cause." Instances of hot pursuit also constitute an exception to the warrant requirement. Thus police officers chasing a suspect need not turn back and acquire a warrant. Finally, a police officer need not ignore evidence accidentally discovered; the officer may seize that which is in plain sight.

Before 1961 there were few effective checks on police searches. An individual subjected to an illegal search could sue the police for civil damages, but juries rarely sympathized with criminal suspects. Evidence was admissible in state trials even if it had been gathered illegally. In 1957 police officers in Cleveland, Ohio, broke into the home of Dollree Mapp and seized pornographic materials (they were looking for a fugitive). They expected to introduce the evidence at trial, even though their search had been conducted without a warrant. This was not to be the case, however. Instead, the Court overturned Mapp's conviction, ruling that evidence gathered illegally was inadmissible in state trials (*Mapp* v. *Ohio*, 1961).[38] This **exclusionary rule** means that evidence, no matter how incriminating, cannot be used to convict someone if it is gathered illegally.

Perhaps no other criminal law ruling stirred as much controversy as the exclusionary rule. Law enforcement officials and political leaders around the country assailed the Court for its coddling of criminals. The exclusionary rule provoked such furor precisely because it dramatizes the conflict between the due process rights of individuals and the interests of a society attempting to control crime. Despite the intense controversy, the Court continues to enforce the exclusionary rule, although lately the justices have limited its reach by creating some broad exceptions. In 1984, for instance, the Court adopted

Preventive detention ruled legal Reputed mob boss Anthony "Fat Tony" Salerno, cigar in mouth, enters a car outside a federal courthouse in New York after being indicted on federal racketeering charges. In one of the most significant decisions of the 1986 term, the Supreme Court ruled that Salerno and other criminal suspects judged to pose a danger to the safety of others or to the community at large could be denied bail pending trial, a practice known as preventive detention.

what is called an inevitable discovery exception: it permits the introduction of evidence collected illegally when such evidence would have been discovered anyway.[39] More important, that same year the Court allowed what is called the good faith exception. If the police conduct a search using a warrant that later turns out to be invalid, the evidence discovered during the search is admissible at trial.[40]

Wiretapping and Eavesdropping

When the Supreme Court first considered whether wiretapping and eavesdropping are constitutional, a majority of the justices concluded that such procedures were fully permissible. Wiretapping and eavesdropping were not, according to the Court, searches and seizures within the meaning of the Fourth Amendment; thus the prohibition against unreasonable searches and seizures did not apply.[41] In 1967, however, the Court reversed this position by ruling that the Fourth Amendment protected "people, not places."[42] Wiretaps therefore are legal if the government demonstrates probable cause to a supervising court.

Cruel and Unusual Punishment

In the 1962 case *Robinson* v. *California*,[43] the Supreme Court made the Eighth Amendment's protection against the imposition of "cruel and unusual punishments" applicable to the states. But beyond noting that the punishment must fit the crime, the justices did little to explain what the terms *cruel* and *unusual* meant. Lawrence Robinson had been convicted under a statute that made it a misdemeanor to be addicted to narcotics. Robinson was not, at the time of his arrest, under the influence of narcotics, nor were any found on him. The police officer made the arrest after observing needle marks on Robinson's arms. Likening this situation to being punished for having an illness, the Court argued that even one day in jail would be excessive. Significantly, however, it gave no hint as to whether the most controversial of punishments, the death penalty, constituted cruel and unusual punishment.

It was not until 1972 that the Court gave an answer to that question. A divided Court concluded, in *Furman* v. *Georgia*,[44] that capital punishment was, in that particular case, a violation of the Eighth Amendment. The Court did not reject the death penalty itself as unconstitutional; instead the justices focused on what one justice referred to as the "wanton and freakish" pattern of imposition. Thus, although the Court declared Georgia's death penalty unconstitutional, it also encouraged states to draft more precise laws that provided standards to guide judges and juries.

Following the Furman decision, several state legislatures rewrote their death penalty statutes in an effort to conform to the Court's guidelines. This turned out to be difficult, however, as the Court seemingly zigzagged through the cases, allowing one statute to stand while ruling another unconstitutional. The justices continued to demand precise standards for the application of the death penalty and yet declared unconstitutional a state law that mandated capital punishment for specific crimes (*Woodson* v. *North Carolina*, 1976).[45] Laws that did not adequately consider mitigating circumstances were also declared unconstitutional because they restricted the discretion of the judge and jury. Thus, although executions have taken place since the Furman decision, the constitutional standards remain unclear.

★ ★ ★

PRIVACY

In a classic law review article published in the 1890s, Charles Warren and Louis Brandeis first articulated the notion of a right to privacy.[46] They hoped to establish the "right to be let alone," but the concept did not come quickly to American law. In fact, the Supreme Court did not recognize or create such a right until the 1965 decision in *Griswold* v. *Connecticut*.[47] Dr. Estelle Griswold had been convicted under a Connecticut law that made it illegal to provide birth control devices or even give instruction on their use. When the case was appealed to the Supreme Court, Justice Douglas, writing for the majority, argued that the law unduly interfered with married couples' right of privacy. Because the Constitution does not specifically mention a right of privacy, Douglas went to great pains to demonstrate that, taken together, several provisions of the Bill of Rights created such a right.

In one of the most controversial decisions it ever delivered, *Roe* v. *Wade* (1973),[48] the Supreme Court extended the right of privacy to cover abortions. The Court ruled that in the first trimester of a pregnancy the decision about abortion resided with the woman. In the second trimester, the state could dictate general rules governing the procedure, such as requiring that it be performed in a hospital. Only in the third trimester could the state prohibit abortion altogether.

Recently, however, the Court has refused to extend the protection of the right to privacy to private homosexual activity among consenting adults. In *Bowers* v. *Hardwick* (1986),[49] the Court upheld Georgia's sodomy law, claiming that the right of privacy does not extend protection to any kind of private sexual conduct between consenting adults. Although the *Bowers* case dealt specifically with homosexual acts, the Court made it clear that the right of privacy does not extend to heterosexuals who may be engaged in illegal acts such as adultery.

★ ★ ★

EQUAL PROTECTION OF THE LAWS

The Declaration of Independence tells us that all men are created equal and the Fourteenth Amendment provides for equal protection of the laws. The fact is, however, that all laws discriminate. Discrimination in its broadest sense involves treating particular categories of people differently from each other, and that is what acts of public policy do. The important question then is what categories are constitutionally impermissible? Invidious, or unconstitutional, discrimination occurs when a category is based on characteristics not fundamentally related to the situation. As you will see, race is such a category. That realization has come slowly to a society dedicated to the myth of political equality, and so racial discrimination persists. Can the same conclusions be drawn with regard to distinctions based on sex? Here the answer given by the Court is not so clear.

The Continuing Struggle Against Racism

An important element of post–Civil War Reconstruction was the adoption of three key Amendments: the Thirteenth, Fourteenth, and Fifteenth. The Thirteenth abolished slavery and involuntary servitude. The Fourteenth, as we have seen, affected several aspects of individual freedom, but its key provision on civil rights is the clause stating that no state shall "deny to any person within its jurisdiction the equal protection of the laws." The Fifteenth guarantees that the right to vote cannot be denied on "account of race, color, or previous condition of servitude."

These three Amendments, plus the congressional acts passed under their authority, promised the recently freed slaves a future of political and civil equality. Indeed, as C. Vann Woodward pointed out in his classic study, *The Strange Case of Jim Crow*,[50] the period immediately following the Civil War was a time of great progress in assimilating the former slaves. But the progress did not last.

In 1883 the Supreme Court struck down the Civil Rights Act of 1875, which forbade the separation of the races in public accommodations—transportation, hotels, and theaters. Congress had assumed it had power to pass the act under the equal protection clause of the Fourteenth Amendment. In disagreeing, the Court argued that the Fourteenth Amendment applied only to state-imposed segregation, not discrimination imposed by private individuals. This interpretation implied that Congress could act if a state affirmatively discriminated, but not if it simply allowed segregation to exist. Thirteen years later the Court dealt another blow to those fighting segregation when it ruled, in *Plessy* v. *Ferguson*,[51] that the Fourteenth Amendment did not even prohibit segregation. On the contrary, the Court argued, separation of the races is permitted as long as they receive equal treatment. This is the noted "separate but equal" doctrine.

The Court's narrow ruling on the Fourteenth Amendment, along with presidential disinterest in racial equality, gave rise to Jim Crow laws. Community after community decreed the separation of the races, and almost no aspect of life was too trivial to escape the reach of these laws. Not only did states require separate drinking fountains and public bathrooms for blacks and whites, but some went so far as to require different courtroom Bibles.[52] The stress was on separation. Even the Court paid little heed to equality. Three years after the *Plessy* decision, the Court let stand as a local matter a Georgia school board decision to close the black high school while leaving open the all-white high school.[53] "Separate but equal," then, meant separate.

Public education. Despite such setbacks, the struggle to end segregation in American society continued. The National Association for the Advancement of Colored People (NAACP) formed in 1909, became the driving force in these efforts. At first the NAACP tried to persuade Congress to pass federal legislation forbidding segregation. Failing in the legislative arena, the organization created a separate unit, the Legal Defense Fund, directed by Thurgood Marshall (now a justice of the Supreme Court). The primary tactic of the Legal Defense Fund was to attack segregation in the courts.

In the late 1930s the Legal Defense Fund began a series of court battles that challenged segregation in all areas of American life. It was most successful in the realm of education. As a result of the fund's efforts, the Court struck down a Missouri law that reimbursed black law students for out-of-state tuition, rather than admit them to the University of Missouri.[54] Then, in 1950, the Court ruled that a separate University of Texas law school for blacks was not equal to the University of Texas law school attended by whites because the former lacked certain intangible factors such as prestige and reputation.[55] Although the Court failed to overturn the "separate but equal" doctrine in its Texas decision, it came close.

Finally, on May 7, 1954, the Supreme Court startled the nation by a unanimous decision in *Brown* v. *Board of Education of Topeka*[56] that the Fourteenth Amendment prohibits a state from compelling children to attend racially segregated public schools. In a brief opinion that specifically overturned *Plessy* v. *Ferguson*, the Court simply declared that "in the field of public education the doctrine of 'separate but equal' has no place." No other conclusion was possible, the justices argued, because "Separate educational facilities are inherently unequal."

Pronouncing segregation unconstitutional was one thing; compelling desegregation another. Recognizing this, the Court set the case for reargument the following term in order to consider remedies, and in *Brown II* (1955) required desegregation of public schools to proceed with "all deliberate speed." All deliberate speed, however, was interpreted by many school districts and lower courts as all deliberate delay.

Between 1955 and 1969 little change occurred in public schools, and such progress as was made exacted a high cost. For instance, in 1957 President Dwight D. Eisenhower used federal troops to protect black students enrolled in a Little Rock, Arkansas, high school. The admission of the University of Mississippi's first black student sparked riots that killed two men. Responding to this resistance to progress, the Court proclaimed in 1969 that "allowing 'all deliberate speed' is no longer constitutionally permissible." Every school district was "to terminate dual school systems at once."[57]

Implementing the *Brown II* decision was hard enough in southern schools, but in the 1970s the Court began to confront seemingly more difficult problems of segregation in the North. By the 1970s many urban school systems in the North were more segregated than their counterparts in the South—because of housing patterns rather than state laws. Having ruled that courts may order remedial action, such as busing, only to correct instances of state-imposed segregation,[58] the Supreme Court made it extremely difficult to remedy segregation due to the movement of white families out of the central cities to the suburbs. This movement created in the North a pattern of largely white suburban school districts surrounding increasingly black and Hispanic city schools. Thus, public school integration remains an illusive goal in many cities.

Public accommodations. The *Brown* decision had little bearing on the widespread practice of private discrimination in public accommodations. As court efforts to eliminate discrimination against blacks continued, public protest against discrimination began to mount. In December 1955, Rosa Parks, a Montgomery, Alabama, seamstress, was arrested for refusing to give up her seat on a bus to a white man. Her arrest sparked a year-long boycott of the Montgomery bus system led by Dr. Martin Luther King. Eventually, the system was integrated, but only after Dr. King's home was bombed and he and several others were arrested for "conspiracy to hinder the operations of business."

The Montgomery boycott was only the beginning, however. In the early 1960s unrest grew among the opponents of segregation: blacks and white sympathizers increasingly turned to public protest. Marches and sit-in demonstrations received wide publicity as police reacted to the protests with greater force. In 1963 President John F. Kennedy proposed legislation to

Marching for freedom Protest marches of the 1960s, led by Martin Luther King, Coretta Scott King, and other members of the Southern Christian Leadership Conference brought a response from Washington in the form of civil rights, voting, open housing, and equal accommodations laws. Despite these gains, racial discrimination continues to burden many individuals in American society.

desegregate public accommodations, which Congress finally passed at the urging of Kennedy's successor, President Lyndon B. Johnson.

When passed, the Civil Rights Act of 1964 made it a crime to discriminate in providing public accommodations. The statute barred racial discrimination in hotels, restaurants, gas stations, at sporting events, and in all places of entertainment. The act also included provisions against discrimination in employment. Though covering similar ground as the Civil Rights Act of 1875, the 1964 statute invoked congressional power over interstate commerce rather than the Fourteenth Amendment. The 1964 act made discrimination a crime because it interfered with the flow of interstate commerce. To justify an attack on discrimination by reference to commerce may seem strange and even dehumanizing, but it was an effective way of getting around the narrow reading of the Fourteenth Amendment given by the Supreme Court in the Civil Rights cases of 1883.

Freedom ride The success of the civil rights movement prompted other disadvantaged groups to adopt the well-tested tactics used by civil rights activists. Here a recent demonstration by differently abled citizens passes the Lincoln Memorial in Washington, D.C.

Voting rights. As we noted earlier, the Fifteenth Amendment guarantees that the right to vote cannot be denied on account of race. Nevertheless, after 1877—the year the federal government stopped supervising elections in the South—southern states excluded the vast majority of blacks from the voter registration rolls. They did so through diverse and inventive means that commonly involved the use of some type of highly subjective test. Potential voters might, for instance, be given portions of the Constitution to read and explain. Because the examiners had complete freedom in selecting questions and answers, rejecting applicants was an easy matter. Even black lawyers sometimes failed the Constitution test. So effective were these efforts that in 1961 less than 10 percent of the black population was registered to vote in 129 counties of the South.

To counter this, Congress passed the Voting Rights Act of 1965. In states and subdivisions covered by the act, all tests were suspended, and the attorney general was empowered to assign federal registrars to enroll all applicants meeting state requirements. In extensions of the act in 1970 and 1975, Congress banned literacy tests nationwide and broadened coverage to areas where Spanish, Asian, Indian, and Alaskan languages are spoken by large numbers of people.[59] Finally, in 1982, portions of the act were extended for twenty-five years. Nevertheless, efforts to disenfranchise minorities continue in several parts of the United States.

Sex Discrimination

The handicapped, the aged, and homosexuals have in recent years become increasingly vocal in their demand for protection from discrimination. But women have been even more visible in pressing the argument that they are deprived of political and social equality.

Women have always held citizenship, but from the beginning it was a strange form of citizenship that carried no political rights. Women could not vote and were recognized by law as subservient to their husbands. A married woman could not own property, contract debts, or even keep the money she might earn. Upon marriage, man and woman became one, and that one was the man. In return for giving up her separate existence, the law guaranteed the wife that the husband would provide for her necessities. He was not responsible, however, beyond what he determined to be the necessities of life.

Women first organized in the effort to abolish slavery. The first generation of feminists, led by Lucy Stone, Elizabeth Cady Stanton, Susan B. Anthony, and others, were dedicated abolitionists. In the organized opposition to slavery, the feminist leaders developed political skills that became the foundation for the first women's movement.

Crucial to the movement was the first women's rights conference, held in 1848 in Seneca Falls, New York. But suffrage—the most dramatic of the many reforms proposed by the Seneca conference—was submerged in the Civil War effort and then in the struggle over the post–Civil War Amendments. Although some feminists wanted to add sex to the provisions of the Fifteenth Amendment's guarantee of the right to vote, others opposed such an effort. Many supporters of the Fifteenth Amendment maintained that the issues of race and sex had to be treated separately if they were to succeed.

Among the many groups that continued to press for suffrage, none was more dedicated than the Congressional Union. Using techniques that would become more common in the 1960s, its members held marches, picketed the White House, and staged hunger strikes. Several members were jailed and beaten for their protests. In 1920 the Nineteenth Amendment was finally ratified. After years of struggle, the Constitution now contained the guarantee that "The right of the citizens of the United States to vote shall not be denied or abridged by the United States or by any state on account of sex."

With the adoption of the Nineteenth Amendment, the women's movement lost steam. The movement had always been broader than the issue of suffrage, but the long and difficult battle for the vote had displaced most other issues. Not until the early 1960s did the women's movement revive. This "second wave" has been seeking the eradication of sexism in all aspects of life.

Paternalism and discrimination. The ratification of the Nineteenth Amendment did not eliminate sex discrimination from American society, partly because sex discrimination, even more than race discrimination, stems from a strong sense of paternalism. Discrimination against women has been routinely defended as a means of protecting them, even when the goal was exploitation.

For many years the Supreme Court rather uncritically accepted distinctions based on sex if they appeared to benefit women. The Court's 1948 decision in *Goesaert* v. *Cleary*[60] illustrates this approach. The Court upheld a Michigan law that prohibited women from working as bartenders unless they were the wife or daughter of the owner. They could, however, work as waitresses. The Court accepted the argument that the statute protected women from the unwholesome elements encountered by bartenders. The exception for wives and daughters was reasonable because the husband or father would protect them. What the Court overlooked was that the statute was motivated by a desire of male bartenders to monopolize the profession. Male bartenders and female servers guaranteed male domination of the better-paying jobs.

Even the liberal Warren Court, which did so much to open American society to racial minorities, succumbed to the paternalistic treatment of women. In *Hoyt* v. *Florida,* the Court upheld the conviction of a woman charged with murdering her husband. Gwendolyn Hoyt claimed that the conviction by an all-male jury violated her rights under the Fourteenth Amendment. Florida law required that both men and women serve on juries, but it also provided that no woman would be called for jury duty unless she had previously registered with the clerk of the court her desire to be placed on the jury list. In declaring the Florida statute constitutional, Chief Justice Earl Warren noted that "woman is still regarded as the center of home and family life."[61] A woman had a right but not a duty to jury service.

In recent years the Court has been less tolerant of statutes that supposedly benefit women. Thus the Court struck down an Oklahoma law that set a lower drinking age for women than men.[62] Nevertheless, the Court continues to accept some classifications that treat men and women differently. For instance, the court accepted as constitutional Florida's tax exemption for widows but not widowers. Noting the economic inequality that existed between men and women, the Court argued that the law was designed to compensate for past discrimination.[63]

Women in the work force. One of the most dramatic changes in society has been the growing importance of women in the work force. Since 1974 the numbers have increased to the point that more than half of all women over the age of sixteen are now in the labor force. Yet women's wages lag behind those of men. Women, in 1982, earned fifty-nine cents for each dollar earned by a male worker. To some extent the wage gap between men and women represents the failure of employers to abide by the Equal Pay Act of 1963, which requires "equal pay for equal work." A large part of the difference, however, is explained by the fact that so many women are found in such low-paying, traditionally female occupations as teaching, nursing, and secretarial work.

The recognition that traditional women's work has long been underpaid has led to calls for a new approach to wage-setting, referred to as comparable worth. Advocates of comparable worth contend that women should receive equal pay for work demanding comparable skill, effort, and education. To date, comparable-worth plans have been introduced in several local governments and in the personnel system of the state of Washington, but resistance to the idea is strong.

Although the Civil Rights Act of 1964 prohibits discrimination in employment on the basis of "race, color, religion, sex, or national origin," its application to women has been slow in coming. Initially, the national government was reluctant to apply the act to cases of sex discrimination. The federal courts often tolerated discrimination based upon sex, plus some other characteristic. For example, the Court used the "sex plus" distinction to justify company policies that provided for compensation for all non–job-related disabilities except pregnancy. Such policies, the Court argued, did not constitute sex discrimination because they are not based simply on sex, but rather on sex, plus the characteristic of pregnancy.[64] In 1978 Congress overturned that decision.

Although the courts were slow to view sexual harassment in the workplace as an issue of discrimination, a 1986 decision affirmed that the Civil Rights Act prohibits harassment. Indeed, the Court's ruling was reasonably broad, arguing that sexual harassment need not result in promotion or job loss to be prohibited. The creation of an offensive or hostile working environment is sufficient to satisfy the definition.

The equal rights amendment. The most conspicuous evidence of this demand for equality was the proposed Equal Rights Amendment. Submitted to the states by Congress in 1972, the ERA read simply: "Equality of rights

controversy continues since affirmative action represents a basic conflict inherent in Americans' ideas about equality.

CONCLUSION: Absolutes and Qualifications

In this chapter, we have seen how inaccurate and inappropriate the myth of absolute liberties is. As we have noted, the Supreme Court, the governmental institution most directly responsible for reconciling conflicting values, has never accepted the myth. For many citizens, however, the myth lives on in regard to First Amendment freedoms and, occasionally, inspires movements to thwart the Supreme Court by amending the Constitution.

In contrast, there is little public support for the myth when it comes to the liberties of criminal suspects. The Court has tried to balance the majority's demand for protection against appropriate constitutional protections for suspects. A society that disregards the rights of defendants risks creating a police state that ignores all individual rights, but at the same time all societies must have the capability to prevent lawless behavior.

Finally, we have seen how the Court has in recent years recognized the reality behind the myth of social and political equality. Using the equal protection clause of the Fourteenth Amendment, it has done much to assure a greater degree of equality for black Americans, although equality is yet to be achieved. But the Court has not expanded the concept of equality to cover other minority groups. Thus women, the aged, the handicapped, homosexuals, and others still face considerable discrimination.

★ ★ ★
SUMMARY

1. Civil liberties are the protections individuals have against excessive or arbitrary government interference. Civil rights are guarantees by the government of protection against discrimination or unreasonable treatment by other individuals or groups.

2. Originally, the Bill of Rights did not restrict the actions of state governments. Through a process known as selective incorporation, however, the Supreme Court has made most provisions applicable to the states, as well as to the federal government.

3. Rejecting the position that all forms of speech are protected, the court has attempted to balance conflicting interests, using a series of tests that considered the impact of the speech. Sometimes the Court has favored speech, but at other times it has not.

4. As with freedom of speech, the Court has rejected the argument that freedom of the press is an absolute, but the justices have been unwilling to permit prior restraint, or the blocking of a publication before it can be made available to the public. After publication, the press can be punished for libel and obscenity.

5. The First Amendment prohibits the government from establishing a religion, and it also guarantees the free exercise of religion. The Supreme Court's interpretation of these provisions has generated considerable controversy in American society.

6. Although it has made some exceptions recently, the Court continues to require that a suspect in a crime be allowed representation by counsel and be informed of that right, as well as the right to remain silent. Evidence seized illegally cannot be used to convict, although the Supreme Court has also made broad exceptions to that rule recently.

7. Racial and sexual discrimination have burdened many in American society. The struggle for equality has led to the end of the separate-but-equal doctrine and some decreases in discrimination, particularly in education, accommodations, and voting. But black Americans and other racial minorities, women, the handicapped, the aged, homosexuals, and others are still subject to discrimination's effects.

8. Among the most controversial of the equality issues is affirmative action. Though many view it as an essential means to ensure equality, others attack it as reverse discrimination.

★ ★ ★

KEY TERMS

civil liberties	prior restraint
civil rights	libel
selective incorporation	slander
clear and present danger	search warrant
bad tendency test	exclusionary rule
preferred freedoms test	affirmative action

★ ★ ★

SUGGESTED READINGS

- Brigham, John. *Civil Liberties and American Democracy*. Washington, D.C.: Congressional Quarterly Press, 1984. An in-depth study of the legal concepts of liberty, due process, property, and equality.

- Corbett, Michael. *Political Tolerance in America: Freedom and Equality in Public Attitudes.* Longman, 1982. A well-written account of public support for political freedom and equality.
- Cox, Archibald. *Freedom of Expression.* Cambridge, Mass.: Harvard University Press, 1981. Commentary on the First Amendment that critiques recent trends in Supreme Court decisions.
- Kluger, Richard. *Simple Justice.* New York: Knopf, 1975. A complete account of the legal and political setting of the Supreme Court's decision in *Brown* v. *Board of Education.*
- Pritchett, Herman C. *Constitutional Civil Liberties.* Englewood Cliffs, N.J.: Prentice-Hall, 1984. A comprehensive history and commentary on judicial enforcement of civil liberties and rights.

5

CHAPTER

Public Opinion and Political Participation

The representative wearily shook her head as she headed out of the meeting room. She was exhausted after five days of traveling through her congressional district, meeting with her constituents. The trip was designed to help her gather opinions about a proposed bill, which would enforce strong and costly industrial pollution control standards. Survey polls, conducted by a reputable firm, showed no clear-cut trends in her constituents' feelings about the bill. She needed to know more, and face-to-face meetings seemed to be the best way to gather information.

She was surprised by the turnout at the meetings. The hearing rooms were packed with people eager to voice their opinions. Apparently, the well-constructed, carefully executed poll had not picked up the depth of opinion on the issue. Although most of those present favored the bill, she had not expected the variety of motivations for that support, nor the number of suggestions for changes in the bill's wording.

Some constituents favored the legislation but wanted its effective date postponed to accommodate nonconforming industries. Environmentalists wanted stronger pollution control standards and immediate implementation. Still others argued that the bill should apply only to new industries in the state. A business group opposed the legislation in any form, insisting that implementation costs would drive many industries into bankruptcy. Finally, a union representative expressed fear that jobs would be lost and that the people of the district would suffer if the bill should pass. Only one important group was missing from the meetings: constituents who knew nothing about the proposed legislation or who did not care about it.

This scenario accurately describes the often varied, competing, or absent public opinions typical of the constituencies of community, state, and national officials. Like our hypothetical representative, members of Congress often assess the public's opinion on a variety of complex programs and issues—occasionally by commissioning polls. Asked to explain their votes on particular bills, they may say that their actions reflect the majority viewpoint in the district.

Indeed, polls and surveys (as well as public hearings) are one important way that politicians, scholars, and the media measure the public's opinions on everything from its favorite presidential candidate to its attitudes on specific issues or laws. A majority of citizens support this use of polls by politicians and the media. In one survey, 75 percent of those responding agreed that most opinion polls work for the best interests of the general public.[1] One reason for this approval is the widespread view that public opinion is majority opinion. Officials who claim that they are following majority opinion when they vote share this perception.

According to some scholars and journalists, only a small portion of the population acts on opinions through participation in the political process. Political action is not a favorite American pastime. A look at voter turnout, a widely used measure of participation, points up the extent of inactivity, particularly when the rates are compared with those in other Western democracies, where almost all eligible voters turn out.[2] For example, the 1984 presidential elections attracted only 54 percent of voting-age adults, and the 1986 off-year general elections had the lowest turnout since 1942—37 percent of the eligible voters.

Some scholars suggest that low participation indicates satisfaction with the political system. Why vote if everything is fine? Many observers, however, suspect that Americans are apathetic. The public may have opinions about politics, the argument goes, but is unwilling (or finds it unnecessary) to participate in the system. Both of these views about public opinion and political participation are strongly influenced by two widely held myths.

The myth of majority opinion frequently surfaces in high school civics books. According to this myth, public opinion "is generally used to refer to the opinion held about any issue by a majority of the people."[3] Most Americans do in fact agree on such general political ideas as the importance of democracy and representative government and the need for majority rule balanced by a concern for minority rights. But they often disagree on specific domestic and foreign policies.

No majority opinion here What should universities do about their investments in companies doing business in racially segregated South Africa? This question has divided opinion on many campuses. At Dartmouth College conservative students tore down this shanty, which was built by supporters of divestment to symbolize the plight of South African blacks. The incident underscores the diversity of American public opinion and also reminds us that the myth of absolute freedom often breaks down when people are faced with real situations.

Consider, for example, the public's views on balancing the national budget. Though in 1986 most Americans recognized the problem—that the deficit was too high and that reforms were necessary—few agreed on any one solution. Almost every specific proposal, ranging from cuts in student loans, farm subsidies, social welfare, and defense programs to the imposition of a national sales tax found its opponents and supporters.[4] In trying to manage the deficit, public officials must balance a diverse set of opinions voiced by a variety of groups. On this issue and many more, "majority opinion" is often unclear or nonexistent. What is more, public opinion is often unstable and difficult to gauge.

The myth of the apathetic public reflects the high value that many journalists, social scientists, and others place on voting in elections. According to this myth, many Americans prefer to leave politics to professionals. Although these observers correctly note the low turnout on election day, their narrow focus on voting, we believe, distorts reality. Participation in politics can take many forms—from joining the school board, PTA, or other community groups to attending political rallies or watching presidential nominating conventions on television. Though political activists may not make up most of the U.S. population, neither are Americans a nation of stay-at-homes.

In this chapter we will look at the origins of public opinion and its content and discuss the ways in which Americans act on their beliefs. By understanding the facts behind the myths of majority opinion and the apathetic public, you will gain a sense of how the public can influence the decisions made by government.

First of all, we will define public opinion and describe its characteristics. Then we will discuss the way political beliefs develop and the use of polls in measuring public opinion. Finally, we will turn our attention to different avenues of political participation and the factors that promote activism in the political system.

★ ★ ★

AMERICAN PUBLIC OPINION

V. O. Key, a respected scholar of public opinion, argued that "to speak with precision of public opinion is a task not unlike coming to grips with the Holy Ghost."[5] No democratic government can afford to ignore public opinion. As you can see in Myth and Reality 5.1, even the Soviet Union polls its citizens, for in order to maintain political stability over the long run, it must pay attention to some of the pressing demands of its people. Public opinion links the values, demands, and expectations of the citizens of any country to the actions of their government. What then is this elusive concept?

MYTH AND REALITY 5.1

Public Opinion Polls in the Soviet Union

In the United States and Western countries, polls are an accepted means of collecting and analyzing public opinion. Most Americans believe that polls provide an important link between the opinions of the people and the actions of government. You may be surprised to learn that polls are also used in communist countries. In fact, the study of public opinion through the use of modern polling techniques has received official encouragement in the Soviet Union.

A number of state party organizations within the USSR, particularly in the Georgian Soviet Socialist Republic, systematically conduct polls to assess the performance of government institutions and officials, to monitor the effectiveness of measures taken to deal with problems, and to justify reversing unpopular decisions made by the government.

In 1981, for example, plans for a new reservoir in the Georgian Republic were canceled after a poll of residents who would have to be resettled indicated overwhelming opposition. When polled in 1983 about municipal services, citizens of the Georgian capital, Tbilisi, complained about housing, transportation, and street crime. The data were used by party officials to criticize local officials and to call for increased government funding so that improvements could be made.

Polling in the Soviet Union is not widespread, however. As one American scholar put it, "most local political leaders have apparently been content to restrict opinion studies to the sphere of ideological work—to help direct the effort to form public opinion, rather than using survey data as a major source for policy guidance and agenda setting." Yet the case of the Georgian Soviet Socialist Republic shows that some party leaders are willing to consider the public's demands and expectations and to use that information in policy decisions on a limited number of issues. What is more, the Soviet Union decided to establish a center for the study of public opinion throughout the entire country. This decision represents a significant effort to expand the use of public opinion polls throughout that nation.

Source: Darrell Slider "Party-Sponsored Public Opinion Research in the Soviet Union," *The Journal of Politics,* 47 (February 1985), 209–227. The article cites additional sources.

What Is Public Opinion?

To state it formally, **political public opinion** is the preferences expressed by people on political issues, policies, and individuals, whereas **public opinion** is the distribution of individual preferences on any topic. As the majority opinion myth suggests, some opinions are widely shared whereas others differ greatly throughout the population.

Characteristics of Public Opinion

Public opinion varies in intensity and saliency, or importance; not every issue evokes a strong opinion because not every issue is equally salient. For example, many Americans share a concern about the treatment of laboratory animals. But few feel intensely about this issue since it matters little in their everyday lives. In contrast, most people feel strongly about unemployment and rising interest rates. These issues are important to them because they affect them directly, and with saliency comes intensity.

Public opinion also varies in stability. For example, public opinion favored President Ronald Reagan's ambitious tax reform and budget-cutting programs when they were first announced. Such changes, it was assumed, would ease everyone's tax burden. But two months later, when it was still unclear who would benefit and who would lose, public support began to wane. On less complex and confusing issues, such as public funding of congressional campaigns or federal funding of higher education, generally favorable public opinion has remained relatively stable over the years.

Public officials use measures of intensity, saliency, and stability as a guide to the public's political preferences. If a majority, or even an active minority, of the public seems indifferent, or if opinions are unstable and shifting, officials may discount the public's views or not act at all. In contrast, salient issues that arouse intense feelings are likely to generate action.

★ ★ ★
HOW PUBLIC OPINION DEVELOPS

What factors influence the intensity and stability of public opinion? People's long-term political convictions—particularly whether they think of themselves as Democrats or Republicans—play an important part. Some of the other key factors are their views on the role of women and minorities in politics, the value of compromise in political process, the appropriate use of money in political campaigns, and the effectiveness of the democratic process.

When we recently asked students about their views on terrorism, we found that most based their opinions on such long-term values as the sanctity of life, concern about the random killing of innocent human beings, and faith in the democratic process. These beliefs affected even students who felt some sympathy for the political concerns of terrorists in the Middle East and in Northern Ireland.

How do long-term political values and beliefs develop? According to social scientists, they are based on the different experiences that people undergo throughout their lives. Growing up and living in New York City, Chicago, Miami, Austin, Boston, Seattle, or Los Angeles is very different from growing up or living in rural Iowa, Texas, Vermont, or Appalachia. And, as you will see when we look at the content of public opinion, there are regional differences in what people believe and value, as well as differences based on gender, race, and other factors.

Nevertheless, most Americans share a common, or core, political culture, including a general faith in democracy, representative government, freedom of speech, and the rights of individuals. The process by which they acquire these important values, as well as their knowledge about politics, is known as **political socialization.** It is strongly influenced by the people with whom they have contact from early childhood through adulthood.

Agents of Political Socialization

Family.   Families, especially parents, transmit to their children basic attitudes, beliefs, and values that shape the children's view of the political world. These general values include perceptions of right and wrong and attitudes toward authority figures—parents, teachers, police officers, judges, and political officeholders. They also include perceptions of one's ability to have an impact on the political system; we call this belief **political efficacy.**

Family feelings Families are central to political socialization, as this young Chicagoan clearly shows. Some social theorists say that parental influence is so strong that what we learn in childhood stays with us forever.

One set of basic beliefs often passed from parent to child is particularly important in understanding political opinions and behavior: **party identification,** or whether people think of themselves as Democrats, Republicans, or independents. Studies in the 1960s and 1970s found that children have a strong tendency to adopt the party identification of their parents. Despite a growing number of eighteen- to thirty-year-olds who call themselves political independents, children tend to make the same party choice as their parents when both mother and father share the same identification.

School.   After the family, no other institution has as great a potential impact on political socialization as the schools. At any given time, about a quarter of the population is enrolled, full- or part-time, in degree-granting educational programs.[6] Public schools reinforce such political virtues as patriotism, compliance with the laws, the importance of voting, and the peaceful changeover of presidential administrations.

The amount of a person's schooling greatly influences the way he or she forms opinions and views the political world. Differences between the better educated and the less well educated cover a wide range of attitudes and behavior. Better-educated men and women know more about politics. Those who have been to college are more likely than others to hold liberal views on civil liberties and rights, foreign policy, and social questions.[7] Education brings confidence that one can affect political and governmental policy and leads to a relatively high level of participation in politics.[8]

There are limits on what the schools can do, however. For example, the educational system does not seem to create civil libertarians who are tolerant of minorities or of others who are perceived as different. Similarly, education does not foster support for the rights of communists or others who believe in forms of government differing from our representative democracy.[9]

The media.   The media are also important socializing agencies. By the age of sixteen, an average child has spent about a quarter of his or her waking hours watching television. The average family television set is turned on for about seven hours a day. Television's potential effect as an agent of political socialization is enormous. But what is its actual influence?

Although television teaches and reinforces general beliefs and attitudes,[10] it has limited political impact, chiefly because such a small proportion of programming has direct political content. For example, extensive coverage of terrorism may show anguished relatives and angry public officials but tell the viewer little about the complex foreign policy issues that underlie the episode. Such programs tend to influence *what* people think about—terrorism is suddenly on their minds—but have much less impact on *how* they think about an issue or policy, for instance, ways of dealing with terrorism. (We will have more to say about the impact of the media in Chapter 9).

Other factors. Although Americans share a common culture, a variety of political subcultures flourish in this vast nation. Individuals grow up and live in different regions of the country; have different religious, ethnic, and racial backgrounds and customs; and undergo different economic and social experiences. A farmer who grew up and still lives in the rural poverty of Appalachia is likely to view the political system as far less responsive than a California lawyer who grew up and prospered in a state that has experienced vast economic growth. These different influences help shape the way a person views the political world.

Despite the existence of widespread agreement on some basic issues, majority opinion is hard to find in our large and diverse nation. Variations in life experience inevitably result in differences in views on political, social, and economic questions. The work of pollsters and public officials would be eased if the myth of majority opinion were true. Reality, it seems, is never simple.

A Word About Adult Socialization

Political socialization is not just a childhood experience. Coworkers, neighbors, and friends start shaping adults' opinions as parents' influence declines. Television, of course, affects adults' political views more directly than it does children's opinions, since so many men and women rely on it for the news. And a variety of additional media—newspapers, magazines, and radio—bring wider exposure to political information.

In addition, adults bring old, established ideas to their assessment of new situations. They are also likely to be influenced by the current conditions of their life. For example, parents may see more merit in a tax increase to support local schools than do childless men and women. Thus, the development of public opinion is clearly a process that continues throughout adulthood.

★ ★ ★
PUBLIC OPINION POLLS

Since polls seem so familiar, you may be surprised to learn that formal and systematic polling has only been around for about fifty years. Informal surveys of public opinion date as far back as 1824, when a reporter from the Harrisburg *Pennsylvanian* asked 532 men on a street corner in Wilmington, Delaware, whom they planned to vote for in the presidential race of that year. But it was not until the 1930s that George Gallup and Elmo Roper first began to experiment with scientific measures of public opinion. By taking into account differences in age, gender, ethnic background, race, religion,

"*And don't waste your time canvassing the whole building, young man. We all think alike.*"

Drawing by Stevenson; © 1980 The New Yorker Magazine, Inc.

social class, and region, Gallup and Roper were able to measure opinion on many issues with a high degree of accuracy.

The pollsters choose their interviewees by the method of **random sampling,** in which every person in the population has the same chance of being selected as every other person. Actually, the procedure is a little more complicated than that, but even the basic idea—that the opinions of individuals selected by chance will be representative of the opinions of the population at large—is highly effective. Since 1936, for example, the Gallup poll has correctly picked the winner in all but one presidential election and has been within a few percentage points of the actual results each time.

In contrast, straw polls rely on an unsystematic selection of people. People are questioned in shopping centers or on street corners, with little or no effort made to ensure that respondents are representative of the population at large. The results are often inaccurate and unreliable. In 1936, for example, a highly respected magazine, *The Literary Digest*, using a straw poll of 2.5

million people, predicted that Republican Alfred Landon would defeat Democrat Franklin Roosevelt in the presidential election. Roosevelt won overwhelmingly, however.

The *Digest* poll failed because it selected its respondents from telephone directories and automobile registration lists. In the midst of the Great Depression, this sample had too many middle- and high-income individuals, excluding voters who could not afford telephones or cars. Gallup's survey for the same election—his first presidential poll—was quite accurate.

Currently, polls are essential to effective campaign strategies. Candidates who can afford their high cost—generally 4 to 6 percent of a campaign budget—typically survey prospective voters to learn their concerns. In fact, a national or statewide candidate who does not use a poll is probably not a serious candidate or, at least, does not face serious opposition. In a recent poll, Senator Charles Percy found that Illinois citizens felt he had ignored their needs and concerns in favor of foreign policy issues. Percy promised to return to Illinois more often if re-elected—a promise that seemed to shift public opinion in his favor.

Major television stations and newspapers also survey the public on issues and candidates. Poll results are frequently the bread and butter of the evening news. In the months before major elections, these reports often have a "horse-race" quality—that is, they focus almost entirely on who is ahead or behind in a contest. How people feel about the real issues of the campaign often goes unreported or is underreported in election coverage.

Like the representative in our opening story, elected officials, including the president, use polls to assess the public's views on a variety of issues. Both Reagan and Jimmy Carter employed full-time pollsters, using the results to help them bolster support for their positions or to fine-tune or eventually abandon policies.

What makes a good poll? As the failure of *The Literary Digest* poll demonstrates, the sample must be chosen with care. In addition, questions must be worded in such a way that their form or content does not influence the response. Beginning a question on a farm issue, for example, with the phrase "Most people believe that farms should be family owned" will increase the likelihood that a respondent will agree with what "most people" believe.

Good questions are another important ingredient. Many surveys ask many questions, allowing for only brief answers—often a simple yes or no. Such questions may improve survey efficiency, but at the expense of more thorough information. Consequently, the intensity, saliency, and stability of opinion may be distorted and complex shades of opinion may be obscured, giving support to the myth of majority opinion when, in fact, there is no such view.

Finally, pollsters must measure what people know about an issue, as

The question of Baby M As the world grows more technologically complex, so do the questions on which the public is expected to have an opinion. The trial that considered the case of surrogate mother Mary Beth Whitehead (shown here with her family and a picture of the baby she did not want to give up) raised a multitude of difficult questions about parental rights. Who should be a mother and who should not? Is it acceptable or right to have a child for someone else or to pay someone to have a baby?

well as what their opinions are, in order to distinguish between informed and uninformed responses. Many Americans recognize the difficulties of keeping up with the issues. In 1984, for 71 percent of the voting public government seemed "so complicated that a person like me can't understand what's going on." [11] Still, failure to understand does not keep people from answering questions. In a classic example, pollsters asked about a nonexistent "Metallic Metals Act." Support was high, although a majority of the people felt that implementation of the act "should be left to individual states." Only 30 percent had no opinion regarding the nonexistent act. [12]

Poorly designed and administered polls provide inaccurate and misleading findings. But when carefully done, professional polls can help link citizens with the officials who represent them.

★ ★ ★

THE CONTENT OF AMERICAN PUBLIC OPINION

Answering the question "What is American public opinion?" is not a simple task. Americans hold strong, weak, or ambivalent opinions—or none at all—on a variety of political issues. Indeed, as we suggested in our discussion of the myth of majority opinion, public opinion is frequently difficult to divide into neat categories. To complicate matters further, public opinion changes as situations change (see Figure 5.1).

Confidence and Trust in Government

In the 1950s and early 1960s Americans viewed government optimistically. The nation had triumphed in World War II, the economy was flourishing, and no domestic or foreign policy problem seemed too difficult to solve. By the late 1960s the country was mired in a seemingly endless war in Vietnam, and protesters mobbed the streets. The 1970s brought economic problems, Watergate and the resignation of President Richard Nixon, and the Iranian hostage crisis. In the 1980s the nation was jolted by exposure of the Reagan

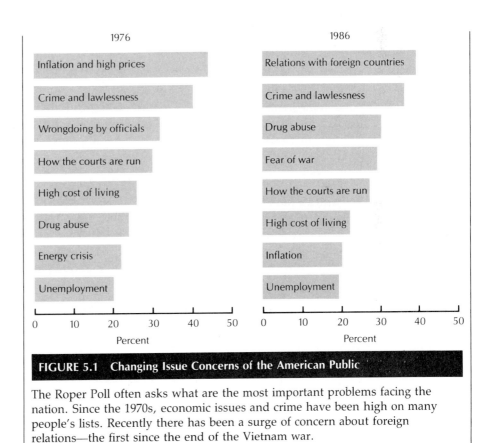

FIGURE 5.1 Changing Issue Concerns of the American Public

The Roper Poll often asks what are the most important problems facing the nation. Since the 1970s, economic issues and crime have been high on many people's lists. Recently there has been a surge of concern about foreign relations—the first since the end of the Vietnam war.

Source: Based on data from *The Washington Post* National Weekly Edition, August 25, 1986, p. 37, © The Washington Post.

administration's covert sale of arms to Iran in exchange for hostages. (See Background 6.1, page 141, for more information on these events.)

Many journalists and scholars believe that these crises have eroded the public's confidence in government and in the people that run it. Poll data seem to support their position. During the mid-1960s 45 percent of the American people claimed that they had "a great deal of confidence" in individuals who were running American's political and nonpolitical institutions.[13] By 1984 only 28 percent expressed that view.

With the decline of confidence in government came loss of trust. In the 1950s most people trusted the nation's leaders. A 1958 survey found that only 23 percent of Americans felt that "government cannot be regularly trusted to do what is right."[14] In the 1980s, however, a significant number of Americans have reached this conclusion. The cumulative impact of Vietnam, Watergate, and Iran, in addition to a number of government scandals at the local and state level, has obviously taken its toll.

The Paradox in Public Opinion

Do these findings suggest that the public no longer believes in democracy and representative government? Interestingly, the answer is no. An overwhelming majority of citizens, 87 percent, are proud to be Americans.[15] A significant percentage feel that the future is bright for the nation, are pleased with their own accomplishments in life, and think that their life is better than that of their parents.[16] Almost everyone—90 percent—is sure that the United States "is the very best place in the world to live."[17] In fact, the legitimacy of the system—that is, the acceptance by the people of the authority of government—has been in jeopardy only once: during the Civil War.

Most contemporary Americans believe that no other nation or government provides the opportunities that exist in the United States. This perception is shared even by minorities who have suffered centuries of discrimination.[18] Although distrust of individuals running the government keeps increasing, support for the Constitution and representative government remains firm.[19] Compared with citizens of other Western democracies, Americans trust their government far more and express far greater pride in their nation.[20]

Opinions on the Issues

Issues change over time, and so does public opinion. For example, during the 1980s support grew significantly for such federally funded social programs as child care and medical insurance (including Medicare and Medicaid), social security, and college student loans. At the same time, strong public backing of military spending declined,[21] although most people oppose substantial cuts in military programs.

This type of contradiction illustrates a certain lack of logic in the public's views. While opposing substantial cuts in social and military programs, the public overwhelmingly favors a reduction in the national deficit. How is that reduction to be accomplished? Not by raising taxes. As we suggested in Chapter 3, on federalism, at times we seem to want to have our cake and eat it too.

Majority opinion is quite clear on these general issues. On other topics, however, majorities are hard to find and opinion is often absent. For example, few people have given much thought to the nation's involvement in Central America, the role of government in assuring employment and a good standard of living for all, or the need for school busing in order to achieve integration.[22] As you can see in Table 5.1, when opinions do exist on subjects like these, a majority viewpoint is not often evident.

Group Opinion

The differences both among and within groups in our society further fragment opinion. Men and women, blacks and whites, young and old do not always

TABLE 5.1 The Indifferent Majority

On specific issues public opinion is often hard to find. Note how many respondents were neutral (category 4) or had not thought about these issues.

	Opinion on Issue (in percent)							
	Greatest agreement with the statement				Least agreement with the statement			Have not thought about the issue
Issue	1	2	3	4	5	6	7	
U.S. should become more involved in internal affairs of Central America	2	3	5	9	7	8	6	61
Government should provide fewer services, even in the areas of health and education	2	4	7	15	7	3	2	58
Government should see that each citizen has a job and a good standard of living	4	3	6	10	10	7	5	55
Government should provide a national health insurance plan	7	4	5	9	6	6	5	59

Source: *American National Election Study, 1984,* Center for Political Studies, University of Michigan, Ann Arbor.

see political questions the same way. Of course, not all women or all blacks or all members of any group are necessarily unified in their views. Nevertheless, some generalizations are possible.

Gender. Compared with men, women express greater concern about the possibility of war and the use of force in armed conflict. Women are also more likely than men to favor social welfare spending and federal aid to cities, and they are less likely to support defense spending.[23]

Surprisingly, no gender differences exist regarding the Equal Rights Amendment and the right to choose abortion; a majority supports both positions.[24] Furthermore, neither major political party has strong gender appeal. The Democrats attract more women than the Republicans, but the differences are marginal (averaging around 5 percent over the past ten years).

Within the two groups, opinions are anything but uniform. In 1984, for example, married women and men were more likely than single people to vote for Republican Reagan,[25] possibly because they prized his strong support for traditional family values. For single independent women (and many, although not all, men), the Democrats' promise to support equal pay for men and women may have had greater appeal. This diversity raises additional doubts about the reality of majority opinion.[26]

College students. Despite popular images of youthful extremism, most college students hold middle-of-the-road political views[27]—opinions that are not much different from those of older generations. Their interest in political affairs is weaker, however. A 1984 survey of college freshmen showed that only 38 percent keep up with politics and government activity.[28]

In the past decade students have moved away from the views held by college men and women of the 1960s and 1970s. Today's undergraduates express greater concern for their future economic well-being, stronger disapproval of extramarital sex, and weaker support for the legalization of marijuana and for affirmative action programs to aid minorities. Contemporary students also register relatively strong support for the death penalty and for defense spending.[29]

As Table 5.2 makes clear, not all their views are conservative, however. Many students favor stronger government action regarding consumer protection and pollution control, equal rights for women, national health, busing to promote school integration, and nuclear disarmament.[30] Thus college students, like the rest of the population, present a diversified opinion picture.

Race. Diversity and divergence also hold true when people are grouped by race, although whites, blacks, Hispanics, and others manifest some group consciousness on important issues.

TABLE 5.2   What Do College Freshmen Think?

Today's generation of college students is relatively conservative on "moral" issues but has retained liberal views on politics.

Issue	Percentage Who Agree Strongly		
	1976	1980	1984
Abortion should be legalized	NA	54	54
Marijuana should be legalized	49	39	23
Death penalty should be abolished	NA	35	26
Government should do more to control pollution	82	80	78
Wealthy people should pay a larger share of taxes	76	70	70
Women should receive the same salary and opportunities as men in comparable positions	92	93	92
A national health care plan to cover medical costs is necessary	NA	58	61
College officials have the right to ban persons with extreme views from speaking on campus	25	26	22

Note: NA = not asked
Source: *American Freshmen: National Norms for Fall* . . . Cooperative Institutional Research Program, American Council on Education and the University of California, Los Angeles, latest that of 1984, as reported in Terry W. Hartle and John Taylor, "What's Big on Campus," *Public Opinion* (August/September 1985), 52. Reprinted by permission.

Most blacks feel that they are making economic and social progress.[31] Nevertheless, they cite unemployment, the high cost of living, and drug abuse as the three key issues facing the nation.[32] Whites agree with this evaluation but differ sharply from blacks on how best to deal with these problems. Compared with whites, blacks favor greater government participation in resolving economic and social issues. For blacks, federal programs remain a key strategy in dealing with civil rights and other pressing problems.

There is agreement across race on many issues. For example, a majority of blacks and whites favor the Equal Rights Amendment, the death penalty for murder, harsher sentencing of criminals, and school prayer. Both groups also describe themselves as middle of the road politically.

Among whites, Republicans hold a narrow edge over Democrats. Blacks have been more heavily Democratic than whites since the 1940s. In 1984, however, only one-third of blacks identified themselves as strong Democrats, a figure that represents a 21 percent decline since 1982 and is the lowest percentage since 1962.[33] Of particular concern to the Democratic party is the decline in strong allegiance to that party among young blacks.[34]

Hispanic opinion is difficult to characterize because the label serves as an umbrella for Mexican-Americans, Puerto Ricans, Cuban-Americans, and others who trace their origins to the diverse cultures of Central and Latin America. Except for Cuban-Americans (a majority of whom identify with the Republican party), Hispanics are Democratic in their politics. But they are not as solidly Democratic as blacks[35] and are more likely than either blacks or whites to call themselves conservative. Hispanics have played an important role in local politics in Florida, Texas, California, and the Southwest, and most certainly will gain political strength in other regions as well.

Religion. Although religion does not necessarily shape political beliefs, members of the same religious groups do share opinions.

Most Jews consistently support liberal social and political policies.[36] Along with most Catholics, they are more liberal than Protestants on civil liberties issues but stand alone in their strong support of social legislation, for which Protestants and Catholics show less enthusiasm. Jewish support for social policies and for equality is no accident. Group opinions grow out of group experiences, and the historical oppression of Jews certainly has contributed to their compassion for the underdog.

Given their liberal bent, Jews and Catholics lean toward the Democratic party, an allegiance stemming from the party's recruitment and support of immigrant groups during the late 1800s and early 1900s. White Protestants tend to identify themselves as Republicans (43 percent), whereas Catholics (30 percent) and Jews (13 percent) make up a smaller percentage of that party's members.[37]

Members of each religious group, however, do differ on many important issues. Catholics are divided on abortion, public support of birth control programs, and the public funding of parochial schools. Many Jews do not support Israel's trade policy with South Africa or U.S. policy toward the Middle East. A number of Protestant fundamentalist groups oppose a broad spectrum of liberal government policies, but other Protestants decry their stand on social welfare and nuclear policy as too conservative and reactionary. Once again, majority opinion is difficult to define within groups.

In recent years some observers have argued that economic and social class influences are more important than religious influences for many Americans.[38] Nevertheless, religion continues to have an indirect effect on political life, influencing tolerance toward disadvantaged groups, moral and ethical opinions regarding political behavior, and conformity with the rules of the system—attitudes related to all the political issues of the day.[39]

Clearly, the development of public opinion is a long and complex process.

A sense of community Not everyone acts on their political opinions by getting involved in party politics. Like these participants in a community meeting on Chicago's Southwest side, many activists devote themselves to solving local problems.

Having opinions is just the beginning. Let us now turn to action. Do Americans act on the opinions that they hold by participating in the political system?

★ ★ ★

AVENUES OF POLITICAL PARTICIPATION

What is political participation? M. Margaret Conway defines **political participation** as "those activities of citizens that attempt to influence the structure of government, the selection of government authorities, or the policies of government."[40] As we indicated earlier, participation covers a broad range of involvement, both active and passive.

Most Americans, for example, participate passively, discussing politics with family and friends and following campaigns, elections, and other political events on television and in the newspapers. Others are more active, writing letters to elected representatives, attending community meetings and legislative hearings, and joining in interest-group activities. A slight majority (54 percent in 1984) vote in presidential elections. Those who are really turned on to politics attend political rallies and speeches, take part in campaigns, and run for political office. A few by-pass traditional avenues of action and engage in civil disobedience.

About one-quarter of all adult Americans do not participate actively in politics. But inactivity does not necessarily support the myth of the apathetic public or indicate a lack of interest in politics. Threats of violence kept some groups, particularly blacks in the South, out of politics until the 1960s. Work and family responsibilities undoubtedly contribute to the inactivity of others— particularly the young. Still others doubt that their participation will have any impact on government; or perhaps they are satisfied with what they see and therefore have no reason for action.

Acting on Opinions

Those who do act fall into six general categories, according to Sidney Verba and Norman Nie.[41] Inactives (22 percent) participate by occasionally casting a vote. Voting specialists (21 percent) vote regularly in presidential, state, and local elections but seldom join other political activities. Parochial activists (4 percent) vote and contact public officials only when their own self-interest is involved. Community activists work hard to solve problems in their localities and vote regularly but do not otherwise participate in party activities or elections (27 percent). Campaigners (15 percent), the mirror image of the community activists, immerse themselves in partisan politics and campaigns rather than in community organizations. Complete activists (11 percent) engage in activities ranging from community affairs to voting, campaigning, and running for political office.

Verba and Nie's categories represent traditional forms of political partic- ipation. What happens when such tactics do not work? In the early 1960s blacks in the South organized sit-ins at segregated lunch counters, boycotted buses, and engaged in other acts of civil disobedience. Since that time protests have become an increasingly common form of participation among those who find traditional avenues of action ineffective or closed. As you may recall from Chapter 4, on civil liberties, these groups have also gone to court to nudge an otherwise unresponsive political system.

Finally, the impact of passive participation should not be overlooked. Over 67 percent of the electorate discuss politics with family or friends. A majority of these individuals do so every week. Of those who watch television news regularly, 86 percent pay some or a great deal of attention to the political news. In the 1984 elections, 33 percent of the electorate tried to persuade others to vote for or against one of the parties or candidates.[42] These forms of political activity may be less dramatic than voting and running for office, but they represent an important form of participation.

Despite this evidence, there is certainly room for skepticism regarding Americans' activism. Few people actually join political clubs or work for parties or candidates. The turnout for presidential elections has dropped during the past twenty years, and only about 40 percent of the eligible electorate currently vote in off-year elections.

Yet this apparent apathy is balanced by activity. When election time rolls around, political meetings are jammed with people, campaign buttons and bumper stickers decorate lapels and automobiles, and money pours into campaign headquarters. Political parties, particularly at the national level, thrive on millions of small contributions—most under fifty dollars. In addition, volunteerism in the United States is alive and well: 36 percent of the adult population now invests time in community work—a rise from 27 percent in 1977.[43] In fact, Americans engage in as much or more campaign and community activity than citizens in four other countries (see Figure 5.2).

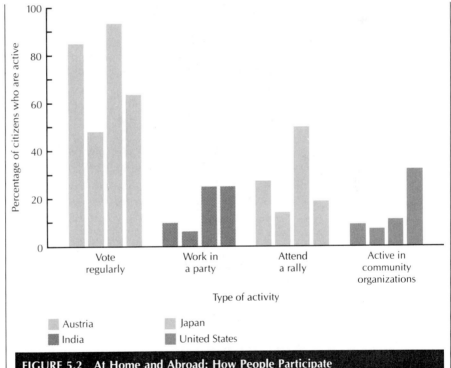

FIGURE 5.2 At Home and Abroad: How People Participate

Despite the myth of the apathetic public, Americans' rates of participation compare quite favorably with citizens of other democracies. Note especially the relatively high level of participation in community affairs.

Source: Kay Lawson, *The Human Polity* (Boston: Houghton Mifflin, 1985), pp. 214–215. Copyright © by Houghton Mifflin Company. Adapted by permission.

What Influences Participation

Why do people participate in politics? After all, an individual act of participation rarely has much impact. One answer is that people participate if the
action does not take much effort. Sending a check or watching the nightly
news is easy to do. People also participate if they care a lot about the outcome.
Black students who took part in sit-ins at lunch counters and marched in
demonstrations in the 1960s had a big stake in the success of the civil rights
movement. Finally, participation depends on life circumstances.

Thus participation is typically low in rural areas, where income and
education are below the levels in larger cities. This has been especially true
in the South, where recent increases in participation can be attributed to
rising educational and socioeconomic levels, as well as enforcement of voting
rights laws. In the past, poll taxes, literacy tests, and other barriers to
registration prevented blacks from voting.

Participation breeds more participation. For example, people who work
in community and fraternal organizations are more likely than the average
citizen to be politically active. A strong sense of party identity also seems to
encourage activism. Indeed, even such passive participation as having an
interest in politics or holding strong opinions on issues and candidates can
serve as a catalyst for political action.

Political activism also depends on age. Those between eighteen and
twenty-six years old are less likely to vote or engage in other forms of political
participation than any other age group through the age of seventy-five. A
higher proportion of those who are fifty and older register and vote in
national elections than of those under the age of fifty.[44] In part, these statistics
reflect the unsettled lives of young people, who often are in school or
adjusting to their status as independent, self-supporting adults. To some
extent, too, political activism is a function of the responsibilities of age. As
taxpayers, parents, and home owners, older people have more immediate
reasons to get involved in politics.

A Closer Look: Women, Blacks, and Hispanics

Women. In recent years barriers against women in national and state
politics have diminished. (Women have a long history of activism in local
and community work.) Currently, as party leaders, candidates, voters, and
community organizers, women are entering politics in greater numbers. They
are slightly more likely to vote than men.[45] Their activity at the state and
national level has increased significantly over the past fifteen years.[46] No
doubt women's activism will continue to grow as elected and appointed
officials become role models for other women and as barriers to the inner
circles of politics continue to break down.

ment, rule by the majority, and concern for minority rights. An overwhelming majority—in most polls, well over 90 percent of the respondents—support a democratic form of government. Polls and elections demonstrate every four years that a majority of the electorate favor one presidential candidate over another.

However, the myth obscures an important attribute of public opinion: that it is often difficult to define clearly. Fuzzy and unstable, it is frequently uninformed as well and sometimes does not exist at all. It rarely comes packaged in neat, easy-to-understand categories. In this vast and varied nation, differences in religious background, region of residence, education, gender, race, and ethnicity produce a broad spectrum of views about the political world. To complicate matters further, even when people have similar backgrounds, they often do not share the same opinions.

In defining majority opinion on any issue, therefore, policy makers must tread carefully. Often the answers to a single survey question or even a series of such questions do not capture the diversity or ambiguity of public opinion. Clearly, the generalization that there is a majority opinion in the United States on many issues is a myth.

What about the myth of the apathetic public? Americans are criticized for their lack of participation in the political process. That criticism often focuses on the relatively low voter turnout in the United States, particularly when compared with higher turnout figures for many other nations.

We agree that if activism is defined by voting, the American public seems apathetic indeed. But by broadening the definition to include nonelectoral, as well as electoral, activities and active and passive forms of participation, we depict a reality of politically and socially concerned citizens and lay the myth to rest.

★ ★ ★
SUMMARY

1. Public opinion is defined as the shared preferences expressed by people on political issues, policies, and individuals.

2. Three important characteristics of public opinion are its intensity, saliency, and stability.

3. Political socialization is the process by which people acquire political values and opinions about the political world. The socialization process is strongly influenced by people and events, from early childhood on through adulthood. The family, school, and the media are three important factors that influence our political beliefs and opinions.

4. Public opinion polls are a major instrument for measuring public opinion. Poorly designed and administered polls can provide inaccurate and misleading findings. When carefully designed and administered, however, professional polls offer sound and meaningful information about public opinion. Nevertheless, on many issues clear and unambiguous majority opinion is often difficult to assess from polls.

5. Americans show a lack of confidence and trust in government and politics but an overwhelming faith in our political system.

6. The opinions of Americans are often influenced by ethnic, religious, racial, regional, and educational backgrounds, although opinions can and do vary widely within any group.

7. Political participation is defined as those activities by which citizens try to influence the structure of government, government policies, or the selection of government authorities. Participation in politics in the United States is extensive if we include both active and passive forms of participation.

★ ★ ★
KEY TERMS

political public opinion
public opinion
political socialization
political efficacy

party identification
random sampling
political participation

★ ★ ★
SUGGESTED READINGS

- Conway, M. Margaret. *Political Participation in the United States.* Washington, D.C.: Congressional Quarterly Press, 1985. A well-crafted and readable study of political participation. The book explores who participates, patterns of participation, the effects of participation on the political system, and the ways in which participation differs from the assumptions of classical democratic theory.

- Hennessy, Bernard. *Public Opinion,* 5th ed. Monterey, Calif.: Brooks/Cole, 1985. A readable text on the content, substance, dynamics, and measurement of public opinion. Good overview of political socialization, political culture, and polling methods, as well as the relationship between public opinion and public policy.

- Holloway, Harry with John George. *Public Opinion: Coalitions, Elites, and Masses,* 2nd. ed. New York: St. Martin's, 1986. A systematic study of concepts and theories of public opinion. The book focuses on elite theory and pluralism.

- Jennings, M. Kent and Richard G. Niemi. *The Political Character of Adolescence: The Influence of Families and Schools.* Princeton, N.J.: Princeton University Press, 1974. A classic study of the impact of family and school on the development of political attitudes of high school students.

- McClure, Robert D. and Linda Fowler. *Political Ambition: Unseen Candidates for Congress.* New Haven, Conn.: Yale University Press, 1988. An excellent and readable study of how and why each of a group of individuals sought the party nomination to run for a seat in the U.S. House of Representatives. This book introduces the reader to the relevance of political ambition in choosing to campaign for political office.

- Milbrath, Lester W. and M. L. Goel. *Political Participation,* 2nd ed. Chicago: Rand McNally, 1977. Focuses on political participation as a function of personal, social, and environmental factors. The book also examines the relationship between political participation and constitutional democracy.

6

C H A P T E R

Political Parties

As the 1968 presidential race got under way, it was clear that one of the major campaign issues facing Democrat Hubert Humphrey and Republican Richard Nixon was the Vietnam War. By all accounts, voters were deeply concerned about U.S. policy in Vietnam. The candidates, too, were concerned. But according to many political observers, as well as many voters, their positions on the issue were indistinguishable.[1]

George Wallace, a disaffected Democrat, former governor of Alabama, and the presidential candidate of the American Independent party, agreed. Surprisingly, he did not focus his attack on Humphrey and Nixon, even though he thought they shared the same opinions on many issues. For Wallace, the problem was the parties the candidates represented. On numerous occasions he charged that there is not "a dime's worth of difference between the two major parties," and many people agreed with him.

Today, twenty years later, many Americans are no less skeptical about party officials and party organizations. According to some scholars, the past three decades have been an "anti-party age," marked by public alienation from parties.[2] Yet many Americans claim some identification with a party, while at the same time arguing that it does not sway their vote.

What is the source of these contradictions? Recent polls suggest that two misconceptions are influencing Americans' views about the Republican and Democratic parties: that there isn't "a dime's worth of difference between the two major parties" and that parties have little impact on domestic and foreign policy.[3] Forty-two percent of Americans questioned in a recent survey sided with Wallace's claim. In fact, 45 percent of the public believed that their concerns were better represented by organized special interest groups than by parties.[4]

Apparently, many Americans see little value in parties even at election time. Nearly three out of every four voters agree that "the best way to vote is to pick a candidate regardless of party label." In addition, a majority of the public blames parties for confusing the issues rather than providing a clear choice, and 50 percent of the electorate would like to see party labels taken off the ballot.[5]

How can we explain this deep-seated skepticism about parties? We argue that public criticism of the Democrats and Republicans reflects two widely believed myths. The myth of Tweedledum and Tweedledee holds that the parties resemble each other so closely that they are practically indistinguishable. (In Lewis Carroll's *Through the Looking Glass*, Tweedledum and Tweedledee are the fat identical twins who tend to agree on everything.) The myth of party irrelevance holds that the Democrats and Republicans are unnecessary, perhaps even worthless, in our political system.

If these are myths, what is the reality? We will demonstrate in this chapter that the two major parties *are* different in several aspects, although not all these differences are significant. We will also show that parties still matter in the country's politics, despite the fact that fewer people now strongly identify with them. We will begin by defining political parties and tracing their history. Then we will look at the two-party system and at what parties do and how they are organized. Finally, we will evaluate the parties and their impact on American politics.

★ ★ ★

WHAT PARTIES ARE AND WHAT THEY DO

Political parties differ from country to country. In most Western democracies, parties are highly centralized, stable, and tightly knit coalitions of men and women who share opinions based on commonly held beliefs. In these countries, parties take clear-cut, sometimes extreme, ideological positions. (As you may recall from Chapter 1, ideologies are coherent sets of beliefs about what government should do.) For example, Karl Marx's ideas about the economic struggle among social classes provide a frame of reference within which communists can interpret events. In countries like Italy, the Communist party is a strong political force, facing a spectrum of ideologically conservative parties on the right. In the United States, the situation is quite different.

Unlike many of their European, African, and Middle Eastern counterparts, parties in the United States historically have not based their positions on ideology. Although some minor parties are strongly ideological—for example, the Libertarian party, the Conservative party, and the Socialist Workers party—no clear-cut Democratic or Republican ideology guides the major-party activists. Each party's position includes a wide range of beliefs about what government should do. Consequently, the Democratic and Republican parties may seem alike and, in fact, do share a number of positions—particularly, a strong democratic, capitalist tradition—while seeking to attract a broad spectrum of supporters. But they differ on many economic and social issues and attract differing proportions of liberals, moderates, and conservatives to their political umbrellas.

Political parties in the United States are coalitions of people organized formally to recruit, nominate, and elect individuals to office and to use elected office to achieve shared political goals. The Republicans and Democrats, the two major parties, are decentralized organizations, regulated at the state level.[6] By **decentralized** we mean that the decision-making power is dispersed. No single individual or organization controls the entire system. The comments of one local party leader perhaps describe this structure best: "No state leader, not even the president of the United States, is going to dictate to us whom we slate for local office. They can't even tell us what issues are

Fair game The decentralized nature of political parties in the United States has meant that state and even county and city organizations have been able to develop their own patterns of organization and their own outreach techniques. For the Democrats of Illinois, one way to hold the attention of voters is by pitching a tent at the annual state fair.

important." All state party organizations and most local party organizations operate more or less independently of each other, although the authority of one party organization may overlap that of another. Compared with other nations, the United States has one of the most loosely integrated party systems in the world.[7]

American parties are loosely regulated, as well as loosely structured. The Constitution makes no mention of parties, and Congress has passed few laws restricting party activities. For the most part, individual states are free to define the characteristics and rules for their own state parties.

The Three-headed Giant

In trying to describe party coalitions, political scientist Frank Sorauf has described them as "three-headed political giants."[8] Sometimes the heads cooperate, and at other times they pull in different directions. The heads represent three different alliances of members: the party-as-organization, the party-in-the-electorate, and the party-in-government.

The **party-as-organization** actually has few members. Unlike many European parties, which have enrolled, dues-paying members and extensive professional staffs, American party organizations are small and relatively informal. The organization consists primarily of state and county chairpersons and ward and precinct captains (sometimes paid, but more often volunteers), who work for the party throughout the year recruiting candidates and participating in fund-raising activities.

The **party-in-the-electorate** is anyone who identifies with a particular party, tends to vote for that party's candidates, and may even contribute to its campaigns. Anyone of voting age can choose to be a member of the party-in-the-electorate. American parties depend for their electoral strength on this public support.

The **party-in-government** comprises the individuals who have been elected or appointed to a governmental office under a party label. Contrary to the myth of party irrelevance, parties play a major role in organizing government and in setting policy. From 1981 until 1986 the U.S. Senate was controlled by the Republicans, who cooperated closely with Republican President Ronald Reagan. When the Democratic party regained control of the Senate in 1987, the Senate was reorganized, and the Democrats supported different policy alternatives than the Republicans.

A successful party can attract people to each of these coalitions. Parties need paid and volunteer workers to ring doorbells, distribute campaign literature, register voters, and staff party headquarters. They need voters who will support the party's candidates, donate money to campaigns, and volunteer their services around election time. Finally, parties need candidates who can successfully run for office and, once elected, work to attain the party's policy goals.

Who Belongs to the Parties and Why?

Despite the widespread belief that the two major parties are alike, many Americans identify with the Republican or Democratic party. As you can see in Figure 6.1, attachment to the Democratic party seems to be weakening, Republican identification has remained steady, and the percentage of independents has increased over the past three decades.

What difference does party identification make? It often determines citizens' political choices. In a typical election, for example, a voter may face a ballot listing candidates for ten, twenty, thirty, or more offices. Since no one can thoroughly study every issue and every office seeker's record, many voters put aside the myth of Tweedledum and Tweedledee and select candidates along party lines. Sometimes they find to their disappointment that the candidate does not represent their views, but often the party label indicates with reasonable accuracy a candidate's political philosophy and positions on issues. As one party loyalist in Michigan recently put it, "If you are a Democratic candidate in this state and don't support labor, you won't be a Democratic candidate for very long."

Who are the Democrats and Republicans? The parties tend to attract

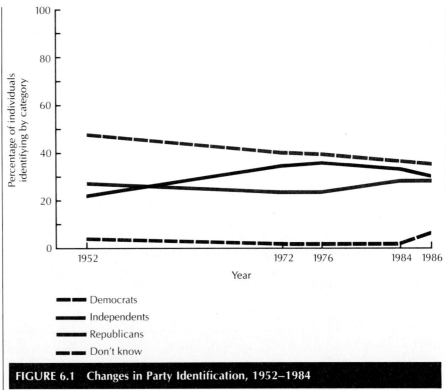

FIGURE 6.1   Changes in Party Identification, 1952–1984

During this period, the Republicans have held their own, while independents have increased and identification as a Democrat has decreased.

Source: Inter-University Consortium for Political and Social Research, University of Michigan, Ann Arbor, Michigan, 1952, 1972, 1976, 1984 and CBS News/New York Times Poll, December, 1986.

different groups of supporters. Democrats maintain their greatest strength among residents of the Northeast, blacks and Hispanics, Catholics and Jews, members of the working class, and individuals over the age of thirty. White southerners, once a critical part of the Democratic coalition, have moved to the Republicans in recent presidential elections, although Democrats still maintain a majority foothold in the South because of the strong support of blacks.

Republicans are scattered across the rest of the country. They tend to be white, Protestant, and middle- to upper-class. They are younger and better educated than the Democrats, and their views are comparatively conservative.

The issue that most sharply divides Democrats and Republicans is the role of government. Since the 1930s Democrats have favored a large role by government in such policy areas as social welfare programs and the regulation

Temporary members of the party-as-organization A major task for candidates is recruiting volunteers to do the grassroots campaigning essential for rounding up the vote. Here congressional candidate Kathleen Kennedy Townsend fires up her volunteers before they set out for a morning's work in suburban Baltimore, Maryland.

of business. For example, in the 1930s Democrats took the lead in supporting the social security program. They are also more willing than Republicans to support nonmilitary foreign aid programs. Republicans, on the other hand, are more likely to favor reducing government services, including aid to minorities and social welfare programs. They also prefer a lesser government role in regulating business but are more likely than Democrats to support government spending on military foreign aid. Indeed, the reality behind the myth of Tweedledum and Tweedledee is that Democrats and Republicans are divided on many important issues.

Independents

Independents—individuals who do not identify with any party—claim that their voting patterns are influenced by issues and leadership qualities, not by party labels. The rise in the percentage of independents over the last thirty-five years reflects the myth of party irrelevance—that is, the tendency of many Americans to question the ability of party and government to solve the nation's major problems. The United States has faced a series of major crises in the past three decades. The Vietnam War, Watergate, and the Iran-Contra scandal (see Background 6.1), political assassinations and terrorist attacks, urban decay, crime, environmental pollution, the energy crisis in the 1970s, and nuclear proliferation in the 1980s—all have contributed to a feeling that the political system is ineffective. This loss of faith has coincided with an increase in indifference toward parties.[9]

Independents make up an important part of the voting population, especially in presidential elections. There is less evidence, however, that they maintain an independent position in state and local elections. In these contests, voters often lack information on candidates' policy positions or leadership qualities. Indeed, party label is one of the best predictors of voter choice in such elections.

A majority of Americans appear to accept the Democratic and Republican parties as relevant symbols, particularly when it comes to voting. In fact, when independents who lean toward one of the parties are included, about 85 percent of the electorate identify to some extent with either the Democratic or the Republican party.[10] Alike or different, relevant or irrelevant, parties seem to be here to stay.

What Parties Do

The basic task of political parties is to win elections. But parties also offer a way to organize the political world and provide elected officials with a means to organize the government. Had parties not developed as a link between the public and the institutions of government, they would have had to be invented.[11] Let us look more closely at some of the functions of parties.

Building electoral coalitions.   Parties exist to organize people into **electoral coalitions**—groups of loyal supporters who agree with the party's stand on most issues and vote for its candidates for office. As we have said, party labels remain an important electoral symbol in the United States, and for many Americans, no other institution or organization embraces as broad a range of issues and goals as the Democratic and Republican parties.

Developing public policy.   Parties also play a major role in developing positions on what government should do about various problems and in seeing those positions translated into legislation. Although the parties may look like Tweedledum and Tweedledee, research on presidential and state platforms indicates that opposing candidates usually differ distinctly on specific policies. **Platforms,** which are statements of goals for the party and specific policy agendas, are taken very seriously by the candidates and the

BACKGROUND 6.1

Vietnam, Watergate, and the Iran-Contra Affair

Throughout this book, you will find references to the Vietnam War and to the Watergate and the Iran-Contra affairs—three events that made Americans lose faith in the federal government.

Public confidence in government began to fall in the 1960s, during the Vietnam War. The United States became involved in Vietnam's affairs in the late 1940s. Our government saw the Vietnamese struggle for independence from France as a test in containing communism. After the French pulled out and the Southeast Asian country was divided into North and South Vietnam, Presidents Dwight D. Eisenhower and John F. Kennedy sent billions of dollars in aid and thousands of military "advisers" to South Vietnam.

Despite American intervention, rebels backed by the North Vietnamese took over more and more of South Vietnam. Finally, in 1968, they occupied the American embassy in Saigon. As the war escalated, so did questions about American involvement. President Lyndon B. Johnson responded by asking for peace negotiations, but it was not until 1973 that a settlement was worked out. In the end more than fifty thousand American lives and hundreds of thousands of Asian lives were lost, and Americans' confidence in their government dropped.

The Watergate scandal further undermined this confidence. In the early 1970s it was discovered that members of the White House staff and President Richard Nixon had engaged in covering up a politically motivated break-in at the Democratic National Headquarters in the Watergate apartments in Washington, D.C. The burglars had rifled the files and bugged the headquarters' telephones—just one of many dirty tricks used by the Nixon forces in an attempt to influence the outcome of the 1972 presidential election.

When the Watergate burglars were arrested, the White House staff worked furiously to destroy incriminating evidence and discourage investigation of the crime. However, diligent probing by reporters, government prosecuters, members of Congress, and federal judges slowly began to reveal that Nixon and his aides had conspired to cover up the crime. On September 4, 1974—with taped evidence against Nixon available and the House Judiciary Committee on record as favoring his impeachment—Nixon resigned from office. He was the first president in the nation's history to do so. Many of his aides went to jail, but Nixon escaped punishment when his successor, Gerald Ford, pardoned him.

Then in 1986 the nation was jolted by the news that Ronald Reagan's administration secretly sold arms to Iran in exchange for hostages. Reagan had promised that he would never negotiate for the release of hostages with nations supporting terrorist activities. Iran was regarded as one of those nations.

When an Iranian newspaper publicized the negotiation process, which involved the United States supplying Iran with sophisticated weapons in exchange for six Americans held hostage, the public was shocked. Not only had a promise been broken, but it was unclear whether the arms sale had anything to do with the release of two hostages. What further complicated the situation was the illegal transfer of money gained in this sale to revolutionaries fighting in Nicaragua. Aid to the Nicaraguan Contras was explicitly prohibited by a law of Congress. A majority of Americans felt that Reagan had lied to them. Whether he broke the law remained an open question.

parties, although they are not binding on the candidates.[12] Gerald Pomper and Susan Lederman argue that

> the parties do not copy each other's pledges, but make divergent appeals, thereby pointing to the differences in their basic composition. [The platform] is important because it summarizes, crystallizes, and presents to the voters the character of the party coalition. We should take platforms seriously because politicians seem to take them seriously.[13]

As you can see in Table 6.1, the Republican and Democratic platforms differed significantly in 1984. Note that the Democrat's positions are relatively liberal, with strong support for minority rights and social spending. In contrast, the Republican platforms are relatively conservative, with emphasis on individual enterprise. Although the platforms show some similarities, it is clearly a myth to characterize the parties as simply Tweedledum and Tweedledee.

Winning elections. A party's ability to recruit the strongest possible candidates and to win elections determines its success. Party organizations do not monopolize this process, however, for many candidates seek nomination on their own. Parties offer them training and support, help them raise funds, and try to turn out voters on election day. But many candidates also rely heavily on paid professional consultants to manage and finance their campaigns.

Today the nomination of candidates rests in the hands of the voters who take part in **primaries**—elections to select candidates to run for office under the party banner. (We will discuss primaries in detail in Chapter 7, on elections.) Although primaries limit the direct role of the party-as-organization in the nomination process, partisanship prevails as the party-in-the-electorate makes it choices.

Organizing government. Parties also organize the legislative and executive branches of government. Congress, and most state legislatures, are structured along party lines. Leadership and committee assignments in those bodies are usually by party, and executives—including mayors, governors, and the president—often work closely with party leaders to pass bills and implement programs.

Congressional voting often follows party lines as well, but changes in the internal processes of Congress have in some ways made it difficult for party leaders to control members. Looking ahead to the next election, many members of Congress are more committed to their constituents than to the party. In addition, self-recruitment and the use of independent campaign consultants decrease reliance on the party as the source of nomination and campaign support. As a result, members of Congress do not necessarily put

TABLE 6.1 Comparison Between the 1984 Democratic and Republican Party Platforms

The Democratic positions reflected traditional party ideas and values. The Republicans' planks largely supported the views of the Reagan administration.

Policy Areas	Platform Planks	
	Democrats	Republicans
Abortion	Freedom of choice on abortions	Constitutional amendment banning abortions
Budget deficit	Reducing deficit through increase in taxes and reduction in defense spending and some domestic spending	Constitutional amendment requiring that the federal government balance its budget
Foreign policy	A policy on Central America emphasizing negotiations and political, social, and economic reform	Maintenance of current policy of support for El Salvador and opposition to the Nicaraguan government
National security	Increased efforts toward arms control through negotiations; less emphasis on defense spending	Achievement of peace through increased defense spending and arms superiority
School prayer	Separation of church and state	Voluntary prayer in public schools
Welfare	Social welfare aid for the poor, including food, health care, job training, and education	Work programs for welfare recipients, to be required whenever possible
Women's rights	Strong support of the Equal Rights Amendment and affirmative action programs for women	No mention of the Equal Rights Amendment

Source: *Congressional Quarterly Weekly Report*, July 21, 1984, pp. 1738–1741, 1747–1780, and August 18, 1984, pp. 2023–2027. Adapted from John H. Aldrich, Gary J. Miller, Charles W. Ostrom, Jr., and David W. Rohde, *American Government: People, Institutions, and Policies* (Boston: Houghton Mifflin, 1986), p. 226. Reprinted by permission.

party first and ignore their district's or their own interests. (See Chapter 10, on Congress, for a detailed discussion.)

In short, party control over the vote of a member of Congress is far from absolute—in stark contrast to countries like England, where the party's domination of the nominating process almost always guarantees loyalty among its legislative members. Nevertheless, most members of Congress have a pronounced sense of party loyalty, and, as Figure 6.2 demonstrates, the average Democrat or Republican usually votes with his or her party.[14]

★ ★ ★

THE TWO-PARTY SYSTEM

The Constitution makes no mention of parties. In fact, many of the founders viewed them as dangerous. In his farewell address to Congress, George Washington warned his colleagues and fellow politicians of the "baneful effects of the spirit of party." John Adams, his vice president, complained that "there is nothing I dread so much as the division of the Republic into two great parties, each under its own leader." And Thomas Jefferson, often

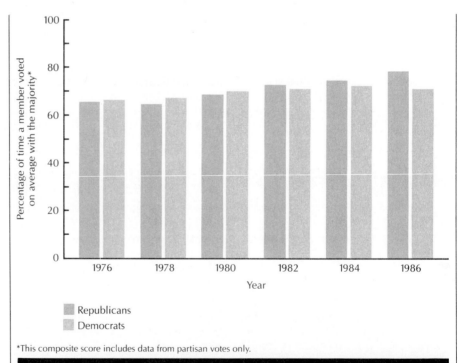

■ Republicans
□ Democrats

*This composite score includes data from partisan votes only.

FIGURE 6.2   Party Unity Voting in Congress: 1976 to 1985

Note that siding with the majority party on partisan votes has actually been increasing despite the myth of party irrelevance.

Source: Congressional Quarterly Weekly Report, January 11, 1986, p. 88. Reprinted by permission of Congressional Quarterly, Inc.

referred to as the "father" of the American party system, exclaimed in the early 1790s that "If I could not go to heaven but with a party, I would not go there at all."

The comments of an anonymous Philadelphian around the time of the nation's founding reflect the widespread fear that parties would split the government into factions. The author wrote in a local paper: "We want no Ticket Mongers: let every citizen exercise his own judgment, and we shall have a good representation—intrigue, favoritism, cabal and party will be at rest."[15]

These fears diminished as parties formed in response to economic and philosophic differences between the merchants and traders in the northern half of the new republic and the planters in the South. By 1800 the United States had a two-party system. In the years that followed, parties evolved into a mechanism for expressing public opinion and organizing support among the citizenry. By 1908 New Jersey Governor Woodrow Wilson, soon to become president, argued that parties are "absolutely necessary to . . . give some coherence to the action of political forces" and that they "have been our real body politic."[16]

The Federalists and the Jeffersonians

American parties grew slowly and cautiously at first.[17] The early parties were stable but short-lived coalitions of like-minded individuals who were drawn together in a conflict over the power of the national government.[18] The Federalists, led by Alexander Hamilton, favored a strong central government with taxing powers, a national bank, and a favorable foreign policy toward England. They attracted most of their support from the Northeast and the Atlantic seaboard and found it chiefly among bankers, industrialists, northern landowners, and merchants who believed that a strong central government would produce a stable economy.

The Jeffersonians (also known as the Democratic-Republicans), organized by Thomas Jefferson and James Madison, favored limited national government and strong states' rights. They argued for a foreign policy that supported France over England and opposed a national bank. Although the Jeffersonians drew considerable support from the Middle Atlantic states, their greatest strength came from the South, particularly Virginia. They attracted small farmers, businessmen, and craftsmen.

The Federalists elected their last president, John Adams, in 1796. In the next few years the party was torn apart by internal disputes between Adams and Hamilton over the direction of the party (particularly regarding foreign policy). As their base of support narrowed, the Federalists gradually faded from national politics. Thus from 1800 to 1820 the United States was a one-party nation.

The Democrats and the Whigs

The Jeffersonians and their heirs dominated national politics from 1800 to 1860, but their reign was not peaceful.[19] A crucial split occurred with the election of Andrew Jackson in 1828. Known as "Old Hickory," Jackson was a tough, ambitious man—the first American president to rise from humble beginnings.

The Jacksonians, who now called themselves Democrats, favored increased participatory democracy, limited central government, and strong state power. Jackson's supporters attracted farmers and other working people to the party. By the end of his presidency, the Democrats were truly a national party. Many of the members of the opposition party, the Whigs, were former Federalists who opposed Jackson's attempts to decentralize the government. Supported by commercial and manufacturing interests, the Whigs successfully elected two presidents during the 1840s. Later the Whigs collapsed in the conflict over slavery, which eroded their support in the North and also split the Democrats into northern and southern factions.

The Whigs and the Democrats laid the foundation for the American two-party system. Like modern parties, they were well organized, with local and state committees. They held national conventions, constructed national party platforms, and had a relatively broad base of support, with participation by an expanded white male electorate. Although the period of strong rivalry between the two parties lasted only twenty years, it marked the real beginning of the two-party system in the United States.

The Democrats and the Republicans

The Republican party was born in 1854 in opposition to slavery. It drew its support from former elements of the Whig party, including business and merchant interests, abolitionists, and small farmers in the North and West. With the election in 1860 of Abraham Lincoln of Illinois, the Republicans established themselves as a major party. Since then the Republicans and Democrats have alternately dominated party politics. The Republicans won most (fourteen of eighteen) presidential races between 1860 and 1928. Their dominance was due in large part to their pro-business policies, which attracted a strong base of support in the industrial North. The Democrats remained powerful in the South, although in 1924, when their popularity was at its lowest, they were able to win only four of the former Confederate states.

The party balance changed in 1932 with the election of Franklin D. Roosevelt of New York. His victory stemmed from the Republicans' inability to deal with the hardships of the Great Depression. The Democrats' new power rested on a coalition of voters from the urban North and white Southerners. Attracted by Roosevelt's New Deal policies, blacks, too, joined

A disaster for the Democrats Antiwar protests, which developed into riots at the 1968 Democratic national convention, contributed to the party's defeat in that year's presidential election. Here police use rifle butts, tear gas, and clubs to battle antiwar demonstrators.

the coalition. With one interruption (the two-term presidency of General Dwight D. Eisenhower in the 1950s), this coalition held onto the White House until Republican Richard Nixon became president in 1969.

Since the late 1960s scholars, reporters, and political pundits have raised questions about the future of the two-party system. Before Nixon's triumph, the Republican party seemed doomed to fail in presidential elections. His victory turned the tide, and the Republicans won four of the following five presidential races. Democrat Walter Mondale's exceptionally poor showing in 1984, in turn, led to further questions about the majority party status of the Democratic party at the presidential level.

Realignment of Parties

Are we experiencing a major shift from one party to another? Do the Republican victories mark a realignment of power? **Party realignments** occur (1) when a political, social, or economic development prompts those groups that traditionally support one party to shift their support to another party or (2) when large numbers of new voters enter the electorate, causing a shift to a new majority party.[20] For a realignment to take place, one party must become dominant in the political system, controlling the presidency and Congress, as well as many state legislatures. The democratization of parties, slavery, and the Great Depression are three of the economic and social issues that precipitated major party realignments of the past. There have been four major American realignments altogether, marked by the election of Andrew Jackson in 1828, Abraham Lincoln in 1860, William McKinley in 1896, and Franklin Roosevelt in 1932.

The realignment that brought Roosevelt's Democrats to power was, in part, the result of a shift in population away from rural small towns, where traditional Republican support rested, to the big cities. New immigrants living in the big cities strongly rejected the Republicans' traditional pattern of nonintervention in economic and social problems. They joined Catholics and other traditional Republicans in a new coalition that gave the Democrats an overwhelming victory in 1932. Together with blacks, they formed a lasting reservoir of support for the Democratic party.

You can see in Table 6.2 that realigning elections seem to occur approximately every thirty years. If history provides an accurate picture of the future, a realigning election, projecting the Republican party into the majority, should have occurred around 1968. Indeed, many observers thought that Nixon's victory marked the beginning of a new realignment.

Conditions favored a Republican resurgence that year. The Democratic party was bitterly divided over the Vietnam War, and riots marred its national convention. Urban unrest, particularly in black ghettos, spelled disaster for the Democrats. Some unusual events, however, may have helped postpone a shift in power to the Republicans. As the result of the civil rights movement of the 1960s, many southern blacks joined the electorate, and their entry strengthened the Democrats' position. People were also living longer, which meant that New Deal Democrats remained in the electorate to support their party's candidates. On the other hand, the Watergate scandal eroded the Republicans' position in the 1970s and probably contributed, in part, to Georgia Governor Jimmy Carter's election to the presidency in 1976. The Democrats continued to dominate both houses of Congress until 1981.

Do Republican President Reagan's impressive victories in 1980 and 1984 and the Republicans' control of the Senate between 1981 and 1986 mean that a realignment has occurred? Two characteristics of our contemporary political scene warn us against any quick judgments regarding realignment.

First, despite the Republicans' success in dominating the presidency, the Democrats have maintained control over the House of Representatives. They have also taken back the Senate, and they dominate a majority of state houses. Second, we may be going through a period of **dealignment,** in which the public disassociates itself from either party and splits its votes between the parties. The growth in the number of independents and weak party

TABLE 6.2   Electoral Party Systems in the United States

Despite the shifts documented in this table, the American party system has been remarkably stable. The Democratic party has been around for more than one hundred and fifty years, and the Republican party has been in existence for more than a century.

Stage of Development	Period	Leading Parties	Events and Developments
First party system	1790s–1824	Federalists Jeffersonians	Parties evolved; powers of national government grow
Second party system	1824–1860	Whigs Democrats	National nominating conventions; national bank; regional conflicts; national party committees; state and local party committees
Third party system	1860–1896	Republicans Democrats	Urban political machines; states' rights; role of political bosses
Fourth party system	1896–1932	Republicans Democrats	Nonpartisan local elections; government reform; U.S. role in world affairs; formal voter registration systems; use of direct primary; weakening of congressional party controls
Fifth party system	1932–?	Republicans Democrats	Changes in convention rules; civil rights; Vietnam; welfare state policies; nominating rules (Democrats)

Source: Alan R. Gitelson, M. Margaret Conway, and Frank B. Feigert, *American Political Parties: Stability and Change* (Boston: Houghton Mifflin, 1984), pp. 26–27. Adapted by permission.

identifiers supports this argument. If the pattern prevails, neither party may be able to regain a solid hold on the title of "majority party" in the near future. At this stage, then, no clear realignment has occurred at the voter or officeholder level.

Why Two Parties?

One thing is clear: for most of its history America has had a two-party system. We have many minor parties, but they rarely elect anyone to a major office. Why has this been the case? Other democracies, including Israel, Holland, France, and Italy, have several important parties. What factors limit significant party activity in the United States to the Republicans and the Democrats?

Winners take all.   According to one explanation the rules that govern the electoral system in the United States are responsible for the two-party system.[21] Early in our history we adopted what is known as a **single-member, plurality electoral system.** In all federal and state elections and in most local elections, we elect officials from districts served only by one legislator. In order to gain office, a candidate has to win a plurality—the most votes. (Occasionally a candidate must win a majority of the votes.) Thus, only one U.S. representative or state legislator is elected from each congressional or legislative district— no matter how close the vote.

In contrast, most European nations use a system of **proportional representation.** In this system, legislative seats are assigned to party candidates in proportion to the percentage of the vote that the party receives within electoral districts. If a party receives 35 percent of the vote in a district, it is allocated approximately 35 percent of that district's legislative seats. Minor or third parties may accumulate enough votes to gain representation in the legislature, even if they are not able to attract a plurality or only have strong pockets of support.

The winner-take-all system in the United States has worked against the development of minor parties. Because it is so difficult for even the most successful minor parties to accumulate pluralities, their candidates rarely win. Recognizing that minorities have so little chance, voters tend to be drawn to the major party coalitions at election time, and those parties try hard to maintain middle-of-the-road positions that will attract voters.[22] The result has been two broad-based party coalitions like the Republicans and Democrats of today.

A division of interests.   A second explanation, advanced by V. O. Key and Louis Hartz, points to a natural division of interests in our nation, as the source of the two-party system.[23] From the time of the country's founding until recently, the North and South have been divided politically. The division stemmed from tensions over the power of the national government and over questions of economic and social policy. This situation, according to Key and Hartz, has fostered the two-party competitive system, which is really a response to the national duality of interests.

A similarity of goals.   Still another view focuses on the over-riding consensus that exists in the United States regarding our political, social, economic, and governmental systems. Basically, most Americans believe in capitalism; virtually no Americans want to institute a monarchy; and most

Americans regard religion as a private matter. By contrast, in many European countries, the people support a variety of radically different social and economic alternatives, ranging from Marxism to anarchy, and differences in social class and religion have given rise to a broad range of parties.

Divisions do exist in the United States as well—for example, between blacks and whites. But a basic acceptance of the political and governmental system by most Americans makes compromise possible. As a result, the two major parties can adequately serve us all, and we do not need a complex multiparty system.

Third Parties in the United States

Despite the strength of the two-party system, minor parties have always existed in the United States. Historically, there have been more than nine hundred of these "third" parties, yet only one former minor party—the Republicans in 1860—developed into a permanent national party. Occasionally, third parties even do well in national elections. As Table 6.3 shows, the American "Know-Nothings" party received over 21 percent of the popular vote in the 1856 presidential election, and the Bull Moose party received over 27 percent of the popular vote in the 1912 presidential election.[24] Sometimes minor parties form around a single issue like prohibition or an ideology like socialism. Others are splinter groups that leave a major party because they feel that their interests are not well represented. An example is George Wallace's American Independent party, which split off from the Democrats in 1968.

Third parties succeed in elections mostly at the state and local level. But even at that level, many barriers must be overcome. Dominated by the two major parties, state legislatures have created complicated electoral rules that make it hard for the minor parties to obtain funding and to place their candidates on the ballot. In California, for example, a new party must submit a petition containing more than seven hundred thousand signatures before its candidates can be listed on the general election ballot. In Florida, a third party must pay the state ten cents for every signature submitted.[25]

Federal election laws also work against the minor parties. For example, major parties automatically receive guaranteed funding for presidential campaigns. A third party cannot obtain such funding until its candidate has demonstrated the ability to garner a minimum (5 percent) of the popular vote.

Despite these obstacles, third parties flourish, attracting devoted members and serving as a force for change in American politics. Third parties put new issues on the political agenda—issues that the major parties may overlook in their search for the broad middle ground, where most voters are perceived

TABLE 6.3 Major Third Parties in Elections

Minor parties with a real chance of electoral success are a rarity in American politics, but that does not stop them from trying. Theodore Roosevelt, the most successful third party candidate, outpolled the Republican incumbent and ensured the election of a Democrat, Woodrow Wilson.

Party	Year	Percentage of Presidential Vote
Anti-Mason	1832	8.0
Free Soil	1848	10.1
American "Know-Nothings"	1856	21.4
Breckinridge Democrats	1860	18.2
Constitutional Union	1860	12.6
Populists	1892	8.5
Bull Moose (Theodore Roosevelt) Progressives	1912	27.4
Socialists	1912	6.0
Robert La Follette Progressives	1924	16.6
George Wallace American Independent	1968	13.5
John Anderson National Unity*	1980	6.6

Source: Daniel A. Mazmanian, *Third Parties in Presidential Elections* (Washington, D.C.: The Brookings Institution, 1974). Data are from *Statistical Abstract of the United States,* U.S. Department of Commerce, Bureau of the Census. Reprinted by permission.
* Anderson ran as an independent candidate in most states. The National Unity party did not have any formal organizational structure other than as a vehicle for slating the candidate in most states.

to be. For example, social security, unemployment insurance, the five-day workweek, workmen's compensation, national health insurance, and government aid to farmers were first introduced by the Socialist party in its 1932 party platform and only later recognized as important programs by both the Republicans and the Democrats.

With so many possible issues of importance to small groups of voters, why do we not have more minor parties? Why, for example, did the civil rights movement not produce a minor party? The answer is that those involved in the movement (like many other underrepresented groups) found support within a major party. Democratic Presidents John F. Kennedy and Lyndon B. Johnson responded to the movement's strategy of civil disobedience and became strong advocates for civil rights. Of course, the Democrats wanted to retain the support of a growing black constituency. When issues are narrower and voter support less widespread, third-party advocates may have few political options except to form a minor party.

★ ★ ★
PARTY STRUCTURE

Decentralization is the key word to remember when thinking about the structure of parties. Just as in our governmental system, power in the parties is fragmented among local, state, and national organizations. The two national parties are loose confederations of state parties, and state political parties are loose confederations of city and county political organizations.

For a long time the most influential party leaders were heads of local party organizations. Bosses like Mayor Richard Daley of Chicago ruled their cities with an iron hand, distributing favors and flattening any opposition. It was said of Daley that he controlled even assignment of the job of running the elevators in city hall. There are still strong local politicians and mayors today, although Daley, who died in 1976, was the last of the old-style, undisputed bosses.

Local Parties

At the bottom of the typical local party structure is the **precinct,** a voting district generally covering an area of several blocks. An elected or appointed precinct captain may oversee electoral activities in the precinct, including voter registration, passing out leaflets, and get-out-the-vote efforts. Above the precinct level, several different organizations exist. **Wards** (city council districts) are important in big cities like Chicago. Elsewhere, party organizations exist at the city, county, congressional district, state legislative, or even judicial level. Members of these committees may be elected or appointed. Their responsibilities include raising money, recruiting candidates, conducting campaigns, and handling **patronage** (providing services, jobs, or contracts in return for support).

In many places around the country, local parties scarcely exist at all. Nonpartisan elections are the rule, and politics is relatively informal. Indeed, two-thirds of cities with populations of over five thousand use the nonpartisan form of election. In these communities, formal or informal "political clubs" raise money and run campaigns. These clubs actively compete with each other in elections and may identify with either major party.

Even in communities where partisan elections are the rule, party organization and strength vary tremendously. If one party dominates, the weaker party may find it impossible to recruit workers and candidates and to raise money for elections. Until its resurgence in the 1960s, the Republican party had to cope with this kind of handicap throughout the Democratic South. In communities that show little interest in politics, neither party may be able to put together a strong local organization.

Machines and Reforms

Local politics was once a far more lively affair. In the late nineteenth and early twentieth centuries powerful but often corrupt machines ran the cities. These **political machines** were centrally controlled and tightly structured organizations that used rewards such as jobs and lucrative contracts to recruit and retain many of their supporters. Indeed, they maintained their power by giving poor immigrant and ethnic groups access to services and the rich access to cash and contracts—in return for their votes and other favors.

One of the oldest and best-known local machines was Tammany Hall of New York City, founded in 1786 and led in the mid-1800s by William (the Tammany Tiger) Tweed. Tweed's ties to business made him and his associates—Richard "Slippery Dick" Connolly, the city comptroller; Abraham "Elegant" Oakey Hall, the mayor; Peter "Brains" Sweeney, the city chamberlain; and John "Toots" Hoffman, the governor—very rich men. When a city contract was put out to bid, for example, they typically received a kickback of 65 percent of the fee. Other local machines were equally corrupt as were many state machines.

An obscure but powerful machine operated in rural Plaquemines Parish, Louisiana (a parish is similar to a county), where the late Leander Perez and his sons were local political and economic bosses until the late 1970s. It was said of Perez—with some humor—that he was so powerful and influential that you could not buy a toothbrush in Plaquemines Parish without checking out the color with him first.

Disillusionment with machine politics led to the rise of a reform movement around the turn of the century. The reformers had mixed motivations. Some wanted to fight the corruption and waste that appeared to come hand in hand with machine-type government. Others resented the power that machine organizations frequently gave to the new immigrants and the lower class. Whatever their motives, the reformers aimed to eliminate, or at least reduce, the power of machines.

The reform movement, also called the **Progressive movement,** mounted a two-pronged attack: it pushed for changes in the way candidates were chosen and in the way government jobs were filled. Many states established direct primary voting, so that the voters rather than the bosses would select the party nominees. Some cities hired professional city managers to run their affairs. Later cities adopted civil service codes, so that jobs could be filled on the basis of merit and not patronage.

The growth of federal and state social welfare programs since the 1930s reduced the need of the poor and unemployed to barter votes for services and slowly eroded the power of urban machines. Nevertheless, some vestiges of party machines remain, despite primaries and civil service and welfare reforms, and it is important to point out that not all machines are corrupt.

State Parties

The influence and power of state party organizations vary from state to state. State parties in Alabama, California, and Maryland, for example, have almost nothing to say about which candidates run for office or how they run. In contrast, parties in states like Connecticut, Indiana, and Michigan wield considerable power.[26] Often a good deal of that power is in the hands of the state chairperson. Party organization varies from state to state, however, and depends on the wishes of officeholders and other influential party members and on state laws and party rules and regulations.

In recent years state party organizations have assumed an important role on the political scene. State parties have increasingly begun to offer fund-raising, polling, and research services to state and local candidates (see Myth and Reality 6.1). They may also provide computer analyses of voting behavior. In addition, most state party organizations help orchestrate the state presidential campaigns.

National Parties

The national party organizations come into their own every four years, when they organize the national conventions and support candidates for major office. Although less visible the rest of the time, the national party staffs, directed by the national chairpersons and the national committees, which include representatives from all the states, are hard at work. They raise money for national and state elections, run workshops on campaigning and fund-raising techniques for congressional candidates, and maintain the loose decentralized structure that is the national party.

The electoral role of the national party organizations, always rather limited, has been challenged in recent years by interest groups and their **political action committees (PACs).** Because federal laws, as well as many state laws, prohibit various interest groups from donating money to political campaigns, such groups have set up affiliated PAC organizations solely for the purpose of contributing money to the campaigns of candidates who sympathize with their aims. (See Chapter 8, on interest groups, for a more detailed discussion of the role of PACs.) The involvement of professional consultants and the media in the campaign process has also diminished the role of the national organizations. (See Chapter 7, on elections, for more on this topic.)

MYTH AND REALITY 6.1

The Arrival of Modern Technology

For the Missouri Democratic Party, the computer age has finally arrived. And right now the future looks a little tattered around the edges. With the help of a grant from the Democratic National Committee, the state party for the first time is building a computerized list of the state's voters. There is only one problem: voters in Missouri do not register by party. To learn which voters to court and which to ignore, the party has to telephone all 3 million registered voters and ask.

This dilemma highlights the limits of modern technology in an age when many people believe the myth that computers can resolve most problems. Both the Democratic National Committee and the Republican National Committee are pouring hundreds of thousands of dollars into computer-based voter files. They have found that such efforts do not always bear fruit. The political director of the Democratic committee, Jeffrey Ely, in discussing the committee's efforts to help thirty-one state parties build meaningful computerized operations, indicated that "only a scattering of state parties were actually providing what Democrats would consider state-of-the-art services."

Computers are useless, for example, in states that do not keep records on who has voted in recent elections. Other problems arise in attempt-ing to establish voter files. Using computers to match names and phone numbers produces only mixed results. In Texas, "you just can't reach half the state because you don't have good phone numbers," says Royal A. Masset, political director for that state's Republican party. Speaking to the broader difficulties faced by many state party organizations, the Republican committee's development director, William D. McInturff, points out that "in most cases, the problem is that the source [voter registration] documents filed by the counties are not terribly accurate."

Clearly, computers and modern technology are useful. They can ease administrative tasks and record keeping, and when the appropriate data are available, they can facilitate targeted mailings and telephone calls to specific groups. The role of computers in these tasks will no doubt grow in importance. But as Republican computer consultant John Brady has indicated, "this stuff [technology] is out there. But we're just scratching the surface."

The material and quotes for this essay were adapted from Ronald Brownstein, "Party Workers in the Computer Age . . . Still Find the Voters To Be Elusive," *National Journal,* August 8, 1986, pp. 2002–2003. Reprinted by permission of the *National Journal.*

Despite these challenges, both national organizations, and especially the national Republican party, have refused to accept a secondary role in national politics and recently have worked to revitalize themselves.[27] Under the leadership of National Committee Chairman Bill Brock, whose tenure lasted from 1977 to 1981, the Republicans strengthened their fund-raising and candidate support systems. They now provide sophisticated technical campaign expertise to state and local parties. They have concentrated particularly

Eagle on the rubber chicken circuit "Rubber" chicken is tough and so is raising campaign funds, but the Republicans have strengthened their collection techniques in recent years. To say thank you for organizing a dinner that raised $7 million for Republican candidates, President Reagan presents a statuette to his former Transportation Secretary Drew Lewis (center).

on increasing Republican representation in state legislatures and building computer-based lists of grassroots contributors.

The Democrats have redefined the rules governing the selection of presidential convention delegates to make the party's decision-making structure more democratic and to increase grassroots participation in the party. This process has involved, among other things, systematic efforts to achieve broad-based representation of women and minorities at the national conventions. The Democrats also increased, in 1984, the number of U.S. Senators and representatives who attend the national convention as delegates. Since the early 1980s the national Democratic party has also tried to offer more fund-raising and campaign support to its own candidates.

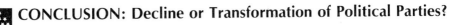

CONCLUSION: Decline or Transformation of Political Parties?

What is the future of the Democratic and Republican parties? Some scholars insist that both parties are in a period of decline and see them as weak, inconsistent in their policies, lacking accountability for their actions, disorganized in pursuing their goals, and less effective than in the past in organizing government.[28] Given the decrease in party identification and the loss of party control over the campaign and election process, it is not surprising that many people believe in the myths of Tweedledum and Tweedledee and party irrelevance.

Are the parties identical? It sometimes seems that way because some of their policies can be difficult to distinguish. On some broad issues like supporting reductions in the national deficit and narrow issues like social

Young Republicans If political parties are to survive in American politics, they will have to attract support from young people. That goal is by no means impossible, as this scene from the 1984 Republican national convention attests.

security for the elderly, their positions are often the same. To confuse matters further, groups of legislators from both parties occasionally join forces to support or oppose legislation.

Nevertheless, the evidence suggests that the parties are not alike. The fact that they attract different coalitions of voters and office seekers and that Democrats and Republicans in the electorate and in government tend to view many issues differently—see Table 6.1 dealing with party platforms—repudiates the notion that the parties are as much alike as Tweedledum and Tweedledee.

The increase in independents and in ticket splitting suggests that parties are less relevant than in the past, as does the takeover of many traditional party roles by interest groups, political action committees, and professional political consultants. The parties, however, have changed in response to such challenges. Furthermore although parties attract fewer strong supporters, particularly among college students, a significant majority of voters still feel some attachment to either the Democrats or the Republicans and believe that one party can do a better job than the other in tackling the nation's most serious problems.[29]

If parties are still viable, what kind of change is taking place? How can we explain, for example, the growing independence of political candidates and legislators from their party? Some scholars have suggested that a transformation is taking place in the roles and functions of parties in our society.[30]

While they are now sharing many traditional functions with other groups, parties have taken on new tasks. Both national and state organizations have enhanced their roles in the campaign process and have continued to play a major role at the local level. In fact, most of the elections held in our nation during the four years between presidential races—and they number over five hundred thousand—are not touched by any other organized group. Party influence in the Senate and House remains strong, and the members vote along party lines more often than not. This pattern is also typical of state legislators.

Thus, despite the myth of party irrelevance, parties remain a key institution in American politics and are still the single most important cue for voters making electoral decisions. They also play a dominant role in organizing and coordinating public policy on literally thousands of issues. Finally, parties represent many individuals and groups that are not adequately served by other organizations. These groups include the poor, the aged, and minorities; all of them have benefited from strong party platforms and legislative action. Challenged by the entry of new and competing institutions into the electoral process, parties have increasingly adapted to these challenges and have maintained their unique role in our political system.

★ ★ ★
SUMMARY

1. American political parties are coalitions of people organized formally to recruit, nominate, and elect individuals to office and to use elected office to achieve shared political goals.

2. Parties represent three different alliances of members: the-party-as-organization, the party-in-the-electorate, and the party-in-government.

3. Although many Americans' identification with the Republican or Democratic parties seems to be weakening, the parties remain relevant symbols, particularly when it comes to voting.

4. Parties organize citizens into electoral coalitions, develop policy positions, work to win elections, and organize government.

5. Parties developed slowly in the United States, but by the mid-1800s, the Whigs and Democrats had laid the foundation for the two-party system. There have been four major realignments, or major shifts from one party to another, in U.S. history. Currently scholars are debating whether another realignment has occurred.

6. Explanations for the existence of the two-party system include winner-take-all electoral rules, a division of social and economic interests, and a basic consensus on political goals.

7. Despite the strength of the major parties, minor parties thrive and present program alternatives that are often adopted by the Democratic and Republican parties.

8. Local political parties are not as strong as they were in the days of machine politics, whereas state parties have grown in importance in recent years. Although the national party organizations have been challenged by competing groups, they have responded to the challenge and in changing have revitalized themselves.

★ ★ ★
KEY TERMS

political parties	platforms
decentralized	primaries
party-as-organization	party realignments
party-in-the-electorate	dealignment
party-in-government	single-member, plurality electoral
electoral coalitions	system

proportional representation
precinct
wards
patronage

political machines
Progressive movement
political action committees (PACs)
retrospective voting

★ ★ ★

SELECTED READINGS

- Chambers, William N. and Walter Dean Burnham, eds., *The American Party System.* New York: Oxford University Press, 1967. A collection of essays reviewing the history and development of the American party system.

- Gitelson, Alan R., M. Margaret Conway, and Frank B. Feigert. *American Political Parties: Stability and Change.* Boston: Houghton Mifflin, 1984. An overview of the structure and functions of political parties. The authors argue that parties are not on the decline but rather are undergoing a transformation in their roles and functions.

- Janda, Kenneth. *Political Parties: A Cross-National Survey.* New York: Free Press, 1980. A comprehensive study of comparative party systems throughout the world.

- Jewell, Malcolm E. and David Olson. *American State Political Parties and Elections,* rev. ed. Chicago: Dorsey Press, 1982. An extensive study and analysis of political parties and elections in the fifty states.

- Riordon, William L. *Plunkitt of Tammany Hall.* New York: Dutton, 1963. An entertaining and often amusing story of an infamous member of the legendary Tammany Hall machine organization of New York City.

7

C H A P T E R

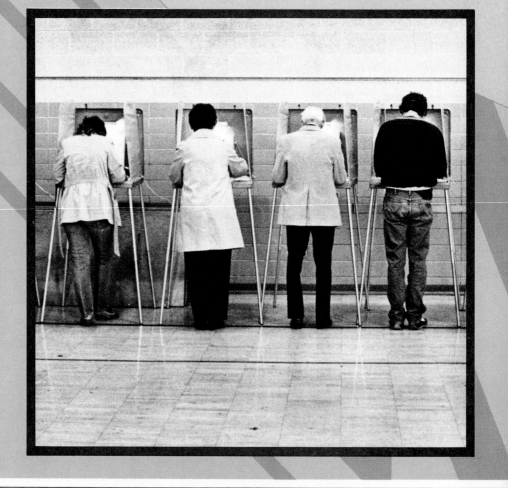

Campaigns and Elections

T he excitement of the election was overwhelming. Millions of people turned out to see and hear the presidential candidates as they traveled around the nation, speaking on the issues of the day. Between July and November the Democratic candidate "made five hundred speeches . . . addressing thirty to forty million people . . . traveling 18,000 miles in four swings around the country."[1] One scholar wrote of the Republican candidate that this was a classic case of a "modern advertising campaign. . . . Cartoons, posters, inscriptions, were turned out by the carloads, more than "120 million campaign documents" were distributed to the people and "an army of 1,400 trained speakers" was engaged to speak in favor of the candidate.[2] The Republicans canvassed voters and targeted specific ethnic groups with campaign literature written in German, Spanish, French, Italian, and Yiddish, as well as other languages.[3]

This campaign story may seem familiar. The campaign strategies and hoopla may remind you of recent presidential races. Yet the campaign took place almost one hundred years ago, in 1896, when the Democratic presidential candidate, William Jennings Bryan, ran against Republican William McKinley.

Rallies, use of the media, and appeals to special interests remain a basic part of modern-day campaigns and elections, and the intensity and excitement have stayed the same. The electoral system itself is quite different, however. An array of regulations, restrictions, and constitutional amendments has changed the way candidates are nominated, how campaigns are run, and who is eligible to vote. Unlike McKinley or Bryan, today's candidates for president have to contend with presidential primaries, campaign-spending limits, and an expanded voting population. In 1896 most voters were middle- and upper-class white men. Today candidates must appeal to men and women, black and white, rich and poor, and young and old.

Despite the excitement of the campaigns and the widespread media coverage, the American public has some misgivings about the election process. Poll findings suggest that Americans do not believe that their elected representatives respond to their demands and expectations. For example, when asked whether "having elections makes the government pay attention to what the people think," 56 percent of those questioned said that it does so only "some" of the time or "not much."[4]

The public also strongly disapproves of the way candidates run their campaigns, particularly the way they finance them. Indeed, 67 percent of those questioned in a recent survey agreed that limitations should be set on election expenditures in congressional campaigns.[5] Such views are reinforced when, for example, the press reports that the 1984 Senate race in North Carolina cost the candidates over $26 million.

Why have so many Americans come to doubt the usefulness of elections? Why do so many citizens stay home on election day? Two myths seem to be at the root of public criticism of the electoral process. The myth of broken promises holds that elections do not affect government policies—that candidates, once elected, fail to keep the promises they made during their campaigns. The money-buys-elections myth stresses the power of funding: if a candidate simply spends enough, he or she will win.

The reality of the election process, however, differs considerably from either myth. We will demonstrate in this chapter that politicians seek to achieve not only their own career goals, but also the social and political goals of their campaigns. We will show, moreover, that although money is important in elections because it buys television time, polls, consultants, and the like, a variety of other factors have a significant impact on who wins office.

We will begin by looking at the way the selection process works: why people run for office and how they are nominated. Then we will describe the strategies candidates use to get elected and the voters' response to their campaigns. We will end with a discussion of the links among campaign promises, elections, and public policy.

★ ★ ★

NOMINATIONS: THE SELECTION PROCESS

Every year thousands of individuals decide to run for political office. Before they can get on the ballot, most must be selected, or nominated, by a political party, often after a costly, time-consuming, and exhausting primary campaign. What motivates these individuals?

Seeking Political Office

"The stakes are too high for government to be a spectator sport," former Texas Representative Barbara Jordan told a commencement audience a decade ago. Few who run for office would disagree. Both personal ambition and policy goals motivate people to enter the proverbial election ring. Personal satisfactions include the power that elective office confers and the prestige of holding public office.[6] These rewards often drive politicians to climb what Joseph Schlesinger refers to as the **opportunity structure:**[7] the political ladder of local, state, and federal offices that brings greater prestige and power as one moves toward the presidency at the very top.

Politics is more than a career, however. Candidates also have a commitment to public service and to policy goals. For example, Ronald Reagan's presidential campaigns made clear his deep conviction that the American public needed financial relief. Its main affliction, he believed, was high taxes. His efforts, along with those of Congress, to reduce taxes, reflect his commitment to that goal—a goal achieved, in part, by the 1986 tax reforms.

Ambition and motivation alone are not enough to ensure election, however. Anyone who wants to run for political office in most partisan elections (including the presidency) must first secure a party nomination.

Promise them . . . With the price of farm products down and agricultural production up, U.S. farmers have faced severe economic hardships in the 1980s. To win their sizable vote, presidential candidates like Ronald Reagan (shown here at a rally in Pennsylvania) characteristically have been unable to resist the temptation of promising solutions to the farm problems.

The Caucus

One of the oldest nomination methods is the **caucus** (the word means "meeting"). A diary entry written by John Adams in 1763 gives a less-than-flattering description of this process:

> This day learned that the caucus club meets at certain times in the garret of Dawes. . . . There they smoke tobacco till you cannot see from one end of the garret to the other. There they drink flip . . . and they choose a moderator who puts questions to the vote regularly; and selectmen, assessors, collectors, fire wardens, and representatives are regularly chosen before they are chosen in the town.[8]

Until the progressive era, all party nominations were decided by caucuses or conventions. These meetings were closed to the public, and party leaders usually chose the nominees. Contemporary caucuses are local meetings open

... and hope you can win their vote In fact, many observers believe that government "solutions" have created the farm problem in the first place. These policies, which included price supports for farm products, have left farmers dependent on the federal government for most of their income. It is failures such as these that lead to the myth of broken promises, but that does not stop candidates like Walter Mondale (front left) from courting the farm vote.

to all who live in the precinct. These citizens "caucus"—that is, discuss—and then vote for delegates to district and state conventions, who then nominate candidates for congressional and statewide offices. In almost half of the states, representatives to the national presidential conventions are also chosen by the caucus-convention method. Many of these delegates are committed in advance to a particular presidential candidate. Some, however, choose to run as uncommitted delegates, awaiting the national convention to declare their candidate preference.

Primaries

Except in presidential nominations, caucuses are relatively uncommon in contemporary politics. As we pointed out in Chapter 6, on parties, most federal, state, and local nominees are chosen in a **primary**—an election in which party members (and sometimes nonparty members) select candidates to run for office under the party banner. The first recorded primary was held in Crawford County, Pennsylvania, in 1842, but the first statewide primary system was not enacted until 1903, in Wisconsin. In about half of the states delegates to the Democratic and Republican national conventions are chosen by primary.

An important turning point for presidential primaries was the violent 1968 Democratic National Convention in Chicago. Outside the hall, club-swinging police attacked crowds protesting the Vietnam War. Inside, conservative and liberal Democrats denounced each other. A divided convention nominated Vice President Hubert Humphrey, the party leaders' choice, frustrating the hopes of two peace candidates, who had won considerable primary support. After Humphrey's narrow defeat in the November election, the Democrats changed the party rules to make the nomination system more democratic. One result was an increase in the number of primaries, which rose from a low of twelve in 1960 to a high of thirty-six (including a primary in Washington, D.C.) in 1980.

The **open primary,** in which any qualified voter may participate, regardless of party affiliation, now prevails in nine states. On entering the polling place, voters choose a Democratic, Republican, or other ballot and vote for the listed candidates.* The **closed primary,** used in thirty-eight states and Washington, D.C., allows voters to obtain only a ballot of the party in which they are already registered. In a **partisan primary,** candidates run for their own party's nomination. In a **nonpartisan primary,** candidates are listed on a ballot with no party identification. All presidential primaries are partisan. Many local primaries and the Nebraska state primary are nonpartisan.

In most states, a successful candidate need only get the most votes in order to win the primary. In ten southern states, a majority (more than 50 percent) of the vote is needed to win. There, if no candidate receives a clear majority, a **run-off primary** between the top two vote getters determines the party's candidate in the general election.

Presidential Nominating Conventions

When Humphrey was nominated in 1968, he had entered no primaries, counting instead on support from President Lyndon Johnson and other party leaders. His defeat in the November election ended a century-old tradition in which the presidential and vice presidential candidates were in effect chosen every four years at their party's national convention by delegates

---

* A variation on the open primary is the blanket primary, found in three states—Alaska, Washington, and Louisiana—where voters do not disclose their party affiliation and where they may participate in the Democratic primary for one office and the Republican primary for another office.

The chilly road to the convention Nomination campaigns begin long before the parties' national conventions. Here Massachusetts governor and Democratic candidate Michael Dukakis tours the Iowa countryside one year before that state's caucuses.

from the fifty states, the District of Columbia, and (in the case of the Democrats) offshore territories and Americans abroad.

The rise of the presidential primary has meant that the national party conventions no longer select the candidates, but rather ratify the presidential and vice-presidential choices already made in statewide presidential primaries and caucus-conventions.[9] (In 1984 alone, fourteen presidential aspirants spent over $107 million in these nomination campaigns.[10]) Conventions still serve a number of traditional functions, however. They give the party faithful a place to transact business, including changing rules and writing the party platform. When the conventions are run smoothly, with minimal disputes and conflicts, they serve as an important "media event," publicizing the party's candidates and the issues to a nationwide audience.

Until the rule reforms of the late 1960s and early 1970s, state and local party leaders appointed most convention delegates. The delegates were largely well-educated, white, male professionals. One survey in the 1940s showed that nearly 40 percent of them were lawyers.[11] By 1984, 62 percent of the Democratic delegates and 66 percent of the Republican delegates were selected through primaries.[12] They were a relatively diverse group, with men and women almost equally represented—and fewer lawyers. Loyal supporters of one of the major candidates, most delegates had stood for election in a primary or caucus in that candidate's name.

The excitement surrounding the 1984 Republican National Convention was tempered by its obvious outcome. No one doubted that the incumbents, President Ronald Reagan and Vice President George Bush, would be nominated. Despite friction over some platform planks, approval of the platform was also a foregone conclusion. At best, the convention served as a media event and as an opportunity for delegates from around the nation to celebrate what they perceived (accurately) would be a successful outcome in the November election.

As has often been the case in recent years for the party without an incumbent running for president, the Democrats fielded a large group of presidential hopefuls. The front runner, former Vice President Walter Mondale, faced six serious opponents, including two southerners, one black, two westerners, and a senator who had been an astronaut. After a long and divisive series of primary battles, Mondale came to the convention with a clear lead over his closest rival, Colorado Senator Gary Hart. The national convention was simply a formality.

Primaries and caucuses were critically important to Mondale's victory. Mondale won most of the large industrial states, from which most convention delegates are selected. By the time the convention opened in San Francisco, he was virtually assured of the nomination. The preconvention contests affected his rivals as well. Many political analysts, for instance, favored John Glenn, the U.S. senator from Ohio and a former astronaut. Yet Glenn soon fell by the wayside as it became clear that he could not win any primaries or caucuses.

In contrast, Gary Hart, who was relatively unknown before seeking the nomination, was catapulted to the front of the race with a well-publicized second-place finish in the early Iowa caucus, followed by a first place in the New Hampshire primary. The latter is the first, and symbolically the most important, primary of the nomination cycle. His New Hampshire victory gave Hart considerable media attention and the necessary publicity to attract campaign contributions and public opinion support.

Although the nomination process is critical to the success of any presidential aspirant, apparently it matters less to most voters. In 1984 an average of 14 percent of the eligible electorate voted in state presidential primaries. This group consisted mainly of well-educated and older voters with higher incomes than the average citizen and a greater interest in politics.[13]

Who Gets Nominated?

In the past, almost all the Democratic and Republican presidential nominees were white, male, wealthy Protestants. The barrier against Catholics fell with the election in 1960 of Senator John Kennedy of Massachusetts, but Protestant candidates still remain the rule. Furthermore, with the exception of General Dwight D. Eisenhower, a World War II hero who was elected in 1952, all presidential candidates for the last hundred years had held high elective office—the vice presidency, a seat in the U.S. Senate, or the governorship of a large state. These elected positions give candidates the visibility and prestige necessary to attract campaign financing and to mount a national campaign.

Social barriers to the nomination of women, blacks, Jews, and other ethnic candidates seem to be weakening. For example, Jesse Jackson, a well-known black minister and civil rights activist, ran an impressive, although unsuccessful, campaign for the Democratic presidential nomination in 1984. That same year Democratic Representative Geraldine Ferraro of New York became the first woman to be nominated for vice president by a major party. Recent polls indicate that a majority of Americans would consider voting for a female presidential candidate.

Ferraro's nomination may mark a breakthrough for women in politics. In 1986, for example, sixteen women were candidates for governor, compared with only two in 1984. In Nebraska, where both the Republican and the Democratic parties nominated a woman to run for the highest office in that state, Republican Kay Orr defeated Democrat Helen Boosalis. Democratic Governor Madeleine Kunin won re-election in Vermont, while Democrat Barbara Mikulski defeated Republican Linda Chavez for the Senate race in Maryland.

<hr />

★ ★ ★

THE RACE FOR OFFICE

Campaign watching is a favorite pastime for many Americans. A controversial candidate, a close race, or any presidential campaign brings headlines, television interviews and debates, and other media coverage. The public may

Crossing the bar Rev. Jesse Jackson (left) is not the first black American to run for president, but thus far he is the most visible and successful. Whether his campaigns are merely symbolic expressions of black power and prestige is an open question. Many observers believe that currently no black candidate can overcome racial bigotry to win a national election in the United States.

be skeptical about the value of elections and the way they are financed, but it still enjoys the excitement of campaigns.

Financing Campaigns

Much of the public subscribes to the money-buys-elections myth and regards the financing of many, if not most, campaigns as suspect. The feeling prevails that campaigns consume far too much money. The Watergate scandal in 1974 increased this discontent. An investigation disclosed that the Committee to Reelect the President (CREEP), President Nixon's campaign committee, had accepted hundreds of thousands of dollars of illegal individual and corporate contributions, some made in the hope of winning the president's favor. One major corporation, International Telephone and Telegraph, was accused of offering to offset the costs of the 1972 Republican national convention in order to favorably influence antitrust policy. George Steinbrenner, owner of the New York Yankees, was convicted of making hundreds of thousands of dollars of illegal contributions to the Nixon campaign. CREEP also spent a great deal of money on illegal campaign tricks that included breaking into and bugging the Democratic national headquarters (see Background 6.1, page 141).

Candidates often face lucrative offers of campaign contributions in return for a favor. No doubt, some candidates accept such offers. Others do not. One would-be contributor to Edmund Muskie's 1972 presidential campaign offered two hundred thousand dollars with the following stipulation: "You understand, there will be a quid pro quo. I want to be an American ambassador. Not a big country, you understand, not France or England. I couldn't afford those anyway. But can you give me a little one, Switzerland or Belgium?"[14] Muskie summarily dismissed the offer.

Of course, financing campaigns is usually an expensive proposition, especially given the cost of television and the high fees charged by pollsters and various campaign strategists. Between 1964 and 1984 campaign costs in all elections in the United States rose from around $200 million to approximately $1.2 billion. In 1972 the major presidential candidates spent more than $100 million on the general election alone. At that time, federal laws governing campaign contributions and expenditures were loosely written and, for all practical purposes, unenforceable.*

In 1971 and again in 1974 and 1979, Congress stepped in to limit the amount of money presidential candidates can receive and spend. The problem Congress tried to solve was not the overall size of campaign expenditures,

---

* Until 1971 the Corrupt Practices Act of 1925 (43 Stat. 1053, ch. 368, sec. 301–19) regulated disclosure of Senate and House of Representative campaign receipts and expenditures. What weakened the bill was that it did not apply to committees set up by the candidates to collect and distribute funds, nor did it apply to presidential and vice-presidential campaigns.

but rather the imbalances created when some individuals and groups can afford to contribute far more than others. The new law ensured that a single individual would no longer be able to contribute $2.1 million to a presidential campaign, as did W. Clement Stone to Nixon's campaign in 1972.

The Federal Election Campaign Act. The new law, the Federal Election Campaign Act of 1971, as amended in 1974 and later, created a system to monitor the flow of funds and set limits on individual contributions. It also provided for public financing of campaigns and restricted total spending by those candidates who accept federal funding. The spending limits, however, apply only to presidential campaign finances. Congress has never restricted its own election expenditures.

The Act has four key features:

- It set up the Federal Election Commission (FEC), a bipartisan, six-member commission, to administer and enforce federal regulations regarding the contribution and expenditure of campaign funds. The contribution limits apply to congressional, as well as presidential, candidates.

- It limits individual contributions to one thousand dollars per candidate per race, five thousand dollars per year to any one political action committee (PAC), and twenty thousand dollars per year to a national party committee. The total amount of contributions per year by an individual must not exceed twenty-five thousand dollars.

- It provides for total public funding of the major parties' presidential election costs, including the Democratic and Republican national conventions. Funding is also provided for presidential primaries—up to half the amount a major contender can spend.

- It places important controls on the amount of money that can be spent in presidential primaries and general elections.

Congress, however, did not intend to reduce the importance of money in the election process. In 1984 each presidential candidate spent approximately $40 million on the general election. Candidates for the House of Representatives spent $203.6 million; candidates for the Senate spent $170.5 million.[15] Expenses covered by campaign funds included the rental and furnishing of campaign headquarters, communication and transportation costs, polls, television and newspaper advertisements, political consultants, and of course accountants to keep track of how the money was collected and spent.

Although these figures seem to support at least part of the money-buys-elections myth, keep in mind that the $1.2 billion spent on all elections in 1984 is relatively small when compared, for example, with the advertising budgets of many large companies. In one year alone Procter and Gamble and Philip Morris, two of the largest corporations in the United States, had a combined advertising budget of $948 million. Furthermore, no matter how much a candidate spends, he or she may still lose. For example, several years ago, California Republican Robert Dorman spent over $1.9 million on a race for the House of Representatives and yet was defeated.

Sources of campaign funding.   Where does the money come from? Some wealthy candidates finance their own campaigns or lend themselves the needed funds. This can give them an advantage over their opponents, since there are *no limits* on this kind of contribution. Most candidates, however, must solicit gifts and loans from interested individuals, their party, or other groups, particularly political action committees (PACs).

One of the major consequences of the Federal Election Campaign Act has been the rise of the PACs. They were set up as a way of by-passing a provision of the act prohibiting unions, corporations, and other groups from contributing directly to congressional candidates.* PACs distribute voluntary contributions from such groups to congressional candidates. In 1986 senatorial candidates received about 19 percent of their campaign funds from these committees, and House candidates received about 30 percent (see Figure 7.1).

PACs can legally spend any amount of money on candidates, as long as they do not coordinate their spending efforts or otherwise cooperate with the candidate's campaign. Thus their participation can circumvent the spending and contribution limits of the campaign act. As important as PACs have become, however, they are overshadowed by individual contributors, who supply the bulk of election funds.

Does money buy victory?   Since 1976 the federal government has funded presidential campaigns, with the Democratic and Republican candidates each receiving equal support. As a result, the major party candidates have entered the race for president on a more or less equal financial footing. This has greatly reduced the amount of money spent in presidential campaigns but not entirely controlled it, since spending by private individuals and groups is still permitted. In the 1984 presidential race, 90 percent of the $23.4 million spent by independent committees and individuals was either pro-Reagan or anti-Mondale.[16]

Money plays a large part in congressional campaigns, which are not funded by the federal government. In 1984, for example, total campaign spending for all Senate races came to more than $172 million. Individual high spenders include North Carolina's Senator Jesse Helms, who spent $16 million on a recent winning campaign, and Mark Dayton, who spent more

---

* Because of its loopholes, a 1907 law prohibiting corporate contributions to federal elections, as well as the Smith-Connally Act of 1944 applying this law to labor unions, had been essentially unenforceable.

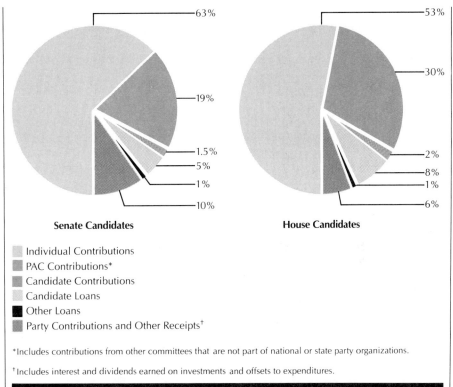

Individual Contributions
PAC Contributions*
Candidate Contributions
Candidate Loans
Other Loans
Party Contributions and Other Receipts†

*Includes contributions from other committees that are not part of national or state party organizations.

†Includes interest and dividends earned on investments and offsets to expenditures.

FIGURE 7.1 Where Did the Money Come From?

Gifts to House and Senate candidates in the 1986 elections came overwhelmingly from individual donors. Note that both PACs and parties are overshadowed by private contributors.

Source: Federal Election Commission Record, October, 1986, page 8.

than $7 million but did not win a Senate seat in Minnesota. In contrast, Wisconsin Senator William Proxmire retained his seat in a recent campaign that cost him a mere $150. Proxmire is a very popular senator whose opponents have not been able to launch effective campaigns against him. Dayton, on the other hand, was an unknown for whom money was a passport to visibility—or at least to the television exposure needed to mount an effective challenge.

Although these campaigns illustrate extremes, they make the general point that money is not the sole factor determining the outcome of congressional elections. Who wins also depends on the circumstances of the race—particularly whether one of the candidates is an **incumbent** (in office at the time of the election). Incumbents are hard to beat because they usually are well known to voters and because they have already served the state or district. In 1982 and 1984, 92 percent of incumbent members of Congress who sought re-election succeeded in their attempts. In 1986, more than 98 percent of incumbent candidates in the House of Representatives won re-election. The retention rate of incumbent senators running for re-election is about 80 percent.

Spending has the greatest impact on elections where there is no incumbent in the race and where the outcome—who will win and who will lose—is uncertain. Still, a strong and competitive challenger with sufficient funds to mount an effective campaign may have a chance against an incumbent.[17] Unfortunately for such challengers, their incumbent opponents may find it relatively easy to raise funds. Unless the challenger can raise enough money— anywhere from two hundred thousand to over $1 million, depending on the district—to create name recognition, the race may be lost before it begins.

Thus, despite the money-buys-elections myth, the reality is that money is a necessary, but not a sufficient, factor in a successful bid for many political offices. As Gary Jacobson, a student of campaign financing, has pointed out,

> [Money] is not sufficient because many factors quite apart from campaigns . . . affect election outcomes: partisanship, national tides, presidential coattails, issues, candidates' personalities and skills, scandals, incumbency, and many others. Money is necessary because campaigns do have an impact on election results, and campaigns cannot be run without it.[18]

Organizing Campaigns

In Boston and its suburbs in the weeks before any election, busy street corners are crowded with silent partisans holding signs that promote their candidate. This unusual ritual, commonplace to Boston natives, assures the wavering voter that the candidate has support. Campaign tactics range from such homey local traditions to highly sophisticated media shows. Even though most state and local campaigns are unorganized or underorganized and lurch from one improvisation to another as the campaign progresses, most visible campaigns—including the campaigns for the presidency, the Senate, and many House seats and governorships—are highly organized.

Campaign organizations.   John Kennedy's 1960 presidential campaign saw the first significant use of an organization recruited from outside the party structure. Kennedy hired a young pollster named Lou Harris (later head of the Harris Poll) to join his inner circle of strategists. He also relied heavily on a personally selected team of advisers and staff, including his brother Robert, to take on the major burdens of running the campaign. This model has been followed in most presidential campaigns since the 1960s and in many state and local races as well.

Candidates assemble personal staffs because the parties have been slow to develop polling and media consulting programs and other support systems. The presence of such staffs also reflects the growing sophistication of campaigns. Staff members write speeches, schedule appearances, plan strategy, and recruit additional talent as needed. In recent years both major parties, and especially the Republicans, have made considerable progress in providing these services. Major state and local candidates now receive sophisticated training and support. Nevertheless, presidential candidates and many congressional and statewide candidates still seek the guidance of their own professional consultants, as well as their personal advisers.

Campaign strategy.   A critical part of the campaign process is the development of themes (reasons why the public should support the candidate) and campaign strategies. The plausibility of such themes is critically important to candidates' success. If voters do not believe that campaign promises will be fulfilled—if the candidates' words evoke the myth of broken promises—the election game is lost. In the 1984 presidential election, Reagan showed that he had learned that lesson well. Having already succeeded in reducing the rate of growth of inflation, he promised to raise the country's standard of living still higher. The majority of voters believed that he could—and would.

In most presidential, House, and Senate races, campaign strategy depends on whether the candidate is an incumbent or a challenger. Congressional incumbents generally have the advantage of name recognition and a record of accomplishments. They often start with a loyal constituency, and, as we have noted, their established position and visibility make it relatively easy for them to raise funds. Not surprisingly, then, most incumbents in the House—between 80 and 98 percent since World War II—have succeeded in their quest for re-election.

Incumbency is also important in presidential elections. No other officeholder in the United States has the same visibility, name recognition, prestige, and opportunity to speak to voters on the issues, and incumbent candidates take full advantage of these assets. Incumbency does not guarantee a second term, however. Since World War II, five out of eight incumbent presidents have not served a second term. In 1952 Harry Truman chose not to run for a second full term. In 1968 an exhausted Lyndon Johnson, overwhelmed by the problems of the Vietnam War, dropped out of the presidential race and initiated peace talks. Gerald Ford, who took office after Nixon's resignation, and Ford's successor, Jimmy Carter, failed to win elections to second terms in office. In 1976 Carter had suggested that the public blame Ford for anything they did not like about Washington. In 1980 the public apparently blamed him.*

---

* The fifth president, John Kennedy, was assassinated on November 22, 1963.

"I should like to depart from my prepared text and speak as a human being."

Drawing by Richter; © 1986 The New Yorker Magazine, Inc.

Carter's opponent, Reagan, selected a typical campaign strategy: he challenged Carter's effectiveness and convinced the voters that his leadership and positions on issues would be superior. Challengers always emphasize a past record of accomplishments, a record that may already have given them considerable visibility and a constituency base. Not surprisingly, most presidential challengers since World War II have previously served as senators (John Kennedy, Barry Goldwater, George McGovern), governors (Thomas Dewey, Adlai Stevenson, Carter, Reagan), or vice presidents (Nixon, Humphrey, Mondale).

Incumbents are most vulnerable when domestic or foreign policy problems call their leadership qualities into question. This was Carter's predicament. Not only was the economy a mess—inflation had risen to 12.4 percent and the country was in the throes of a recession—but also rebels in Iran were holding a large group of Americans hostage. Reagan's campaign hit hard at those issues.

Differences among elections reflect something more than incumbency, however. Winners and losers alike are profoundly affected by the political environment: the partisan leanings of the electorate; presidential coattails;

the candidates' experience, personality, and leadership skills; and their positions on policy issues. Most candidates try to ensure that none of these factors polarizes the electorate and drives away potential supporters. Thus they are unlikely to take stands that are either strongly conservative or strongly liberal, although on balance Republican candidates are more conservative than Democratic ones.

The new campaign style. Use of the media, particularly television, has almost become a way of life in recent presidential, congressional, and gubernatorial races. The organization of a campaign often centers on media coverage. Candidates make decisions about trips, rallies, and press conferences with an eye to attracting the press and meeting its schedules. Because advertising costs so much, campaign managers work hard to maximize free television news coverage to promote their candidate's virtues. Consequently, a candidate's speeches and rallies before large crowds are often scheduled so that he or she can appear on the early evening local and network news programs.

Media people try to structure election news to attract and hold the biggest possible audience. Often this means highlighting, even promoting, conflict. Candidates are encouraged to attack one another's policies, and television debates, especially between presidential candidates, are turned into major contests with "winners" and "losers." The Kennedy-Nixon debates in 1960 marked the beginning of face-to-face discussion between presidential candidates.* Over the years the debates have produced many dramatic moments, including an irreparable blunder by Gerald Ford in 1976. He claimed that Poland was *not* under Soviet domination—an assertion that may have lost him some support.

Of course, candidates do not rely on free coverage alone. Advertising is also a crucial part of campaigns. Media consultants like Ed Blakely, who manages a television production studio for the National Republican Congressional Committee, and David Sawyer, a media consultant for many Democratic candidates, provide their clients with a full range of services—from the production of television spots to the purchase of advertising time on local and network stations. Because television advertising is so expensive—a local thirty-second spot on the popular television program "60 Minutes" costs anywhere from two thousand dollars if aired in Tulsa to nine thousand dollars if aired in New York City—it is used primarily in visible and well-funded campaigns.

Polls are another expensive and relatively new campaign tool that can dramatize or establish proof of the viability of a candidate for major office.[19]

---

* In 1984 a new dimension was added to the televised debates: a debate between the vice-presidential candidates, Geraldine Ferraro and George Bush.

In Chapter 5, on public opinion, we looked at the way candidates use polls to evaluate their strengths and weaknesses, assess the relevance of specific issues, and determine the campaign's impact on the voters. Positive poll results can energize a campaign and draw new support and funding.

Professional pollsters like Republican Robert Teeter and Democrat Patrick Caddell have established strong reputations for the accuracy of their estimates of candidates' standing and the voters' views on the issues. A pollster's services are now almost universally used in presidential and many congressional and statewide races. Costs depend on the size of the state and the kind of polling. A statewide campaign can run from twenty-five thousand to fifty thousand dollars.

Newspapers, magazines, and television often commission their own polls, and the results can be big news. Whether these polls help or hurt candidates is an open question. As you can see in Table 7.1, polls had little effect on voters' choice of candidate in the 1984 presidential election.[20] Even if polls do not change the outcome, they certainly heighten the hoopla and intensify the horse-race nature of the contest.

TABLE 7.1 Do Polls Change Voters' Minds?

According to this *Washington Post*/ABC News poll, most people were unaffected by the news that Ronald Reagan was ahead of Walter Mondale in the 1984 presidential election. The shifts that did occur tended to cancel each other out.

Question: There were many public opinion polls in the weeks before the election for president. Do you remember who the polls said would win the election, Ronald Reagan or Walter Mondale?

	Percentage		
	All Voters	**Reagan Voters**	**Mondale Voters**
Polls picked Reagan	78	74	84
Polls picked Mondale	7	9	4
Other/no opinion	15	17	12

Question: What effect did those polls have on you: Would you say they helped you decide to vote for Reagan, to vote for Mondale, not to vote in the election, or would you say the opinion polls had no effect on your voting one way or the other? (Results shown are for the 78 percent who stated that polls showed Reagan ahead.)

Helped in decision for Reagan	3.8
Helped in decision for Mondale	3.7
No effect/other	92.5

Source: *The Washington Post National Weekly Edition*, June 10, 1985, p. 37. From a survey of 1,503 adult Americans, May 9 to May 13. Reprinted by permission.

A final "miracle" of modern campaign technology is computer-assisted, direct mail fundraising and advertising. A candidate or party buys mailing lists from state motor vehicle registration departments, magazines, membership organizations, and a variety of other sources. Then advanced data and word-processing techniques are used to send letters soliciting campaign funds and providing information on the candidate. Shrewd campaign managers sometimes even include a few typographical errors to make the letter seem hand-typed.

The letters can be individualized, focusing on the interests of a specific audience. For example, a voter on the membership list of an environmental protection group might get an original-looking, personally addressed letter that focuses on the candidate's desire to support the acquisition of park land or some other environmental cause. The signature is often the work of a machine that produces perfect replicas of the candidate's handwriting.

Technological changes over the past three decades have added new dimensions to campaigns. The new technologies have been accompanied by the rise of a new political animal—the political consultant. These individuals, often trained in public relations, media, or polling techniques, have replaced the traditional campaign manager in the most visible elections. Some consultants organize all aspects of the race, from the physical appearance of the candidate to the strategies the candidate adopts in presenting positions on issues. Most consultants specialize in certain aspects of the campaign—for example, media or polling or fund raising.[21] Ultimately, however, the voter still determines which candidate will win.

The Electoral College

Before beginning our discussion of voting and elections, it is important to describe the constitutional environment in which presidential campaigns take place—the **electoral college.** While the founders believed in representative government, they were very hesitant to place the selection of the president directly in the hands of the people. The system that evolved provides for the election by the people of *electors* in each state equal to the number of U.S. senators and representatives representing that state in Congress. For example, California has two U.S. senators and 45 members in the House of Representatives. Thus, in presidential elections, that state elects 47 electors to the electoral college. The presidential candidate winning the majority vote in a state receives all of its electoral college votes. (The one exception is Maine, which awards its electoral college votes according to who wins in each congressional district.) A total of 538 electoral college votes are cast in the fifty states and the District of Columbia, with the presidential candidate receiving the majority of the votes winning the election. The vice president is selected in the same manner.

Because of the possibility of a president being elected with a majority of the electoral college vote but not a majority of the popular vote—such was the case in 1888 when Benjamin Harrison was elected president with 233 electoral college votes whereas his opponent, Grover Cleveland, received more popular votes—a number of reforms have been proposed, including the selection of the president by popular vote. Yet no consensus for a constitutional amendment has emerged, and thus the indirect election of presidents through the electoral college has remained intact.

When campaigning for the presidency, candidates well appreciate that it is not enough to receive a majority of the popular vote. A candidate must be successful in garnering majority votes sufficiently distributed among the states to ensure receiving a majority of the electoral college vote (see Figure 7.2). Not surprisingly, most candidates focus much of their attention on the larger states, such as California, New York, Illinois, and Texas, states which have significant numbers of electoral college votes.

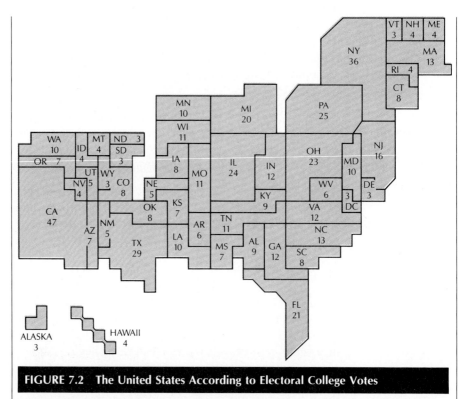

FIGURE 7.2 The United States According to Electoral College Votes

This distorted map will give you a sense of the electoral power of the most populous states, such as California, New York, Texas, and Pennsylvania.

Source: Adapted from *The Boston Globe*, September 29, 1984, p. 16.

★ ★ ★
VOTING AND ELECTIONS

Voting rules and regulations have changed considerably in the past two hundred years. Until the 1920s women could not vote. Blacks and women faced voting restrictions during most of the country's history. Although the vote has now been extended to all adult citizens, everyone does not choose to exercise this option. Let us look at who votes and why.

Who Is Permitted to Vote?

The Constitution originally left the decision on voting qualifications to the individual states. Article I, Section 4, specifies that Congress may regulate by law only the time, place, and manner of federal elections. Any extension of voting rights by the federal government must come in the form of a constitutional amendment or a federal law.

State leaders in the 1780s had little sympathy or inclination to provide universal voting rights. Indeed, John Jay, a New York delegate to the Constitutional Convention, summed up the view of many of the Founding Fathers when he wrote in 1787 that "the mass of men [in the new United States] are neither wise nor good—those who own the country ought to govern it."[22]

All thirteen states restricted voting rights to white males, and only three of the new states—New Hampshire, Pennsylvania, and Georgia—admitted adult males into the electorate without a property requirement. In these states, however, the voter without property had to be a taxpayer. As a result, in 1789 only about 10 percent of the population could cast ballots.[23]

Over the past two centuries, voting rights have been extended to those who do not own property to blacks, Native Americans, women, and young people aged eighteen to twenty. Equality was not achieved without an intense struggle. It took a civil war to give citizenship to blacks. And although the passage of the Fifteenth Amendment to the Constitution gave black males the right to vote, they waited another hundred years before most barriers to voting came down.

Women fought for another half century for voting rights. In 1878, human rights activist Susan B. Anthony managed to have introduced in Congress a proposed constitutional amendment that said: "the right of citizens of the United States to vote shall not be denied or abridged by the United States or any state on account of sex." The wording of the Twentieth Amendment, which finally became part of the Constitution in 1920, was identical.

In 1971 passage of the Twenty-sixth Amendment lowered the voting age in federal, state, and local elections from twenty-one to eighteen. Several states already had similar regulations. There is nothing in the Constitution that prohibits states from setting their own voting standards, as long as these regulations do not violate the Constitution or federal law. Thus women in Wyoming had the vote some forty years before the Twentieth Amendment enfranchised women in other states. In fact, any state could, if its legislature wished, lower the minimum voting age to sixteen or even ten.

Congress has intervened to lower barriers set up by the states to prevent blacks and others from voting. The 1970 extension of the 1965 Voting Rights Act banned the use of literacy tests and other similar qualifying devices. The 1975 extension of the act increased the opportunities for participation for Hispanics. The act, which was strengthened and extended for twenty-five years in 1982, resulted in increased electoral participation by southern black voters and other minorities, including Eskimos. In addition, Supreme Court decisions have laid the remaining voting restrictions to rest. During the 1960s the Supreme Court struck down property ownership requirements and poll taxes; it also shortened residency requirements.*

Voting Turnout

Americans are proud of their free electoral system. Indeed, many citizens would argue that the freedom to select political leaders is one of the most important differences between a democracy and a fascist or communist government. Yet, as we saw in Chapter 5, on public opinion and political participation, relatively few Americans vote. On the average, a little over 50 percent of Americans can be counted on to take part in presidential elections (see Background 7.1). By contrast, 95 percent of Australians regularly go to the polls, and turnout in other Western democracies ranges from 70 to 80 percent.

Comparisons are not entirely justified, however, since voting is easier and simpler in other nations. Americans face much longer ballots and relatively brief and inconvenient polling schedules. Europeans can vote on weekends. Many European nations also have automatic universal registration, which is not widespread in the United States. As a final incentive to ensure voting, some European countries levy fines on stay-at-homes.

Demographics and voter turnout. Chapter 5 also discussed the social and economic factors that influence political participation patterns, and particularly voter turnout. Individuals who vote regularly are more likely to be white and have higher educational backgrounds, larger incomes, and better jobs than nonvoters.

---

* Today a citizen needs only to have resided in a state for thirty days in order to vote in federal elections and in most state elections.

━━━━━━━━━━━ **BACKGROUND 7.1** ━━━━━━━━━━━

Why Don't People Register to Vote?

In the 1984 presidential election, only about 50 percent of eligible citizens cast a vote. Many people stay home on election day because registration laws make it hard for them to vote. The problem has a long history.

Beginning in the 1860s, in response to claims of voter fraud, states began to require citizens to preregister with their local boards of elections. Some states have made it relatively easy to register, allowing registration on the day of an election. Most states, however, close off registration thirty days before an election. When states simplify registration—providing easily accessible registrars, short residency requirements, evening and weekend registration, and mail-in forms—more citizens register. This is the case in Connecticut, North Dakota, South Dakota, and Minnesota, where the voting rolls include more than 60 percent of those eligible. When states make registration difficult, fewer eligible voters register—generally well below 50 percent. According to some observers, easier registration would increase turnout in presidential elections by as much as 9 percent.

State laws and regulations, however, are only part of the reason for low registration. Forty-eight percent of nonregistrants say they ignore politics because it does not interest them. The remaining stay-at-homes give as their excuse illness or disability, inconvenience, or a recent move, and some offer no reason at all.

Source of data: U.S. Bureau of the Census, "Voting and Registration in the Election of 1980," *Current Population Reports* (April 1982), Series p-20, No. 370, p. 89, and Raymond E. Wolfinger and Steven J. Rosenstone, *Who Votes?* (New Haven, Conn.: Yale University Press, 1980), p. 88.

Education seems to be the key to voter turnout.[24] As Raymond Wolfinger and Steven Rosenstone point out, education,

> imparts information about politics . . . and about a variety of skills, some of which facilitate political learning. . . . Educated people are more likely to be well informed about politics and to follow the campaign in the mass media.[25]

In addition, for non–English-speaking citizens, including those of Puerto Rican, Mexican, Cuban, and Vietnamese extraction, education provides fluency in English, a tool necessary for following and participating in the electoral process. In 1984 only 33 percent of the adult Hispanic population voted. There is some evidence, however, that Hispanics are turning out in growing numbers, particularly in large urban areas.

Younger citizens are less likely to vote than older people (except those who have difficulty getting to the polling booths because of the infirmities of very old age). For example, citizens between the ages of twenty-four and thirty are 30 percent less likely to vote than those aged thirty-seven to sixty-nine.[26] Reasons for this pattern are rather complex. Young people are frequently preoccupied with the demands of school, military service, or new careers. They also tend to believe that they have little impact or influence on the political system.

Technology and turnout As President and Mrs. Reagan watch television coverage of his reelection bid on November 6, 1984, their intensity belies the fact that the three major networks had early declared him the winner.

A difference of opinion exists on whether the results of exit polls influence people who have not yet voted. Would you vote for a candidate who you knew had already lost?

Historically, turnout among women has trailed behind that for men. Today, however, women vote in elections in slightly higher percentages than do men.

The disappointed electorate. As indicated earlier, barriers such as pre-registration requirements and long ballots reduce the numbers of citizens who turn out to vote. But another obstacle is the myth of broken promises. Many Americans do not take part in elections because they do not believe that government in general and elected officials in particular can solve the country's problems. They also question the honesty and integrity of many political leaders.[27]

This lack of confidence in government is relatively new. As you may recall from our earlier discussion, it began with the Vietnam War in the 1960s and the Watergate scandal in the early 1970s. The energy crisis, high unemployment, inflation, and crime kept it alive in the late 1970s. It persists today as citizens contemplate the government's apparent inability to cope with world terrorism, maintain an effective public education system, or even help the average American to fulfill a traditional dream—the purchase of a home.

In this atmosphere of cynicism, many potential voters doubt that their vote would matter and simply stay home on election day. Several recent studies have clearly documented the reasons that people do not turn out to vote. First, they believe that government cannot resolve the nation's problems. In addition, as we pointed out in Chapter 6, on political parties, they are less likely than before to identify with parties, which once got out the vote. Finally, they have even begun to question whether it makes any difference who wins elections.[28]

Should we be concerned about the disappointed voter? Some observers say yes, arguing that low turnout undermines representative government, which depends on full electoral participation. Others disagree, suggesting that people who are ill informed may make poor choices when they vote. It has even been argued that low levels of voter turnout are a sign of a healthy system—that is, they show that people are satisfied with their government.

Voter Choice

What draws voters to the polls? What influences their choices of candidates? Why did so many voters pick Reagan in 1980 and 1984? Obviously, his supporters thought he was a better candidate, but that is not the full answer. Reagan supporters put aside their skepticism about the usefulness of voting and supported his positions, believing that he had or would fulfill his promises (see Myth and Reality 7.1).

Issues. Political observers often accuse American voters of focusing on frivolous aspects of campaigns. In fact, many American voters pay attention to issues and often take them into account in making their choices. Of course, no one can review all the issue positions of every candidate who is running for every office. Given the thousands of issues that arise at the local, state, and national level each year, no one could possibly follow or even have an interest in most of them.

Many voters, however, do focus on issues. In presidential elections there is a relationship between citizens' issue preferences and the candidates they support.[29] In 1976 a serious economic recession worked against the incumbent, Ford, and for the challenger, Carter. In 1980 Reagan took strong positions on reducing interest rates and inflation, building a stronger defense program,

MYTH AND REALITY 7.1

Elections as a Mandate

We often hear people speak of elections as providing a mandate, or instruction, for our political leaders—a map of public views on specific issues for elected officials to use in developing public policy. We suggest that this belief represents the myth of the mandate. The election process does provide the nation's political leaders with general guidelines for directing domestic and foreign policy, but these directions are strictly limited.

The mandate is restricted by the size of voter turnout. In recent presidential elections only a little more than 50 percent of the eligible electorate has voted. This means that of the entire eligible electorate, less than 30 percent votes for the winning presidential candidate—a phenomenon that is typical of almost all elections. With so few actual supporters, winning candidates can scarcely argue that they have a mandate from the people.

Voter motivation also limits the mandate. People vote for candidates for different reasons. Few voters support all of a candidate's positions. You may agree with your senator's economic policies and disagree with his or her positions on the environment, trade tariffs, and defense. Your friends may vote for the same candidate but for different reasons. The diversity of the voters' positions makes it impossible to assume that an election victory represents a mandate on any single issue.

Finally, retrospective voting further decreases the mandate. As we have said, voters often choose candidates on the basis of their past record of accomplishments. This happened in the 1980 presidential elections, when many voters rejected the incumbent, Jimmy Carter, because of his record, and in 1984 when a majority voted for the incumbent, Ronald Reagan. A victory, then, may not be based on issues at all but on past performance, which also invalidates the notion of mandate.

Despite these restrictions, winning candidates must assume that they have been given some direction from the voters. They even have the right to assume that they have received the support of a majority of those who turn out on election day and that the support can be translated into action. As you can see, like most myths, the concept of election mandates creates complex dilemmas for elected officials.

and waging a more aggressive, anticommunist foreign policy. Many Americans voted for Reagan or Carter on the basis of the candidates' positions on these three issues. When Reagan was re-elected in 1984, many of his supporters cited one issue as determining their vote: his economic policies. Many voters believed he reduced interest rates, controlled inflation, and stabilized unemployment. In 1986, 45 percent of the electorate claimed that they voted for their representative on the basis of that candidate's position on national, state, or local issues. Others based their vote on the character and experience of the candidates (41 percent) or on party identification, while the rest gave no specific reason.[30]

Candidate image. Clearly, the candidate's personal qualities also count, particularly leadership. Voters also ask themselves how well the candidate would represent their interests and whether the candidate is honest, trustworthy, and approachable by the electorate. One observer labels this process "politics by psychoanalysis."[31]

In 1976 and in 1980 Ford and Carter were seen as weak leaders. Reagan looked determined and effective, and voters liked his optimistic, honest, and approachable manner. The problems of his first administration—a Middle East policy that resolved few of the tensions of that region and the death by bombing of over 250 Americans marines in Lebanon—did little to shake the confidence of a majority of the voters. Indeed, in a survey during the 1984 campaign, 48 percent saw Reagan as providing a great deal of leadership, while only 16 percent responded similarly to Mondale.[32] As we mentioned earlier, a candidate's experience and character were the second most important factor—after issues—in influencing voter choice in the 1986 House races.[33]

Party identification. In Chapter 6 we showed that party identification gives voters a general sense of how candidates are likely to approach various

Image matters Vice presidents are automatically considered major contenders for their party's presidential nomination, but the office is fraught with electoral perils. A vice president must be a good team player, loyally supporting the administration, while simultaneously establishing an image of independence that will impress the electorate. Vice President George Bush, seen here greeting Republican party activists, struggled with these contradictory expectations throughout his campaign.

issues and policies. This label can be misleading, however, since opinion within the parties is quite diverse. Nevertheless, in a world in which voters may know nothing about many of the candidates, the party label serves as an approximate cue to policy positions.

Retrospective voting. The process by which individuals base their vote for candidates on the candidates' or parties' past record of performance is referred to as **retrospective voting**.[34] Incumbents are judged on their records in the office; challengers may be judged on their records in previously held offices. In effect, voters are looking back at the past in order to evaluate the future—one rational way to make judgments. Such information is relatively easy to acquire, particularly in races covered by the media.

Is retrospective voting a common occurrence? Poll findings suggest that it is. In 1980, for example, the public was dissatisfied with Carter's performance in office; 63 percent saw that election as a rejection of Carter.[35] In contrast, only 24 percent of the public believed that the election was a mandate for winner Reagan's conservative philosophy. In 1984 many voters supported Reagan because of the way they perceived his record. When asked, for example, who would best keep the country prosperous, 60 percent of the voters said Reagan would, as compared with 32 percent for Mondale. Obviously, those opinions were directly influenced by the public's perception of the record of the past few years.

Group support. As can be seen in Figure 7.3, economic and social factors affect how people vote. In 1984, for example, Reagan drew strong support from college-educated voters. Because educational level is related to participation, the Republicans have profited from this demographic pattern.

Republican Reagan received a majority of the support of whites, Catholics, white Protestants, the middle and upper class, professionals, white-collar and blue-collar workers—indeed, every demographic and regional group except blacks, Hispanics, the poor, the less educated, and Jews. With the exception of Jews, Democratic supporters come from groups with the lowest turnout rate in the United States. The Democrats had hoped that Geraldine Ferraro's nomination as vice-presidential candidate in 1984 would attract the women's vote. Reagan was able to win a majority of that vote, too.

These data raise a number of important questions about future voting patterns. Will the Republicans continue to attract a majority of the vote in the 1988 presidential race? In 1986 Republicans increased the number of gubernatorial seats they control to twenty-four, while the Democrats won the Senate after six years of Republican control. Democratic candidates for the House and for seats in state legislatures continue to attract wide support. Will these majorities be maintained? The results of the 1988 elections may tell us more.

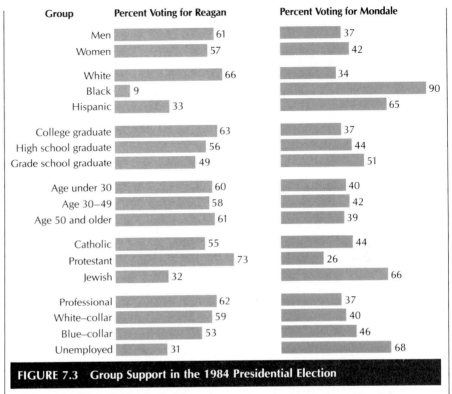

Group	Percent Voting for Reagan	Percent Voting for Mondale
Men	61	37
Women	57	42
White	66	34
Black	9	90
Hispanic	33	65
College graduate	63	37
High school graduate	56	44
Grade school graduate	49	51
Age under 30	60	40
Age 30–49	58	42
Age 50 and older	61	39
Catholic	55	44
Protestant	73	26
Jewish	32	66
Professional	62	37
White–collar	59	40
Blue–collar	53	46
Unemployed	31	68

FIGURE 7.3 Group Support in the 1984 Presidential Election

Who you are has a major impact on how you vote. As you consider these figures, keep in mind that party identification, candidate characteristics, and issues also explain voter choice.

Source: Adapted from *New York Times/CBS Poll*, November 8, 1984; Gallup Poll, December, 1980; and *The National Journal*, November 10, 1984, page 2132.

★ ★ ★

PROMISES, PROMISES: THE LINK BETWEEN CAMPAIGNS AND PUBLIC POLICY

You may recall our earlier discussion of public skepticism about the responsiveness of government. The poll results that we presented describe a public that questions whether any significant relationship exists between the promises that candidates make in campaigns and the policies that they follow once they are in office. We believe that this perception of broken promises is a myth—a simplification of the facts.

Of course, candidates do not fulfill all the promises they make. How could they? The collective wish list of Americans is endless. But candidates try very hard to keep many of their promises.[36] Party platforms are, in effect, their agreements with the electorate. It is as if they were saying: "This is what I think. This is what I will try to do. If you agree with what I think, at least on many of the issues, then vote for me." (One slight alteration to this monologue is: "Even if you don't agree with me, give me a chance. I'm right.")

As Table 7.2 shows, presidents have been reasonably successful in fulfilling their campaign promises and persuading Congress to act on those promises. For example, Reagan pledged to shore up the economy, increase defense spending, and appoint conservatives to the federal court system. He accomplished all those goals.

Reagan also made a number of promises he could not keep—but not for want of trying. Why did he fail? Why was he unable to decrease the size of the bureaucracy or of the budget deficit, both of which increased during his administration? A president's programs can fail because they are poorly conceived or ineffective. Reagan's plan to reduce the federal debt is an example. Programs also fail because Congress refuses to cooperate. Sometimes one or both houses are controlled by the opposition party. Sometimes the president is not able to persuade his own party to support his programs. Carter had that experience during the early part of his administration when he tried to implement his energy conservation program.

In short, the politics of implementation is complex, but successful candidates try and often manage to deliver on many of their promises.

TABLE 7.2   A Score Card on Campaign Promises

Presidents try to keep their promises and often succeed. Some failures reflect poorly conceived plans rather than lack of effort.

Performance on Promises	Percentage				
	Kennedy	Johnson	Nixon	Carter	Reagan*
Full or partial fulfillment of promises	68	63	59	66	53
Little or no action taken	23	24	36	22	30
Promises turned into legislation	53	62	34	41	44

* Data through February, 1984.

Source: Jeff Fishel, *Presidents and Promises: From Campaign Pledge to Presidential Performance* (Washington, D.C.: Congressional Quarterly Press, 1985). Recalculated from Table 2.3, p. 39, and Table 2.4, p. 42. Reprinted by permission of Congressional Quarterly, Inc.

CONCLUSION: Do Elections Matter?

Americans are ambivalent about elections. The public acknowledges their importance in the democratic process but takes part in elections in relatively low numbers as compared with many other Western democracies. To understand the election process better, we have examined in this chapter the facts behind two myths—that candidates break their campaign promises and that money buys elections. Although these myths contain some truth, they are by and large inaccurate.

What is the reality? First, although some campaign promises are not fulfilled, many are. Furthermore, although candidates run for office for personal reasons—power is a strong motivator—they also run in order to implement promised policies. And they are quite successful in achieving that goal. An analysis of presidential performance, for example, shows that recent presidents have managed to fulfill a majority of their promises either partially or completely.

Regarding the money-buys-elections myth, the conclusion is clear. Money is an important—indeed, a necessary—part of most campaigns, but it is not the decisive factor in most elections. Other elements, such as incumbency, issues, personalities, skills, national trends, and partisanship, strongly influence election outcomes. In addition, voter characteristics—religion, ethnic identity, race, age, and so forth—also appear to have some bearing on the way in which voters view the political world and the way they vote.

★ ★ ★

SUMMARY

1. Elections begin with the nomination of candidates. Those who run for office are motivated by personal ambition and by a commitment to policy goals.

2. Candidates are nominated in open meetings (caucuses) and, most commonly, in primary election campaigns.

3. Presidential nominations take place at national conventions, which frequently ratify the outcome of often complicated primary campaigns. Walter Mondale, the nominee of the Democrats in 1984, had to overcome six serious opponents to win his party's nomination. Typically, the incumbent, Ronald Reagan, faced no real opposition. Mondale's choice of a woman as running mate signaled a breaking of societal barriers to nomination.

4. The escalation of campaign costs in recent years led Congress to pass the Federal Election Campaign Act, which set limits on contributions and

expenditures in federal elections. The law has given rise to a growing source of funds from political action committees (PACs).

5. Most highly visible election campaigns—including those for the presidency, the U.S. Senate, and governorships as well as many U.S. House, statewide, and large-city mayoral races—are highly organized, with staffs that include a variety of professional consultants and personal advisers. The shape of the campaign depends on whether the candidate is an incumbent and on other factors in the political environment, particularly the presence of the media.

6. All women and nonwhite males have faced voting restrictions for most of the nation's history. Voting rights have been extended to these groups and to young people between the ages of eighteen and twenty by constitutional amendment and by federal law.

7. Turnout to vote in American elections is low compared with that in other countries. Well-to-do, well-educated, older individuals are more likely to vote than other groups. Low turnout has been attributed to laws and institutional factors (such as preregistration requirements and long ballots), as well as to voters' loss of faith in government.

8. People base their choice of candidate on issue preferences, the personal qualities and past records of the candidates, and on their own sense of party and social identity. The candidates' positions are not idle promises. Once elected, candidates try to fulfill their campaign pledges.

★ ★ ★

KEY TERMS

opportunity structure

caucus

primary

open primary

closed primary

partisan primary

nonpartisan primary

run-off primary

incumbent

electoral college

retrospective voting

★ ★ ★

SELECTED READINGS

• Crotty, William and John S. Jackson, III. *Presidential Primaries and Nominations*. Washington, D.C.: Congressional Quarterly Press, 1985. A careful and detailed examination of the presidential nomination process.

- Darcy, R., Susan Welch, and Janet Clark. *Women, Elections, and Representation.* New York: Longman, 1987. A careful analysis and inquiry into why so few women are elected to public office. The book serves, too, as an excellent review of the workings of the American electoral system.

- Flanigan, William H. and Nancy H. Zingale. *Political Behavior of the American Electorate,* 6th ed. Boston: Allyn and Bacon, 1987. A basic analysis of who votes and why and how the American electorate is influenced by parties, issues, candidates, and the mass media.

- Malbin, Michael J., ed. *Money and Politics in the United States: Financing Elections in the 1980s.* Chatham, N.J.: Chatham House, 1984. An excellent collection of essays discussing the role that money plays in elections in the United States.

- McClure, Robert D. and Linda Fowler. *Political Ambition: Unseen Candidates for Congress.* New Haven, Conn.: Yale University Press, 1988. An excellent and very readable study of how and why each of a group of individuals sought the party nomination to run for a seat in the U.S. House of Representatives. This book introduces the reader to the relevance of political ambition in choosing to campaign for a political office.

- Salmore, Stephen A. and Barbara G. Salmore. *Candidates, Parties, and Campaigns: Electoral Politics in America.* Washington, D.C.: Congressional Quarterly Press, 1985. Presents a framework for understanding the campaign process, including discussions on the role of television, incumbency, campaign themes, the mass media, parties, consultants, and political action committees.

8

CHAPTER

Interest Groups

WHAT ARE INTEREST GROUPS?

TYPES OF INTEREST GROUPS

Economic Interest Groups: *Corporations, associations, others*
Citizen Activist Groups: *Public interest, causes, advocacy*
Government-related Interest Groups: *Cities, states, nations*

RESOURCES OF INTEREST GROUPS

Group Dynamics: *The importance of cohesion, leadership, information, expertise, and size*
Money: *Money and the free-rider problem*
Power and Influence: *Its origins and importance*

INTEREST GROUP TACTICS

Lobbying: *Definition, lobbying, and lobbyists*
Political Action Committees (PACs): *Funding campaigns*
Electioneering: *Scorecards and other tactics*
Building Coalitions: *Collective action by interest groups*
Grassroots Pressure: *Influence from constituents*
Litigation: *Using the courts*

INTEREST GROUPS, PACs, AND PUBLIC POLICY

Interest Groups and Public Policy
The Cozy Triangle: *The mutually supportive network of interest groups, Congress, and the bureaucracy*

CONCLUSION: CORRUPT OR CONSTRUCTIVE?

The office is decorated simply. The surroundings are modest. Located in Ballston, Virginia, a twenty-five-minute metro ride from Capitol Hill, it has none of the glamour of Washington, D.C., where one might expect to find an interest group's headquarters. The man sitting behind the desk, William Axtman, is executive director and lobbyist for the American Boiler Manufacturers Association. With fewer than one hundred members, the group is not the largest or most imposing lobby in Washington. But in many respects, Axtman represents the average interest group, and he is a typical lobbyist.

Axtman's job is to keep on top of rules and regulations that affect the boiler industry, quickly passing this information on to the members of his association. He then reports the association's objections to the right congressional staff member. He has never met the president or had dinner with any major congressional leader. His total contribution to political campaigns in 1984 was five hundred dollars—from his own pocket.

Axtman receives a salary of fifty-seven thousand dollars a year, plus the use of a 1985 Buick that he drives himself. His idea of wining and dining influential people is to take knowledgeable congressional staff specialists to see a working boiler at a suburban utility plant, and offer each of them a two-sandwich lunch in a gift-lunch pail, a container of hot coffee, and an apple. " 'I tell my [association] members that once in a while you can maybe make a bill change from here to there,' [says Axtman] . . . pointing his right hand like an arrow and allowing a minuscule shift in the vector. 'But never from here to there,' he [says] . . . pivoting around 180 degrees. At least I never have.' "[1]

Axtman represents only one of many styles of lobbying. There are twenty thousand or so lobbyists in Washington, D.C., representing the interests of different groups and individuals before members and staff of Congress and before executive officials. Among them are some whose style conforms more closely to the conventional stereotype of lobbyists as powerful, wealthy, and influential.

Few Americans are aware of the Axtman style of lobbying. Most see lobbyists as wheeler-dealers. They also suspect interest groups of dishonesty and of corrupting the political process by unduly influencing government, most often through campaign contributions. In a recent national poll, 55 percent of the respondents agreed that government is pretty much run by a few big interests looking out for themselves.[2] Another survey found that 57 percent of those responding thought that limiting the money spent on congressional campaigns is one way to keep members of Congress from being bought by special interests.[3]

Apparently, then, a majority of Americans believe in the myth that interest groups are a corrupting influence. Though undoubtedly interest groups have become central actors in the American policy-making process, whether they are a corrupting influence in politics remains questionable. We will return to this issue at the end of the chapter. Before we can evaluate the myth and reality of interest groups, however, we must look at the role they play in American politics and the resources and techniques they use to influence politics.

★ ★ ★
WHAT ARE INTEREST GROUPS?

A political **interest group** is any organized group of individuals who share one or more common goals and who seek to influence government decision making.[4] Such diverse groups as the National Rifle Association, the Sierra Club, the U.S. Chamber of Commerce, and the League of Women Voters all fit this definition. Even college students have interest groups to represent them—for instance, the Coalition of Independent College and University Students and the United States Student Association.

Interest groups differ from political parties.[5] In Chapter 6, on parties, we emphasize that parties are broad-based coalitions whose policies cover a wide range of issues. The party's ultimate goal is to contest and win elections in order to control and operate government. In contrast, interest groups put forth a limited set of demands.* Although they sometimes try to affect the outcome of certain elections, interest groups do not run candidates for office or attempt to control or operate government. Their primary concern is to influence policy that affects their own area of interest.

★ ★ ★
TYPES OF INTEREST GROUPS

Differing in size and make-up, interest groups pursue varying objectives. One commonly held belief about interest groups, however, is that they serve as an organizational link between their members and elected and appointed government officials. What justifies the existence of interest groups in a democratic, representative form of government is their role in making members of the executive and legislative branches of government more aware of the needs and concerns of various segments of the population. Many people join together in these groups to promote their own economic well-being and to effect political and social change. They believe that common goals are best served by collective action.

---

* Some interest groups like Common Cause and the Liberty Federation support a wide range of issues. Even these two groups, however, most often direct their focus and resources to a few key issues.

Economic Interest Groups

Business, labor, and agricultural interest groups are the most enduring and powerful type of group. This should not surprise you when you consider the intensity of most people's interest in their own economic welfare (see Myth and Reality 8.1).

Corporations and business and trade associations. More than three thousand individual corporations and businesses employ lobbyists in Washington.[6] Companies with lobbyists range in size from giants like the Rockwell International Corporation and IBM to small companies like the Lake View Trust and Savings Bank of Chicago and the 47th Street Photo Company in New York City.

The concerns of this fastest growing type of group depend on the business in question and on the political climate. Tax laws, government subsidies, antitrust laws, tariffs on imported goods, and consumer product and environmental regulations—all may affect the cost of doing business. The Michigan Knife Company, for example, cares particularly about duty-free treatment of imported steel.[7] The Potato Chip and Snack Foods Association protects the producers' right to tempt you with junk food.

Business and trade associations are one of the oldest forms of interest group. Under the umbrella of business associations are the large and influential U.S. Chamber of Commerce, with a membership of over 250,000 individuals and companies; the Business Roundtable, made up of the approximately two hundred largest industrial, commercial, and financial businesses in the nation; and many other groups. These associations represent the collective interests of corporate America. They are particularly concerned with issues involving taxes and a ballooning federal budget that affects interest rates for business loans.

The conflicting demands and goals of the members complicate the business associations' task. For example, the interests of a "mom and pop" grocery store do not necessarily coincide with the interests of multinational corporations like American Airlines or Mobil. Not surprisingly, then, the interests of the National Small Business Association and the goals of the National Association of Manufacturers are often at odds with each other. Thus it is a rare issue on which there is a unified business voice.

The trade associations, which represent entire industries, also have widely divergent interests. For example, the Fertilizer Institute's views on water pollution controls are likely to clash with the ideas of a group like the Texas Shrimp Association. The Atomic Industrial Forum, representing industries associated with the manufacture, construction, and use of nuclear power plants, may lock horns with the National Coal Association, a trade association promoting the use of coal-burning power plants. Whatever the concerns of the association, all of these groups are interested in government

MYTH AND REALITY 8.1

Business Versus Labor

A commonly held myth about business and labor interest groups depicts them as natural enemies when it comes to making policy. They do, in fact, take opposite sides on such issues as federal regulation of minimum hourly wages. But on some other issues, such as the establishment of tariffs to control the import of foreign goods, labor and business interests frequently coincide.

When the Chrysler Corporation came close to bankruptcy in 1977 and sought a federally guaranteed loan, one of its strongest allies was the United Auto Workers (UAW) union. The loan

not only rescued the economically troubled company but also made secure the jobs held by UAW members at the Chrysler automobile plants.

Interestingly, business groups, which are often perceived as unified on most issues (another myth!), were divided on the question of the guaranteed loan. A number of conservative groups opposed the loan, fearing that it might result in increased federal regulation of a major corporation. Many businesses object in principle to such regulation.

regulations that may affect the way a company does business. The National Coal Association, for example, closely monitors government regulations covering environmental pollution that may increase the costs of operating coal-burning plants.

Labor organizations. Labor organizations represent a vast segment of society. The American Federation of Labor and Congress of Industrial Organizations (AFL-CIO), an umbrella organization of ninety-six labor unions, has approximately 15 million members. Along with the United Automobile Workers, the Teamsters, and many other labor organizations, the AFL-CIO for many years has represented the interests of labor in the state capitals and in Washington.

Individual labor unions also lobby independently of the umbrella groups. Thus, for example, the Brotherhood of Locomotive Engineers keeps on top of transportation issues, while representatives of the Sheet Metal Workers International Association follow legislation on import tariffs.

Though still a potent force in the political system, labor unions have lost strength in recent years. Their power has diminished for two main reasons: a decline in union membership in key industries such as mining, steel production, and automobile manufacturing, and an increase in the number of corporate and business interest groups.

Professional associations. Professional associations bring the interests of their particular membership to the government's attention. Two of the most

Fueling public protest Bread-and-butter issues make strange allies in the world of interest group politics. Although organized labor has not been in the forefront of environmental activism, these union coal miners see nuclear power as a social as well as economic issue and lend their enthusiastic presence to a protest rally.

powerful—the American Medical Association (AMA) and the American Bar Association (ABA)—have huge lobbying budgets, as well as full-time staffs in Washington and in many state capitals. Smaller, less powerful associations, such as the Clowns of America, have fewer resources but also try to protect their members' interests in regard to workers' compensation, tax laws, and other legislation affecting their professions.

Agricultural interest groups. Farmers make up less than 5 percent of the working population of the United States, but they are a relatively strong economic force in contemporary American politics. One of their major goals is protection from fluctuating prices for meat, grain, fruit, and other produce.

As in the case of trade associations and business interest groups, the interests of farmers are highly diversified, ranging from dairy farming and the raising of chickens and hogs to the growing of wheat, soybeans, and other produce. The interests of small family farmers are often at odds with those of companies like the Quaker Oats Company and the Campbell Soup Company, two large companies—agribusinesses—closely associated with the business of farming. This diversity is often reflected in the competing interests that farmers have with each other over issues like farm subsidies and federal farm loan programs.

Two of the nation's largest farming interest groups are the American Farm Bureau Federation (AFBF) and the National Farmers Union (NFU). The AFBF, which represents the owners of large farms, generally opposes federal regulation of agriculture. The smaller NFU includes many low-income farmers and favors federally supported and guaranteed farm loans and other government intervention. Size of membership is not necessarily related to power, for the NFU is as significant a force on government farm policy as the AFBF.

Citizen Activist Groups

Not all shared interests are purely economic. In recent years there has been a proliferation of citizen activist groups, which rely on public opinion to back up their demands and expectations. Some of these groups try to represent what they deem to be the interests of the public at large and thus they are referred to as **public interest groups**.[8] Other organizations focus on specific causes or serve as advocates for those who are not able to represent themselves.[9]

"Looks as if the clean-air crowd turned out in force."

Drawing by Richter; © 1987 The New Yorker Magazine, Inc.

Public interest groups. Common Cause—a grass-roots organization supported by member dues—and Nader's Raiders—a loose affiliation of groups formed by the consumer activist, Ralph Nader, and supported by foundation grants—were part of an explosion of citizen lobbies in the 1960s. These groups have always tried to represent what they see as the public's interests on such issues as civil rights, consumer protection, and environmental regulation.

A Harvard Law School graduate, Nader received public acclaim in 1965 for his book *Unsafe at Any Speed.* The book attacked unsafe production designs in the automobile industry. Regarded as a champion of consumer interests, Nader established a dozen public interest lobbying organizations, including the Health Research Group, the Tax Reform Research Group, the Public Citizen Litigation Group, and the Center for the Study of Responsive Law. All have become prominent and effective actors in Washington politics.[10]

Cause groups. Some citizen groups focus on small clusters of issues. One such group, the Moral Majority (now a division of the Liberty Federation), a conservative, religious organization, seeks action on constitutional amendments that would ban abortion and permit voluntary prayer in schools.[11] Opposing this conservative agenda are liberal, multi-issue organizations like the American Civil Liberties Union and People for the American Way (founded by television producer Norman Lear).

A cause group with an extremely narrow focus becomes known as a **single-issue group.** The National Rifle Association (NRA) and the Gun Owners of America work to preserve the right of Americans to own handguns and rifles. The National Abortion Rights Action League (NARAL) fights for legislation and court decisions that protect the right of women to have abortions. Still another active cause group, MADD—Mothers Against Drunk Driving—persuaded Congress to deprive states of federal highway funds if they did not set the minimum drinking age at twenty-one. MADD's tactics included the direct lobbying of members of Congress by local constituents, the distribution of pamphlets on the loss of life due to drunk driving, and emotionally packed public forums where the mothers of teen-agers killed by drunk drivers appealed for public support to raise the minimum drinking age.

Advocacy groups. Some citizen activist groups serve as advocates for individuals who alone may be unable to represent their own interests.[12] For instance, the National Association for the Advancement of Colored People (NAACP), the Child Welfare League of America, and the American Cancer Society assist their target populations by lobbying, providing the public with information, and taking cases to court. Other advocacy groups focus on such issues as women's rights, gay rights, and racial equality, as well as the rights

Advocacy for the elderly Among the least organized in society are the elderly poor. The Gray Panthers have attempted to redress this inequity by organizing protests and grassroots lobbying efforts.

of Hispanics, various ethnic and religious groups, college students, and senior citizens. Many of their supporters do not benefit directly from their advocacy role but believe in the goals of the group.

The effectiveness of these groups in the political system has been demonstrated over and over again. The NAACP was instrumental in originating the 1954 Supreme Court case, *Brown* v. *Board of Education*, which declared unconstitutional the segregation of public schools based on the race of a student. In 1982 the United States Student Association was one of several advocacy groups that successfully lobbied against Reagan's proposed reductions in student aid programs in higher education.

Government-related Interest Groups

Governments not only receive pressure from lobbyists; they also act as lobbies. In the 1970s and early 1980s, when New York City seemed on the brink of bankruptcy, it lobbied Congress, the president, and its own state legislature for financial relief. Few major cities remain unrepresented in Washington. Indeed, the offices of more than a hundred cities and states are listed in the *Washington Representatives Directory*.[13]

In addition, a number of government associations represent the collective interests of their members. These organizations include the U.S. Conference of Mayors, the International City Management Association, the National League of Cities, the National Association of Counties, the Council of State Governments, and the National Governors Association. The U.S. Conference of Mayors, for example, meets every year with an agenda that frequently calls for increased federal spending for the cities. Its efforts include the lobbying of members of Congress in support of programs ranging from social welfare services and housing to public transportation. As local governments have come to depend on Washington for funds, the need for effective representation has increased and lobbies have become the principal means of achieving that representation.[14]

Even foreign nations have lobbyists looking after their interests. For example, Canada recently hired lobbyists to represent its concerns about U.S. sources of acid rain. More typically, foreign diplomats directly lobby members of Congress and other officials. Takis Theodoracopoulos of Greece was a familiar sight in congressional hearing rooms and members' offices as he effectively fought off a 1986 effort to reduce U.S. aid to his country.[15]

★ ★ ★
RESOURCES OF INTEREST GROUPS

What accounts for the success of interest groups? What are the resources on which they draw to influence the policy-making process?

Group Dynamics

The groups' power is strongly influenced by their internal cohesion. The AFL-CIO can be sure, for example, that its large membership is united in opposition to the lowering of federal minimum hourly wages. Such unity gives the AFL-CIO enormous strength. Congress, the president, and the bureaucracy cannot ignore the intense preferences of 15 million organized individuals.

When an interest group lacks unity on an issue, its influence on the policy-making process drops considerably. As we noted in discussing trade associations, internal disagreements often work against group cohesion. Even within particular industries lack of consensus sometimes causes problems. For example, agreement is rare across the petroleum industry.

The lonely crowd Lobbyists mill impatiently in the hall outside the room where a House-Senate conference committee is putting finishing touches on a major tax revision bill. The crowd includes lobbyists from banking, real estate, insurance, and other interests—all hoping for a last minute chance to plead their cause.

> Many proposals pertaining to the oil industry affect companies quite differently because they vary in size, ranging from [giants] like Exxon and Mobil to the small independent wildcatter. . . . As a result, says one API [American Petroleum Institute] lobbyist, consensus on many issues is a "long time coming." On broad issues cutting across the membership, API's stand is sometimes "no stand" due to lack of consensus.[16]

Leadership. Consensus does not necessarily ensure success, however. Interest groups must also have leaders who can articulate and represent the issues and demands of the organization.

Sometimes leaders attempt to be democratic, giving members a say in the decisions. Large membership groups like Common Cause regularly pool their members. But individual opinions generally have little impact in such groups, which puts most decision making in the hands of the leadership. Other groups pay even less attention to the members' views. For example, individual rank-and-file members of the Teamsters' Union, the largest union in the nation, have little or no opportunity to influence the union's policies. Of course, responsibility for their lack of power rests to some extent with interest group members. If they have no real interest in the policy positions of the organization, they can create a power vacuum in which the leaders and their staffs find it easy to act on their own.

Information and expertise.   What lobbyists know—their ability to collect information, evaluate its importance, and pass it on to appropriate government officials—is critical to their success. Faced with decisions on a variety of issues, public officials need credible and trustworthy information. An interest group that can provide its expertise cogently and convincingly has a distinct advantage over less-informed and less-articulate organizations. Pat Healy, formerly the powerful and successful chief lobbyist for the National Milk Producers' Federation, argues that facts are the major resource of lobbying and that being able to provide accurate information to members and staff in Congress is the key to a lobbyist's success. Few of his colleagues would disagree with him.

Size.   Size can also be a major resource in establishing an interest group's base of power. Large organizations like the AFL-CIO have the potential collectively to mobilize vast resources of money, information, time, and energy in the service of an issue. The success of unions' defense of federally mandated minimum wages is a measure of the importance of size as a component of political force.

In evaluating the impact of size, the key word is *potential.* Many large interest groups have little or no influence over the political opinions and participation of their membership. Indeed, a large constituency is often an organizational burden—difficult both to manage and to influence.[17] If the leaders of large interest groups can convince elected officials, administrators, and congressional staff that they can mobilize their membership behind a policy, size becomes very important. Otherwise, large groups have relatively little clout with elected officials. Although the U.S. Chamber of Commerce has a membership of over 250,000 individuals and companies, internal disputes and dissension have weakened the organization in recent years. As a result, its effectiveness in lobbying for or against certain federal programs has diminished.

Money

Lobbying, collecting information, and other activities cost money. Besides the lobbyists' salaries, expenses include office space, supporting staff, telephones, office equipment, and travel. Some groups hire professional lobbying firms to conduct their business, and the costs of these services can be significant. A large budget may not be the most critical resource of interest groups, but adequate funding is essential.

Fund-raising tactics differ from group to group. Citizen activist groups like the Sierra Club rely on an annual membership fee. For these groups, finding enough members to maintain the organization can be a problem. A hiker or camper need not join the club in order to benefit from its efforts at improving environmental conditions and preserving national parks. To get around this problem of **free riders**—those who benefit from the actions of interest groups without expending effort or money for the groups—groups often seek foundation support and provide special services and resources.[18] These special services and resources help recruit members. An interest group may provide its members with free publications, technical journals, informative newsletters, reduced insurance rates, and even the opportunity to combine business with pleasure at annual meetings held in vacation resorts. For example, the American Judicature Society, an organization seeking reforms in the selection of state and local judges, offers its members, including lawyers and judicial scholars, low-cost insurance policies. The members of the National Rifle Association can buy ammunition, handguns, and rifles at discount prices.

Economic groups often have easier access to funds. Groups like the U.S. Chamber of Commerce and the National Association of Manufacturers receive dues from their corporate and individual members. Many companies use corporate funds to pay for the cost of maintaining a staff lobbyist or hiring a lobbying firm. Still others can count on financial support from members who must join the organization in order to keep their jobs. This is typical of many trade and industrial jobs and even some professions. Carpenters and plumbers must join their unions, and physicians, lawyers, and other professionals find themselves under pressure to join their associations.

Finally, a number of interest groups, including the National Council of Senior Citizens, the National Governors Association, and the American Council on Education, rely on government grants for financial assistance.

Power and Influence

Interest groups are as powerful as their cohesion, leadership, expertise, funds, and size enable them to be. All of these resources need not be present, but the more, the better. In addition, a group's power often depends on what it has to offer the beholder. Members of Congress from the farm belt respect the expertise of agricultural interest groups, whereas urban legislators have less interest in such groups. Power also depends on the perception of the groups' motives. When, for example, the American Medical Association (AMA) takes a position on smoking or some other public health issue, Congress and the public heed their views. When the AMA comes out against medical insurance for the elderly, however, its lobbying may be received with some skepticism and even with talk of the corrupting influence myth.

Lobbyists are aware of and work hard to overcome the myth of corruption. When 175 of them were asked which resources were most important to their success, an overwhelming majority singled out the reputation for being credible and trustworthy.[19] Interestingly, they placed a large budget and membership size at the bottom of the list. (See Figure 8.1.) Most leaders of interest groups feel that effective leadership is much more of an advantage

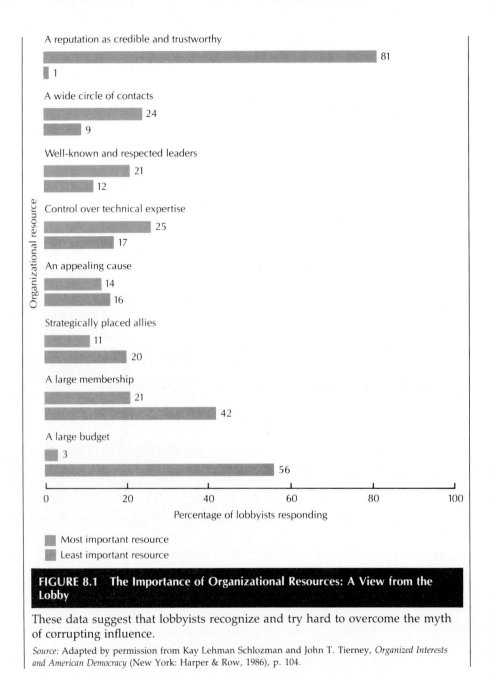

FIGURE 8.1 **The Importance of Organizational Resources: A View from the Lobby**

These data suggest that lobbyists recognize and try hard to overcome the myth of corrupting influence.

Source: Adapted by permission from Kay Lehman Schlozman and John T. Tierney, *Organized Interests and American Democracy* (New York: Harper & Row, 1986), p. 104.

than a large budget. The low ranking of membership size can be explained by the fact that the largest types of interest groups, that is, corporate interest groups (which are not membership organizations) and trade associations (which generally have relatively few members) do not place a high value in the importance of membership size. On the other hand, unions and citizens' groups, which traditionally claim large membership and mass representation, do place a high value on membership size.[20] Of course, no single resource can make or break a group. More often than not, success comes from effectively combining organizational resources and the tactics used to influence policy making.

★ ★ ★
INTEREST GROUP TACTICS

"You don't lobby with hundred-dollar bills and wild parties. You lobby with facts," says lobbyist Patrick Healy. As you will see, however, money counts, although it is only one of many tools used by interest groups to influence government.

Lobbying

Lobbying is the act of trying to influence government decision makers. Named after the public rooms in which it first took place, lobbying now goes on in hearing rooms, offices, and restaurants—any spot where a lobbyist can effectively present a case.

Lobbyists' stock in trade is their relationships with government officials and their staffs. (See Table 8.1.) That relationship is not maintained with bribes and favors, as the myth of corruption implies, but with data—technical information that members of Congress and bureaucrats need to carry out their committee and administrative assignments. Their work demands a level of expertise that few can muster, and so they come to depend on lobbyists' information and recommendations on the thousands of issues that they must decide.

Once an interest group proves itself as a source of dependable information, it has easier access to officials. Lobbyists also share that expertise at congressional hearings, presenting research or technical information or discussing the impact of the bill on national interests. Knowing how important constituents' concerns are to legislators, they are quick to point to the impact of a bill on a representative's home district or state. Whenever they can, interest groups mobilize the folks at home to write and call members of Congress to stress the importance of particular issues to the district. When the Chrysler Corporation was threatened with bankruptcy in the late 1970s, thousands of

TABLE 8.1 What Lobbyists Do

Despite the myth of corrupting influence, lobbyists do not spend much time "endorsing candidates" or contributing to their campaigns. As these data demonstrate, disseminating information is the major focus of their work.

Type of Technique	Percentage of Organizations Using Technique
Testifying at congressional hearings	99
Contacting government officials directly to present your point of view	98
Engaging in informal contacts with officials over lunch, and so on	95
Presenting research results or technical information	92
Helping to draft legislation	85
Mounting grassroots lobbying efforts	80
Alerting congressional representatives of the effects of a bill on their district	75
Filing suit or otherwise engaging in litigation	72
Publicizing candidates' voting records	44
Contributing work or personnel to electoral campaigns	24
Making public endorsements of candidates for office	22
Engaging in protests or demonstrations	20

Source: Kay Lehman Schlozman and John T. Tierney, *Organized Interests and American Democracy* (New York: Harper & Row, 1986), p. 150. Reprinted by permission.

letters and telephone calls came from constituents to members of Congress whose districts included a Chrysler plant. These letters and calls urged that a federally insured loan be granted to the company. The tactic, which was part of a larger strategy, succeeded very well.

Increasingly, lobbying is a professional, full-time occupation. Many lobbyists are lawyers and former members of the executive branch and Congress. (See Figure 8.2.) A number of Reagan's former staff members have joined or formed their own lobby firms. They include such high-ranking personnel as Michael Deaver, former deputy chief of staff, Edward Rollins, former assistant to the president on political and governmental affairs, Richard

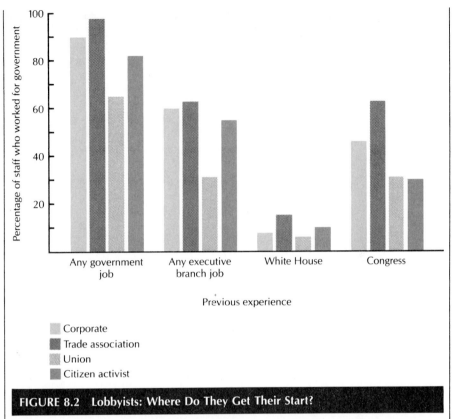

FIGURE 8.2   Lobbyists: Where Do They Get Their Start?

The vast majority of interest group staffers have previously worked for the federal government. Note that union lobbies are least likely and trade associations most likely to employ former government officials.

Source: Kay Lehman Schlozman and John T. Tierney, *Organized Interests and American Democracy* (New York: Harper & Row, 1986), p. 269. Reprinted by permission.

Allen, former head of the National Security Council, and Sheila Tate, First Lady Nancy Reagan's former press secretary. In 1986 Deaver, who was president of the lobbying and public relations firm Michael K. Deaver and Associates, represented, among other groups, the governments of Singapore and South Korea and the Korean Broadcasting Advertising Corporation.

Lobbyists even draft legislation, write speeches, and help plan legislative strategy. For most lobbyists, however, presenting research results or technical information to public officials is the most important and time-consuming part of their job.[21]

Clearly, the existence of bad lobbyists supports the myth of corruption (see Background 8.1). The Watergate hearings (see Chapter 6, on elections)

BACKGROUND 8.1

Regulating Interest Groups

In the early years of the republic, presenting gifts to or bribing willing legislators were not uncommon ways of influencing the passage of a specific bill. Indeed, in the early 1800s, as prominent a senator as Daniel Webster was on retainer to the Bank of the United States, which was fighting for its survival. Webster wrote to the bank president: "My retainer has not been renewed or refreshed as usual. If it is wished that my relation to the Bank should be continued, it may be well to send me the usual retainer."

Despite their reputation for bribery and corruption, most interest groups function within the law. Nevertheless, Congress has found it necessary to pass laws regulating the groups and their representatives.

In 1887 Congress first required lobbyists to register with the House of Representatives. Additional laws mandate that lobbyists file reports listing their clients, as well as describing their activities and recording the amount of money spent on them. The 1946 Federal Regulation of Lobbying Act is the most recent comprehensive attempt to regulate the groups. Efforts to add further restrictions have not succeeded.

Under the 1946 act, lobbying is vaguely defined and the regulations are minimally enforced. Of the estimated twenty thousand lobbyists active in Washington, D.C., only fifty-five hundred are actually registered. One reason is a loophole in the law: only individuals paid to lobby for someone else must register. Thus, for example, an official who works directly for a corporation and lobbies for the interests of that company need not register. In addition, only lobbyists who have direct contact with members of Congress must register. A great deal of the lobbying that goes on, however, targets the staff people who work for and advise members of Congress.

In the more than forty years since the law was enacted, it has been violated only six times. Whether this fact reflects the vagueness of the statute or the honesty and rectitude of contemporary lobbyists is anybody's guess.

The source for Daniel Webster's quote is *Guide to Current American Government* (Washington, D.C.: Congressional Quarterly Press, 1986), p. 45.

---

revealed that some interest groups, through their lobbyists, were willing to make illegal campaign contributions to the Nixon presidential campaign in 1972 in order to gain favor with the president. Such willingness was also demonstrated in 1977 when a South Korean businessman was accused of providing several members of Congress with expensive gifts in exchange for legislative favors.

The norm of behavior for the vast majority of lobbyists, however, is to act within the law, and their actions are governed by one major rule: a lobbyist should never lie. As one member of Congress put it,

> It doesn't take very long to figure which lobbyists are straightforward, and which ones are trying to snow you. The good ones will give you the weak points as well as the strong points of their case. If anyone ever gives me false or misleading information, that's it—I'll never see him again.[22]

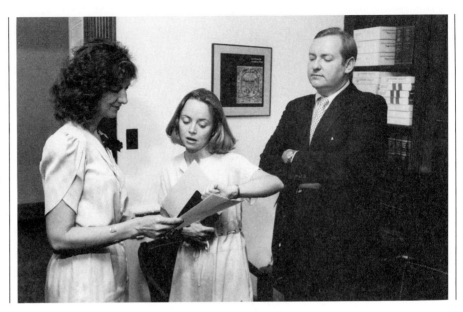

Lobbyists in action Republican Representative Claudine Schneider of Rhode Island discusses a fundraiser with two lobbyists in her Capitol Hill office. Scenes like this one are common as representatives of special groups try to influence policy making.

Political Action Committees

If the myth of corruption has tainted interest group politics in recent years, a major source of that concern has been **political action committees (PACs).** These independent organizations are set up to collect campaign contributions from group members and pass them on to candidates. PACs resulted from a change in campaign finance laws designed to limit interest groups' financial involvement in elections.[23]

The change came about in the 1970s when Congress, pressured by public interest groups, passed the Federal Elections Campaign Act. The act provides for a rigid reporting system covering PAC money raised and spent for campaigns; it drastically restricts campaign contributions and prohibits corporations and labor unions from directly raising funds for or making contributions to political campaigns. However, Congress permitted unions and corporations to set up and administer independent organizations designed to collect and disburse campaign contributions.

Unions invented PACs, but, as you can see in Figure 8.3, corporations rapidly surpassed them in numbers. Currently, virtually every kind of group uses PACs. Unaffiliated groups (such as the National Conservative Political Action Committee), trade and professional groups (including the Tobacco Institute Political Action Committee and the American Medical Association Political Action Committee), and cooperative groups (for example, the

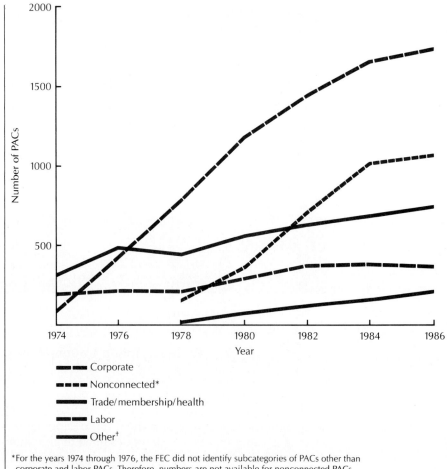

*For the years 1974 through 1976, the FEC did not identify subcategories of PACs other than corporate and labor PACs. Therefore, numbers are not available for nonconnected PACs.

†Includes PACs formed by corporations without capital stock and cooperatives. Numbers are not available for these categories of PACs from 1974 through 1976.

FIGURE 8.3   An Explosion of PACs

Unions invented them but corporations forged ahead with them when political action committees were in their infancy. Corporate, union, and trade PACs have tended to support candidates, whereas nonaffiliated PACs have worked on negative campaigns.

Source: Federal Election Commission Record, February 1987, p. 10.

Committee for Thorough Agricultural Political Education of Associated Milk Producers, Inc.) solicit and contribute money to political campaigns.

PAC money has become very important to candidates. During the 1983–1984 election cycle, PACs contributed slightly more than $100 million to

Senate and House candidates. That figure represents an increase of $70 million—or more than 200 percent—over 1977–1978.[24] In the 1984 congressional elections, more than a third of the incumbent House members relied primarily on PAC contributions to fund their campaigns.[25] Few congressional candidates, incumbent or not, refuse PAC funding of their expensive campaigns for office. (See Table 8.2 for a list of major PAC contributors).

PACs' patterns of giving reflect their partisan persuasions. In 1980, for example, labor PACs, traditionally strong supporters of the Democratic party, channeled their contributions primarily to Democratic candidates. Corporate PACs, on the other hand, gave nearly twice as much to Republican candidates as to Democrats.[26] Corporate gifts to Democrats were not insubstantial, however. When Democrats control Congress, business knows that it must cultivate that party's support.

Do PAC contributions matter? Do the recipients of campaign funds support the donors' programs? Apparently, interest groups think they do. In one recent study, 58 percent of interest group representatives said they used campaign contributions as a means of exercising influence on the policy-making process.[27] Despite this belief, there is no evidence that campaign contributions guarantee support or votes on a bill.[28] In general, a gift normally just ensures easier access to elected officials.

TABLE 8.2 Top Ten PAC Contributors

These PACs (political action committees) contributed the largest amounts of money to candidates for federal office in 1983–84.

1 Realtors Political Action Committee	$2,429,852
2 American Medical Association Political Action Committee	1,839,464
3 Build Political Action Committee of the National Association of Home Builders	1,625,539
4 National Education Association Political Action Committee	1,574,003
5 UAW Voluntary Community Action Program	1,405,107
6 Seafarers Political Activity Donation	1,322,410
7 Machinists Non-Partisan Political League	1,306,497
8 Active Ballot Club, a department of United Food and Commercial Workers International Union	1,261,974
9 Letter Carriers Political Action Fund	1,234,603
10 National Association of Retired Federal Employees Political Action Committee	1,099,243

Source: Federal Election Commission, November, 1985 press release, p. 8.

According to the Federal Election Campaign Act, PACs can donate no more than five thousand dollars per candidate per election, a restriction motivated by a history of interest group contributions that could reach tens of thousands of dollars for a single candidate. Since now candidates must seek out a larger number of contributors to their campaigns to ensure sufficient funding, a single group's influence on a candidate may be less than it expects. However, the five-thousand-dollar restriction per candidate makes it possible for PACs to support more candidates, for there is no limit on the number of campaigns a PAC may contribute to. This outcome disturbs many reformers who had hoped to restrict, not increase, the involvement of interest groups in campaigns.[29]

Electioneering

Interest groups support campaigns in other ways besides PAC contributions. Labor, trade, and professional associations supply candidates with volunteers and offer public endorsements. The AFL-CIO, the Americans for Democratic Action, and the National Conservative Political Action Committee (NCPAC) are just three of the many interest groups that give their members and the public voting scorecards on candidates they support or target for defeat. By listing key votes, the cards can praise or damn the candidate. NCPAC specializes in the so-called negative campaign, or putting down the opposition. The group has spent large sums, particularly on television advertisements, in an effort to defeat liberal candidates.

Interest groups do not limit their activities to congressional races. Besides pressuring the major parties to include in its goal their platforms, an interest group may turn out in force at the national conventions. Of the 2,067 delegates at the 1984 Democratic National Convention, 220 were members of the National Education Association (NEA); 280 were members of the National Organization for Women (NOW); and 573 belonged to unions affiliated with the AFL-CIO.[30] Not surprisingly, the party took strong platform positions on education, women's issues, and labor concerns.

Building Coalitions

A tactic of interest groups that has gained increasing importance is **coalition building**—the bringing together of diverse interest groups in a common lobbying effort. Such cooperative action has proved very successful. In 1985 the Daylight Saving Time Coalition successfully lobbied for the passage of federal legislation that would extend the number of days covered by daylight saving time. Groups forming this coalition—amusement parks, the 7-Eleven convenience food store chain, the Kingsford charcoal company, and lawn and garden outlets—had all concluded that the "more daylight in the evening hours—the better to snack, grill, play, and till the soil."[31] Their efforts paid off when federal legislation was passed extending daylight saving time. It now begins on the first, rather than the last, Sunday of April.

Coalitions are often temporary alliances keyed to a particular issue. For instance, the Quaker Oats Company, interested in keeping down the price of grains used in many of their cereal products, and Common Cause, the public interest group seeking to control the retail costs of food, have at times testified jointly against certain farm support bills. Yet Quaker Oats and Common Cause are on opposite sides of the fence on many other issues, such as federal safety laws regulating the manufacture of children's toys.

Most signs point to an increasing use of coalition building by interest groups and PACs in an effort to influence the policy-making process.

Grassroots Pressure

The word *grassroots* used to have a rural flavor, an up-from-the-people, down-with-the-bosses connotation. The urban associations are gone, but the term remains people-centered. In interest group politics, **grassroots pressure** refers to lobbying by rank-and-file members of an interest group, who use such tactics as letter writing and public protests to influence government.

When the National Beer Wholesalers Association (NBWA) wanted exemption from antitrust legislation, it mobilized grassroots support for a massive letter, telephone, and telegram campaign. Truly a "bottoms-up" effort to stimulate pressure from the grassroots level, the campaign was supported by political contributions from the NBWA political action committee—which no doubt you have guessed is called SIXPAC.[32]

Grassroots activity includes face-to-face meetings between members of Congress and selected constituents, as well as demonstrations and protests. In one such demonstration, more than three thousand members of the American Agricultural Movement drove their tractors through the streets of Washington, D.C., to protest proposed reductions in farm price supports.[33] When interest groups mobilize grassroots mail and telephone campaigns, they tend to focus on narrow issues and direct their efforts to specific members of Congress.

Grassroots lobbying has become highly sophisticated, and the activities of the U.S. Chamber of Commerce illustrate this change. The group maintains a closed-circuit television network linking local affiliates all over the nation. When it wants to mobilize support for or against a bill, it can beam its views to congressional and community leaders, as well as to its members.

On any given issue, "lobbyists understand intuitively what political scientists have demonstrated empirically: members of Congress are more influenced by their constituents than by Washington lobbies."[34] For this reason, many interest groups stress grassroots efforts.

Pressure from the grass roots Florida Representative Claude Pepper sits in front of six tons of petitions protesting Social Security cuts. To make his support for the cause more graphic, he has decorated the mound of boxes with a photograph of President Franklin Roosevelt signing Social Security into law.

Litigation

Many pressure groups, particularly public interest and advocacy groups, also use the courts to influence policy. They bring direct suit, challenge existing laws, or file briefs as "friends of the court" to support one side in cases already before the court.

Though it is expensive and time consuming, litigation can bring about remarkable political change. Perhaps the outstanding example is the use of the courts by the National Association for the Advancement of Colored People (NAACP) in the 1940s and 1950s. In a series of cases, culminating in the *Brown* v. *Board of Education* decision in 1954, NAACP lawyers argued and the Supreme Court affirmed that school segregation is illegal in the United States. Women's groups, consumer groups, environmental groups, and others have followed the civil rights movement's lead in taking their causes to the courts. Corporations and trade associations have also engaged in litigation.

However, the high cost restrains many groups. Recently, one interest group, the Women's Equity League, could not appeal a court ruling against it in an important case because it could not afford the forty thousand dollars necessary to pay for copies of the trial transcript.[35]

One way to get around the cost problem is to threaten a lawsuit; often that is enough to dissuade opponents from acting. In another approach, groups try to influence the philosophy of the court by opposing or supporting judicial nominees. Two of President Richard Nixon's nominees to the Supreme Court, Clement Haynsworth and G. Harrold Carswell, were bitterly opposed—Haynsworth by labor unions and Carswell by civil rights groups—because of their records as federal District Court judges. Neither candidate was approved by the U.S. Senate.

★ ★ ★

INTEREST GROUPS, PACS, AND PUBLIC POLICY

Interest groups pose a number of problems for a democratic society. James Madison argued in *Federalist No. 10* that the rise of factions is inevitable in a democracy. Although he felt that factions could destroy the policy-making process, he did not want to prohibit them, for that would undermine the basic tenets of a participatory republic. Instead, Madison hoped that the divisiveness of factions would be tempered both by built-in checks and balances and by a political system that would assure the creation of competing factions.

Interest Groups and Public Policy

Interest groups do distort the democratic process, mainly because their membership is clearly biased toward the upper half of the socioeconomic ladder. The groups that have the most clout in Washington are dominated by business and professional lobbies working on economic issues that benefit the already advantaged in society. The poor, the young, and the elderly have much less PAC representation. Thus the haves gain more, while the have-nots remain unrepresented or underrepresented by interest groups. To the extent that the business, labor, and professional groups have exceptional influence, policy is similarly distorted.

Interest groups and PACs are essentially middle- and upper-class institutions representing middle- and upper-class values in the policy-making process. Though they may intend to serve the nation's interests, they generally design their goals and limit their commitments to suit a relatively small group of private interests.

The Cozy Triangle

Interest groups can also distort the policy-making process by joining a **cozy triangle**—an informal network of interest groups, congressional committee members and staff, and bureaucrats. By exchanging information and advice, and providing mutual assistance, each group, working on behalf of its own interests, also works for the advantage of the others.*

In the defense industry, for instance, contractors, the U.S. Department of Defense, and the Senate Armed Services Committee share a strong interest in expanding national defense programs. The interest groups lobby the Armed Services Committee in support of the Department of Defense's various budget requests. The committee sponsors legislation requested by the Department of Defense. The weapons manufacturers and other interests profit from the Defense Department contracts that result from the legislation.

President Dwight D. Eisenhower, a former army general, warned that this network of mutual support could undermine the national interest by creating an environment in which members of the cozy triangle only look after their narrow self-interest. He may have been right. It is not unusual for retiring civilian and military Defense Department officials and retiring or defeated members of the Senate or House Armed Services Committee to seek or accept jobs with defense contractors or their interest group representatives. Thus some Defense Department officials and members of Congress may support the industry's programs in expectation of possible future employment in the defense industry sector.[36] Eisenhower's concern regarding these supportive relationships applies to cozy triangles in many different policy areas.

CONCLUSION: Corrupt or Constructive?

Unquestionably, interest groups have come to wield increasing political power, and Americans' fear of these groups has some basis in reality. With large treasuries to disburse and an inside track with public officials, they are potentially a distorting influence on the functioning of the political system. Not every group with a shared interest is self-interested, however. To see only the biasing effects of interest groups is to perpetuate the corrupting influence myth.

---

* As you will see in Chapter 10, on Congress, members of both the House of Representatives and the Senate serve on committees that specialize in specific subjects—agriculture, military affairs, and so on. These committees study a bill and recommend to the House or Senate, as a whole, whether the bill should be passed or not.

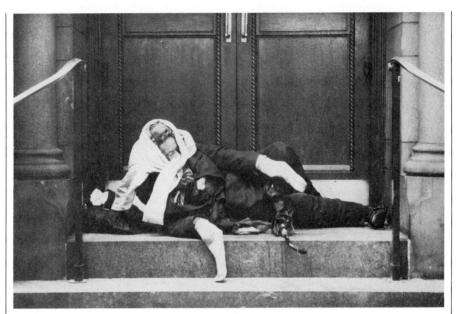

Sanctuary An elderly woman huddles in the doorway of a New York City church. Scarcely anyone speaks for the homeless, among whom are a disproportionate number of the mentally ill and substance abusers. In a political system in which interest groups are increasingly important, who will represent the needs of this growing group?

As with the proverbial concept of beauty, an interest group's "goodness" or "badness" rests in the eyes of the beholder. To the extent that the interest group system favors those individuals and groups in our society that are most affluent and have the greatest resources, it does promote an unbalanced, if not corrupt, society. To the extent that broad, national interests are lost in the clamor of pressure group activity and narrow self-interest, the system compromises the ideals of democratic government.

Interest groups, however, are also a healthy feature of the political process. They are organizations that give voice to the voiceless and represent the unrepresented. Advances for blacks, the poor, the young, and the aged, and others who are disadvantaged, as well as farmers, laborers, and owners of small businesses, can be attributed, in large part, to the effective activities of interest groups.

Many interest groups promote causes that benefit us all. For example, a coalition of environmental groups, including the Sierra Club, the Wilderness Society, and the National Resources Defense Council, have for more than two decades lobbied effectively for federal and state laws regulating air and water pollution, forest, rangeland and coastal land management, strip mining, and the production and use of pesticides and toxic substances, as well as for laws protecting endangered species.

Madison warned of the pitfalls of interest groups. He also argued that they are an inevitable cost in any democratic system. We argue that the groups link citizens and public officials through corporate, labor, trade, and professional associations and through citizen activist groups; such linkage may be worth the price of real (and imagined) distortions that inevitably occur when interest groups are active in the policy-making process. Certainly, the groups are too useful to dismiss by invoking the myth of corrupting influence.

★ ★ ★
SUMMARY

1. Interest groups are organized groups of individuals who share one or more common goals and who seek to influence government decision making.

2. Political parties deal with both specific and general policy development. Interest groups usually focus on narrow policy areas.

3. While they may attempt to influence the outcome of certain elections, interest groups do not run candidates for elective office, their names do not appear on the ballot, and they do not attempt to gain control over or operate government.

4. Types of interest groups include economic organizations, citizen activist groups, and government-related interest groups.

5. Resources that interest groups rely on to influence the policy-making process include group cohesion, strong leadership, information and expertise, strength in numbers, money, and power and influence in their specific area of interest. In general, however, given different issues and different political environments, no single resource determines the success of an interest group. A group's influence is usually strongest when a combination of organizational resources is brought to bear on the policy-making process.

6. Interest group tactics include lobbying, financing and supporting campaigns through affiliated political action committees, electioneering, coalition building, grassroots pressure, and litigation.

7. Political action committees (PACs), cousin organizations of interest groups, serve as affiliated or independent organizations with the prime function of collecting and disbursing campaign contributions. Candidates, particularly for Congress, have become increasingly dependent on this source of campaign support.

8. Interest groups can pose problems for a democratic society because they often represent narrow interests that are biased toward the higher economic groups, and they form unhealthy coalitions (a cozy triangle) with Congress and the bureaucracy.

9. Interest groups are important to the political process because they can and do enhance our representative process, focusing our attention on important issues.

★ ★ ★
KEY TERMS

interest group
public interest group
single-issue group
free riders
lobbying

political action committees (PACs)
coalition building
grassroots pressure
cozy triangle

★ ★ ★
SELECTED READINGS

- Berry, Jeffrey M. *The Interest Group Society*. Boston: Little, Brown, 1984. A well-written examination of how interest groups operate within the context of democratic theory. The author places special emphasis on the relationship between interest groups and political parties and the changes in campaign finance practices.

- Cigler, Allan J. and Burdett A. Loomis. *Interest Group Politics*, 2nd ed. Washington, D.C.: Congressional Quarterly Press, 1986. An excellent collection of essays by leading scholars, focusing on the policy-making roles of interests and groups, interest group participation, organizations and elections, political action committees, interest groups and the courts, and lobbyists.

- Sabato, Larry J. *PAC Power: Inside the World of Political Action Committees*. New York: Norton, 1985. A careful evaluation and analysis of political action committees (PACs) drawing on extensive interviews with PAC officials.

- Schlozman, Kay Lehman and John T. Tierney. *Organized Interests and American Democracy*. New York: Harper & Row, 1986. A skillful study broadly covering the role of organized interests in the United States. The authors draw on several sources of information, including a set of interviews with 175 Washington interest group representatives.

9

CHAPTER

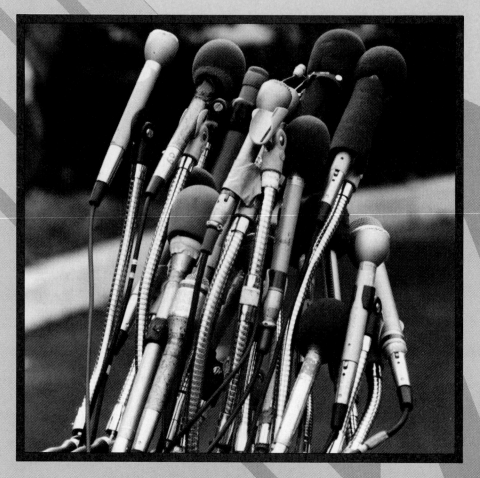

Media and Politics

Back in 1971 a CBS television crew traveled to Johnson City, Texas, to film an interview with former President Lyndon Johnson. During the taping, John Sharnik, a senior editor for CBS, casually asked Johnson what changes he had seen in his thirty years of politics. Without a moment's hesitation, he exploded: "You guys! All you guys in the media! All of politics has changed because of you. You've broken all the machines and ties between us in Congress and the city machines. You've given us a new kind of people. . . . They're your creations, your puppets. No machine could ever create a Teddy Kennedy. Only you guys. They're all yours. Your product."[1]

Perhaps Johnson was reflecting on the evening in 1968 when Walter Cronkite, anchor of the "CBS Evening News," presented a half-hour news special on the failure of the war effort in Vietnam. Cronkite—the most trusted man in America according to several polls—told the nation that Johnson's optimism was wrong. The war could not be won, and committing more troops would not change the situation. America, Cronkite argued, should begin to negotiate, "not as victors, but as honorable people who lived up to their pledge to defend democracy, and did the best they could."[2] As another journalist observed, "It was the first time in American history a war had been declared over by an anchor man."[3]

Whatever the immediate cause of his outburst, the former president was expressing the thoughts of many observers of American politics. That the media have changed American politics seems beyond question. But in what ways? On this subject there is much disagreement and perhaps misunderstanding.

In part, the popular views of the power of the mass media rest on the myth of media manipulation: that television, radio, and the print media dominate and direct the public's thinking about politics. Consequently, conservatives worry about the effects on the public of what they see as a liberal bias. On the other hand, those pursuing revolutionary goals complain that the media present an uncritical view of the capitalist system. To defend themselves, journalists often perpetuate the mirror-to-society myth, which portrays journalists as simply reflecting the world. They just cover the story. Thus Roan Conrad, political editor for NBC News, argues that "the news is what happens. . . . The news is not a reporter's perception or explanation of what happens; it is simply what happens."[4]

As you will see in this chapter, although the choice of stories does much to define public concerns, the media cannot dictate the political beliefs of the country. At the same time, journalists are not simply passive instruments through which events called news pass. Instead, the decisions they make define what the public calls news. Interestingly, the standards that journalists use to decide what is newsworthy often work to the advantage of officials and candidates who use the media to achieve policy and electoral goals.

We will begin our examination of the mass media with a brief account of how the modern press developed. Then we will look at the elements that make a story newsworthy and the individuals who decide what is news. We will conclude by examining the effect of media coverage on the public and on political leaders.

★ ★ ★

THE RISE OF THE MEDIA

Americans buy nearly 60 million newspapers and keep their television sets on an average of more than six hours each day. Simultaneously, they can choose among ten thousand or so weekly and monthly periodicals and almost nine thousand radio stations. The attentive media watcher faces an incessant flow of information on topics ranging from foreign affairs to domestic scandals. Yet it has not always been this way. A mere 150 years ago news of Washington or the state capital arrived, if at all, days, weeks, or even months after the events occurred.

"Sorry, but nobody around here reads anymore."
Drawing by Levin; © 1984 The New Yorker Magazine, Inc.

The Early Days

Before 1830, the American press consisted of specialized publications designed to reach elite audiences. Many papers were simply organs of political parties or individual candidates. Appearing once or twice a week, these partisan papers rallied the party faithful and denounced political opponents, often through vicious personal attacks. The only alternative sources of news were commercial papers, which appealed to merchants and traders. Although short on politics, the commercial papers provided extensive accounts of business activities. Covering shipping dates, commodity prices, and business transactions, rather than local news, the commercial press made no attempt to reach a wide audience.

With the publication, in 1833, of the *New York Sun,* American publishing entered the age of mass journalism. Capitalizing on technological advances that made printing relatively fast and cheap, the *Sun* was the first paper that appealed successfully to the public at large. Sold on street corners for a penny a copy, the *Sun* and its many imitators (together they became known as the penny press) cultivated readerships in the thousands. A breezy style and an emphasis on local news, especially scandalous events, ensured the papers' popularity. Each vied fiercely with the others to produce the most sensational stories. At one point the staff of the *Sun* invented a hoax about life on the moon.[5]

Toward the end of the nineteenth century, the emphasis on sensationalism became even more pronounced. Joseph Pulitzer, a crusading spirit who owned the *New York World,* and William Randolph Hearst of the *New York Journal* created yellow journalism—named for the "Yellow Kid" comic strip that appeared in the *World* and then in the *Journal.* Yellow journalism utilized large bold headlines, illustrations, cartoons, and color features to promote its tales of scandal and corruption. Not content with reporting the news, both Pulitzer and Hearst often made the news by committing the considerable resources of their papers to various political causes. For instance, Hearst is usually credited with arousing in the American public the strong anti-Spanish feelings that led to the Spanish-American war. Just before the war Hearst sent an artist to Cuba to cover the conflict between Spain and Cuba. When the artist wired that war did not seem likely, Hearst replied, "Please remain. You furnish the pictures. I will furnish the war."[6] Many people believe that he did just that.

Even as Hearst and Pulitzer inflamed public opinion with their sensational appeals, a new style of journalism was developing. A conservative paper, *The New York Times,* attacked the excesses of yellow journalism as indecent and stressed objectivity in its reporting. Newspapers, according to *Times'* owner Adolph Ochs, had the responsibility to "give news impartially, without fear or favor, regardless of any party, sect or interest involved."[7] Although its circulation was small in comparison with the yellow journalism, the *Times* became a standard by which journalism was judged, and objectivity became the goal of journalists. As any trip to the supermarket will show, however, yellow journalism did not die; it just became less prevalent.

The Broadcast Media

Even as newspapers were undergoing change, the technology of the broadcast media was being developed. The first regularly scheduled radio station, KDKA in Pittsburgh, began operation in 1920. Its owner, Westinghouse—the nation's leading manufacturer of home receivers—initially viewed it as a means of creating a market for home receivers. Entertainers like Bob "Pepsodent" Hope soon demonstrated that advertisements linked with entertainment could be immensely popular and profitable.

Although broadcasters stressed entertainment, government leaders were quick to grasp the political potential of radio. President Franklin D. Roosevelt employed the medium skillfully during the Great Depression to deliver his famous fireside chats: speaking in a warm and informal manner Roosevelt sought to reassure millions of Americans, by making his broadcasts sound like friendly discussions of the problems. Roosevelt demonstrated the vast possibilities of radio, as well as its potential for overt manipulation. During

Master of the media
On Sunday evening, March 12, 1933, millions of Americans tuned their radios to the comforting voice of President Franklin Roosevelt. In the first of many fireside chats, he restored people's faith in the nation's economic system. Roosevelt skillfully used the medium during his long tenure in office. Here he is shown in a 1938 broadcast.

the 1944 election, for instance, Roosevelt learned that his opponent, Thomas Dewey, had purchased airtime immediately following his own. Although scheduled to speak for fifteen minutes, Roosevelt stopped after fourteen minutes. Millions of puzzled listeners turned their dials away from the silence and missed Dewey's address.

Despite the interest shown by political leaders, most broadcasters resisted programming news until the fledgling CBS network entered the business. Its owner, William Paley, saw news as a cheap source of programming and a means of competing with NBC, the more established radio network. His team of journalists, including Edward R. Murrow and Eric Sevareid, quickly established a reputation for superior news coverage. Murrow's broadcasts from London during World War II captured the imagination of the entire nation; they also made Murrow a national celebrity.

Like radio, television was from the beginning a commercial venture that stressed entertainment and advertising. (It is, perhaps, appropriate that Philo T. Farnsworth, the inventor of television, used a dollar sign as his first test pattern.) Throughout the 1950s, the television networks provided one fifteen-minute news program five evenings a week. The format was expanded to thirty minutes in 1963. Even CBS, which had pioneered radio news, was reluctant to use valuable airtime for news and public affairs, preferring the popular and extraordinarily profitable quiz shows.

In 1960, however, the situation changed when all three television networks covered the debates between presidential candidates John F. Kennedy and Richard M. Nixon. Although there is still disagreement as to which candidate won, the debates definitely enhanced television's news potential. By drawing an audience of 60 million to 75 million viewers, the debates demonstrated the commercial potential of news and public affairs programming. News programs ceased to be viewed simply as a means of improving a network's public image. Instead, the networks began competing to produce the most highly rated news programs, using such advanced technology as small cameras, wireless microphones, and videotape recorders. As their coverage broadened, their audiences grew into the millions, and most Americans came to depend upon television as their prime source of news.

Diversity and Concentration

Although the media present a staggering array of choices, simply reciting the number of outlets can be deceiving. The real issue, say media critics, is the increasing concentration of ownership in a few hands—a change that threatens to limit diversity of expression. About two-fifths of all daily newspapers published in the United States belong to the twelve largest chains. The largest chain, Gannett, owns approximately seventy-five news-papers, including *USA Today*. (Gannett also owns television stations.)

In addition, although the number of newspapers has stayed the same in recent years, newspaper competition has decreased markedly. Only 2 percent of American cities have more than one newspaper,[8] and the vast majority of newspapers rely on one or both of the national wire services—Associated Press (AP) or United Press International (UPI)—for stories from outside the local area. The wire services, with reporters scattered throughout the world, transmit stories to their subscribers, who often use them word for word.

Concentrated ownership and influence are even greater in the television markets. About 85 percent of the nation's commercial television stations are affiliated with ABC, CBS, or NBC.[9] Affiliated stations contract with the networks for the right to broadcast network programs. In exchange, the network pays the affiliate a fee for each program it uses. The affiliates may refuse to broadcast certain network programs, but that is rare. On a typical day stations present from twelve to fourteen hours of network programming, including national news. In addition to affiliates, each network is allowed to own five stations. Not surprisingly, all three own stations in America's largest cities—New York, Los Angeles, and Chicago.

The increasing concentration of outlets means that decisions about the news are controlled by a powerful few, a situation that raises for many people the specter of the myth of media manipulation.

★ ★ ★
WHAT IS NEWS?

Prominently displayed on the front page of *The New York Times* is the company motto: "All the News That's Fit to Print." Admirable as this sentiment may be, it is not, nor can it be, true. Indeed, a more accurate rephrasing of the motto might be "all the news that fits." No form of mass media can carry every newsworthy event; all are constrained by costs and availability of space and time. For instance, the average daily newspaper fills approximately 62 percent of its space with advertising, leaving a mere 38 percent for news accounts, along with human interest stories, and pure entertainment features.

Network television news is even more limited. Each half-hour program contains only twenty-two and a half to twenty-three minutes of news and human interest stories. Contrary to the mirror-to-society myth, news is not simply out there; it must be picked from a multitude of happenings, only a few of which will ever be covered. What then is news? Perhaps the best explanation is "that news is what reporters, editors, and producers decide is news" (see Myth and Reality 9.1).[10]

Although the basis of news judgment often seems vague and unarticulated, Doris Graber has identified five criteria most often used in selecting stories.[11]

MYTH AND REALITY 9.1

Hard News and Television Campaign Coverage

Television news representatives often argue that their networks' coverage of political events, including presidential elections, represents hard news: the issues and substance of a political event. Indeed, for years the three major networks boasted in their advertisements of their complete and thorough coverage: "All You Need to Know," an ad for NBC News; "That's tonight's news," closing commentary for ABC; and "That's the way it is," CBS Evening News.

Networks do cover the hard news, but if you assume that it is usually the focus of campaign broadcasts, you are perpetuating a myth.

Political observers charge that network news coverage of campaigns is often superficial, focusing on the hoopla and the crowds—the "game" of the election—rather than on the issues and substance of the race. During the last ten months of the 1976 presidential campaign, the three major networks devoted only 29 percent of their coverage to the substance of the race, that is, to issues, policies, records, and endorsements. They spent 58 percent of their coverage on the game aspects of the campaign—who was winning or losing in the polls, strategy, appearances, hoopla.

One study of the 1972 presidential election offers the following network report on the Nixon campaign as showing the "lip service paid to election issues." Many believe that the charge of superficial coverage is as relevant today as it was then:

VIDEO (picture)	AUDIO (voice)
Anchorman	ANCHORMAN: President Nixon made one of his frequent campaign trips today, this time going through traditionally Republican communities in the New York area promising to do all he can to block what he called "a Congressional spending spree."
Motorcade moving through crowded streets *Crowd cheering President* *McGovern supporters and protesters picketing Nixon's appearance* *Motorcade winding its way through countryside* *Motorcade moving through business district* *People racing in and out of moving buses* *The Nixons shaking hands with crowd*	REPORTER: The Nixon campaign rolled through the wealthy northern suburbs of New York City, attacking Congress, which of course was not there, and warmly embracing the crowds which were on hand. In a written statement issued on arrival in Westchester County, the Republican candidate contended "the time has come to stand up to the big spenders in Congress." He promised to use every weapon to hold down federal spending. The economy, though, wasn't as much a focus of protest as the bombing and Vietnam war, especially among small pockets of pro-McGovern supporters along the way. The fifty-mile motorcade route wound through eleven small cities in the solid Republican county, which Nixon carried by 28,000 votes in 1968. With the Veterans Day holiday, schools out, and the route directed through the heart of business districts, the crowds were standing deep at the curbs and, at times, raced dangerously in and out among five photo trucks and seven press buses packed with newsmen trying to observe the action of the most extended day of Nixon campaigning thus far. At a couple of points the President's limousine stopped, and as he worked one side of the crowd, Mrs. Nixon worked the other.

Source: Network news report, ABC Evening News, October 23, 1972. Material reported and analyzed in T. E. Patterson and R. D. McClure, *The Unseeing Eye: The Myth of Television Power in National Elections* (New York: Putnam, 1976), pp. 36–39.

What's too personal?
Candidates' personal lives have been a hot campaign topic since the question of Gary Hart's infidelity was raised by *The Miami Herald* in spring 1987. Candidates have been asked for their medical records and FBI files as well as about their personal friends since high school. Critics wonder how much the public needs to know and whether the media has embarked on an era of voyeurism.

- To qualify as news the story must have a *high impact* on the audience, that is, the events covered must be relevant to people's lives. Events in the Middle East, for example, are news when they have a measurable effect on American hostages there or on the supply of oil at home.

- Newsworthiness is heightened by the presence of *violence, conflict, disaster, or scandal*. Violent crime, for example, was a staple of the penny press and continues to dominate contemporary news. Even nonviolent conflict makes news. Larry Speakes, former deputy press secretary to President Ronald Reagan, once noted that no one pays attention when one hundred members of Congress come out of a White House meeting and say that the president's program is great. "But if one says it stinks, that's news."

- *Familiarity* is also an element of newsworthiness. Events are more likely to be covered as news if they involve individuals that the public already knows. Approximately 85 percent of the domestic news stories covered by television and news magazines involve well-known people—mostly those holding official positions.[12] Unknown people are most newsworthy as victims of crime or natural disasters.

- *Local events* are more newsworthy than those far away. In a nation linked by instant communications, however, close to home may also include such familiar locations as Washington, D.C., and Wall Street.

- Stories must be *timely and novel* to capture the attention of the media. They must be what reporters call breaking stories, and they must also be unusual. The routine is considered unworthy of coverage even though it may have a significant impact on people's lives. As a former editor of the old *New York Sun* put it, "When a dog bites a man, that is not news, because it happens so often. But if a man bites a dog, that is news."

To this list might be added the availability of individuals for interviews. Reporters rely almost exclusively on interviewing and only occasionally on the reading of documents. The dependence on the interview results partly from the need to personalize the news—especially in television journalism, with its demand for visuals. Interviews with adversaries also increase the sense of conflict, adding a dramatic element to the story. The fact that most reporters find document analysis dull and boring also increases their dependence on interviews.[13] Whatever the cause, the result is a bias in favor of those willing and able to talk.

These criteria have little to do with the intrinsic importance of news stories and stress mainly ways of keeping the audience interested. Because media outlets make their profit from the sale of advertising, they must keep their ratings or circulations high. As you will see, this concern for audience appeal has an impact on the way politics is conducted in the United States.

★ ★ ★

WHO DECIDES WHAT IS NEWS?

If it is true "that news is what reporters, editors, and producers decide is news," then the social backgrounds and beliefs of editors, reporters, and producers should be of great interest to us.

Perhaps the most obvious characteristic of journalists is that they are overwhelmingly white males. A recent survey of more than a thousand journalists around the country found that only about five percent of the working press is black.[14] Stephen Hess notes a similar absence of black reporters and editors in the Washington press corps. Hess further argues that the hiring of black reporters and editors has been directly proportional to the extent of racial conflict in society. When civil rights demonstrations faded as a source of breaking news, so too did attention to recruiting black employees.[15]

In recent years women have gained highly visible positions, especially at the three television networks. Nevertheless, men still dominate the press corps. The gender ratio among Washington reporters is roughly four males for every female. More important, female editors and reporters tend to be employed by the less prestigious specialized publications, and those who do work for the more notable outlets are concentrated in less desirable assignments. Few women, for example, have served as foreign correspondents. Women reporters in Washington are most likely to be assigned to cover those domestic departments, like education, that supposedly deal in "women's issues."[16]

Reporters are far more likely than the general public to have completed college and to identify themselves as liberals. In a 1985 *Los Angeles Times* survey of staff members from 621 newspapers, 55 percent of the reporters and editors said they were liberals, as compared with 23 percent of the general public. Journalists' liberal values were most pronounced on social issues: affirmative action, gay rights, gun control, and abortion.[17]

What effect do these characteristics have on the news? It is difficult to draw clear conclusions. Certainly journalists—solid members of the middle and upper middle classes—tend to emphasize white middle-class values and, except when conflict emerges, generally neglect the poor and minorities. The predominance of male journalists may also explain the heavy emphasis on male sports. Nevertheless, as Doris Graber points out, journalists may simply be catering to the kinds of people advertisers most want to reach.[18]

★ ★ ★
THE EFFECTS OF THE MASS MEDIA

For many citizens, concern about media manipulation rests on the belief that the media have an extraordinary effect on public opinion. Critics of television have been particularly prone to imagine it as dictating the attitudes of a largely passive audience. Indeed, the argument goes, if the media were not influential, why would companies spend so much money on advertisements? Social scientists who have examined the issue are far less certain about the media's impact. In fact, contrary to the myth, most research suggests that the media by and large fail to change people's political beliefs.

The media's power to change political beliefs is limited because people exercise selective exposure, absorbing only information that agrees with their own existing beliefs.[19] Such information is more easily incorporated than data that contradict preconceived ideas, which may be dismissed or even entirely ignored. Existing beliefs also influence the way people interpret what they see. Thus, to supporters, a candidate's actions may demonstrate complete integrity, whereas opponents may view the same events as proof of the candidate's dishonesty.[20]

Nevertheless, the media do sway individual beliefs. In matters where a person has neither experience nor a firmly held opinion, the information and interpretation supplied by the media may shape that person's political attitude. Lacking knowledge on a particular subject, citizens often adopt the views expressed by media commentators.[21] Increasingly, the media also influence the political agenda and the conduct of politics.

Setting the Agenda

Although the media have only limited power to change people's beliefs, they influence quite strongly their audience's view of what is politically important. In deciding what to cover, journalists focus attention on some aspects of public life and ignore others. Because the media's choices usually constitute the public's only source of knowledge, what journalists do not report as news may as well not happen. As Austin Ranney suggests, the appropriate riddle for the media age may well be this: "If a tree falls in a forest but the event is not videotaped or broadcast on the nightly news, has it really happened?"[22]

When the public knows events and issues well, the press has less impact on its attitudes. For example, in a study conducted in 1981 and 1982, individuals exposed to stories alleging that the nation's defenses were weak grew more concerned about national defense. On the other hand, stories about inflation had no effect on their opinions, undoubtedly because inflation affects everyone personally.[23] Thus the media wield the most influence in shaping the public agenda when the events and issues are either outside an individual's experience or new to the society.

The Conduct of Politics

Politicians are much more attuned to the media than the public. The conduct of politics is changing in the United States as candidates and public officials increasingly tailor their activities to meet journalists' needs. Thus they plan and time speeches, rallies, and personal appearances to win maximum media coverage, especially on television. These **pseudo-events**—staged simply to produce media coverage—have become an important part of American politics. Candidates for public office, and particularly presidential candidates, plan their campaigns with the media firmly in mind (see Figure 9.1).

To ensure coverage, reporters are provided with daily schedules designed to help them anticipate stories. Major announcements are spaced during the day to allow time for filing stories. Additionally, the staging of events takes into account the special needs of television. Knowing that television producers dislike "talking heads" (scenes of the candidate simply delivering a speech), campaign organizations work hard to provide interesting and symbolic visuals for the evening news. Whether candidates visit farms to symbolize their concern for the family farmer or retirement centers to emphasize their commitment to social security, the picture is the thing.

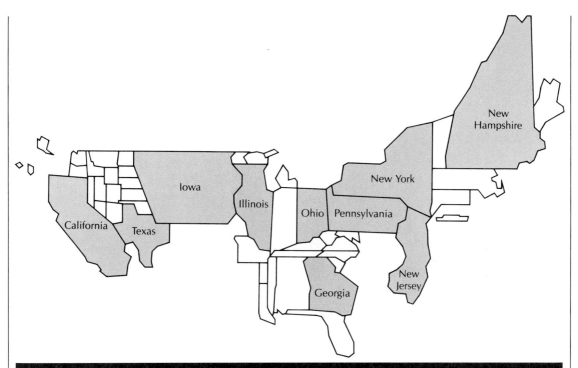

FIGURE 9.1 **The States in Proportion to Media Coverage in the 1984 Presidential Nomination**

The sequential nature of state primaries and conventions creates a chain of media events that results in more extensive coverage of earlier contests than the later ones. This map, picturing the states in proportion to their media coverage in the 1984 election, shows the importance that the media place on the early contests in Iowa and New Hampshire.

Source: W. C. Adams, "As New Hampshire Goes . . . ," in G. R. Orren and N. W. Polsby, eds., *Media and Momentum: The New Hampshire Primary and Nomination Politics* (Chatham, N.J.: Chatham House, 1987), p. 43. Used by permission.

Among the many pseudo-events of American politics, few rival the national party nominating conventions. Obviously, a convention in which the eventual choice of nominee is in doubt contains enough drama to attract widespread public attention. Since 1952, however, the parties have nominated their presidential candidates on the first ballot. To compensate for the lack of surprise, candidates and parties carefully stage their conventions, hoping to retain media attention.

The 1972 Republican convention serves as a case in point. The incumbent president, Nixon, was unopposed as nominee. To provide the missing drama, the convention managers drafted a minute-by-minute script for the convention. Speakers were instructed when to pause for spontaneous ovations. The

A monster pseudo-event Contrived news that is orchestrated for the publicity it may attract has become a feature of American political life. Here a Republican candidate for mayor of Chicago seeking news coverage rides a circus elephant.

script even noted that the secretary of the convention would be interrupted in midsentence. Nixon's nomination at precisely 10:33 P.M. was to be followed by a "ten-minute spontaneous demonstration with balloons."[24]

Despite the parties' efforts to dramatize the conventions, the television networks began in 1984 to restrict convention broadcasting to selected events. This decision has not lessened the conventions' importance to candidates, however. As Ken Reitz, manager of the Republican party's 1980 convention, said, "The whole idea is to make the event into a TV production instead of a convention. The most important thing we can get out of our convention is TV coverage."

Still, the national nominating conventions would take place with or without television coverage. Presidential debates, however, would probably not occur without it. They have become major media events, as the 1976 debates clearly demonstrated. Supposedly, the confrontation between Gerald Ford and Jimmy Carter was a news story rather than a staged event. This fiction relieved the networks of the burden of providing equal time for third party candidates. Yet when the networks lost their audio connection during the first of the debates, the proceedings stopped. The two candidates stood silently for twenty-six minutes while the networks worked to restore sound. Neither the League of Women Voters, which sponsored the debate, nor those present in the auditorium mattered nearly so much to the candidates as the millions of viewers watching at home.

Besides affecting the candidates' conduct, media-oriented politics also diverts attention from issues and toward campaign strategies. Because journalists define news as involving conflict and the unexpected, they pay special heed to the "horse-race" characteristics of elections. Media attention focuses on who is winning and why. When issues are discussed, the question is how the candidate's position will help or hurt the campaign. According to one study, the television networks devoted about nine times as many minutes to the strategic elements of the 1972 campaign as to the personal qualifications of the candidates.[25] As Graber has demonstrated, newspapers also stress campaign strategy rather than issues, but they give more coverage to the issues than does television.[26] To defend this preoccupation with strategy, journalists invoke the mirror-to-society myth, arguing that the audience prefers to hear about the campaign (see Background 9.1). Whether they are correct or not, it is also apparent that campaign strategies possess the elements necessary for news as defined by reporters, editors, and producers.

The heart of the convention The press booth has replaced the smoke-filled room as the source of convention excitement. Now that presidential candidates are no longer chosen by cigar-smoking party bosses, the big talkers at political conventions are anchormen like John Chancellor, shown at his desk high above the convention floor.

BACKGROUND 9.1

One Insider Views the Television News

How do television news producers view the role of television news reporting? Avram Westin, who was director of the 1972 campaign coverage for the ABC Evening News, states one viewpoint:

> Television is show business. Television news is part of show business. As long as show business techniques can be used to convey information without distorting it, I believe it is perfectly all right. As a "show," a television news program requires pacing and style. Pacing, in my view, means letting the audience breathe a little between periods of high and intense excitement. A vivid pictorial report of battle action should be followed by an interlude of less exciting material. . . . Pacing can be achieved in a number of ways. The length

of time on the air for [the anchorman] is one way. The length of time for the film and videotape reports is another. The frequency of switches from one man to another or from one film to another creates the sense of forward movement and pace. In my view, the audience has a very short attention span and it welcomes the change. . . . The result is that the audience never gets bored or finds its attention span taxed.

Source: Quoted in Thomas E. Patterson and Robert D. McClure, *The Unseeing Eye: The Myth of Television Power in National Elections* (New York: Putnam, 1976), pp. 84–85. Quoted from a working paper provided to one of the authors by Avram Westin, a former executive producer of ABC News.

★ ★ ★

THE UNEASY ALLIANCE BETWEEN GOVERNMENT AND MEDIA

Government officials and journalists are often portrayed as adversaries locked in combat, each trying to best the other. This is an accurate picture at times when their goals conflict—as when journalists, wanting the big scoop on governmental waste, fraud, or incompetence that will bring instant fame, confront government officials who want the press to present their actions in the most favorable light possible. At other times their goals overlap, and cooperation is the name of the game. The journalists court officials to obtain the information that is their livelihood, and government officials woo the mass media in order to build public support for their policies.

Government officials, more than the general public, are consumers of journalism, and this fact creates additional incentives for cooperation. The mass media provide an important communications link among officials, informing them of what others in and out of government are doing and saying. John Kenneth Galbraith, a former ambassador to India, described this process when he observed: "I found it easier to bring my views to bear on the President of the United States by way of *The Washington Post* and its New Delhi correspondent than by way of the State Department."[27]

Given this mutual dependence, the media and government form an uneasy alliance. Journalists report the actions of government officials, particularly the president and to a slightly lesser degree members of Congress, while government officials attempt to shape the content of news.

Covering the President

Nowhere is the uneasy alliance more clearly seen than in the coverage of the White House. Almost everything the president does becomes news. Even trivial events, such as President Carter's building of a tree house for his daughter, Amy, receive wide coverage. For presidents this extensive coverage represents a valuable means of reaching the American public on a daily basis, but it also constitutes a source of frustration. No president has ever been completely happy with media coverage. President Kennedy undoubtedly spoke for all presidents when, in response to a question concerning some particularly critical accounts of his administration, he claimed to be "reading more and enjoying it less."[28]

Because the media provide the vital link between the president and the public, and because from the president's perspective journalists cannot be counted on to get their stories right, the White House goes to great lengths to put its view across to the media. Indeed, about one-third of the high-level White House staff is directly involved in media relations.[29]

Most of the responsibility for dealing with the media falls to the president's press secretary, who provides the daily briefing to some seventy-five reporters and photographers who regularly cover the White House. Under constant pressure from editors to file stories on the president, these reporters rely extensively on the briefings and press releases provided by the press secretary. On occasion, the press secretary may also arrange interviews with the president or provide photographers with photo opportunities—a chance to take photographs of the president but not to ask questions. Most White House reporters simply repeat the information given them by the press secretary. According to Bill Moyers, former press secretary for President Johnson, the White House press corps "is more stenographic than entrepreneurial in its approach to news gathering."[30]

Press conferences. Presidents communicate directly to the public through the press conference. Although press conferences often seem spontaneous, they are in fact highly structured events that allow presidents a great deal of control. Typically, these thirty-minute affairs begin with a short statement, which enables the president to speak directly to the public. The opening statement also reduces the time available for questioning and directs much of the audience's attention to a subject of the president's choosing.

Careful preparation and rehearsal further strengthens presidential control of press conferences. Days, even weeks, before a press conference, the president's staff prepares a list of questions most likely to be asked and then provides written answers, so the president can study and rehearse them. Reagan, for instance, practices by holding mock news conferences. Furthermore, presidents can and do frequently call upon reporters known to be friendly to their administration. Such reporters are far more likely than others to ask easy questions or even ask questions that the White House has provided them. At Reagan press conferences, reporters thought to be sympathetic to the administration, called the "known friendlies," are seated in front and to the president's right. If a line of questioning becomes uncomfortable, he need only "go to the right."[31]

Even with a high level of control over what questions are asked and by whom, presidents cannot avoid embarrassing or politically charged queries. As valuable a tool as press conferences can be, they also entail risks. Few presidents are satisfied with press conferences as an institution, and most take part in them with some misgivings.

Leaks to the press.   The relationship between presidents and the media is further strained by the frequent appearance of stories based on information provided by unnamed sources. President after president has been moved to anger at the sight of such leaked stories. Reagan, for instance, dealt publicly with the problem by opening a news conference in January 1982 with these words: "I was going to have an opening statement, but I decided that what I was going to say I wanted to get a lot of attention so I'm going to wait and leak it."[32] A year later an angrier Reagan declared, "I've had it up to my keister with these leaks."[33]

Such reactions are typical of presidents when leaks divulge information they would prefer the media not know. Publicly expressed hostility by presidents should not be interpreted as a dislike of all leaks, however. Presidents most certainly object to some leaks but applaud others. In fact, it is not unusual for the president or someone acting on his instructions to be the source of many leaks. For instance, during the 1984 presidential campaign, a story that Reagan was going to meet with Soviet leaders was leaked to the press on the same day that the president's opponent, Walter Mondale, was scheduled to announce a major policy proposal. The leak upstaged Mondale's speech and allowed the president a second day of news coverage when he publicly announced his plans to meet with the Soviets.

More typically, presidents plant stories with reporters in the form of "trial balloons." A story is leaked concerning a proposal under consideration. If the public or congressional reaction is negative, the president can disclaim the story and the proposal is dropped. From this perspective then, leaks can be quite useful. Of course, since the president has no monopoly on leaks, they may also constitute a source of embarrassment and frustration.

A public conversation Congressional leaders are nearly as interesting to the press as is the president. Here former Senate Majority Leader Robert Dole of Kansas is the focus of rapt attention as he talks to President Reagan about Senate passage of a major tax reform bill.

Covering Congress

Compared with their coverage of the executive branch, the press and the media do not seem to pay much attention to Congress. This apparent imbalance is due to some extent to the nature of the institution itself. Presidential coverage deals primarily with one person. Unlike the presidency, Congress has no single leader who can be expected to speak authoritatively, although its members are generally more willing to talk and far less secretive than executive branch officials. Reporters cope with the size problem by concentrating their attention on party leaders, committee chairs, and others who hold key leadership positions or are clearly identified as experts on a particular issue. Thus many senators and representatives receive little or no national media attention. To Stephen Hess, this focus suggests that "Where You Sit Determines How Often You Will Be Photographed."[34]

Another reason for the apparent difference in coverage is that Congress is hard for the media to reach. The House of Representatives did not permit radio and television coverage even of its committee hearings until the 1974 impeachment hearings of Richard Nixon. In 1979 the House finally allowed live coverage of floor action, though with restrictions. For example, cameras must focus solely on the representative who is speaking. The Senate has allowed some committee hearings to be broadcast since the 1950s, but not until 1986 was floor action open to television coverage.

Despite these constraints, the media do not ignore Congress. In fact, Congress and the president receive about the same amount of media coverage. Reflecting the president's superior ability to provide good visual copy, television coverage slightly favors the presidency over Congress. But newspaper stories pay more attention to Congress.[35]

Covering the Courts

The least-covered branch of government is the courts. Although specific decisions of the U.S. Supreme Court may receive substantial media attention, most go unreported. When decisions are reported, the discussion is often superficial, concentrating on who won and who lost.

The complex nature of the decisions and the specialized knowledge necessary to interpret them make judicial opinions particularly subject to misinterpretation by journalists, and, in fact, justices often complain about such misinterpretation. Nevertheless, the justices remain indifferent to the needs of journalists. The justices, for instance, do not hold press conferences or grant interviews to explain their decisions. Reporters are expected to read the decisions and draw their own conclusions. Most justices accept Justice William Brennan's observation that their opinions "must stand on their own merits without embellishment or comment from the judges who write or join them."[36]

Government Regulation

The American mass media are freer of government restrictions than those of any other nation. Nevertheless, the government exercises some control, especially over radio and television. In the case of printed materials, regulation applies only to obscenity and libel, which the Supreme Court has permitted in narrowly defined circumstances (see Chapter 4, on civil liberties).

Government licensing. Because there is a limited number of frequencies over which radio and television signals can be transmitted, Congress created the Federal Communications Commission (FCC) in 1934 to monitor and regulate the use of the airwaves. Besides assigning frequencies so that stations' signals do not interfere with each other, the FCC issues licenses, which must be renewed every five years for television and every seven years for radio. According to statute, license renewals depend on "satisfactory performance" that "serve[s] the public interest, convenience, and necessity." The vagueness of this mandate gives the FCC tremendous discretion in awarding or denying license renewals, but as a matter of practice it has denied few applications and exercised little control over broadcasting content. For instance, the FCC refused to require television broadcasters to limit early evening hours to family programs.

Fairness requirements. Even though the FCC has generally refrained from regulating broadcast content, license holders are required, under specified conditions, to provide public access to the airwaves. The most controversial of these rules is the **fairness doctrine,** which states that broadcasters must provide reasonable time for reply to opposing interests in matters of controversial nature. Although it is somewhat unclear what constitutes a controversial issue, the fairness doctrine often has the effect of discouraging broadcasters from airing subjects that might require a reply.

Similarly, the FCC required broadcasters to abide by the **equal-time rule.** This provision stipulated that broadcasters who permit a candidate for political office to campaign on the station (including through paid advertisements) must allow equal time at identical rates to all other candidates for the same office. Deregulation was advanced in 1987 when the FCC, responding to congressional failure to override the president's veto of an act making the equal-time provision a statutory requirement, revoked the provision.

Recently, industry leaders and others have pushed for relaxation or elimination of the fairness doctrine and the equal-time rule. Opponents of these rules have argued that the increased competition among the numerous radio and television stations ensures access for all points of view. Indeed, critics note that electronic media are far more competitive than newspapers. Very few cities in the United States are served by more than one newspaper, but most citizens have several choices among stations, especially since the introduction of cable television. This argument for deregulation has been supported by the Reagan administration, but Congress has not significantly altered the fairness or equal-time rule.

CONCLUSION: Manipulator or Mirror?

We began this chapter by noting the general belief that the mass media have dramatically altered the conduct of American politics. But the increasingly sophisticated technology that made possible inexpensive newspapers and then the transmission of voice and images over the airwaves also changed the media. Slowly, newspapers began to emphasize objective reporting of

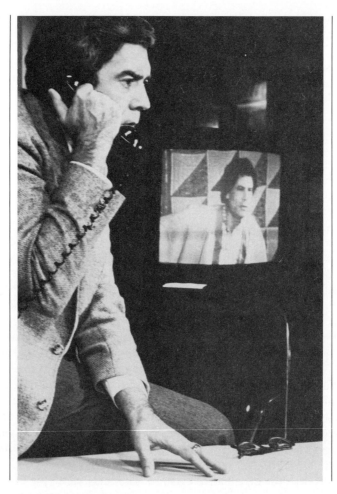

The newshound as news TV news commentators like Dan Rather (shown here talking with Libya's Colonel Moammar Gadhafi) are as celebrated as the people they cover. Sometimes their participation in news events becomes the focus of media reports and ultimately obscures the reality that gave rise to the original news story.

public events. Similarly, radio and television turned into important sources of news, but only when it became apparent that there was an audience for such programming.

Along with the development of the mass media has come the fear, expressed as the myth of the manipulative media, that Americans are in danger of being indoctrinated by journalists. Journalists, for their part, have countered with the mirror-to-society myth, according to which they reflect the world as it is. Neither of these myths quite describes the complexity of the situation. The political views of reporters are not necessarily irrelevant to the definition of the news, but by and large reporters must appeal to a wide audience.

The fears expressed as the myth of the manipulative media exaggerate the power of the mass media to alter political opinions. Citizens are not so susceptible to being told what to think as the myth suggests. Consumers of the mass media are not uncritical receptors of the media product. Nevertheless, the media do play an important role in setting the political agenda. Journalism may not change political attitudes, but it does have a significant effect on what people think is important. The story choices that journalists make in many cases define the political reality.

Furthermore, the mass media have greatly affected the conduct of political campaigns and government business. The media do not simply hold up a mirror to these processes; the reporters and cameras are not invisible observers. On the contrary, media coverage introduces distortions. But again there is little evidence that the distortions are journalistic attempts to manipulate the news. In fact, journalists often feel that they are being manipulated when political candidates and public officials attempt to get their story across to the public—and often succeed.

★ ★ ★
SUMMARY

1. Early American newspapers were either organs of the political parties or commercial papers that reported business news to merchants. True mass media did not come into being until the 1830s, with the rise of the sensationalist penny press.

2. Both radio and television began as instruments of mass entertainment, but soon started to exploit news and public affairs programming as ways of reaching millions of viewers.

3. The American mass media consist of thousands of alternative outlets. Nevertheless, critics worry that the increasingly concentrated ownership of media outlets threatens the diversity of information.

4. Journalists do not just find news; they apply identifiable criteria for selecting stories. Among the criteria are high impact, conflict, familiarity, timeliness, and novelty.

5. The journalists who report the news are mostly white, college-educated males. Despite some improvements, women and racial minorities are still underrepresented.

6. The power of the media to change public opinion is limited because many people accept only the information that confirms their previous beliefs. The less familiar the issue, the more likely are the media to have an impact on people's attitudes.

7. American political candidates orient their campaigns to ensure media exposure. Candidates often create pseudo-events solely for the purpose of attracting media attention. Journalists, in turn, are more likely to cover the horse-race elements of political campaigns than the policy issues.

8. Government officials use the media to build public support for their programs, but reporters are often viewed as adversaries that must be controlled.

9. The president is the prime focus of media coverage. Presidential administrations expend a great deal of time and effort in dealing with the media.

10. Although Congress is a more difficult institution for the media to cover, it receives about the same amount of coverage as the president. The Supreme Court is the least covered institution of American government, in part because the justices are not particularly attentive to the needs of journalists.

11. Television and radio are subjected to government regulation by the Federal Communications Commission (FCC), which has been reluctant to control the content of broadcasts.

★ ★ ★
KEY TERMS

pseudo-events

fairness doctrine

equal-time rule

★ ★ ★
SUGGESTED READINGS

- Gans, Herbert J. *Deciding What's News: A Study of CBS Evening News, NBC Nightly News, Newsweek and Time.* New York: Vantage Books, 1980. An important study of journalists that concentrates on the values and ideology prevalent in the profession.

- Graber, Doris A. *Mass Media and American Politics,* 2d ed. Washington D.C.: Congressional Quarterly Press, 1984. A wide-ranging discussion of the impact of the mass media on American politics.

- Hess, Stephen. *The Government/Press Connection: Press Officers and Their Offices,* Washington, D.C.: The Brookings Institution, 1984. An examination of the production of news about government by the government itself.

The author discusses the organization and staffing of government press offices and details how press briefings are prepared and conducted.

- Ranney, Austin. *Channels of Power: The Impact of Television on American Politics.* New York: Basic Books, 1983. An engaging exploration of the impact of television on national politics.
- Spear, Joseph C. *Presidents and the Press: The Nixon Legacy.* Cambridge, Mass.: The MIT Press, 1984. Laced with inside stories and entertaining ancedotes, this book explores the relationship between the president and the national press.

10

CHAPTER

Congress

At precisely noon Eastern Standard Time on Friday, October 17, 1986, thousands of federal workers in Washington, D.C., and across the nation walked off their jobs to begin an unscheduled long weekend. In the nation's capital, the shortened work day created a midday rush hour that strained the mass transit system. At the Washington Monument, tourists were turned away as guards closed and locked entrances to the memorial. Visitors to other attractions suddenly found them closed or operating on a limited basis. Nature tours were canceled at the national parks, and park rangers were few and far between. Citizens calling federal offices heard recorded messages informing them that the offices were closed indefinitely.

What caused this walkout? Did federal employees suddenly decide to demand higher wages or improved working conditions? Was the nation confronted with a newly militant bureaucracy demanding change? No, October 17, 1986, was simply the day the federal government ran out of money. According to statute, the new federal budget begins on October 1 of each year. (The federal government's fiscal year—that is, its budget year— runs from October 1 through September 30.) October 1, 1986, came and went without congressional passage of any of the appropriation bills needed to fund the new year's activities.

The president and Congress had tried to ward off the walkout. To keep the government operating, Congress passed and the president signed a continuing resolution—a temporary law appropriating money at the previous year's level. Unfortunately, the resolution expired before Congress could agree on the necessary appropriation bills. Congress passed two more continuing resolutions—the final one set to last only twenty-four hours. When the twenty-four hours elapsed without agreement on a bill, President Ronald Reagan issued the order to shut down all but essential federal services.

Even as the national government was closing down, the Senate was engaged in a furious debate over a final item—the funding of a training plane known as the T46. After nearly twenty-four hours of debate, the Senate reached a compromise, and the months of bargaining came to an end with the passage of a 1,200 page, $576 billion spending bill. Thus two weeks after it was scheduled to adjourn and seventeen days into the new fiscal year, Congress finally appropriated the funds needed to keep the government operating.

The funding crisis was over, or so everyone thought, when Reagan signed the massive appropriations bill. As it turned out, however, a further complication developed. The bill that the president signed had been rushed to the White House missing two pages. The two pages provided the General Services Administration with about $2.39 billion for the over four thousand buildings that it leases for government offices. And so, twelve days after the first signing, White House aides sent a complete version of the bill to Spokane,

Government shutdown
A building guard stands watch at the Federal Communications Commission on October 17, 1986—the day the government ran out of money. FCC employees were sent home at noon after the White House ordered the government shut down.

Washington, where the president was campaigning for Republican candidates. Unceremoniously, he signed the bill once again.

For many Americans, this tale of delay and confusion seems all too typical of the workings of the U.S. Congress. Indeed, the perception of congressional ineffectiveness is widespread. Television commentator David Brinkley, discussing the possibility of congressional passage of an important measure in a month, summarized what many feel when he observed: "It is widely believed in Washington that it would take Congress thirty days to make instant coffee work."[1] The image of Congress paralyzed by its own internal bickering and lack of effective leadership pervades almost all discussion of the institution. For example, when the magazine *Newsweek* asked citizens to rate eighteen institutions in terms of efficiency, they rated Congress last, well below the Postal Service. Only 8 percent of the respondents in the 1986 poll thought Congress efficient.[2]

Given this general displeasure, it is not surprising to find a rather widely held myth of congressional ineffectiveness. Whether Congress is called the "sapless" branch or the "broken" branch matters little, for both terms reflect disdain for the institution's capabilities. Members of Congress often seem to perpetuate the image when they run "for Congress by running against Congress."[3] As you will see, a narrow view of the functions of Congress, which ignores its full range of responsibilities, offers some support for the myth of congressional ineffectiveness. But the myth does an injustice not only to what Congress does, but also to what it is supposed to do.

We begin our examination of Congress by discussing who serves in it and what roads lead to a seat in the House of Representatives or in the Senate. Then we look at what Congress does, and how it is organized to fulfill its responsibilities.

★ ★ ★

WHO SERVES IN CONGRESS AND THE PATHS THAT LEAD THERE

Article I of the Constitution specifies only three criteria for membership in the U.S. Congress. Before taking office, senators must have reached the age of thirty, must have been citizens of the United States for at least nine years and must reside in the states from which they are elected. Representatives may enter office at a slightly younger age, twenty-five, and after only seven years of citizenship. Members of the House must also reside in the states from which they are chosen, but the Constitution does not require residence in the districts they represent.

Despite these rather minimal requirements, a group portrait of Congress reveals an institution composed of individuals drawn from the upper levels of American society. The typical member is a middle-aged, highly educated white male, previously employed in a high-status occupation, which earned him an income well above the national average. Congress may not be, as Mark Twain suggested, the only "distinctly native American criminal class," but it is distinctly an American elite.

Education and Occupation

As befits an elite, virtually all members of Congress hold a college degree, and a majority have completed some form of graduate work. Senators and representatives come from several different occupations, but lawyers outnumber all other professions. When the one hundredth Congress convened in 1987, 46 percent of the members were lawyers. Although the percentage is lower than it was in the 1970s, when more than half of all national legislators were lawyers, it nevertheless demonstrates that the legal profession is still a steppingstone to Congress.

Legal expertise can be useful to the members in performing their legislative duties. Just as important, however, is the fact that lawyers, unlike most other professionals, can interrupt and resume their careers at little cost. In fact,

"Listen, pal! I didn't spend seven million bucks to get here so I could yield the floor to you."

Drawing by Dana Fradon; © 1987 The New Yorker Magazine, Inc.

seeking public office—win or lose—is a form of advertising that can be professionally profitable. Next to law, business and banking are the most common occupations of legislators. Members of such occupational groups as manufacturing workers, farm laborers, and domestic servants are rarely found in Congress.

Race and Sex

In the period immediately after the Civil War, more than twenty blacks served in Congress (all of them Republicans). By the late nineteenth century, restrictions on the voting rights of blacks had eliminated their congressional representation entirely. No black Americans served in Congress from 1900 until 1928, when Oscar DePriest, a Republican from Chicago, was elected to the House of Representatives. During the next twenty-five years only three more blacks entered Congress.

In the 1970s the number of black legislators began to grow significantly, reaching an all-time high of twenty-three representatives in 1987. At present, there are no black senators. Despite recent gains, blacks account for only 4 percent of congressional membership. Furthermore, almost all the black representatives come from districts with a majority of black voters. Because only two districts with black majorities are currently represented by whites, the prospects for additional gains seem slight without substantial political change.

Faring slightly better by comparison is the Hispanic community, which had twelve representatives in the House in 1987. Though this is a threefold increase since 1980, when the House contained only four Hispanics, it still underrepresents what amounts to 5 percent of the population. As with blacks, the Hispanic minority has no senators.

The first woman to serve in Congress, Representative Jeanette Rankin, a Montana Republican, was elected in 1916, four years before the Nineteenth Amendment guaranteed women the right to vote. Although Representative Rankin was defeated in 1918 when she sought the Republican nomination for a Senate seat, she returned to Congress for one term in 1940. Since Rankin's election, slightly more than a hundred women have served in the Congress. In many cases, the women were appointed to Senate seats to fill midterm vacancies created by the death of their husbands—a practice known as the *widow's mandate*. Several of these women went on to have careers far more distinguished than those of their husbands.[4]

The use of the "widow's mandate" has declined considerably as the number of women elected on their own account has increased slightly. The fact that in 1986 women won election to twenty-three seats in the House illustrates the change. Two women serve in the Senate. Although the twenty-three women representatives constitute the highest number ever elected to the House, it is a gain of only four seats in a decade. As Eleanor Smeal of the National Organization for Women (NOW) noted, at that rate it will take women 217 years to reach equal representation in Congress.[5]

Getting Elected

Despite the myth of the ineffective Congress, the American public demonstrates considerable faith in individual members by consistently re-electing incumbents—proving, as Albert Cover put it, that "one good term deserves another."[6] From 1946 through 1986 more than 90 percent of the House incumbents who sought re-election won. In 1986 the figure was a record-breaking 98 percent.

Accompanying the extraordinary success rate of incumbents has been a trend away from close elections. House incumbents who win usually win big. In 1986, 85 percent of the House incumbents won with at least 60 percent of the vote or had no major party opposition at all. Senate incumbents do not fare quite as well. Reflecting the more competitive nature of Senate campaigns, the re-election rate of senators during the same period averaged

The incumbency advantage Incumbent members of Congress are generally successful in pursuing reelection because they work hard at maintaining a favorable impression among the constituents. Here Senator Barbara Mikulski of Maryland greets constituents from the back of an open car.

75 percent. Furthermore, senators were involved in a greater number of close elections.

Just why incumbents do so well is the subject of much speculation. One frequent explanation is that House incumbents are "safe by design," that is, they run in districts that have been drawn to maximize their voter strength. The process of designing districts does, in fact, have a major impact on political power within Congress.

Every ten years, in response to the census, House districts are redrawn by state legislatures at the same time as House seats are redistributed among the states. In drawing the new boundaries, state legislatures must create districts of approximately equal population.[7] In addition, the districts may not be designed to dilute minority voting strength.[8] However, since these requirements do not specify the shape of a district, legislatures have considerable freedom to engage in the time-honored practice of **gerrymandering**— the drawing of district boundaries in ways that gain political advantage.

The party controlling state government generally attempts to draw boundaries that maximize the number of seats it can win. It tries to concentrate opponents in the fewest possible districts and create majorities of supporters in as many districts as possible. In 1981, for instance, Indiana Republicans, who controlled the state legislature and the governor's office, produced a reapportionment plan that placed three Democratic incumbents in the same district and required all five Democratic incumbents to move their residences

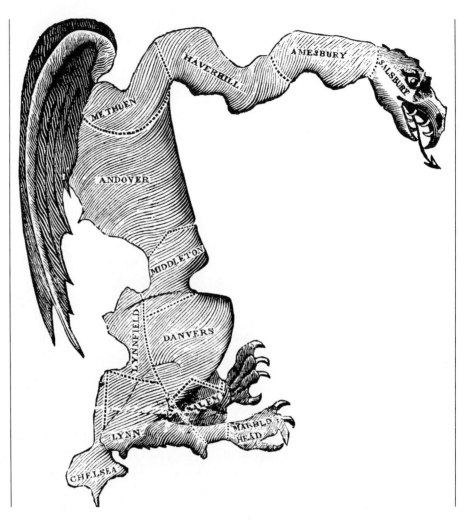

The original Gerrymander The rule in drawing gerrymandered district lines is to achieve the largest number of seats for one's own party and the smallest number of seats for the opposition. Poor Elbridge Gerry, for whom the technique is named, had nothing to do with its creation.

to have a chance of winning.[9] Clearly, some incumbents benefit from these practices, but gerrymandering alone cannot explain the increased success of incumbents.

Incumbents have been receiving larger percentages of the vote even in states that did not redistrict.[10] With or without gerrymandering, they have a variety of resources on which to draw. They find it easy to get their names before the public, and they are almost always better known and viewed more favorably than their challengers. Speaker of the House Jim Wright may have been correct when he said that outside their districts members of the House are individuals of "widespread obscurity," but within their districts they are conspicuous.[11] This visibility is the result of hard work and the skillful use of the resources of office. As one observer notes, "When we say Congressman Smith is unbeatable," we mean "Congressman Smith is unbeatable as long as he continues to do the things he is doing."[12]

Members of Congress have a wide array of official resources that can be used to pursue reelection. Incumbents can, for example, send out mail free of charge. Using this **franking privilege** for newsletters or questionnaires enables them to cultivate a favorable image among constituents. A long-distance WATS line, shared use of a completely equipped television studio, an allowance to maintain district offices, and funding sufficient to permit weekly visits to the district further help incumbents to enhance their name recognition. The dollar value of these services and privileges is conservatively estimated at more than $1 million over a two-year House term.

Sitting members of Congress also have opportunities to engage in "credit claiming"—taking credit for benefits constituents receive from the national government.[13] Whether a representative or Senator is announcing an award of federal money for a new dam, a highway extension, or an important defense contract, the effect is to portray him or her as someone working hard for the district and getting results. Legislation appropriating funds for local projects is often referred to as **pork-barrel legislation.** Securing such benefits for the districts is "bringing home the bacon."

Finally, incumbents' success depends on what Richard Fenno calls their **home style** or the way incumbents present themselves to their constituents. As Fenno says, "It is the style, not the issue content, that counts most in the reelection constituency."[14] Although incumbents may differ in the ways they present themselves, their purpose is the same: to win the voters' trust. This kind of bond does not develop overnight; it takes time and constant attention, but the rewards can be great. An incumbent trusted by the voters is relatively safe from political attack and likely to find constituents sympathetic to occasional political mistakes. In the brief time span of a campaign, challengers find it difficult to establish this kind of relationship.

Although incumbents have a strong advantage, challengers can and do defeat them, but to win they generally have to spend a great deal of money. Just how much varies from race to race. Between 1972 and 1984, however, more than $250,000 was needed to have even a one-in-four chance of defeating an incumbent representative. As we mentioned in Chapter 7, on elections, money does not buy elections, but it may buy the name recognition that is essential to competing against a well-known incumbent.[15]

No matter how well financed their campaigns, challengers face the difficult task of undermining the incumbents' support. Occasionally, a challenger may benefit from an incumbent's involvement in scandal or corruption, but in most cases the challenger needs to find some other weakness. Often incumbency itself becomes the issue. Frequently, challengers charge that the incumbent is too interested in Washington politics and neglects the district. Similarly, a challenger may successfully associate the incumbent with unpopular policies or political leaders. Noting that longevity itself "is a good reason to get rid of you," Representative Morris Udall probably expressed the feelings of many incumbents when he claimed that "Being an incumbent's not all it's cracked up to be."[16]

★ ★ ★

THE WORK OF CONGRESS

Even though the Constitution establishes a government in which three branches share power, the framers were united in the belief that the legislature should play the central role in governing. As a result, Congress is charged with several different kinds of duties. In large part, the myth of the ineffective Congress rests on a failure to understand the range of governmental functions with which it is entrusted.

Making Laws

Article I of the Constitution charges Congress with making binding laws. Additionally, Section 8 of Article I lists a series of specific powers, known as the enumerated powers—for example, the power to establish post offices, and to coin money. Section 8 also gives Congress the power "To make all laws which shall be necessary and proper for carrying into Execution the foregoing Powers, and all other Powers vested by this Constitution in the Government of the United States. . . ." This necessary and proper clause has been interpreted by the Supreme Court in such sweeping terms that Congress can legislate in nearly every aspect of American life.[17]

Taxing and Spending Powers

Foremost among the duties of Congress is the setting of taxing and spending policies for the nation. According to the Constitution, bills raising revenue (taxes) are to originate in the House, but since the Senate may amend these bills, the distinction is not particularly significant.

Tax policies—always an important issue—took on still greater prominence in 1981 as Congress, at the urging of President Reagan, passed what was at the time the largest tax cut in U.S. history. But in 1982 concern over the growing national deficit led to changes that constituted the largest peacetime tax increase in U.S. history. Congress followed these measures with the Tax Reform Act of 1986, a bill that completely overhauled the federal income tax system. Hailed by supporters, including Reagan, as promoting a fairer tax system, the bill cut individual tax rates and dramatically reduced the number of income tax brackets. Despite or because of the 1986 reforms, tax policy remains a controversial issue in Congress.

Equally controversial are the spending decisions (appropriations) made yearly by Congress and incorporated as the federal budget. Throughout most of the nation's history, Congress had no means of coordinating the federal budget. The budget was simply the total of the separate appropriations made to each department of government. Recently, however, Congress has attempted to centralize the budget process and place restraints on overall spending levels.

With the passage in 1974 of the Budget and Impoundment Control Act, Congress created a new budget committee in each house. These committees receive the president's budget and recommend to their respective houses spending ceilings for the major funding categories. As various appropriations committees of the two houses formulate the funding bills for specific departments and programs, they are expected to follow the overall spending guidelines set by the budget committees. If recommendations exceed those in the guidelines, the appropriations must be reduced or the House and Senate must agree to amend the guidelines.[18]

The act created a new sense of coherence in the budgeting process, but did not reduce the budget deficit. Then in the 1980s combinations of tax cuts and spending increases brought record deficits. In response, Congress passed, in 1985, the Gramm-Rudman Act, which set a series of deficit-reduction targets. The head of the congressional General Accounting Office, the comptroller general, was empowered to withhold funds already appropriated if Congress and the president had not enacted either spending cuts or tax increases sufficient to meet the year's target. The Supreme Court quickly ruled that the delegation of such power to the comptroller general is unconstitutional. Nevertheless, many members of Congress continue to express hope that the deficit-reduction targets can be met.

Representation

Congress is a representative assembly, but the term *representation* has several different meanings. Generally, as applied to members of Congress, representation is defined as "acting in the interests of the represented, in a manner responsive to them."[19] But even this definition leaves much in dispute.

There are two distinct points of view on how representatives can act in the interests of others. According to one view, representatives are delegates; their job is to reflect the policy preferences of their constituents, and therefore they should do what the constituents want done. The other view stresses the representative's role as a trustee: members should do what they think is in the best interests of the constituency, acting on their own opinions even if these opinions conflict with those of the constituency.

The public tends to expect representatives to conform to the first of these views. However, a major study of the House of Representatives found that the members take a relatively practical approach. Forty-six percent of those interviewed claimed that they act as either delegate or trustee depending on the situation.[20] Nevertheless, few members of Congress have been as willing to ignore their constituents' desires as was Representative Davey Crockett in 1836. When some of his constituents demanded that he not join the forces at the Alamo, Crockett supposedly wrote to them: "I am going to Texas, and you can go to Hell."[21]

Casework

Besides representing constituents on policy questions, members of Congress are expected to provide constituents with personal services, called **casework.** Senators, representatives, and their staffs spend a great deal of time and energy helping constituents through the maze of federal programs and benefits. Leaving the country and need a passport in a hurry? Contact your representative. Need help with a small business administration official who will not return your phone call? Having problems getting a Veterans Administration or social security check? Have a son or daughter in the Army who has not written home in several weeks? Call the district office of your representative or senator. Many members complain that casework reduces them to the role of an errand runner, but few refuse to do the work.

Though it may be tiresome, casework is good electoral politics. As Morris Fiorina points out "the nice thing about casework is that it is mostly profit;

Happiness is a helpful senator In this example of casework, Democratic Senator Frank Lautenberg of New Jersey (right) helped Aina Reilly leave the Soviet Union to join her American husband, Robert, one of Lautenberg's constituents.

one makes many more friends than enemies."[22] But casework is more than simply good politics. It is also a form of representation. Richard Fenno reminds us that constituents may want "good access or the assurance of good access as much as they want good policy."[23]

Congressional Oversight

The passage of a law rarely ends congressional involvement in the matter. Congress is responsible for overseeing the activities of the executive agencies charged with implementing the policy. This process of legislative oversight, which has become a crucial aspect of congressional work, takes many forms. Congress may, for instance, require executive officials to prepare periodic and detailed reports of their activities. Often, however, the oversight function is performed as part of the appropriation process. The hearings to consider agency budgets give members of both houses an opportunity to question executive officials extensively. As one member of the House Appropriations Committee remarked, "You keep asking questions just to let them know someone is watching them."[24]

More dramatically, Congress may exercise oversight by conducting committee investigations. Committees of both houses can compel testimony and evidence from government officials and private citizens for the purpose of proposing new legislation. Committees can also demand testimony and evidence when conducting hearings about specific bills. In the famous Watergate investigation, the specified purpose of the committee was to propose changes in campaign laws governing presidential elections. Although the committee proposed little new legislation, its televised hearings shed considerable light on the illegal acts and dirty tricks that occurred during the 1972 election campaign.

In the 1970s Congress increasingly relied for oversight on the **legislative veto**—a device in a bill that allowed Congress or a committee of Congress to veto the actions of an executive agency or the president in an area covered by the bill. Using the legislative veto, Congress would pass a statute granting the president or an administrative official wide discretion in formulating specific policies, but these policies would be subject to congressional approval. Thus, in the War Powers Resolution of 1973, Congress gave the president the authority to send troops into a hostile situation for sixty days. The troops must leave at the end of that period unless Congress declares war or provides specific statutory authorization.

In 1983 the Supreme Court declared the legislative veto unconstitutional.[25] Nevertheless, Congress is reluctant to give up this form of oversight. Since the language of the Supreme Court opinion is not entirely clear, Congress has continued to include the legislative veto in statutes. Whether these laws will survive court scrutiny remains to be seen.[26]

★ ★ ★
ORGANIZATION OF CONGRESS

The U.S. Congress is an example of a **bicameral** legislature: a legislature divided into two separate houses. Our Congress differs markedly from bicameral legislatures in other countries. Unlike most two-house assemblies, Congress contains bodies of near equal power. This arrangement was set up to divide power and to strike a balance between the large and small states.

Limits on Power

The Founders also designed the two houses to represent different elements in American society. The House of Representatives, with its membership based on frequent and popular elections, was to be the voice of public opinion. James Madison saw the House as "the grand repository of the democratic principles of government." In contrast, senators, originally chosen by state legislatures, were expected to curb the radical tendencies of House members. Perhaps George Washington best described the purpose of the Senate. When asked by Thomas Jefferson why the constitutional convention had agreed to the second body, Washington replied: "Why did you pour that coffee into your saucer?" "To cool it," responded Jefferson. "Even so," said Washington, "we pour legislation into the senatorial saucer to cool it."[27]

The Seventeenth Amendment, ratified in 1913, changed the mode of electing senators so that they too would be chosen by the mass electorate. Although the Founders' expectations for the two bodies may not have been completely fulfilled, the bicameral structure is still an important feature of the American legislative system. Because the two houses are nearly equal in power, public policies are the product of two distinct legislative processes, with two sets of rules, politics, and internal dynamics. These differences fragment power, and Congress has a decentralized organization. Let us examine the two different sets of processes and consider what bearing they have on congressional effectiveness.

Congressional Leadership

Although the Constitution does not mention the political parties, congressional leadership is party leadership, for the political parties organize Congress.

Leadership in the House.　The most powerful position in the lower body is that of the **speaker of the House.** The speaker is the presiding officer of the House, the leader of its majority party, and second in line, behind the vice president, to succeed the president. The only House position created by the Constitution, the speaker was supposed to be elected by the entire body but is actually chosen by a vote of the majority party.

Because the speaker serves as majority party leader and presides over the House, the position is the most powerful in Congress. Nevertheless, the speaker's power has greatly diminished from what it once was. In the early 1900s speakers dominated the business of the House. The last of the truly powerful speakers, Joseph "Uncle Joe" Cannon, assigned members of both parties to committees, appointed and removed committee chairs at will, controlled the flow of bills to the floor, and exercised complete authority to recognize members' right to speak on the floor. Cannon's almost dictatorial control of the House precipitated the 1910 "revolt against the speaker," which stripped the office of all committee assignment powers and drastically limited the power of recognition. Modern speakers have regained some power. Since 1975, for instance, Democratic speakers have chaired the party's Steering and Policy Committee, which assigns Democrats to committees.

The holder of the second-ranking party position, the **majority leader,** schedules floor action on bills and guides the party's legislative program through the House. The majority leader also works with the speaker and other party leaders to develop the legislative agenda for the party. The majority leader generally succeeds the speaker; at least this has been true of the last four Democratic speakers. Not surprisingly, the contest for majority leader in the Democratic party is often intense. The current speaker, Jim Wright of Texas, was elected majority leader in 1977, beating the last of three other candidates by a single vote.

The **minority leader** heads the opposition party in the House and represents its interests. The minority leader also consults with the speaker and the majority leader over the scheduling of bills and rules for floor action. Like their counterparts in the majority party, minority leaders are generally seasoned legislators. When Robert Michel of Illinois, minority leader in the one hundredth Congress, was first elected to that post in 1981, he had already served twenty-four years in the House. The majority and minority leaders have the assistance of the **party whips,** who support the party leaders by communicating the party positions to the membership and keeping the leaders informed of members' views.

Senate leadership. The Constitution makes the vice president of the United States president of the Senate. This is largely a ceremonial position; the Senate's presiding officer votes only to break a tie. Of greater importance are the positions of majority and minority leader. Much like their counterparts in the House, the majority and minority leaders of the Senate are expected to organize support for party initiatives. Furthermore, the majority leader is expected to manage floor activity, whereas the minority leader is expected

The ins and outs of government At this 1986 conference, Majority Leader Robert Dole of Kansas (center) and Minority Leader Robert Byrd of West Virginia confer with President Reagan. Some months later the Democrats gained control of the Senate and the two senators exchanged jobs.

to represent the "loyal opposition." The Democratic majority leader heads the party in the Senate and chairs the committees that assign members to committees and schedule floor debates. In the Republican party, these tasks are assigned to three different senators; therefore the Republican majority leader has less opportunity to exercise power. The Senate also has whips, although they have fewer responsibilities than House whips.

Party leaders in both houses struggle to bring organization to a fragmented institution. In their efforts to manage the Congress, the leaders must contend with a committee system that distributes power to many others.

★ ★ ★
THE COMMITTEE SYSTEM

Work in the modern Congress is mostly carried out in committees and subcommittees. These "little legislatures," as Woodrow Wilson referred to them, screen the thousands of bills introduced in each session and decide which should be recommended for consideration by the larger body. The few bills that the committees recommend for floor action define Congress's agenda. Bills passed over by committees rarely reach the floor.

It has not always been this way. In the early days of Congress temporary committees considered specific legislative proposals and then disbanded.[28] These committees possessed little independent power and could not withhold a bill from floor consideration. Only gradually did Congress come to rely on permanent committees.

Types of committees. The most important committees in Congress are the **standing committees**—permanently established committees that consider proposed legislation in specified policy areas and decide whether to recommend passage by the larger body. It is to the standing committees that nearly all legislation is referred. Table 10.1 lists the standing committees of the one hundredth Congress (1987–1988).

Subcommittees of the standing committees are increasingly important in the work of both the House and the Senate. Each subcommittee covers a portion of the policy area controlled by its larger committee. Each of the eight agriculture subcommittees, for example, deals with specific agricultural commodities. Having their own staff and jurisdiction, subcommittees often function as small standing committees. In fact, most decisions about proposed bills come out of subcommittees. Some parent committees routinely approve and send to the floor any proposal passed on by their subcommittees. As a result, small groups of members have great power in extremely specialized areas, which fragments the work of the larger body.

Select, or **special, committees** are temporary committees established by the House or Senate to study particular problems. For instance, in 1986 both the House and the Senate created select committees to investigate the Reagan administration's sale of arms to Iran and the diversion of funds from the sale to forces seeking the overthrow of the government of Nicaragua. In 1986 there were also four permanent **joint committees,** composed of an equal number of members from both houses. One of these was the Joint Library Committee, which oversees the activities of the Library of Congress. Finally, temporary **conference committees** are formed to reconcile differences between House and Senate versions of a bill. Sometimes called the "third house of Congress," conference committees are composed of members of both bodies. Because a bill may be sent to the president only if passed in identical form by both houses, the conference committees often take on great importance in shaping legislation.

Committee size. Questions of committee size and the numbers of Democratic and Republican members are settled by negotiations between the party leaders. Both houses can adjust the size of their committees from session to

TABLE 10.1   Standing Committees of the House and Senate, 100th Congress (1987–1988)

Almost all of these committees have subcommittees. The number of members ranges from the low teens to nearly sixty.

Committees	Number of Members	Number of Subcommittees
House		
Agriculture	43	8
Appropriations	57	13
Armed Services	51	7
Banking, Finance and Urban Affairs	50	8
Budget	35	8*
District of Columbia	11	3
Education and Labor	34	8
Energy and Commerce	42	6
Foreign Affairs	42	8
Government Operations	39	7
House Administration	19	6
Interior and Insular Affairs	37	6
Judiciary	35	7
Merchant Marine	42	6
Post Office	21	7
Public Works	50	6
Rules	13	2
Science and Technology	45	7
Small Business	44	6
Standards of Official Conduct	12	none
Veterans' Affairs	34	5
Ways and Means	36	6

session, and many committees have grown larger to satisfy congressional members seeking good assignments. Determining the ratio of majority to minority party members on each committee causes far more controversy than committee size. Generally, the allocations reflect party strength in the full House or Senate. On occasion, however, the majority party may be unwilling to accommodate the opposition. In 1981, for instance, House Democrats refused to readjust the ratio on certain key committees, despite the substantial gains made by the Republicans in the 1980 elections. Although the Democrats held only a 5-to-4 advantage in the 1981–1982 House, they insisted on a 2-to-1 ratio on the all-important Rules Committee. (As will be seen later in the chapter, no bill goes to the floor of the House without favorable action by

Committees	Number of Members	Number of Subcommittees
Senate		
Agriculture, Nutrition and Forestry	18	6
Appropriations	29	13
Armed Services	20	6
Banking, Housing and Urban Affairs	18	4
Budget	24	none
Commerce, Science and Transportation	20	8
Energy and Natural Resources	19	5
Environment and Public Works	16	5
Finance	20	7
Foreign Relations	20	7
Governmental Affairs	14	5
Judiciary	19	6
Labor and Human Resources	16	6
Rules and Administration	16	none
Small Business	18	6
Veterans' Affairs	11	none

TABLE 10.1 Standing Committees of the House and Senate (continued)

* 8 task forces.

Source: Committees and Subcommittees of the 100th Congress (A Congressional Quarterly Special Report; a supplement to *Congressional Quarterly Weekly Report,* May 5, 1987. Reprinted by permission of Congressional Quarterly, Inc.

the Rules Committee.) Fearing that such an unfavorable mix would stifle the Reagan administration's legislative program, Republicans took the matter to the House floor. Their efforts were defeated by a straight party vote, with only one Democrat defecting. The Republicans then filed suit in federal court, charging that the Democratic leadership unconstitutionally discriminated against Republicans and their constituents. The District Court for the District of Columbia dismissed the suit.[29]

Committee assignments.   The House and Senate rules specify that the full membership is responsible for electing individuals to committees. By custom, however, the parties make the assignments, and the chambers simply ratify their choices.

Because of the key role committees play in controlling the flow of bills to the floor of Congress, competition for places is often keen. Junior members struggling for a desirable assignment seek allies among the senior members, as well as among outsiders who have an interest in the committee's area.

Oversight: investigating the executive The word *oversight* can mean vigilance or an omission. In this case it means both as the House Foreign Affairs Committee asks Secretary of State George Shultz what he knew about events surrounding the Iran-contra affair.

For example, in 1981 Democratic Representative Phil Gramm enlisted the aid of fellow Texan Jim Wright (at that time majority leader) in his bid for a seat on the House Budget Committee. Wright persuaded members of the steering committee to award the seat to Gramm, though he came to regret his assistance when Gramm supported Reagan's economic policies. House Democrats pursuing a seat on the Education and Labor Committee commonly seek recommendations from organized labor.

Additionally, the members' goals play an important part in committee assignment. Legislators seeking re-election and constituency service choose committees that serve the district interests. Members who want to acquire influence in the House show a different set of committee preferences. Still others may pick committees that allow them to pursue certain policy objectives.[30]

Committee leadership. Following the principle that the parties organize Congress, chairs of committees and subcommittees are always members of the majority party in the body. Furthermore, the committee leadership reflects the **seniority system,** a tradition through which the member of the majority party with the longest continuous service on a committee automatically becomes its chair. Similarly, the most senior member of the minority party is generally the ranking minority member.

The seniority system gave extraordinary power to Democratic members from safe districts in the South, who achieved re-election easily. In the early 1970s liberals, dissatisfied with the system, altered it by requiring the election of committee chairs and ranking minority members. These changes have been more apparent than real, however, since the party caucuses have routinely voted for the members with the most seniority. In 1975 House Democrats did remove three particularly autocratic chairs, one of whom insisted upon addressing freshman members as boys and girls, but these removals have proven to be the exception.

House Democrats also limited their members to one subcommittee chair, which meant that committee chairs could no longer chair several subcommittees. In addition, House Democrats required referral of legislation to subcommittees and stripped committee chairs of the power single-handedly to appoint subcommittees.

Before the reforms of the 1970s, chairs could and often did completely dominate their committees. They could refuse to act on legislation favored by committee members; they could even refuse to convene committee meetings. More than one committee chair echoed the sentiments of House Rules Committee Chairman Philip Campbell. When attacked for blocking legislation favored by his own committee, Campbell reportedly replied: "You can go to hell. It makes no difference what a majority of you decide. If it meets with my disapproval, it shall not be done. I am the committee."[31] Such total domination is now less likely, but the committee chairs still wield considerable power. As the chair of the House Interior Committee, Morris Udall, Democrat from Arizona, said, "If you work hard, you can still win most of what you want."[32]

The Nonofficial Groups

Informal groups within Congress also help it shape its public policy goals. The modern era of nonofficial groups began in 1958 with the formation of the Democratic Study Group (DSG) to enhance the power of Democratic liberals. The DSG has its own whip system, publishes a newsletter to keep members informed, and even provides campaign and fund-raising assistance for its members.[33] Conservative Democrats have countered with the less organized Conservative Democratic Forum. Recently, the number of groups with a relatively narrow focus has increased significantly. Groups such as the Steel Caucus, the Rail Caucus, the Copper Caucus, and the Mushroom Caucus are linked to outside interests and often receive financial support from them.

Members frustrated by the decentralized nature of Congress have also joined together to pursue common goals. For many years the larger state delegations have routinely met—often at weekly breakfast sessions—to discuss legislation. These groups frequently mobilize to pursue federally funded projects for their states or favorable committee assignments for their members. A recent development is bipartisan regional delegations such as the Northeast-Midwest Economic Advancement Coalition, a sixteen-state group that works together to obtain federal money for its states.

Although the unofficial groups represent an effort to compensate for the fragmented committee system, they have actually made things worse. The effect of creating numerous unofficial groups is to increase the decentralization of the House and to increase the importance of single-issue politics. As Burdett Loomis has noted, "while members decry the increases in single-issue politics, they have only to consider their own behavior."[34] It may be that the former speaker of the House, Thomas "Tip" O'Neill, was correct when he complained that the "House has over-caucused itself."[35]

★ ★ ★
HOW A BILL BECOMES LAW

The most obvious congressional function, lawmaking, is also the function that Congress has the most difficulty performing. For those who wish to pass legislation, the congressional process is an obstacle course.[36] The maze of complex rules and multiple points of power overwhelmingly favors the opponents of legislation. Ignoring the warning of former Democratic Representative Wayne Hays from Ohio that the public should never see the making of sausages or legislation, we now will look at the making of laws. Figure 10.1 shows the process schematically.

Any member of Congress—but only members—may introduce legislation. To aid in this important task, each house has an Office of Legislative Counsel that assists in the actual drafting of legislation; members need only present their ideas to the counsel. In any case, the bills introduced may have been drafted elsewhere by constituents, interest groups, or the presidential administration.

Regardless of a proposal's source, the formal process of introduction is the same. Representatives simply drop the proposal in a box called the hopper. Senators hand the proposed law to a clerk for publication in the *Congressional Record*. Once this action is taken, the bill will be numbered (by

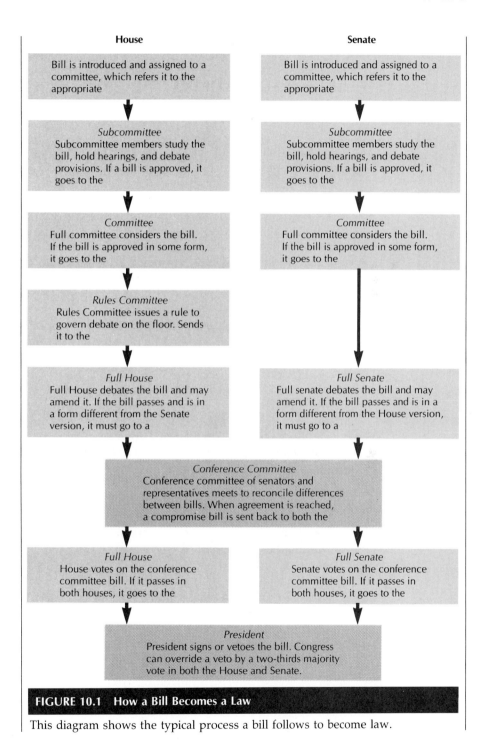

House   **Senate**

Bill is introduced and assigned to a committee, which refers it to the appropriate

Bill is introduced and assigned to a committee, which refers it to the appropriate

Subcommittee
Subcommittee members study the bill, hold hearings, and debate provisions. If a bill is approved, it goes to the

Subcommittee
Subcommittee members study the bill, hold hearings, and debate provisions. If a bill is approved, it goes to the

Committee
Full committee considers the bill. If the bill is approved in some form, it goes to the

Committee
Full committee considers the bill. If the bill is approved in some form, it goes to the

Rules Committee
Rules Committee issues a rule to govern debate on the floor. Sends it to the

Full House
Full House debates the bill and may amend it. If the bill passes and is in a form different from the Senate version, it must go to a

Full Senate
Full senate debates the bill and may amend it. If the bill passes and is in a form different from the House version, it must go to a

Conference Committee
Conference committee of senators and representatives meets to reconcile differences between bills. When agreement is reached, a compromise bill is sent back to both the

Full House
House votes on the conference committee bill. If it passes in both houses, it goes to the

Full Senate
Senate votes on the conference committee bill. If it passes in both houses, it goes to the

President
President signs or vetoes the bill. Congress can override a veto by a two-thirds majority vote in both the House and Senate.

FIGURE 10.1   How a Bill Becomes a Law

This diagram shows the typical process a bill follows to become law.

order of introduction) and sent to the Government Printing Office, which will make multiple copies for future referral. An "HR" (House of Representatives) preceding the number identifies bills introduced in the House; Senate bills are marked with an "S."

Committee Consideration

After a bill has been properly introduced, the speaker of the House or the Senate's presiding officer refers it to a committee. Because both houses have elaborate rules that restrain the leaders' choice of committee, most proposed bills automatically go to the committee that specializes in the area. On occasion, however, the presiding officer may be able to choose among rival committees. Perhaps the most notable example of the exercise of this option occurred in 1963 when the Kennedy administration's civil rights bill was referred to the Senate's Commerce Committee rather than its Judiciary Committee, with a predominantly southern membership. In the House, the bill was given to the House Judiciary Committee, whose chair strongly supported civil rights legislation. If the subject matter is broad enough, proposed bills may be referred to more than one committee.

When a bill reaches a committee, it is usually referred to the subcommittee that has jurisdiction. For the vast majority of bills, this is the final resting place. Woodrow Wilson best described the fate of bills in committee when he said: "As a rule, a bill committed [to committee] is a bill doomed. When it goes from the clerk's desk to a committee room, it crosses a parliamentary bridge of sighs and dim dungeons of silence whence it will never return."[37]

If the subcommittee chooses to hold hearings, then members of the president's administration, congressional colleagues, representatives of interest groups, and (time permitting) private citizens are invited to testify. Afterward the subcommittee meets in what is called a **markup session,** in which it votes on amendments to the bill and settles on the precise language. Sometimes this process involves a line-by-line analysis of the bill, with debate on the language or intent of virtually every sentence. In other cases, the subcommittee may substitute an entirely new version of the bill. Subsequently, most bills go to the full committee, where the process of hearings and markup may begin again or the full committee may accept the subcommittee version. The full committee may also take no action, thus killing the bill, or send the bill back to the subcommittee for further work.

If the committee orders the bill reported—that is, votes to approve it—the bill is sent for consideration to the body from which it first came. A committee report accompanies it, explaining the bill and justifying the committee action. These reports can be crucial since for some members of Congress they may be the main source of information about a bill. Senators and representatives not on the committee are unlikely to possess a great deal of expertise in the subject matter. Thus they often look to the committee reports for guidance.

Floor Action

When a committee orders a bill reported, it is placed on a calendar. What happens next is different in the House and in the Senate.[38]

The House floor. In the House, the Rules Committee determines the scheduling of controversial bills that are unlikely to receive unanimous consent from the floor or bills requiring the expenditure of public funds. This committee grants motions that specify the time allocated for debate and any limitations on amendments. In formulating the rules for a bill, the committee may conduct hearings of its own or kill the bill by doing nothing.

The actions of the Rules Committee are stated in a resolution that must be approved on the House floor before the bill can be considered. Often the battle over the resolution is the most important floor action. In 1981, for instance, a fierce struggle developed over the rule for Reagan's budget cuts. A Democratic-sponsored rule would have required the House to vote on individual spending cuts separately. Republican leaders opposed it, fearing that a majority would not vote to cut popular social programs if they were separated from the larger package. With the help of conservative Democrats, they managed to reject the resolution and substitute one that permitted the cuts to be voted up or down as a whole.

Once a rule is accepted, the House can begin debate, which is strictly limited by the rules adopted. The time allotted for debate ranges from an hour or two for a noncontroversial bill to ten hours for difficult legislation. Votes on amendments are crucial because they can alter the bill sufficiently to attract or lose supporters. Once debate is over, the full House votes on the bill and any amendments that have been attached to it.

The Senate floor. Because the Senate is a smaller body than the House, the floor procedures are considerably more casual. The Senate has no counterpart to the House Rules Committee. Bills come off the Senate's calendars when the majority leader schedules them. The Senate also allows its members to engage in unlimited debate. This privilege of unlimited debate can lead to a **filibuster**—a prolonged debate intended to prevent a vote on a bill and thus kill it. Filibusters can be broken, but only with difficulty, since the rule for **cloture**—or ending of debate—requires a vote of at least sixty senators to cut off the discussion. When it comes to the filibuster, no one has yet topped the performance of South Carolina Republican Strom Thurmond who, while leading the opposition to the 1957 Civil Rights Act, held forth for twenty-four hours and eighteen minutes. (See Background 10.1.)

BACKGROUND 10.1

The New Filibuster

The room grew quiet as the Senate's Democratic majority leader addressed the Republican minority leader: "Would the distinguished Republican leader be in a position to indicate to me as to whether or not he could give comment to proceed to the Defense Department authorization bill?" The response was brief and to the point: "I will say to the majority leader that I am not in a position to do that at this time." What might appear to most observers as a courteous, benign exchange of words was in fact the first salvo of a carefully orchestrated Republican effort to prevent the passage of a Democratic bill, sections of which the Republican president and his party strongly objected to.

A filibuster had begun. But those who had braced themselves for an old-fashioned filibuster would be disappointed. A Senate custom backed by written rules that allow individuals or groups of members an unlimited amount of time to speak before the Senate, the filibuster can prevent action on a bill. The filibuster, however, is no longer "an endurance contest, in which a senator . . . stood and read the telephone book for hours, holding the floor against" an objectionable piece of legislation. Probably no one will ever see the likes of South Carolina Senator Strom Thur-

mond's speech against a civil rights bill—a speech that lasted twenty-four hours and eighteen minutes.

Now filibusters are conducted "not so much by voice as by rules." If an individual or coalition of individuals wishes to block the actions of the Senate, an intimate knowledge of its 1,325-page manual of procedures can help the most in accomplishing the task. A bill's opponents can use multiple amendments, consecutive roll calls, and other parliamentary devices to filibuster and delay a vote. Often the very threat of such maneuvers is enough to keep a bill's sponsor from bringing it to the floor of the Senate for consideration.

Although many senators bemoan the rules that allow for parliamentary gridlock in the Senate, a strong tradition seems to guarantee little support for fundamental changes in the rules. "Senators insist that in contrast to the House of Representatives, where the majority dominates, their rules protect minority interests." As Republican Senator Alan K. Simpson of Wyoming put it, "One person can tie this place into a knot, and two can do it even more beautifully." The nature of the game may have changed, but the effect remains the same.

Conference Work

Before a bill can be sent to the president, it must be passed by both houses of Congress in identical form. Usually, this requirement poses little difficulty. If the last house to act on the bill makes only slight changes, it is generally sent back to the originating house for approval. On occasions when the two versions differ significantly, a conference committee will be appointed to work out the differences.

If the members of this committee cannot reach agreement, the legislation may die in conference. More commonly, the committee reports a compromise bill that must then be accepted by both houses. At this point so much work has gone into producing the legislation that rejection of the bill and the committee report is infrequent. The bill is then sent to the president, who either signs or vetoes it.

Masterminds of collaboration Oregon Senator Robert Packwood (left) and Illinois Representative Dan Rostenkowski (right) shepherded tax reform through their respective houses of Congress. Although the resulting bills were similar in intent, it took weeks of hard negotiation for them to get a compromise bill out of their joint conference committee.

As we noted earlier, the lawmaking process is an obstacle course studded with complex rules and multiple points of power. In fact, many of these rules reflect the original intent of the founders, which was to create a legislative system that works slowly and is not unduly influenced by the passions of minorities. As it has evolved, the system is best designed for preventing the passage of legislation, and so has reinforced the myth of an ineffective Congress. Yet Congress does make this system work, and not just in small matters. Congress is capable of initiating great changes. One has only to think of the civil rights bills of the 1960s to recognize that Congress can and does respond when a consensus forms in society.

★ ★ ★

INFLUENCES ON CONGRESSIONAL VOTING

Members of Congress cast thousands of votes every year on a staggering array of issues. Understanding how they vote and why they vote as they do has long been a preoccupation of students of Congress. This task is made difficult by the fact that each vote represents not a choice but more accurately a set of choices. As one observer notes, "The predicament of the legislator is that every vote is a dozen votes upon as many issues all wrapped together, tied in a verbal package, and given a number of this bill or that."[39] In addition, legislators are routinely asked to vote on an incredibly broad range of subjects.

Except in selecting its leaders, Congress rarely engages in straight party-line voting. Nevertheless, the party remains the single best predictor of how a member will vote. On the average, the members support party positions on better than two out of three votes. Given the extensive party organizations within Congress, this outcome is not surprising. Of course, since members of the same party are likely to attract the same kinds of supporters, they may vote alike out of loyalty to these supporters rather than to their party.

Does the constituency influence legislative decision making? The answer is difficult to determine, in part because constituents' views are not clearly expressed. When an issue arouses deep feelings, the constituency may well sway a senator's or representative's decision. In most instances, however, members of Congress receive little or no instruction from their districts. Even so, a district's majority usually exerts at least indirect influence, since most members of Congress share their constituents' views. That is why they were elected to begin with.

The threat of electoral defeat also ensures a measure of constituency influence. A single vote in Congress rarely ends a career, and a senator or representative—particularly one who has cultivated an effective home style—can now and then take a position at odds with constituents' views. But a string of such votes may well tarnish even the most polished home style and spell disaster in the next election. Hence few members of Congress frequently vote against the wishes of their districts.

Given the time restraints under which senators and representatives operate, no member can be fully informed on every issue. Therefore members turn to each other for information and guidance on how to vote. Most members develop a set of colleagues with whom they are in general agreement and who can be trusted to provide honest and knowledgeable advice. These experts are often members of the subcommittee or committee in charge of the area in question. Thus members are usually extremely well informed when they vote on the narrow range of issues with which they are familiar but heavily dependent on trusted colleagues in regard to other legislation.

CONCLUSION: Is Congress a Failed Institution?

We began this chapter by noting that Congress is generally perceived as an ineffective institution. This is not a recent perception, but rather a constant complaint. For instance, the nineteenth-century House of Representatives struck Woodrow Wilson as "a disintegrated mass of jarring elements."[40]

Yet individual members of Congress seem to be pleasing their constituents. While bemoaning the conditions of Congress in general, voters return the same members to the institution election after election. Despite the myth of an ineffective Congress, then, voters appear to be satisfied with the incumbents. This situation is not an accident. Incumbent members of Congress are safe because they work hard at carrying out their constituents' wishes, that is, they work hard at representing their constituents. In this area of activity, surely Congress cannot be deemed a failure.

Congress works slowly because it was designed that way. Its complex rules and maze of procedural hurdles were set up to frustrate immediate responses. George Washington's talk of cooling legislation in the Senate might well describe the entire process. Congress will never move quickly. No institution wedded to representing the great diversity of this nation can move quickly.

Nevertheless, Congress is capable of fomenting great change. Perhaps Republican Representative William Cohen from Maine best summed up the problem: "Congress is designed to be slow and inefficient because it represents the total diversity of this country. Yet people are accustomed to instant gratification, and when they don't get it, they have instant cynicism. I don't know if we will ever be able to measure up to public expectations."[41] The real problem with Congress may well be that in representing the multitude of constituents it mirrors the conflicts within American society. Finally, it may well be that Congress fails in comparison only to citizens' inflated view of presidential effectiveness.

★ ★ ★
SUMMARY

1. Members of Congress tend to be wealthier and better educated than the public they represent. Furthermore, Congress includes proportionately fewer minority group and women members than the general population.

2. Despite the public's seeming dissatisfaction with Congress, incumbents are greatly favored in congressional elections. Incumbents use the opportunities and resources available to them to win the voters' trust.

3. Members of Congress perform many roles. For example, Congress is responsible for creation of taxing and spending policies for the nation. The members are also expected to represent the interests of their constituents and oversee the actions of the executive branch.

4. As a bicameral institution, Congress is highly decentralized. The two houses of Congress have developed their own rules and internal dynamics.

5. The most powerful position in the House of Representatives is that of the speaker of the House. Elected by the majority party, the speaker is assisted by the majority leader and the majority party whips. Leadership of the minority party in the House falls to the minority leader and minority party whips.

6. Although the Constitution provides that the vice president shall preside over the Senate, the majority and minority party leaders are of greater importance.

7. Most of the work of Congress is done in its committees and subcommittees. The reliance on committees and subcommittees results in decision making by highly specialized members.

8. Committee leaders are generally those members of the majority party with the greatest seniority on the committee. In the 1970s Congress instituted reforms that gave the majority party the right to elect committee leaders, but the seniority rule is still strong.

9. A bill becomes law only after it has passed through a maze of complex procedures. Though they resemble an obstacle course, these rules and procedures are in keeping with the Founders' intent that Congress not act in haste.

10. Members of Congress make decisions on a broad range of issues. In so doing, they take into account the desires of party leaders and constituents. The members also accept and seek out the advice of trusted colleagues who have expertise in the subjects under consideration.

★ ★ ★
KEY TERMS

gerrymandering
franking privilege
pork-barrel legislation
home style
casework
legislative veto
bicameral
speaker of the House
majority leader
minority leader

party whips
standing committees
select, or special, committees
joint committees
conference committees
seniority system
markup session
filibuster
cloture

★ ★ ★
SUGGESTED READINGS

- Congressional Quarterly. *Origins and Development of Congress.* Washington, D.C.: Congressional Quarterly Press, 1982. A brief but comprehensive history of Congress.

- Fenno, Richard F. Jr. *Home Style: House Members in Their Districts.* Boston: Little, Brown, 1978. An important study of House members' relationship to their constituents in their districts.
- Jacobson, Gary C. *The Politics of Congressional Elections.* 2d ed. Boston: Little, Brown, 1987. A systematic account of congressional elections.
- Reid, T. R. *Congressional Odyssey: The Saga of a Senate Bill.* San Francisco: Freeman, 1980. A well-written account of how one bill became law. In following the bill from drafting to final passage the author takes the reader through the legislative maze.
- Ripley, Randall B. *Congress: Process and Policy.* New York: Norton, 1983. A textbook on Congress that provides a complete discussion of congressional elections, committees, leadership, and presidential relations.
- Smith, Steven S., and Christopher J. Deering. *Committees in Congress.* Washington, D.C.: Congressional Quarterly Press, 1984. A complete account of the structure and role of committees and subcommittees in the modern Congress. The authors pay particular attention to the reforms of the 1970s.

11

C H A P T E R

The Presidency

After concluding a brief review of some U.S. marines bound for duty in Vietnam, President Lyndon Johnson headed for a helicopter to take him away. Before the president reached the helicopter, he was intercepted by a marine officer. The officer, pointing to another helicopter, said, "That's your helicopter over there, sir." "Son," said the president, "they are all my helicopters." Although it is tempting to pass this off as an idle boast, the fact is that Johnson was expressing a general conception of the American president's power.

Presidents are set apart not only from average citizens but also from other leaders because for many citizens the president *is* American government. Of course, Congress and the Supreme Court are government too, but the White House is the focus of attention. When things go well, it is because the president is exercising leadership; when they go badly, it is because the president is weak or incapable. Somehow, if we could just get the right president—perhaps another Lincoln or a Roosevelt—all would be well. Whether called the "textbook presidency,"[1] the "imagined presidency,"[2] or the "savior" model of the presidency,[3] this view projects the myth of the all-powerful president. Its imagination fueled by legends of great presidents, the public has come to believe that all of the country's problems—social, economic, and international—can be solved by the immense power available to the president. Even presidents succumb to this myth. Jimmy Carter contended that "The President is the only person who can speak with a clear voice to the American people and set a standard of ethics and morality, excellence and greatness."[4]

In this chapter we will consider the expectations placed on presidents and the powers at their disposal. We will begin by examining the evolution of the presidency, for even though the Constitution has changed little with respect to presidential power, the modern presidency is a far different institution than it was in the nineteenth century. Next we will turn to the roles that a modern president is expected to fill and to the organization of the institutionalized presidency. Finally, we will discuss the president's need to persuade others.

★ ★ ★

THE GROWTH OF THE PRESIDENCY

On April 30, 1789, General George Washington stood before the assembled Congress in New York City's Federal Hall and repeated the oath of office administered by Robert Livingston. The oath completed, President Washington lifted the Bible to his lips as Livingston cried out, "It is done." But just what had been done must have been a mystery to all present. For none could be sure what shape the presidency would take or what influence presidents

A man of mythic proportions A host of myths surround the presidency of Abraham Lincoln. He was not alone in embracing his humble origins, however. Log cabins have figured in other political autobiographies. John Nance Garner, a two-term vice president under Franklin Roosevelt, once observed, "That log house [in which he was born] did me more good in politics than anything I ever said."

would have. Nor were these questions answered quickly. The character of the modern presidency did not develop in an instant. Rather the office evolved over the course of two centuries, and during this period the balance of power moved back and forth between the presidency and Congress.

The First Presidents

As the first president, Washington was keenly aware that he was building a new institution and that his every act created a precedent. Although he respected the need to cooperate with others, he was careful to protect the dignity and strength of the office. Once, while on a visit to Boston, Washington was informed that John Hancock, the governor of Massachusetts, was ill and would be unable to call on the president. Believing that governors should defer to the office of the president, Washington canceled his dinner engagement at the governor's mansion and proceeded to outwait Hancock. The next day an apologetic Hancock, carried by four men, appeared at Washington's door to pay his respects.

During his presidency, Washington gave a notably broad interpretation to executive power. Although he stayed aloof from congressional politics, he was quite active in formulating legislation. Using his secretary of the treasury,

Alexander Hamilton, to build congressional support, Washington successfully steered his program of economic development through Congress.

Washington also established a number of presidential roles and customs, including the practice of meeting with the heads of his executive departments as a cabinet. His response to international threats established a dominant role in foreign affairs for the presidency. Finally, by refusing to seek a third term, Washington eased fears that the presidency might become a monarchy, and in the process he created the precedent, not broken until 1940, of a two-term limit.

Washington's strength contrasts sharply with the weakness of his successor, John Adams. Although Adams was one of the great American patriots (during the American Revolution he was known as the "Atlas of Independence"), failure marked his presidency. At odds with the opposition party (the Jeffersonians) and with members of his own Federalist party, Adams lasted only one term as president. He lost his re-election bid to Thomas Jefferson.

As the leader of the Jeffersonians (the predecessors of the modern Democratic party), Jefferson advocated restrictions for the national government. Yet as president, he enlarged the powers of the office and skillfully used the political party in Congress. During his presidency, he planned his party's legislative strategy and worked diligently to elect party faithful to Congress. By these actions, he greatly enhanced the president's effectiveness as a legislative leader. Furthermore, without consulting Congress, he doubled the land mass of the United States through the Louisiana Purchase of 1803. Jefferson's immediate successors were comparatively unsuccessful at leading their party. The so-called era of good feelings (1812–1824) was a period of congressional and one-party governance.

The Jackson presidency. With the election of Andrew Jackson in 1828, the United States had its first president who was truly elected by the people. Until then state legislatures appointed most members of the Electoral College, but by 1828 only Delaware and South Carolina refused to select delegates by popular vote. At the same time, the elimination of the requirement that only property owners could vote significantly expanded the eligible electorate.

Capitalizing on his popularity, Jackson established a popular base for the presidency and strengthened the executive's role. He styled himself the only representative of all the people and appealed over the heads of congressional leaders directly to the public, which supported him in confrontations with Congress. He vetoed twelve acts of Congress, more than all his predecessors combined. More important, he claimed the right to veto legislation simply because he disagreed with Congress; previous presidents had vetoed bills only when they thought them unconstitutional. Commenting on his battles with Congress, critics complained that the presidency had become an elected monarchy. The president, claimed Daniel Webster, "carries on the government; all the rest are subcontractors."[5]

Although Jackson offered little by way of policy initiatives, he profoundly influenced the office by demonstrating that a strong and independent presidency could be founded on popular support. Few of his successors could apply the lessons, however. For the next hundred years the presidency, with a few exceptions, dwelled in obscurity.

Congress Reasserts Power

As soon as Jackson retired, Congress re-established its power over the less flamboyant Martin Van Buren (1837–1841)—a man so famous for his political evasiveness that the noun *noncommittalism* was coined to describe his usual public stance.[6] Van Buren, a Democrat, was no match for his opponents in the Whig party. The Whig theory of presidential power held that Congress is the center of government and that the president's job is simply to execute the laws.

Van Buren was not alone in his failure to maintain an independent presidency. The years from the end of Jackson's presidency to Lincoln's were marked by a string of remarkably mediocre presidents. Even their names are difficult to remember. The reputation of Millard Fillmore (1850–1853) illustrates the lack of power of these presidents; his only claim to fame, that he installed the first bathtub in the White House, is not even true. The one exception was James Polk (1845–1849), who annexed Texas through war with Mexico, and the Oregon territory by peaceful means from the British. When he left office, the nation was half again as large as when he entered.

In Abraham Lincoln (1861–1865), however, the nation found a president of immense influence. Although Lincoln was a Republican when elected president, he had earlier been elected to Congress from the Whig party. As a Whig, he had continually challenged executive authority, even attacking the war with Mexico as an unconstitutional act initiated by Polk. (Indeed Polk had provoked the Mexican army into an attack.)

On taking office, Lincoln used the powers of the presidency in new and extraordinary ways. He blockaded southern ports, called up the militia, closed opposition newspapers, ordered the arrest of suspected traitors, closed the mail to "treasonable correspondence," and issued the Emancipation Proclamation—all without prior congressional approval. Throughout the war, Lincoln did whatever he thought necessary to win. In conducting the war, he demonstrated that in times of national emergency the American presidency possessed virtually unlimited powers.

Lincoln, like Jackson, was followed by a series of weak, easily forgotten presidents—known collectively as the Bearded Presidents—who were easily dominated by Congress. So complete was congressional control that for the next forty years all important legislation, including the decision to enter the Spanish-American War (1898), was initiated in Congress.

Only the vigorous tenure of Theodore Roosevelt briefly interrupted the era of congressional government. Viewing the presidency as a "bully pulpit" from which he could educate and appeal to the American public, Roosevelt skillfully used public opinion to build support for his actions. Known for his articulation of the "stewardship theory" of presidential power, Roosevelt argued that, as the only official elected by the entire nation, the president has the duty to take whatever action was necessary so long as it was not specifically forbidden by the Constitution or law.

The Modern Presidency

Theodore Roosevelt argued for a strong presidency, but it was Franklin D. Roosevelt who infused the office with power. Confronting the Great Depression and then World War II, the second Roosevelt rallied the American people to accept his leadership and, in the process, the legitimacy of the powerful president. Immediately after his inauguration in 1933, Roosevelt called Congress into special session and in the First One Hundred Days introduced fifteen major pieces of legislation, all of which were passed by a willing Congress. (One of the most important of these, the administration's banking bill, passed in just seven hours.)

World War II helped expand Roosevelt's power still further. The mobilization effort needed to fight a total war led to such a spectacular growth in government size and authority that the federal government became involved in every aspect of life. Struggling to deal with the emergency of war, Congress willingly turned to the president for policy leadership. By the end of the war, political power had dramatically shifted from Congress to the White House, and the Whig theory of the active Congress dominating the passive president was dead. More important, the heroic image of Roosevelt rescuing the nation so changed the presidency that the nation came to expect action from its vigorous presidents as the norm. As one scholar put it, rather than being a threat to democracy, the strong executive was the "savior" of democracy.[7] The argument was simple: the more power the executive had, the more good he could do.

Ironically, the "savior" quickly turned into what a critic has called a "Frankenstein monster"[8] when Lyndon Johnson and Richard Nixon used the power of a strong executive to prosecute an increasingly unpopular war in Southeast Asia. Revelations of secret bombings of Cambodia and the Watergate scandal led to a general disenchantment with the presidency. Suddenly, presidential government seemed harmful to the republic. Many of the same scholars who had glorified the expanded presidency of Franklin D. Roosevelt began to argue that the office had grown too strong. Arthur M. Schlesinger, Jr., whose biographies of Andrew Jackson, Franklin D.

Roosevelt, and John F. Kennedy had done so much to build myths around the presidency, began to warn of the dangers of the *imperial presidency*—the increased authority and decreased accountability of the presidency in the 1960s.[9]

In the wake of these concerns, leadership passed to two successive presidents who were anything but imperial. Gerald Ford assured the nation that he was "A Ford, not a Lincoln," and Jimmy Carter, with his cardigans and blue jeans, sought to reduce the pomp surrounding the president. Failing to project an image of a strong leader, both were rejected by the voters, and presidential observers began to worry about the *tethered presidency*—a presidency too constrained to be effective.[10] Increasingly, these observers became alarmed at the inability of presidents to meet public expectations.

The election of Ronald Reagan in 1980 seemed to confirm the concerns over the tethered presidency. Elected on the promise to dismantle much of the federal government, Reagan seemed unlikely to manifest the characteristics of the strong president. His first term saw major legislative victories on tax and budget reductions, but deepening economic problems soon overshadowed these triumphs. Midway through Reagan's first term, the number of unemployed reached 11 million, and the president could command only a 37-percent approval rating in the Gallup Poll. Yet those who wrote off Reagan as another one-term president obviously misjudged the situation. Riding the wave of an economic recovery, Reagan scored a landslide victory in 1984. At the beginning of his second term, he garnered higher public opinion approval ratings than had the popular Dwight D. Eisenhower, the last president to serve two full terms.

★ ★ ★

PRESIDENTIAL ROLES

Tethered or free, presidents are central to American politics, and perhaps the strongest evidence of their importance is the variety of roles that the president is expected to play. Scholars have identified as many as forty-seven different roles, which, when combined, create the appearance of what has been called "the awesome burden" of the presidency. Indeed, as one scholar has pointed out, "All that is missing is Mover of Mountains and Raiser of the Dead."[11]

Chief of State

Presidents are not just celebrities; they are the American version of royalty.[12] Lacking a royal family, Americans look to the president to symbolize the uniqueness of their government.

A profile in courage Despite a back problem that caused him constant pain, John Kennedy was an active president who reached out to his constituents. This scene at a White House garden party was typical of the public life of presidents before Kennedy's assassination in Dallas, Texas, in November 1963.

As chiefs of state, presidents lavishly entertain foreign dignitaries and prominent Americans, throw out the first baseball of the season, review parades, issue proclamations, and carry out other ceremonial duties. To some these activities may seem a waste of valuable time, but presidents view them as enhancing prestige. Ever mindful of the value of pageantry, Washington regularly rode through the streets of Manhattan (New York then being the nation's capital) in an elaborate carriage pulled by six cream-colored horses. On the days he chose to ride horseback, he mounted a white steed draped in leopard skin and a saddlecloth bound in gold. His flair for pomp and circumstance was such that John Adams once said of Washington, "if he was not the greatest President, he was the best actor that we ever had."[13]

Chief Executive

Article II of the Constitution clearly specifies that "the executive power shall be vested in a President of the United States of America" and that the

On guard Bulletproof podiums, closed automobiles with bulletproof glass, and stringent Secret Service protection of presidents and presidential candidates is now the order of the day. Here the crowd listening to President Reagan is subject to intense scrutiny by three Secret Service agents.

president shall "take care that the laws be faithfully executed." On the surface, then, the president appears all-powerful as a chief executive. After all, no other official shares executive authority. Yet the notion that one person can manage an executive branch of some 3 million civilian employees is an illusion. Presidents quickly discover that management is considerably more difficult and time-consuming than they had imagined. Indeed, management functions often become low in priority for presidents facing more immediate and rewarding political concerns.

Powers to appoint and remove.   Given the president's role as the chief executive, it stands to reason that he would possess enormous power to staff the executive branch. Such is not the case, however. Since the vast majority of federal employees are protected by civil service (see Chapter 12, on the bureaucracy), the president has fewer than two thousand positions to fill by appointment. Moreover, many of these appointments require senatorial approval, and the Senate occasionally denies that endorsement. Reagan's nomination of Ernest Lefever as assistant secretary of state for human rights illustrates the Senate's power over appointments. Widely perceived as supporting regimes that violated human rights, Lefever met stiff opposition in the Senate, and his nomination was eventually withdrawn.

Likewise, the president has limited power to remove officials—an issue on which the Constitution is silent. The president can hire and fire agency heads and others who perform purely executive functions. Officials who perform legislative or judicial functions, however, are protected by Congress from presidential discharge, although the line between purely executive functions and those that are legislative or judicial is somewhat unclear.[14]

The president's power to pardon. The president's power to grant pardons and reprieves is one of the few executive powers that Congress may not limit. It may be used to correct what the president sees as mistaken convictions or, as Alexander Hamilton put it, to "restore the tranquility of the commonwealth." Reagan demonstrated the first of these uses of the pardoning power when, in 1981, he granted pardons to two FBI agents who had been convicted of burglarizing the homes of Americans suspected of harboring terrorists. Reagan claimed that the agents had acted in good faith, believing their actions to be legal. In contrast, after the Civil War President Andrew Johnson used the power to restore tranquillity to a divided nation by granting full amnesty to all confederate veterans, except those guilty of treason or felonies.

Executive privilege. Even though the Constitution makes no mention of this power, presidents since Washington have claimed **executive privilege**— the right to withhold information from the legislature. Justifying their claims either by the need for secrecy in foreign affairs or by the necessity of keeping advice confidential, presidents exercised the power without serious congressional challenge for almost two hundred years.

The issue came to a head, however, when the Nixon administration greatly expanded the meaning of executive privilege. As the events of Watergate began to unfold, Nixon tried to deflect inquiry by claiming that executive privilege applied to all executive officials. At one point, Nixon even claimed coverage for all who had worked for the executive branch in the past.

The Nixon version of executive privilege was challenged in court when the Watergate special prosecutor requested tape recordings of White House conversations. The president, citing executive privilege, refused to turn over the tapes, and the special prosecutor pursued the matter in federal court. In the case of *United States* v. *Nixon* (1974), the Supreme Court ruled that presidents could rightfully claim executive privilege but not when facing a criminal investigation. Thus while the Court recognized the need for executive privilege, it also set limits on this power.

Chief Diplomat

According to Article II of the Constitution, the president is authorized to make treaties with the advice and consent of the Senate; to receive foreign ambassadors and ministers; and, with the advice and consent of the Senate, to nominate and appoint ambassadors, ministers, and consuls. As chief diplomat, the president plays a leading role in shaping U.S. foreign policy, but he is seldom free to do as he wishes. Although President Harry Truman once claimed that "I make foreign policy," most presidents have found their role as chief diplomat far more constrained than it appears.

Treaties. The power to make treaties illustrates the limits of the role. A literal reading of the Constitution suggests that both the president and the Senate are to take part in all phases of the treaty process. Such was Washington's initial understanding, but he soon changed his mind. While negotiating a treaty with the Indians, Washington appeared before the Senate and requested advice on certain provisions. The Senate, however, withdrew to discuss the matter without Washington. Angered by the Senate's refusal to engage in face-to-face discussions, Washington reversed his position.

Since Washington's time, no president has appeared before the entire Senate seeking advice on treaty provisions. Nevertheless, presidents do consult prominent senators. As former Secretary of State Dean Acheson said, "anybody with any sense would consult with certainly some of the members of the ratifying body before he got himself out on the very end of a limb from which he could be sawed off."[15] At times individual senators are even included in the delegation appointed by the president to negotiate a treaty. The 1963 nuclear test-ban treaty was negotiated in the presence of a panel of senators. In contrast, President Woodrow Wilson did not include senators in the delegation to the conference that created the League of Nations at the end of World War I. Many observers believe that this oversight angered members of both his own and the opposition party and led the Senate to reject U.S. membership in the new international organization.

Consulting leading senators is imperative because every treaty must be approved by two-thirds of the Senate before it can take effect. Even if the Senate does not reject the treaty, it can modify it in ways that may not be acceptable to the president. Carter, for instance, won the necessary Senate support for his Panama Canal treaties only after agreeing to several Senate modifications that he initially opposed.

Executive agreements. To avoid the uncertainties associated with treaty ratification, presidents frequently turn to **executive agreements,** which are agreements with other nations made by the president without the Senate's consent. Such accords have all the legal force of treaties but, unlike treaties, are not binding on succeeding presidents.

Chief diplomat President Richard Nixon exchanges one of many toasts with Chinese Premier Zhou Enlai. For Nixon, the Cold War between the United States and communist nations was the central issue in foreign affairs. In February 1972 he made an historic trip to China to normalize diplomatic relations, which had been broken since shortly after World War II.

Even though the Constitution does not provide for executive agreements, presidents since Washington have used them more and more, for both trivial and important matters. Because executive agreements can be made quickly and secretly, presidents resort to them to avoid rejection by the Senate. Thus in 1905, when Senate Democrats, fearful of foreign commitments, blocked consideration of a proposal for American operation of custom houses on the Caribbean island of Santo Domingo, Theodore Roosevelt implemented the proposal as an executive agreement.[16]

More recently, Carter let it be known that he intended to convert the Second Strategic Arms Limitation Treaty (SALT II) into an executive agreement if the Senate rejected or significantly altered the accord he negotiated. In the end Carter withdrew the SALT II treaty from Senate consideration as a reaction to the Soviet Union's invasion of Afghanistan. His successor, Reagan, never resubmitted the treaty for consideration.

Legally, anything the president and Senate can do through treaty can be accomplished by executive agreement. The political reality is sometimes quite different, however, since the implementation of executive agreements often requires congressional action. A dramatic demonstration of this political reality occurred during the Vietnam War. Nixon assured President Thieu of South Vietnam that the United States would "respond with full force should the settlement (i.e., the Paris Peace Agreement) be violated by North Vietnam."[17] This secret agreement between the two presidents ultimately proved futile because Congress refused to provide the South Vietnamese with the promised assistance when, in 1975, the North Vietnamese resumed their attack on the South.

Power of recognition. As an element of their constitutional power to receive foreign ambassadors and ministers, presidents possess the power of recognition. The simple act of receiving a foreign diplomat signifies the official recognition of the sponsoring government. As one observer has noted, "Throughout the entire course of our national history the President has performed dozens of acts of recognition of new governments without consulting, or being expected to consult, Congress."[18] Thus Washington granted recognition to the new French Republic without consulting Congress. Similarly, Carter extended recognition to the People's Republic of China (Communist China) and at the same time withdrew recognition from Taiwan.

Diplomatic appointments. A final aspect of the president's role as chief diplomat is the power to make diplomatic appointments. According to Article II of the Constitution, the president "shall nominate, and by and with the advice and consent of the Senate, shall appoint ambassadors, other public ministers and consuls." By and large, the Senate automatically approves the nominees, allowing the president to fill diplomatic posts with people who share his views. On occasion, however, members of the Senate delay and even obstruct the confirmation of presidential nominees as a way of expressing displeasure with administration policy. In reaction to Nixon's efforts to normalize relations with the People's Republic of China, several senators used confirmation hearings to block the administration's initiative. Nevertheless, David Bruce and George Bush, Nixon's liaisons to Beijing, were confirmed in the end.

For most Americans, the president is the maker of foreign policy, single-handedly directing the United States in world affairs. Even presidents succumb to this view. As former Secretary of State Henry Kissinger has said, each new president enters office "not only with plans to change the world, but acting as if he created it."[19] As chief diplomat, the president is clearly the major force in shaping foreign policy, but to assume that only the president makes foreign policy is to exaggerate presidential power—and yield to the myth of the all-powerful president. Presidents may create the foreign policy initiatives to which Congress responds, but Congress is not just a powerless spectator.

Commander in Chief

Of all the president's roles, the most controversial is that of commander in chief. Under the provisions of Article II of the Constitution, the president is the "commander-in-chief of the Army and Navy of the United States, and of the Militia of the several states, when called in the actual service of the United States." The president thus is, without doubt, the supreme commander of the military forces. The Constitution, however, clearly assigns the power to declare war to Congress, and not to the president. Alexander Hamilton stressed in *Federalist* 69 this division of responsibilities when he said of the role of commander in chief, "It would amount to nothing more than the supreme command and direction of the military and naval forces, as first general and admiral of the confederacy." Thus the president was to command the troops once they were committed to battle, but Congress was to make the decision to wage war.

Although the Founders restricted the role of commander in chief, presidents have come to view this power quite expansively. In fact, presidents have regularly committed troops to action without asking Congress to formally declare war. For the most part, these actions have been small in scale, as when Jefferson sent ships against the Barbary Pirates in 1805. On other occasions, however, presidents have unilaterally embarked on major war efforts. Convinced that he possessed all the powers necessary to win the Civil War, Lincoln undertook a series of extraordinary actions that included the blockade of southern ports, the expenditure of $2 million from funds not appropriated by Congress, and the drafting of 300,000 militiamen. All of this was done without explicit statutory authorization, although later Congress did approve most of the president's actions.

In the period preceding World War II, Franklin D. Roosevelt issued several orders of doubtful constitutionality. The most famous of these was his "shoot at sight" order given to U.S. naval vessels transporting military material to Great Britain. Roosevelt's directive, issued without congressional approval, empowered the U.S. naval forces to fire at German submarines even though the United States had not yet entered the war. A formal declaration of war did not come until three months later, after the attack on Pearl Harbor.

Roosevelt's successor, Truman, went a step further in exerting presidential power when he ordered U.S. troops to repel an attack on South Korea by North Korean troops. On learning of the North Korean assault, Truman did not seek a congressional declaration of war but immediately committed thousands of American soldiers to combat in what was called a "police action." Truman moved with such haste that his order to the troops preceded both the South Korean and the United Nations requests for intervention. Although the administration later justified American actions as necessary to fulfill the U.S. commitment to the United Nations, a State Department publication of the time noted that the dispatching of military forces ̄ really based on the "traditional power of the president to use the Armed Forces of the United States without consulting Congress."[20]

Presidents have taken over the power to make war because Congress and the public have let them do so. Even though specific presidential actions have at times generated controversy, Congress has been willing to surrender its constitutional authority to the president. Not until the U.S. involvement in Vietnam divided the nation did Congress begin to reassess its own role.

Johnson's and Nixon's continuation of that war led Congress and the public to question presidential power to make war. Yet the initial commitment of American military forces to Vietnam had followed a familiar pattern of executive leadership and congressional docility.

In August 1964 Johnson reported to Congress that the USS *Maddox* had been attacked while patrolling in international waters off the coast of North Vietnam. At the president's request, Congress responded to the event by passing, with only two dissenting votes, the Gulf of Tonkin Resolution, which authorized the president "to take all necessary measures to repel any armed attack against the forces of the United States and to prevent further aggression." Thus, with little knowledge of the actual events and only nine hours of debate, Congress provided the president with a blank check to increase American involvement as he saw fit.

Nine years after the Gulf of Tonkin Resolution, Congress moved to limit the war-making powers of the president by passing the War Powers Resolution of 1973. Enacted over Nixon's veto, the War Powers Resolution provided that the president could send troops into hostile territory for a period not to exceed sixty days (Congress can provide a thirty-day extension). If within that time Congress does not approve the actions or if by resolution it votes to withdraw the troops, they must be removed. Another important provision of the resolution requires the president "in every possible instance" to consult with Congress before dispatching troops into hostile or potentially hostile situations.

Years after its enactment, the effectiveness of the War Powers Resolution remains questionable. Gerald Ford, the first president to initiate actions that could be said to fall under its provisions, refused to acknowledge the legitimacy of the resolution. In 1975 he ordered air and ground forces to rescue an American ship, the *Mayaguez,* and its crew from Cambodian communists. Ford did not consult with members of Congress before committing the troops but merely informed Congress of actions already under way.

A more serious challenge to the War Powers Resolution came in 1982, when Reagan detailed a "peace-keeping" force of marines to Lebanon. Like Ford, Reagan refused to acknowledge the validity of the resolution and therefore did not formally notify Congress of his actions. After substantial congressional protest, Reagan and congressional leaders worked out a compromise. It allowed the marines to stay in Lebanon for eighteen months on the understanding that the president would recognize the legitimacy of the resolution. Thus the usefulness of the War Powers Resolution depends less on its wording than on congressional response to presidential actions.

Chief Legislator

These days the mass media, the public, and even members of Congress look to the president as a kind of grand legislator who initiates public policy and then guides it through Congress. As soon as they take office, presidents are expected to formulate and present a well-defined legislative program that promises to solve all that ails the nation. As the chairman of the House Foreign Affairs Committee told an Eisenhower administration official in 1953, "Don't expect us to start from scratch on what you people want. That's not the way we do things here. You draft bills and we work them over."[21]

These assumptions suggest that the president possesses broad legislative powers, but such is not the case. Article II of the Constitution gives the president only four rather narrow legislative duties: (1) to "convene both Houses, or either of them" in special sessions; (2) to adjourn Congress if the two houses cannot agree on adjournment; (3) to "from time to time give Congress Information of the State of the Union;" and (4) to recommend such measures "as he shall judge necessary and expedient." Additionally, Article I arms the president with a veto.

The president no longer uses his powers to convene and adjourn Congress, owing mostly to the extended length of the legislative year. Congress was last called into special session July 26, 1948—the day turnips are planted in Missouri. President Truman barraged this so-called turnip Congress with one reform proposal after another. When, as expected, Congress failed to act, Truman had the issue for his 1948 campaign. Running against the "do-nothing, good-for-nothing" Eightieth Congress, Truman defeated his Republican opponent, Thomas E. Dewey, and scored the biggest political upset of the century.

Recommending legislation. The weak presidents of the 1800s offered Congress few specific policy proposals for fear of appearing to interfere with the legislative process. Modern presidents show no such reluctance, and this attitude certainly contributes to the myth of their unlimited power. The State of the Union message delivered each January illustrates the change in presidential dealings with Congress. During the 1800s presidents typically offered nothing more than a routine report on the work of the previous year. Today this message is a major political statement addressed to the entire nation. The president exalts the administration's achievements and presents legislative goals for the coming year. Carefully crafted to hold the attention of the radio and television audience (a detailed written report is provided a few days after the oral message), the contemporary State of the Union message gives the president an opportunity to mobilize congressional and public support.

The president presents legislative proposals in less conspicuous ways as well. Numerous statutes require the president to submit detailed reports and

Chief legislator Demands for equality by the civil rights movement found an effective champion in President Lyndon Johnson. In 1964 he used his considerable influence with the public and Congress to force a civil rights bill through Congress. Here he shakes hands and gives a pen to Martin Luther King after signing the act.

even specific legislation. Each year, for instance, the president, as directed by the Budget and Accounting Act of 1921, presents a proposed federal budget for congressional consideration. Similarly, the president annually reports on the nation's economic condition as required by the Employment Act of 1946.

As you will soon see, initiating legislation and mobilizing sufficient support to secure passage are two different things. Members of Congress expect presidential initiatives; they even demand them. That does not mean, however, that the president's program will pass. As the committee chairman quoted earlier said, "You (the administration) draft the bills and we work them over."

The veto power. Once a bill has been passed in identical form by both bodies of Congress, it goes to the White House for the president's signature. When the president views a bill as particularly significant, there may be a public signing ceremony. Lyndon Johnson, for instance, dramatized his commitment to education by signing a 1965 education bill in a one-room schoolhouse in rural Texas. A presidential signature is not necessary for a bill to become law, however. If the president fails to act within ten days of receiving the bill (Sundays excepted), the bill becomes law without presidential approval.

During the last ten days of a session, the president's failure to sign has the opposite effect: it kills the bill. The action, known as a **pocket veto,** is particularly effective because Congress, which has gone out of session, has no way to fight back. When presidents exercise their ordinary veto power by sending bills back to the originating house, their vetoes can be overridden by a vote of two-thirds of those present in both houses.

Despite the potential for a congressional override of vetoes presidents enjoy a substantial advantage. The fact of the matter is that Congress overrides few vetoes. Nixon's veto of the War Powers Resolution at the height of the Watergate scandal shows how hard it is for Congress to muster its forces for an override even when a president is in disgrace. Though the scandal seriously undermined the president's public support, the House was able to override his veto by only a four-vote margin.

Because Congress succeeds in overriding vetoes so rarely, presidents can wring concessions from it through the threat of a veto. In such instances, the House and Senate drop provisions that run counter to White House priorities and sometimes even withhold entire bills rather then face certain veto. To achieve these results, however, the president's threats must be credible. Used too frequently, the threat of a veto may lose its effectiveness and take on the appearance of a bluff.

What further weakens veto threats is the fact that presidents do not possess an **item veto:** the power to veto portions of a bill while signing the rest. Since the president must sign or veto the entire bill Congress often attaches provisions opposed by the administration to bills that the president otherwise desires—the attached provisions are known as **riders.** Thus the president must take what he objects to along with what he wants or veto the whole bill. In most cases, the president signs the bill. Occasionally, however, presidents have tried to create a kind of item veto by signing the bill but declaring portions of it unconstitutional and therefore invalid. In 1971, for instance, President Nixon signed a bill that contained a section urging the president to withdraw troops from Vietnam. On signing the bill Nixon announced that he would ignore that part of the act. The constitutionality of this practice has yet to be tested in court.

Impoundment. Presidents have also tried to create an item veto by **impounding** (withholding) funds appropriated by Congress. As far back as

Jefferson, presidents have claimed the right to impound funds either by deferring spending to some later date or by forbidding agencies to spend money. Jefferson postponed spending fifty thousand dollars on gunboats in 1803 so that he could purchase a more advanced model the following year.

Traditionally, impoundment power has been used cautiously, to avoid confrontation with Congress; in most cases the money was eventually released. Taking impoundment further than any previous president, Nixon provoked a series of confrontations with the Democratically controlled Congress. After failing to get Congress to agree to cut spending, Nixon simply impounded appropriated funds, arguing that he had a right not to spend money that he had not requested from Congress. Nixon used the technique to eliminate whole programs that he disliked. By signing the bills that created the programs but refusing to spend the money to implement them, he fashioned a veto that could not be overridden. In fact, his strategy was more than a method of controlling spending. It was a means of controlling Congress.

Congress responded by limiting the president's impoundment power. In the Budget and Impoundment Control Act of 1974, it set forty-five days as the maximum time that funds may be impounded. During that time Congress must pass a new act—a *rescission* bill (as in rescind, or repeal)—to cancel the spending, or the funds must be spent. Reagan has asked to have these limitations lifted, but Congress has ignored his request.

The Seamless Web

For the sake of easier discussion, it is useful to partition presidential responsibilities into distinct roles. Yet presidential activity is not so neatly divided. In fact, the various roles form a "seamless web" of overlapping connections in endless combinations, and doing well in one role may be essential to performing another.[22] For instance, successful performance as chief of state can often benefit a president seeking to fulfill other roles. Similarly, when diplomatic actions involve the threat or use of force, the distinction between chief diplomat and commander in chief may all but disappear.

★ ★ ★
THE INSTITUTIONAL PRESIDENCY

According to the standard organizational charts reproduced in textbooks, the president is the boss of some 3 million civilian employees—the largest administrative organization in the country. Obviously, no single person can control an organization of such size, yet that is exactly what is expected of presidents. Fortunately, they need not perform the task alone, for the modern president is surrounded, perhaps even engulfed, by layers of presidential advisers known collectively as the institutional presidency.[23] Included in this group are members of the cabinet, members of the Executive Office of the President, the White House staff, and the vice president.

The Cabinet

The original advisory group is the cabinet. Not provided for in the Constitution, the cabinet by tradition comprises the heads of the major executive departments and other officials whom the president designates. George Washington created the cabinet by meeting frequently with his attorney general and the secretaries of state, treasury, and war. (James Madison gave those meetings with Washington the title of the president's cabinet.) The modern cabinet consists of the thirteen department heads and generally the ambassador to the United Nations.

As a collective unit, the cabinet has seldom functioned as an effective advisory body for the president. Because the cabinet is not provided for in the Constitution, its role in decision making can be defined by the individual presidents, and it is the rare president who finds the cabinet useful. Many presidents have undoubtedly found themselves in the position of Lincoln when he asked his assembled cabinet for advice. As Lincoln went around the table, each member voted against the president's position. Undisturbed, Lincoln announced, "Seven nays and one aye, the ayes have it."

Most candidates for the presidency have high hopes for the cabinet and promise to revitalize it when elected. Early in the first term there is usually a great show of cabinet meetings, but the president soon grows weary of this attempt at cabinet government. Acting on his promise to create a strong cabinet, Carter held sixty such meetings during his first two years in office. By the spring of 1979 he was so disenchanted that he asked the entire cabinet to resign. (He accepted four of the resignations.)

In 1980 Reagan promised to restore cabinet government. Because Reagan attached great importance to the budget, he added the director of the Office of Management and Budget to the cabinet. Even this did not prevent the inevitable disillusionment. By the end of Reagan's first year in office, cabinet meetings had become largely ceremonial events, with policy developments coming out of the White House.

Even though collectively the cabinet does not often act as an effective advisory body to the president, its members may perform important advising functions. In any cabinet, for instance, there are likely to be individuals who are close to the president. (John F. Kennedy's reliance upon his brother Attorney General Robert Kennedy is an obvious example.) By virtue of the departments they head, members of what Thomas Cronin calls the "inner cabinet" (the secretaries of state, defense, and treasury and the attorney general) are most likely to serve as important counselors to the president.[24]

Executive Office of the President

In 1939 the President's Commission on Administrative Management reported: "The President needs help." Acting on the commission's recommendations, Franklin D. Roosevelt issued an **executive order**—a rule or regulation that has the effect of law—creating the Executive Office of the President (EOP). The EOP is not so much an office as an umbrella for a hodgepodge of organizations performing a wide variety of tasks for the president. Currently, it is composed of ten separate organizations, the most important of which are the Office of Management and Budget, the Council of Economic Advisers, and the National Security Council.

The Office of Management and Budget. The Office of Management and Budget (OMB), until 1971 known as the Bureau of the Budget, is the largest of the organizations within the Executive Office of the President. OMB's primary function is to prepare the president's budget for presentation to Congress each January. The departments and agencies of the executive branch each submit their budget requests to OMB, which screens these requests for fidelity to the president's program and impact on the economy. Since no agency can request appropriations from Congress without clearance from OMB, the director of the office, who is appointed by the president with senatorial confirmation, serves as an important means of controlling the budget and making policy through budgetary power.

In addition to its budgetary responsibilities, OMB routinely reviews all legislation proposed by the executive departments and agencies to make sure that the proposals are consistent with the president's program.[25] Agencies proposing laws and regulations with projected costs of $100 million or more must justify the expense. OMB cannot reject the proposal on the basis of such a cost-benefit analysis, but it can recommend that the president do so. Occasionally, OMB even conducts cost-benefit analyses on its own. Although these procedures help evaluate the effectiveness of new programs and regulations, they heighten tension between the departments and the Executive Office of the President.

The Council of Economic Advisers. Legislated into existence by the Employment Act of 1947, the Council of Economic Advisers consists of three members, generally professional economists, appointed by the president with senatorial confirmation. Its small but highly competent staff advises the president on the full range of economic issues: unemployment, inflation, taxes, federal spending levels, and the value of the dollar abroad. The council also prepares an annual report that contains analyses of current economic data and economic forecasts. Given its wide-ranging responsibilities, the council often finds itself competing for influence in economic policy making with the director of the Office of Management and Budget, the chairman of the Federal Reserve Board, and the secretaries of treasury, commerce, and labor.

National Security Council. Created by the National Security Act of 1947, the National Security Council (NSC) advises the president on foreign and defense policy. By statute, the NSC consists of the president, the vice president, and the secretaries of state and defense. In addition, the heads of the Central Intelligence Agency and the Joint Chiefs of Staff are statutory advisers. The president may also request the attendance of other officials.

The role of the NSC depends greatly on the president's preference. Eisenhower met weekly with the council, but succeeding presidents have preferred to rely on informal groups of advisers and the special assistant for national security affairs. Originally, the job of special assistant for national security affairs was little more than the secretary of the NSC, but President Kennedy placed greater authority in the special assistant. President Nixon's special assistant, Henry Kissinger, rivaled the secretary of state in power. Using an enlarged staff and his considerable political skills, Kissinger soon eclipsed Nixon's secretary of state, William P. Rogers, as foreign policy adviser to the president. Ultimately, Rogers resigned, and Kissinger took on both jobs.

During Reagan's second term, the National Security Council became the subject of controversy over its direction of undercover operations in Iran and Nicaragua. In an effort to secure the release of Americans held hostage in

Controversial council
The Iran-contra affair has focused attention on the National Security Council. Here President Reagan meets with NSC members in the office of National Security Adviser Frank Carlucci (seated at Reagan's left next to White House Chief of Staff Howard Baker).

the Middle East, NSC employees arranged for the sale of weapons to Iran. Profits from these sales were then diverted to Contra rebels attempting to overthrow the government of Nicaragua, despite a congressional ban on such aid. In this instance, rather than serving as an advisory body, the NSC took on the role of policy implementation.

The White House Office

Technically, the White House Office is part of the Executive Office of the President, but in an important sense the two organizations are separate. The White House Office is composed of staff members who are located in the White House and serve the president's personal needs. Smaller than the Executive Office of the President, the White House Office is nevertheless a sizable organization in its own right—for example, Carter's employed over five hundred people. It includes assistants, special assistants, counselors, special counselors, and consultants of varying titles who perform a wide range of personal and political services for the president.

The actual structure of the office depends on the president's organizational preferences. Some presidents have favored a rather loose structure in which several aides report directly to the president. Sometimes referred to as the "wheel," this highly personalized approach is designed to assure the president access to information. The best-known exponent of this organizational style was Franklin D. Roosevelt, who often assigned the same task to different aides. The fierce competition among his aides, each wanting recognition from the boss, maximized the information available to the president and allowed him to extend his influence.

Although valuable as a means of gaining information, the wheel may create confusion and conflict among staff members, creating the impression that the president cannot manage his own office. Carter's early efforts to implement the wheel style of organization led to public battles among his aides and contributed to his image as an ineffectual leader. On the other hand, Reagan's use, in his first term, of a modified version of the wheel style proved generally successful.

Some presidents have favored a tight structure, with staff responsibilities and reporting procedures clearly detailed. Under this organizational style, which resembles a pyramid, only one or two key aides have access to the president. Eisenhower, with his military background, clearly preferred this type of arrangement, delegating much authority to his chief aide, Sherman Adams. Nothing could come to the president unless it was initialed by Adams. Carrying the pyramid style a step further, Nixon used his chief of staff, H.R. "Bob" Haldeman, and his domestic adviser, John Ehrlichman, to seal him off from the rest of government. Haldeman had such tight control over the president's daily schedule that not even members of the president's family could see him without getting Haldeman's permission.

Pyramid structures can reduce the president's burden, allowing concentration on those issues that truly require a president's time. But the relief may come at some cost. Staff members may limit their communications to what the president wants to hear, cutting off dissenting viewpoints. The aides may make important decisions before the questions reach the president. As two critics have put it, "presidential assistants can become assistant presidents."[26]

Reagan's second term was marked by staffing problems that came to light during the investigation of the sale of arms to Iran and the funding of the Contras. He had reorganized his staff, shifting from the wheel to a pyramid style of management. As details of the scandal came to light, his chief of staff, Donald Regan, was forced to resign, with the president claiming not to know what his staff was doing.

The Vice President

Benjamin Franklin once suggested that the vice president be called "His Superfluous Majesty." Daniel Webster, saying that "he did not propose to be buried until he was already dead," refused to accept nomination for the office.[27] Despite the fact that thirteen vice presidents have become presidents, esteem for the office has never been high. The reason rests with the Constitution: it provides the vice president with little to do. The vice president's only constitutionally prescribed task—the presidency of the Senate—offers little real power, except to cast a tie-breaking vote. The vice president has no role in the day-to-day business of that body.

The vice president does, of course, become the president if the president dies in office, resigns, or is impeached and removed from office (see Myth and Reality 11.1). Furthermore, with the passage of the Twenty-fifth Amendment, the vice president can assume the presidency if the president decides that he is disabled, or if the vice president and a majority of the cabinet declare the president disabled. For instance, Reagan, before undergoing cancer surgery, wrote a letter empowering Vice President George Bush to act as president while Reagan was under the anesthetic.

Because the Constitution is silent on the subject, a vice president's duties are determined by the president. Typically, presidents send their vice presidents to advisory panels and ceremonial functions that they want to avoid. Perhaps the most striking example of distant relationship between a president and a vice president was provided by Franklin D. Roosevelt. Although it was known for months that the president was dying, no one informed Vice President Truman of the existence of the atomic bomb. Truman was not briefed on the bomb until after he became president, a mere four months before he made the decision to use it.

In part, presidents have been reluctant to delegate too much to their vice presidents for fear of creating a political rival. Since vice presidential candidates

MYTH AND REALITY 11.1

The Vice Presidency and Presidential Succession

No other office is as close to or as far away from the seat of political power in this nation as the vice presidency. Woodrow Wilson's vice president, Thomas R. Marshall, used to tell the story of two brothers: "one went to sea while the other was elected vice president . . . nothing ever heard of either again." Indeed, the vice president's only constitutional power is that of casting a ballot to break a tie vote in the Senate.

Most people believe that the framers invented the position to provide for the succession in case of death, resignation, or incapacitation of the president. But in fact, originally they had a different solution in mind. Their initial plans did not include a vice president. One draft of the Constitution, written on August 7, 1787, recommended that if the presidency should become vacant "the President of the Senate [no mention is made of a vice president] shall exercise those powers and duties, until another president of the United States shall be chosen."

A number of delegates to the Constitutional Convention objected even to the provisional appointment of the Senate president. Gouverneur Morris wanted the chief justice of the Supreme Court to take over the reins of power, while James Madison preferred that the vacancy be administered by a Council of State. One authority on presidential succession argues that

the framers never intended any officer "to become President by succession," but to serve only temporarily, "until a President should be supplied by special election."

The idea of a vice presidency surfaced two weeks before the convention adjourned, and then not for purposes of succession but as the solution to an electoral problem. To ensure that an individual with national appeal would gain the presidency, presidential electors would vote for two candidates—one of whom could not be from the individual's own state. This method would defeat the natural tendency of electors to vote for a local favorite. Under this system, "the person winning the most votes became President, the runner-up Vice President."

Thus the framers' chief aim was not to create a mode of succession but rather to develop a method of electing a president acceptable to a majority of the electors. Not until 1792 did Congress pass the Presidential Succession Act, which specified that the vice president would act as president if the president died or resigned from office.

Material and quotes for this box are adapted from Arthur M. Schlesinger, Jr., *The Cycles of American History* (Boston: Houghton Mifflin, 1986), ch. 12.

are most often chosen to add to the ticket political supporters that the presidential candidate needs, they constitute a potential competitor for the limelight. The vice president is also a constant reminder of the president's own mortality. Indeed, Lyndon Johnson likened the vice president to "a raven hovering around the head of the president."[28]

Recently, however, presidents have delegated more responsibilities to their vice presidents. Carter provided a greatly expanded role for Walter Mondale by allowing him to influence the selection of several high officials in the administration. Mondale also took a leading role in the development of domestic policy. In the Reagan administration, George Bush has also seemingly benefited from an expanded view of the office. Reagan placed Bush in charge of two important presidential committees: the president's Task Force on Regulatory Relief (the commission designed to eliminate unnecessary government regulation) and the National Security Council's crisis management team. Whether these two examples represent a trend toward expanding responsibilities for vice presidents or are simply exceptions remains to be seen.

★ ★ ★
PRESIDENTIAL INFLUENCE

To those outside the office, the myth of the all-powerful president seems compelling. Yet presidents are most likely to stress the frustrations of holding office. Truman, for instance, describing what it was going to be like for his successor, Eisenhower, said: "He'll sit here, and he'll say, Do this! Do that! And nothing will happen. Poor Ike—it won't be a bit like the army."[29] Similarly, Lyndon Johnson once complained that the only power he had was nuclear, and he could not use it.

The point of these remarks is that presidential desires are not automatically translated into government policy. As frustrating as it may be, power is shared in the American system. Congress, with its different constituency interests, often checks presidential initiatives. The bureaucracy seems to have endless opportunities to circumvent presidential directives. According to political scientist and former presidential adviser Richard Neustadt, if a president is to be effective, he must become adept at persuasion, convincing others that what the president wants of them is in their own interests.[30]

Persuading Congress

Perhaps the greatest and most persistent problem facing any president is working with Congress. According to Lyndon Johnson, "There is only one way for a President to deal with Congress, and that is continuously, incessantly, and without interruption. If it's really going to work, the relationship between the president and Congress has got to be almost incestuous."[31] As you may recall from Chapter 10, on Congress, presidential initiatives are only a starting point for congressional action. Obtaining congressional support is crucial. In pursuing this goal, presidents have three primary resources: party loyalty, staff lobbyists, and personal appeal.

Party loyalty. At the heart of a successful strategy for dealing with Congress is the political party. Presidents must retain the support of members in their own party, while gaining the support of as many of the opposition

One-term president
Media pundits were asking whether Jimmy Carter could be re-elected president less than a year after he took office, even though he demon-strated a commanding grasp of the issues fac-ing the president. His apparent vulnerability stemmed from poor re-lations with Congress. Although his batting av-erage with Congress was no worse than Lyn-don Johnson's, it took him much longer to get key proposals passed.

party as possible. As Figure 11.1 demonstrates, party loyalty is fairly strong in the Republican party, and less so among Democratic members of Congress. Clearly, presidents cannot take their own partisans for granted. There is considerable defection from the president's position by fellow party members. Having a majority of seats in Congress is no guarantee of an administration's success, but it is easier than dealing with a Congress controlled by the opposition party.

Lobbying staff.   Before 1953 contacts between the president and Congress were informal and largely based on personal relationships. Some presidents relied on frequent social occasions to discuss their concerns with members of Congress. Jefferson used this tactic with particular success. His elaborate dinner parties were planned as much for their lively talk as for the superb cuisine. In 1953, however, Eisenhower created the Office of Congressional Relations (OCR) to formalize the administration's lobbying efforts. (The OCR did not, of course, replace the social occasions; rather, it provided the president with a structure to coordinate lobbying activities.)

Since Eisenhower offered few major legislative proposals, the office was small and mostly concerned with heading off the passage of legislation that Eisenhower opposed. During the Kennedy and Johnson years, however, the office began to grow substantially as these administrations took a more aggressive legislative posture. Johnson, in particular, used the office to inform

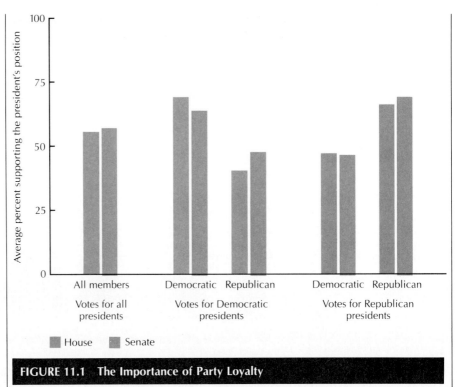

FIGURE 11.1 The Importance of Party Loyalty

These data from *Congressional Quarterly* for the period 1953–1985 show the percentage of time that members of Congress supported the president on roll call votes. Not surprisingly, members tend to side with presidents of their own party.

members of Congress of the administration's position on issues and to solicit congressional support. More importantly, Johnson expanded the role of the office by instructing the administration's lobbyists to help members of Congress with personal service for constituents.

Although talented lobbyists can be quite effective in persuading members of Congress to support administration proposals, they must have presidential involvement in order to succeed. According to Bryce Harlow, legislative liaison chief under both Eisenhower and Nixon, "for real effectiveness a White House congressional man must be known on Capitol Hill as a confidant of the president; he must be in the know."[32] As if to underscore the point, Harlow resigned as Nixon's liaison chief because he lacked the necessary access to the president.

During Carter's first year as president, his Office of Congressional Relations was notorious for virtually ignoring Congress. Complaints of phone calls not returned and a staff of inexperienced aides aggravated tensions between the White House and Congress. Much was made of the fact that Carter's chief liaison officer, Frank Moore, had no Washington experience, but the real problem was that Carter paid little attention to Congress. Congressional relations were not a high priority of the early Carter administration.

Personal appeals. A president's ability to appeal personally to members of Congress can be vital to his success. A little flattery and attention from a president can go a long way in persuading members of Congress. Reagan used this personal approach to great advantage, offering frequent invitations to breakfast at the White House and the gift of cuff links bearing the presidential seal in his persistent effort to cultivate relations with Congress. On important bills the president often made phone calls to wavering members, personally soliciting their support.

Public Opinion

Lincoln once said, "Public sentiment is everything. With public sentiment nothing can fail, without it nothing can succeed." As a tool of persuasion, nothing serves the president quite as well as popularity. One political scientist has argued that members of Congress try to predict the public's reaction to their behavior toward the president and often decide on that basis what tack they should take.[33] Lacking precise information about public attitudes, they look to the president's popularity as a guide. Whether they wish to serve the will of their constituents or merely to assure their own re-election, they are reluctant to defy a popular president. Popularity does not guarantee presidential success, but it does provide leeway in dealing with others.[34]

Naturally, presidents are well aware of the importance of public popularity. (When the polls were good, Lyndon Johnson used to carry the results in his breast pocket, ready to be shown to anyone who needed convincing.) Recent presidents have increasingly tried to translate their popularity into political strength by taking their policy proposals directly to the public. Many of Reagan's early successes in cutting the budget were attributed to his skillful use of this strategy. His televised appeals to the nation for help in cutting taxes put pressure on Congress to act.[35]

As a method of influence, going public has its drawbacks, however. First of all, there is always the danger of overuse. A president who calls for public response too many times may find the audience losing interest. More fundamentally, the effectiveness of public appeals depends on the president's general popularity, and presidential popularity tends to decline during the term of office. In fact, no post–World War II president has left office with a level of popularity as high as when he entered.

At the beginning of their term, presidents traditionally enjoy a honeymoon period of broad public support and favorable media coverage. By the third year in office, however, public approval declines substantially. Carter went from an initial approval rating of 63 percent to a low of 38 percent in his third year. Reagan had similar problems, dropping from 58 percent to 37 percent at the beginning of his third year. Consequently, the president must go public while public approval is still high. As Reagan aide Edwin Meese put it, presidents must "hit the ground running."

The decline in public approval of presidents has been so substantial that no president since Lyndon Johnson has left the office with a majority of the population applauding his performance. Although Reagan began his first term with lower public approval ratings than any postwar president, he managed to win re-election in 1984 by a huge margin. Moreover, he carried substantial public support into his second term, until his administration became embroiled in the Iran-Contra scandal.

CONCLUSION: Awesome Power or Helpless Giant?

According to the myth of the all-powerful president, modern presidents possess awesome powers that, if mobilized, could enable them to solve all of the country's problems. Although this myth has not always prevailed, it has colored public expectations of the presidency in the latter half of the twentieth century. As the office evolved to its current state, the course of change has not been smooth. Presidential power has increased at times of grave emergency and great stress. In calmer periods Congress has generally reasserted its own role in the political system by reining in the president.

The broad range of roles ascribed to the president further enhances the myth of presidential power. As chief of state, the president performs a wide array of symbolic duties that underscore his dominant position, and as chief executive, he is expected to preside over and manage the American bureaucracy. Yet presidents often find such duties more difficult than they imagined. The Constitution, for instance, does provide the president with appointment and removal powers, but these are shared with the Congress.

The president also serves as the nation's chief diplomat. To many, including presidents themselves, foreign policy is the product of presidential action. The myth of the all-powerful president seems most applicable here perhaps, since the Constitution does appear to delegate primary responsibility for foreign affairs to the president. The power to make treaties and executive agreements, as well as the powers of recognition and diplomatic appointments, helps suggest that the president creates foreign policy. Yet, though the president can greatly influence the shaping of foreign policy, Congress is hardly a silent spectator in the process. As chief diplomat, the president may take the lead in making foreign policy but presidents find themselves constrained even in this important area.

Much the same may be said about the president as commander in chief. Although presidents have assumed that as commanders in chief they possess the power to make war, the Constitution assigns declarations of war to Congress. At times Congress has been willing to grant presidents great latitude and thereby enhance the image of the all-powerful president. Recently, however, Congress has attempted to limit presidential power in this area through the War Powers Resolution.

The final role we have discussed in the chapter, that of chief legislator, also enhances the myth of the all-powerful president. The expectation that presidents will not only initiate public policy, but see their proposals enacted into law overrates the president's powers. The veto, along with impoundment and the constitutionally provided powers, gives the president opportunities to promote his legislative programs, but again Congress is not obliged to follow the president's lead.

To give him support in his various roles, the president has acquired a multitude of advisers—in the cabinet, the Executive Office of the President, and the White House Office. In fact, presidents are surrounded by a bureaucracy of advisers, who constitute the institutional presidency. Thus the president does not lack counsel, but with the growth of the institutional presidency, the problem has become that of managing the advisers.

Finally, we have also examined presidential power as persuasion. Although the office itself is generally seen as all-powerful, presidents find that their wishes do not automatically become policy. In this system of shared powers, the president must convince others that what he wants lies in their interest. Invoking party loyalty, effective lobbying, and personal appeals are all potential means of persuasion, but the support of the public is particularly useful. Although popular approval does not guarantee presidential success, it makes it more likely.

★ ★ ★

SUMMARY

1. The powers of the presidency have expanded significantly since the adoption of the constitution. American history has witnessed periods of presidential dominance, usually in times of emergency, followed by congressional efforts to reassert power by limiting presidents.

2. The importance of the modern presidency is seen most clearly in the variety of roles that the incumbent is now expected to play.

3. As chief of state, the president is the ceremonial head of the government.

4. As chief executive, the president must "take care that the laws be faithfully executed" and manage an executive branch composed of some 3 million employees. To perform the duties of chief executive, the

president has the power of appointment, the power to grant pardons, and the power of executive privilege, but none of these is unlimited.

5. As chief diplomat, the president, with the advice and consent of the Senate, can negotiate treaties and make diplomatic appointments. The president also has the power of recognition—that is, to extend diplomatic recognition to other countries—and can make executive agreements with other nations without Senate approval.

6. In the role of commander in chief, the president is supreme commander of the military forces. Presidents have also used this role to claim the power to make war. After the Vietnam War, Congress tried to limit the president's war-making power by passing the War Powers Resolution.

7. As chief legislator, the president can convene special sessions of Congress and adjourn Congress if the two houses cannot agree on a date. The president is also required to give Congress "from time to time" information on the "State of the Union" and to recommend measures for congressional action. Furthermore, the president has the power to veto acts of Congress, although the veto is subject to override. The president, however, does not have an item veto. Presidents have attempted to fashion an item veto on appropriation bills by impounding funds, but in 1974 Congress, through the Budget and Impoundment Control Act, set limits on presidential authority to do so.

8. The modern president is assisted by several advisory groups: the cabinet, the Executive Office of the President, the White House Office, and the office of the vice president. These groups constitute the institutional presidency.

9. The cabinet, consisting of the thirteen department heads, the ambassador to the United Nations, and other officials whom the president designates, is the original presidential advisory group. But the cabinet does not often function effectively, and most presidents hold cabinet meetings for purely ceremonial purposes.

10. Created by an executive order of Franklin D. Roosevelt, the Executive Office of the President (EOP), contains ten separate organizations. The major agencies within the EOP are the Office of Management and Budget, the Council of Economic Advisers and the National Security Council.

11. Also within the EOP is the smaller White House Office, which serves the president's personal needs. The White House Office includes assistants, special assistants, counselors and consultants, who perform a wide variety of personal and political duties. The five hundred or more people employed by the White House Office are structured according to the president's organizational preference. Some presidents have preferred a structure known as the wheel, while others have favored a pyramid structure.

12. The vice president presides over the Senate but votes only to break a tie. The vice president assumes the presidency if the president dies, resigns, is removed by impeachment, or is unable to function because of a disability. Generally, vice-presidential candidates have been selected so that they might draw to the ticket supporters that the presidential candidates need.

13. To be effective, presidents must be skilled at persuasion. In dealing with Congress, the president can rely to some extent on party loyalty, but presidents must also assemble an effective lobbying staff and use them well. Skillful use of personal appeals to legislators is often effective and necessary.

14. Presidents succeed better at persuasion when their public popularity is high, but popularity often eludes them. No president since the end of World War II has left office as popular as when he entered.

★ ★ ★
KEY TERMS

executive privilege
executive agreements
pocket veto
item veto

riders
impounding
executive order

★ ★ ★
SUGGESTED READINGS

- Edwards, George C. III. *The Public Presidency: The Pursuit of Popular Support*. New York: St. Martin's Press, 1983. A comprehensive study of the relationship between the president and the public. The author demonstrates why popular support is necessary for the president to govern effectively.

- Kessler, Frank. *The Dilemmas of Presidential Leadership: Of Caretakers and Kings*. Englewood Cliffs, N.J.: Prentice-Hall, 1982. A study of the presidency arguing convincingly that the presidency is not and never has been as powerful as many observers have assumed.

- Neustadt, Richard E. *Presidential Power: The Politics of Leadership from FDR to Carter*. New York: John Wiley, 1980. A classic study of the elements of presidential power. The author argues that presidential power is the power to persuade and not the power to command.

12

CHAPTER

Bureaucracy

It was one of those horror stories that Americans read about almost daily. On December 30, 1973, Ed Cramer, an official with the San Francisco office of the Social Security Administration, visited the building where government checks are printed and processed for mailing to California residents. Cramer was working on a project designed to change the nation's public welfare system. A year earlier Congress had passed legislation establishing the supplemental security income (SSI) program. Under this program, the national government took on greater responsibility for helping elderly, blind, and permanently disabled citizens. The first SSI payments were to be mailed on New Year's Day 1974.

As he surveyed the tall stacks of printed checks, Cramer thought about the time and effort that this project had consumed. Getting the first checks ready on schedule involved more than sixty thousand federal employees and nearly $120 million in overtime pay. Cramer and his coworkers were proud of completing the important job on time.

But pride turned to panic when Cramer noticed the numbers printed on one stack of SSI checks. Each check was written for somewhere between $600 and $800. Cramer was stunned. The maximum individual payment was supposed to be $235. After checking other stacks and finding similar errors, he realized that he had uncovered a major problem. A daylong search turned up more than 3000 incorrect checks—and that hardly scratched the surface.

The head of the Social Security Administration's regional office decided that too much was at stake to hold up the checks. He ordered them mailed by the deadline, hoping that the financial damage would not be too great. Several months later a government audit showed errors on approximately 55 percent of the 540,000 SSI checks sent to Californians during the first six months of 1974. Overpayment during that period amounted to nearly $50 million.

The Social Security Administration's problems were not limited to California. Vermont residents received more than a quarter of a million dollars in overpayments. A computational error resulted in $10.5 million in overpayments to individuals throughout the country. By 1976 losses reached $547 million. What was once a source of pride for Ed Cramer and the other bureaucrats at the Social Security Administration became a source of profound embarrassment.[1]

The story of Ed Cramer's discovery and the millions of dollars in losses shocked but did not surprise many Americans, who are used to reports of bungling by government officials. On almost any day you can read about the inefficiencies of government agencies and their employees in local newspapers or hear about it on television or radio. These comments are rooted in a widely held myth of American government—the myth of bureaucratic incompetence.

Central to the myth is the view that American government is not managed in a businesslike fashion. According to this view, government agencies are inefficient and wasteful, and are run by people who are overpaid, cannot be fired, and could not make it in the "real world" of private business. Thus the very words bureaucracy and bureaucrat carry negative connotations.

The myth is supported by several studies of the federal bureaucracy conducted by official government commissions. In 1905, for example, a congressionally appointed commission called for reforms in federal agency record-keeping and personnel policies, and in 1910 a presidential body recommended a major reorganization of the federal government as well as a uniform budgeting system. Substantial reforms were also suggested by presidential commissions appointed by Franklin Roosevelt, Harry Truman, Dwight Eisenhower, and Richard Nixon. All these studies concluded that the federal government is grossly mismanaged. A similar conclusion was reached by the Grace Commission, a group established by President Reagan and which reported to him in 1984 that "the federal government is suffering from a critical case of inefficient and ineffective management, evidenced particularly by the hemorrhaging of billions of tax dollars and mounting deficits."[2]

With such support for the myth of bureaucratic incompetence (see Figure 12.1), why should we doubt its truth? In this chapter, we do not deny that federal agencies fail to operate in an efficient, businesslike fashion. Rather, we show that the federal bureaucracy is not designed to be managed like a private corporation and that it was never intended to be operated as efficiently as a business firm. Finally, we show how under our system of government it is more important that we be able to control bureaucratic power than to manage it.

★ ★ ★
A PROFILE OF THE FEDERAL BUREAUCRACY

The myth of bureaucratic incompetence implies that the federal government should operate as efficiently and effectively as a private sector firm. But as we shall see, the size and complexity of the federal bureaucracy is not well suited to being operated like a private corporation.

Who Are the Bureaucrats?

The term **bureaucracy** has wide currency in the United States, and it is usually used to describe both government agencies and people who work in

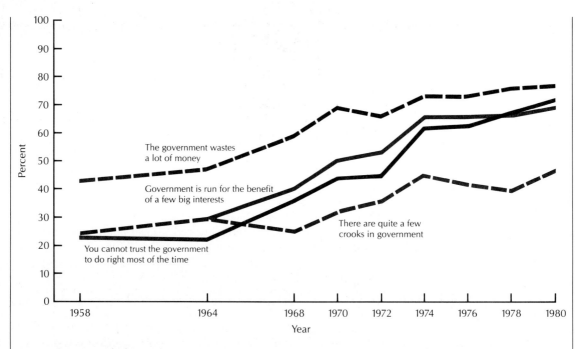

Questions asked in survey:

━ ━ "Do you think that people in the government waste a lot of money we pay in taxes, waste some of it, or don't waste very much of it?"

━ ━ "Do you think that quite a few of the people running the government are a little crooked, not very many are, or do you think hardly any of them are crooked at all?"

━━━ "How much of the time do you think you can trust government in Washington to do what is right—just about always, most of the time, or only some of the time?"

━━━ "Would you say the government is pretty much run by a few big interests looking out for themselves or that it is run for the benefit of all the people?"

FIGURE 12.1 Confidence in Government Bureaucracy

Individuals' responses to survey questions during the period 1958 to 1980 about their confidence in government bureaucracy seem to lend support for the myth of bureaucratic incompetence.

Source: Reprinted with permission of The Free Press, a division of the Macmillan Publishing Company, from *The Confidence Gap: Business, Labor, and Government in the Public Mind,* by Seymour Martin Lipset and William Schneider, p. 17, © 1983 by Columbia University, New York, New York.

BACKGROUND 12.1

What Is a Bureaucracy?

What do we mean when we discuss government bureaucracy? In technical terms, a *bureaucracy* is a type of modern organization. Like other organizational forms, a bureaucracy is a means by which people structure their work and relationships in order to accomplish some common purpose. What makes bureaucracy a unique organizational form are three basic characteristics: hierarchy, specialization, and formalization.

First, a bureaucracy has a hierarchical structure. In a hierarchy, relationships among people are determined by their rank order and status in the organization's pyramidal structure. You are either a supervisor or subordinate in those relationships, and the subordinate is always supposed to seek instructions and guidance from the supervisor. Second, the roles of people in bureaucratic organizations are specialized. Specialization means that each individual has a specific task to perform in the organization, and it is assumed that he or she develops a high degree of skill or expertise in that job. Finally, a true bureaucracy operates according to standardized regulations which are set forth in formalized (written) rules. The formalization of bureaucracies means that each role and task performed in the organization is described in clear and specific terms so that there is no question of what is expected of the worker under most conditions.

Although most of us associate bureaucracies with government agencies, they are just as common in the private sector, especially in large corporations. In fact, one prominent historian who studied the rise of America's corporations argues that the success of companies like Du Pont, Sears, General Motors, and Standard Oil of New Jersey (Exxon) can be attributed to the bureaucratic structures they adopted during the first decades of this century. There are, of course, many differences between business and government organizations. Nevertheless, bureaucracies have emerged as the most widely accepted forms of organizational life in both the public and private sectors.

For more information on the technical nature of bureaucracy, see Peter M. Blau, *Bureaucracy in Modern Society* (New York: Random House, 1956). On the history of bureaucracy in corporate America, see Alfred D. Chandler, Jr., *Strategy and Structure: Chapters in the History of the American Industrial Enterprise* (Cambridge, Mass: MIT Press, 1962).

them (see Background 12.1). Who are these federal bureaucrats that so many of us believe to be incompetent? What do we know about them?

First, we know that more than 3 million of them work in the United States and abroad, primarily (over 81 percent) in full-time, clerical, technical, service, managerial, and professional positions.[3] Equally diverse is the blue-collar work force, which includes electricians, carpenters, maintenance workers, and a variety of other skilled and unskilled jobs. For instance, the federal government employs nearly nineteen thousand plumbers, more than ten thousand paperhangers and painters, and more than twenty-five thousand metalworkers.

In 1986 the average federal bureaucrat had been working for the government for thirteen-and-a-half years. Forty-two percent of the federal civilian work force were women, and just over a fourth of all federal employees were members of minority groups. Approximately one-third held a college degree, and approximately 35 percent were veterans.[4]

With such a large and diverse workforce, the federal government has adopted several different personnel systems to help in managing the government's human resources. The president's major **political appointees** occupy two thousand or so of the most strategically important positions in the government. At the top are the members of the president's cabinet, an official advisory board that is made up of the secretaries (heads) of the thirteen major departments responsible for carrying out most of the federal government's policies and programs. Below them are assistant and deputy department secretaries, deputy assistant secretaries, counselors, and a variety of other positions. Their formal appointments by the president must be confirmed by the Senate. They owe their loyalty to the president, and their tenure in office hinges on how the White House evaluates their performance.

At one time in our history, political appointees made up a vast majority of the federal bureaucracy (see Background 12.2). However, the scandals of one presidential administration and the assassination of another president provided the impetus for reforming the system. In 1883 Congress passed the Pendleton Act, which reduced the number of political appointments a president could make and established a merit system for about 10 percent of existing federal jobs. A merit system stresses employee ability, education, experience, and job performance; political factors are not supposed to be considered. Hiring and promotion depend on competitive examinations or job performance evaluations conducted by a bipartisan Civil Service Commission.

The merit system now covers most federal civilian jobs—approximately 93 percent in 1984. Many of these are found in the **general civil service** system. The general civil service covers government positions from weather forecasters to financial analysts, from librarians to civil engineers. These federal workers usually obtain their jobs through some form of competitive merit system. Almost all of the positions under this personnel system are ranked according to a General Schedule (GS), which ranges from GS1 through GS18 (see Table 12.1).

The highest ranks in the general civil service system (ranks GS15 through GS18, often called the "supergrades") overlap the Senior Executive Service (SES), a select group of public administrators who specialize in managing public agencies. Most of the civil servants in the small SES have made their mark as effective supergrade managers in the highest positions within individual agencies. In joining the SES, those managers agree to transfer to other agencies that need their talents. Before the Civil Service Reform Act of 1978 established the SES, the best executive talent in the federal government could not be efficiently or effectively used because moving from one agency

---

BACKGROUND 12.2

The Remains of Patronage

The political appointments made by the president are the remains of a bureaucratic personnel system that once depended exclusively on patronage. *Patronage* is a system of hiring government employees in which appointments are based on "who you know" rather than "what you know." Patronage was once commonplace throughout the federal bureaucracy. Thomas Jefferson replaced many federal workers loyal to the Federalist Party when he took over the presidency from John Adams in 1801. But the first wholesale application of patronage followed Andrew Jackson's election nearly three decades later. Jackson believed in the "spoils system," that is, giving government jobs at all levels to members of the winning party. He was also committed to opening up government positions to ordinary American citizens. For Jackson, the political appointment process was a means of promoting democracy.

The Jacksonian spoils system influenced the design and operation of the federal government for several decades. Under the system, the federal bureaucracy was probably more than usually responsive to the president's wishes, since loyalty to the White House was the key to getting the job in the first place. Since no one stayed for

very long in any position, government jobs had to be redesigned and standardized so anyone could step in to fulfill the tasks of the position. Thus, the job of being a postal clerk or a tax collector was made much simpler. But the spoils system also led to less desirable outcomes, such as widespread political corruption in the administration of Ulysses S. Grant and the assassination of President James Garfield in 1881 by a disgruntled office seeker.

Very little of the patronage system remains in today's federal bureaucracy. Aside from top-level appointees who hold the highest positions in the executive branch, there is also a small group of presidential appointees who occupy politically sensitive advisory and managerial posts throughout the federal government. For example, these appointees may be special assistants or advisers to the president or some cabinet official. In many instances, however, Congress has placed limits on the behavior of these lower-level appointees. Thus, despite the obvious political nature of their jobs, those who occupy these positions are prohibited from any partisan political activity and must adhere to other politically restrictive standards of behavior.

---

to another was too difficult. Along with a small group of presidential appointees, SES and supergrade personnel fill the major managerial positions in federal agencies. The individuals in these positions represent some of the best executive talent in the federal government.

In addition to the general civil service, there are special **career service** personnel systems for highly specialized agencies such as the Forest Service and the Coast Guard. Perhaps the best known of these career service systems is the Foreign Service, which includes the more than 13,000 State Department officials who serve in American embassies throughout the world. The Veterans Administration operates the largest career service system, employing more than 36,000 physicians and surgeons who work for that agency. All together, approximately 125,000 federal civilian employees occupy positions in these career service systems.

TABLE 12.1 Meritorious Service: The Pay Scale for Federal Employees

Salaries for bureaucrats range from somewhat above minimum wage at the bottom of the scale to salaries comparable with executives in private industry at the top of the scale.

Grade	Salary Range for 1987
1	$ 9,526–11,919
2	10,711–13,482
3	11,687–15,197
4	13,119–17,052
5	14,687–19,079
6	16,360–21,265
7	18,180–23,634
8	20,135–26,174
9	22,240–28,909
10	24,492–31,836
11	26,909–34,982
12	32,251–41,926
13	38,351–49,853
14	45,319–58,918
15	53,308–69,301
16–18	62,522–70,100

Source: Statistical Abstract of the United States: 1987 (Washington, D.C.: U.S. Bureau of the Census, 1986).

Finally, over a million federal workers can be classified as part of the government's **wage systems.** Included in this group are those with blue-collar and related jobs ranging from pipe fitting to metal work. More than 750,000 postal workers make up the largest single organized group in this category. Many of the workers in these wage systems are paid by the hour, and a great many are represented by unions or other associations that have limited bargaining rights under current civil service laws.

What Do Federal Bureaucrats Do?

Directly and indirectly, federal agencies touch almost every aspect of Americans' lives. Their activities range from funding special education programs in the public schools and maintaining major highways to providing for national security and exploring outer space. The federal bureaucracy processes

Bold bureaucrat Surgeon General C. Everett Koop tells a House committee that network television advertisements for condoms would help prevent the spread of AIDS. Koop fought a losing battle within the Reagan administration to deter routine AIDS virus testing and to promote frank "safe sex" education.

the loan guarantees that permit many students to attend America's colleges and universities, monitors the economy, oversees the safety of commercial aviation, regulates the use of television and radio broadcasting, and maintains the vast systems of national parks and forests.

Since bureaucrats' work lacks drama, few people know much about it. White House pronouncements, televised congressional hearings, or history-making Supreme Court decisions are major news events, but you have to dig far back in the *Washington Post, New York Times,* or *Wall Street Journal* to find out that the Food and Drug Administration has given the final approval for the sale of a new drug or that the Interstate Commerce Commission has turned down a request by an interstate bus company to abandon its routes in Kansas. Yet many bureaucratic decisions on these and related matters have a greater impact on our daily lives than the more newsworthy items of the day.

We depend on the federal bureaucracy not only to make decisions, but also to make certain that the policies of Congress and the White House are being implemented. In some instances, federal agencies are directly involved in carrying out those policies. The Internal Revenue Service, for example, has offices located throughout the nation to collect federal income receipts. As discussed in Chapter 3, on federalism, the federal government makes considerable use of the intergovernmental relations system to carry out most of its domestic policies. It funds interstate highway construction and counts on the states to build the roads according to federal specifications. It pays for remedial education for low-income students and expects states to provide special classes according to federally set guidelines. It gives local governments federal money for public housing and expects federal criteria to be followed in constructing and filling such housing units. The role of the federal bureaucracy in these programs is to allocate federal grants to state and local governments and to monitor their use of those funds.

Bureaucracies also provide expertise to policy makers, especially in the design of special policies and highly technical programs. Agencies such as the Bureau of Reclamation and Army Corps of Engineers, for example, develop plans for water diversion and storage projects, which then go to the White House and Congress for revision and adoption as official government programs. In the case of military and defense policy, Congress and the president establish the general outlines of policies, but leave the creation of specific defense programs and systems to civilian and military experts at the Pentagon.

Finally, almost every federal agency provides policy makers and the general public with advice and information, and some agencies specialize in these functions. The Office of Management and Budget, for example, advises the White House on agency actions and budget requests. The Bureau of Labor Statistics and the Bureau of the Census are the principal sources of information on unemployment levels and current population figures.

Where Do They Work?

Where do these federal civil servants work? They can be found in literally hundreds of different agencies (see Figure 12.2).

Executive Office of the President. Closest to the president are the agencies of the Executive Office of the President (EOP), which was created in the 1930s to coordinate the activities of a growing federal bureaucracy. The staff of the Office of Management and Budget (OMB) provides that help by linking the president to most federal agencies. All agencies report to OMB on matters relating to program and budget requests. A smaller (but no less important) group of EOP employees is located in the White House Office. These staff members include the president's key advisers, as well as those who help the chief executive deal with the day-to-day business of the presidency.

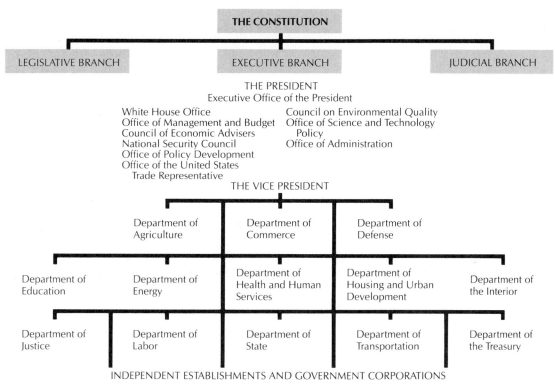

THE CONSTITUTION

LEGISLATIVE BRANCH   EXECUTIVE BRANCH   JUDICIAL BRANCH

THE PRESIDENT
Executive Office of the President

White House Office   Council on Environmental Quality
Office of Management and Budget   Office of Science and Technology
Council of Economic Advisers   Policy
National Security Council   Office of Administration
Office of Policy Development
Office of the United States
   Trade Representative

THE VICE PRESIDENT

Department of Agriculture	Department of Commerce	Department of Defense

Department of Education	Department of Energy	Department of Health and Human Services	Department of Housing and Urban Development	Department of the Interior

Department of Justice	Department of Labor	Department of State	Department of Transportation	Department of the Treasury

INDEPENDENT ESTABLISHMENTS AND GOVERNMENT CORPORATIONS

ACTION
Administrative Conference of the U.S.
African Development Foundation
American Battle Monuments Commission
Appalachian Regional Commission
Board for International Broadcasting
Central Intelligence Agency
Commission on the Bicentennial of the
   United States Constitution
Commission on Civil Rights
Commission of Fine Arts
Commodity Futures Trading Commission
Consumer Product Safety Commission
Environmental Protection Agency
Equal Employment Opportunity
   Commission
Export-Import Bank of the U.S.
Farm Credit Administration
Federal Communications Commission
Federal Deposit Insurance Corporation
Federal Election Commission
Federal Emergency Management
   Agency
Federal Home Loan Bank Board

Federal Labor Relations Authority
Federal Maritime Commission
Federal Mediation and Conciliation
   Service
Federal Reserve System, Board of
   Governors of the
Federal Trade Commission
General Services Administration
Inter-American Foundation
Interstate Commerce Commission
Merit Systems Protection Board
National Aeronautics and Space
   Administration
National Archives and Records
   Administration
National Capital Planning
   Commission
National Credit Union Administration
National Foundation on the Arts and
   the Humanities
National Labor Relations Board
National Mediation Board
National Science Foundation
National Transportation Safety Board

Nuclear Regulatory Commission
Occupational Safety and Health Review
   Commission
Office of Personnel Management
Panama Canal Commission
Peace Corps
Pennsylvania Avenue Development
   Corporation
Pension Benefit Guaranty Corporation
Postal Rate Commission
Railroad Retirement Board
Securities and Exchange Commission
Selective Service System
Small Business Administration
Tennessee Valley Authority
U.S. Arms Control and Disarmament
   Agency
U.S. Information Agency
U.S. International Development
   Cooperation Agency
U.S. International Trade Commission
U.S. Postal Service
Veterans Administration

FIGURE 12.2   The Government of the United States

Also found in the EOP are various council and staff members specializing in particular policy areas. Among the most important of these have been the Council of Economic Advisers, the National Security Council, and the Council on Environmental Quality. These agencies play a key role in formulating, but not in carrying out, public policy. Under the Reagan administration, however, some members of the National Security Council staff crossed the boundary into implementation when they arranged to sell arms to a hostile government in Iran and illegally transfer funds to support rebel groups in Central America. The resulting scandal, which surfaced in 1986, led to several resignations and a political crisis that nearly paralyzed the White House.

The cabinet departments. The most visible agencies in the executive branch are the thirteen cabinet departments. As we have already noted, they are the major bureaucratic institutions responsible for carrying out most of the federal government's policies and programs (see Table 12.2). Each department is headed by a secretary and composed of many smaller agencies. Some of these departments are in charge of basic governmental functions such as defense and foreign relations. Others address the needs of special clientele groups—for example, agriculture and labor—or they coordinate the labyrinth of federal programs in education, energy, social welfare, and other areas.

Independent executive branch agencies. A number of agencies that administer federal programs exist outside the cabinet departments, and many of them carry out important government functions. The Environmental Protection Agency regulates air and water quality, as well as the disposal of hazardous wastes. The Federal Emergency Management Administration helps coordinate federal, state, and local government responses to major disasters. The National Aeronautics and Space Administration runs the civilian space program. The Veterans Administration manages a wide range of health, social, and education programs for individuals who have served in the armed forces. The administrators who head these independent executive branch agencies report directly to the president.

Some independent executive branch agencies help in running the federal government rather than in carrying out specific programs. For example, the General Services Administration acts as the government's landlord and maintenance team, while the Office of Personnel Management has responsibility for overseeing several of the federal government's personnel systems.

Regulatory commissions. Regulatory commissions make policies affecting various sectors of the American economy (see Table 12.3). Their members are appointed by the president, and they employ large professional staffs. Regulatory commissions are formally independent of the White House. That

TABLE 12.2 The Cabinet Departments

The growth of government over the past two hundred years is evident in this list. Originally responsible for foreign policy, finances, defense, and the law, the executive branch agencies now oversee a wide range of activities.

Department	Year Created	Number of Employees[a] (1986)
State	1789	25,482
Treasury	1789	140,669
Defense[b]	1789	1,087,893
Justice[c]	1789	65,285
Interior	1849	76,232
Agriculture[d]	1889	111,927
Commerce	1913	35,408
Labor	1913	17,841
Health and Human Services[e]	1953	136,318
Housing and Urban Development	1965	11,545
Transportation	1966	61,348
Energy	1977	16,674
Education	1979	4,680

[a] Civilian employees.
[b] Previously called the Department of War.
[c] Previously called the Office of the Attorney General.
[d] Although created in 1862, the Department of Agriculture did not achieve cabinet status until 1889.
[e] Prior to 1979, the Department of Health and Human Services and the Department of Education were combined in the Department of Health, Education, and Welfare.
Source: Statistical Abstract of the United States: 1986 (Washington, D.C.: U.S. Bureau of the Census, 1985).

is, they exist outside the cabinet departments and have a special legal status (provided by Congress and supported by the Supreme Court) that protects them from presidential interference. The president cannot fire commission members for political reasons—only for corruption or a similar cause. Of course, the president has some influence over the commissions; since he appoints their members, he can choose individuals whose decisions are likely to accord with the administration's views.

The special legal status of the regulatory commissions derives from the fact that they do more than enforce the law or implement public policy. When they formulate rules that regulated companies or individuals must adhere to, these agencies are also performing lawmaking, or quasi-legislative, tasks. For example, in 1972 the Federal Trade Commission issued regulations requiring that all billboard and magazine advertisements for cigarettes contain a warning from the surgeon general's office about the health hazards of

TABLE 12.3 Major Regulatory Commissions

These agencies have generally been established in response to public demands. Ironically, from the beginning, industries have not suffered adversely from regulatory actions.

Commission	Year Established	Purpose
Interstate Commerce Commission	1887	Regulation of railroads, interstate trucking, bus lines, oil
Federal Trade Commission	1914	Regulation of trade practices and advertising; prevention of unfair competition and price fixing
Securities and Exchange Commission	1934	Regulation of stock exchanges and stock market activities
Federal Communications Commission	1934	Regulation of use of radio and TV airwaves; licensing of broadcast stations
Civil Aeronautics Board	1934	Regulated passenger air service; agency terminated in 1985
National Labor Relations Board	1935	Regulation of relations between labor and management; guaranteeing of rights of workers to organize
Consumer Products Safety Commission	1973	Protection of public from unreasonable risks due to unsafe products
Nuclear Power Regulatory Commission	1974	Regulation of safety in nuclear power industry

Source: Statistical Abstract of the United States: 1987 (Washington, D.C.: U.S. Bureau of the Census, 1986).

smoking. Along with enforcing and making rules, these commissions also have a quasi-judicial function by sitting in judgment of those companies or individuals accused of violating the regulations. Violations of commission rules get their first court-like hearing before commission officials. A company or person found guilty of such violations may appeal directly to the federal court system.

Government corporations. A unique form of bureaucracy, the government corporation, acts more like a private business than a part of government.

The best known of these organizations, the Tennessee Valley Authority and the U.S. Postal Service, exist as independent executive branch agencies. Several government corporations are located within cabinet departments. The Commodity Credit Corporation, for example, is part of the U.S. Department of Agriculture. Most government corporations carry out specific economic or service functions, such as delivering the mail. The Federal Deposit Insurance Corporation insures savings accounts in many local banks. The Corporation for Public Broadcasting helps fund the Public Broadcasting System and National Public Radio.

Other agencies. Besides these five types of federal agencies, literally hundreds of boards, commissions, institutes, foundations, endowments, councils, and other organizations make up the federal bureaucracy. They range in importance from the Federal Reserve Board (better known in the news media as the "Fed"; see Chapter 14) and the National Science Foundation to the National Capital Planning Commission and the U.S. Metric Board.

An Unmanageable Institution

The term bureaucracy is a misleading one, for it implies that we are speaking of a single institution that has a clearly indentifiable membership. Our profile of the federal bureaucracy, however, does not support that image. Instead, we see a federal bureaucracy composed of hundreds of distinct organizations that employ millions of people. It is so large and complex that it defies description. Organizationally, it seems to be a hodge podge of structures and forms. Those who work in it perform almost every conceivable type of work. If the bureaucracy is one of the four basic institutions of our government, it is certainly the most unwieldy.

More important, the federal bureaucracy is obviously an unmanageable institution. Its complexity and size are unmatched in the private sector. There is no corporation as big, nor is there any that attempts to carry out the numerous and myriad tasks that we ask the federal government to perform. We must keep that fact in mind as we consider the suggestion that the federal bureaucracy should be operated in a more businesslike fashion.

★ ★ ★
THE EMERGENCE OF AMERICAN BUREAUCRACY

The fact that the federal bureaucracy may be unmanageable today will not deter some observers from arguing that it was originally intended to remain small enough to be manageable. We will never know what the founders of our government intended for the bureaucracy, for we have little indication that they thought much at all about the administration of government. We do know that they considered bureaucracy to be a vital institution in our constitutional system. For instance, in *The Federalist* No. 70, Alexander Hamilton acknowledged that a badly administered government "must be . . . a bad government." Beyond that, we must turn to the growth of bureaucracy itself in order to assess whether the management of bureaucracy has been a major concern for most Americans.

The Constitutional Roots of Bureaucracy

The U.S. Constitution makes the president responsible for ensuring that the laws and policies of the national government are carried out. When the Constitution's framers met in Philadelphia in 1787 to design the basic institutions of our political system, the tasks of government were relatively few and easy to implement. Executing the law meant keeping the peace, defending the country from foreign intruders, and delivering the mail. To the framers, charging a single individual with overseeing the administration of government did not seem unreasonable. Consequently, in Section 2 of Article II, they made the president both commander in chief of the armed forces and the chief executive officer to whom the heads of all administrative departments would report.

Initially, the framers were not wrong in their views about the administration of the federal government. In the early years of the Republic, the federal bureaucracy was very small and quite manageable. In 1802, for example, there were less than ten thousand civilian and military federal employees. Almost all the civilians worked as tax collectors and postal workers. Of course, those were simpler times. The country was rural and the people self-sufficient; they were less dependent on government than we are today for even the most basic public services. When Americans did turn to government for help, it was usually to state and local governments rather than the nation's newly settled capital in Washington, D.C.

Today the administration of the federal government is no simple chore. It has become an awesome responsibility, especially over the last sixty years as the federal government has become involved in economic and social problems, as well as in world affairs.

The History of Bureaucratic Growth

At first the national government provided only limited services to the public. Although by the 1820s the federal government's civilian bureaucracy had more than doubled, nearly 75 percent of its members worked for the U.S. Post Office. In the late 1800s, however, the number of functions performed

Taxing the "Tingle Tables" As the scope of bureaucrats' activities have expanded, so has the inventiveness of those who supply them with equipment. These specially designed tables are used to sort millions of federal income tax returns at the Chamblee, Georgia, Internal Revenue Service center. The tables are named for their inventor.

by federal officials increased, causing a change in government employment patterns.

After the Civil War, Americans demanded more and better government services from elected officials at all levels. During the last half of the 19th century the number of federal agencies doubled. The major agencies established during this period included the U.S. Department of Agriculture and the Interstate Commerce Commission. Furthermore, federal workers were being hired not just to deliver the mail, but also to regulate railroads, assist farmers, manage the federal government's vast land holdings, survey and help settle newly acquired territories in the west, and promote American commerce overseas. Post office positions had accounted for more than four out of every five federal jobs in 1861, but by 1901 postal workers made up only 58 percent of the bureaucracy.

This pattern of bureaucratic growth continued through the first decades of the twentieth century. By the time Franklin D. Roosevelt took office as president in 1933, the number of major federal agencies had grown from 90 in 1901 to 170.

In response to the economic and social problems of the Depression, Roosevelt helped create many new federal programs and agencies, especially in the area of employment and the regulation of business. The demands of World War II led to further growth in the bureaucracy and the expansion of government responsibilities in domestic and foreign affairs. By 1950 the number of federal civilian employees increased to nearly two million. In the 1960s President Lyndon Johnson's domestic programs caused a huge jump in federal employment—the largest since the years of Roosevelt's New Deal administration. As national defense programs expanded and the public became concerned about environmental quality, consumer protection, public health, and worker safety, federal civilian employment rose to approximately 3 million. It remained at that level throughout the 1970s and during most of the 1980s.

The mounting federal budget also points to the growth of the federal bureaucracy, or at least to the increase in its influence and power. By noting the size of the federal budget, we can judge how much of the nation's resources go to operate government and support the work of federal agencies. George Washington ran the government for about $1.5 million a year. By the time Andrew Jackson took office in 1829, the federal budget had increased tenfold, to over $15 million. By 1940 the budget had climbed to $9.5 billion, and in 1960 the U.S. government spent a little over $92 billion. The greatest growth in federal expenditures, however, took place over the next quarter-century. In January 1987 President Ronald Reagan submitted the first trillion dollar budget proposal to the Congress.

Explaining the Growth of the Bureaucracy

What accounts for this explosion of bureaucracies and bureaucrats? Many observers believe that the growth can be attributed directly to the expansion of the nation itself (see Myth and Reality 12.1). There a great many more of us—242 million, compared with less than five million in the 1790s—and we are living closer together. Not only do the residents of cities and suburbs require many more services than did the predominantly rural dwellers of the early 1800s, but the challenges of urban and industrial life have intensified and outstripped the capacity of families or local and state governments to cope with them. Thus, the American people have increasingly turned to their national government for help.

There is considerable evidence that the growth of bureaucracies is "of our own making."[5] Public opinion polls indicate widespread public support for expanding federal involvement in a variety of areas. Even when public support for new programs is low, pollsters find Americans unwilling to eliminate or reduce existing programs. Furthermore, public expectations about the quality of service they receive is constantly rising. The public wants government to be more responsive, responsible, and compassionate in administering public programs. Officials have responded to all these pressures by establishing new programs and maintaining and improving those that exist.

The federal bureaucracy has also expanded in response to sudden changes in economic, social, cultural, and political conditions. During the Depression and World War II, for example, the federal bureaucracy grew to meet the challenges these situations created. Washington became more and more involved in programs providing financial aid and employment to the poor. It increased its regulation of important industries and during the war imposed controls over much of the American economy. As part of the general war effort, the federal government also built roads and hospitals and mobilized the entire population. When these crises ended, the public was reluctant to give up many of the federal welfare and economic programs implemented during the time of emergency.

Public officials, too, foster bureaucratic growth. Government bureaucracies are often enlarged by presidents wanting to be re-elected in order to leave their mark on history. We have noted the large expansions of federal bureaucracies that occurred under Roosevelt's New Deal and Johnson's Great Society programs. Nor is Congress an innocent bystander in all this activity. The incentives for members of Congress to create new programs and expand the federal bureaucracy are enormous. Bowing to pressure to "bring the bacon" back to the folks at home, even the most conservative members of Congress find themselves voting for new or larger programs to serve their constituents.[6]

The bureaucracy itself plays an ever larger role in developing and expanding government programs. For example, in 1970 staff members of the Department of Labor came up with the idea for the Occupational Safety and Health Administration (OSHA). Some analysts point out that expanding agency programs and budgets is one of the few personal rewards that bureaucrats can seek since compensation is limited and promotion quite slow in government service.

Thus, a number of factors have contributed to the growth of the federal bureaucracy during the past two hundred years. Obviously, the myth of bureaucratic incompetence and the demand for a more manageable bureaucracy has had little impact on the constant pressure to expand government agencies. The American public seems willing to suffer what it perceives as bureaucratic incompetence in order to receive the public services that federal agencies can help provide.

★ ★ ★
BUREAUCRATIC POWER

Inherent in the myth of bureaucratic incompetence is a fear of bureaucratic power. The U.S. constitutional system is rooted in the idea that the people should govern, if not directly, then at least indirectly through elected representatives. Yet over the past two centuries, more and more government power has been placed in the hands of bureaucrats. The myth of bureaucratic incompetence reflects a widespread belief that federal bureaucrats are misusing or even abusing this power. American citizens believe that the only way to restrain the potential abuse of bureaucratic power is through reforms that will make the federal bureaucracy more efficient and businesslike. In this section we discuss the nature of bureaucratic power and how it is currently kept under control.

The Need and Nature of Bureaucratic Power

The existence of bureaucratic power is an inevitable result of the operation of government. Bureaucracies and bureaucrats exist because policy makers create the need for them by passing laws that must be enforced and establishing policies that must be carried out. Enforcement and administration require that government agencies have enough personnel and funding; agencies and bureaucrats also must have the power to influence others so that policy goals and objectives can be attained. The need for bureaucratic power is so great that one student of public administration has called power the "lifeblood of administration."[7]

What is the basis of bureaucratic power?[8] A major source is external support—from the general public, special interest groups, the media, Congress, or the White House. The greater an agency's external support, the more power it is likely to wield. Throughout the 1950s and 1960s, for example, the Federal Bureau of Investigation (FBI), under Director J. Edgar Hoover, had a great deal of support from the general public. After Hoover's death and a series of revelations about questionable actions taken by the FBI and its agents, the agency's reputation and support declined. The directors who succeeded Hoover worked for many years to restore public confidence and so rebuild the agency's power.

An agency's power can also stem from its expertise. As noted earlier, in matters of national defense, America's top policy makers often turn to experts at the Pentagon for advice. On issues involving the public's health, they ask the opinion of the surgeon general or the Centers for Disease Control. Of course, as we mentioned in discussing interest groups, expert information must be accurate and reliable. If the surgeon general announced tomorrow

Consummate bureaucrat Cabinet secretaries are key policy makers in the executive branch. Here Secretary of Transportation Elizabeth Dole and Ford Motor chairman Donald Peterson inspect a model of the first air bags to be installed in automobiles. Dole played a critical policy role in crafting a contract between government and business on this issue in order to save more lives on the highways.

that smoking cigarettes is *not* harmful to your health, questions about that official's competency would immediately arise. Once the credibility of a bureaucrat's expertise is put in doubt, his or her influence is likely to deteriorate.

In performing their administrative tasks, bureaucrats are often permitted to use their own judgment in carrying out public policies and programs. Congress and the White House frequently formulate policies in ambiguous and vague terms. When President John F. Kennedy issued a mandate to the National Aeronautics and Space Administration (NASA) to land an American on the moon by 1970, he could not tell the agency exactly when and how to do it. Those details were left to the discretion of NASA officials. Discretion can be a source of considerable power, for it gives the bureaucracy considerable flexibility in deciding how to do its job.

The merit system, which protects most federal employees from being fired for political reasons, provides still another source of bureaucratic power. Because it is extremely difficult to dismiss a federal civil servant without a good, nonpolitical cause, civil servants usually last long in their jobs. They have the advantage of longevity in office. Meanwhile, presidents and members of Congress come and go, as do the presidential appointees who head federal agencies. Currently, the average bureaucrat has served through four presidential administrations and seven Congressional terms. As a result, elected officials and their appointees find themselves relying on career civil servants

MYTH AND REALITY 12.1

The Oversized Bureaucracy

All the numbers indicate that the federal bureaucracy has grown into an extremely large institution over the past two centuries. No wonder many Americans believe that the federal bureaucracy has grown too big. Many people believe in the myth of the oversized bureaucracy. There is no question that the federal bureaucracy is large. It would be foolish, however, to look at the growth of the federal bureaucracy without considering the growth in other areas of American society.

For example, while the number of Americans employed by the federal government has increased from a few thousand to nearly 3 million, the overall size of the American labor force has grown even faster. Within the total U.S. labor force, federal civilian workers accounted for under 3 percent of all employed individuals in 1983. That is, only 3 of every 100 employed Americans worked for the federal government. During World War II that figure had been as high as 4.7 federal workers for every 100 Americans, and even as recently as 1970 there were 3.7 civilians on the federal payroll for every 100 people in the U.S. labor force. Thus, when viewed as part of the U.S. labor force, the federal bureaucracy does not look quite as big and may not be growing as much as many people believe.

Nor does the size of the federal bureaucracy seem too big when compared with the number of civilian workers employed by state and local governments. In recent years the federal government has employed fewer than one out of every five government workers in the United States. State governments employ 3.8 million public employees, while local governments employ 9.3 million people.

In other words, while 3 million federal employees may seem like a large number, in relative terms the federal bureaucracy is not as big as it seems at first glance. Nevertheless, 3 million is a great many people, and the question of why there are so many federal bureaucrats is unavoidable.

to keep the agencies functioning. Thus, longevity in office can add up to considerable power for the experienced bureaucrat.

External support, expertise, discretion, and longevity in office will not accomplish much by themselves. Potential wielders of bureaucratic power must have the talents and will to use those resources. That is as true for agencies as it is for individuals. Without skills and leadership, even the most resource-rich federal agency will not be able to accomplish its objectives.

The Defense Department, for all its potential power and influence, would fail in its search for White House and congressional support if the secretary of defense did not provide effective leadership. During the Reagan administration, for example, Secretary of Defense Casper ("Cap") Weinberger gained a reputation as an effective salesperson for increasing defense expenditures. When some members of the Reagan administration proposed reductions in requests being made for defense expenditures, Weinberger managed to convince the president that defense "is not a budget issue. You spend what you need." In most instances, Weinberger was able to get the president to protect his department's budget.[9]

In short, power is the fuel that gives bureaucracies the energy to carry out their missions. A bureaucracy without power or the potential to exercise power is truly a waste of public resources. The question is not whether bureaucratic power exists, but whether it can be properly controlled so that it will be used correctly and effectively.

Limiting Bureaucratic Power

The fear that bureaucratic power might be abused or misused is not unfounded. But we should not assume that federal bureaucracies seek to exercise unlimited power or could do so if they desired. Both internal and external checks usually keep bureaucratic influence and authority within acceptable bounds.

Some of the curbs come from bureaucratic self-restraint. For example, in the mid-1970s certain regulatory commissions began to relax the controls they had previously exercised over sectors of the American economy. For example, the Civil Aeronautics Board (CAB) intentionally eliminated many barriers to competition among the nation's major airlines. That initiative was so popular that in 1978 Congress formally deregulated the airline industry and in 1985 eliminated the CAB altogether. Although no other regulatory commission has been abolished, most have exercised similar self-restraint in recent years.

The quantity and quality of available resources also put limits on bureaucratic power. The Internal Revenue Service (IRS), for example, does not have enough auditors and agents to review everyone's tax return and investigate all suspected cases of tax fraud. The competence of the auditors and agents it does have determines how effectively the IRS collects taxes.

As the formal head of the executive branch, the president can also exercise some control over the federal bureaucracy. He can do this by carefully selecting those he appoints to office or promotes. For example, before taking office in 1981, Reagan established an appointment system that selected for office only people who would be loyal to him and willing forcefully to pursue his objectives of reduced government activity.[10]

The White House can also influence the funding of federal agencies and their programs. Typically, federal agencies make their budget requests through the Office of Management and Budget (OMB), which evaluates and often modifies the agencies' proposals to conform with presidential priorities. Even after funds and other resources have been appropriated to agency programs by Congress, the White House retains control over the allocation of funds from the Treasury. In addition, the president can require that federal agencies adopt certain management methods and budgetary techniques. In 1965, for example, President Johnson ordered all federal agencies to adopt an agency planning technique that originated in the Department of Defense. When Jimmy Carter came in to office in 1977 he ordered federal agencies to adopt a budgeting approach he had used when he was governor of Georgia. In both instances, the management techniques were intended to give the president greater control over agency decisions.

Congress can also impose limitations on the power of federal agencies. The Constitution authorizes Congress to establish public programs and arrange for their implementation. Yet it has never been clear how detailed and explicit Congress must be in its instructions to federal agencies. Vague legislation has led many critics to argue that Congress is not working hard enough to limit or control bureaucratic power. Bureaucrats themselves have complained of the lack of specificity in what Congress asks them to do. In 1979, for example, one administrator openly criticized a congressional act that, in a single line of statutory language, required his agency to establish a program to protect the rights of the handicapped. Congress provided no details or guidance. "They're frequently very unhappy with what we do after they give us a mandate like that," he noted. "But the trouble is, the mandate is broad, they deliberately are ambiguous where there is conflict on details and they leave it to us to try to resolve the ambiguities."[11]

Implied in these criticisms is the belief that Congress has a right to exercise much more legislative control than it does today by expanding or contracting an agency's authority to take action. In a few instances, Congress has tried to provide detailed instructions for federal agencies. The Clean Air Act Amendments of 1970, for instance, set a number of specific deadlines for action by the Environmental Protection Agency (EPA). By April 30, 1971, the EPA was to establish a set of rules and regulations that would reduce air pollution. By June 30, 1972, it was to have received and reviewed state plans for dealing with air pollution. By 1975 it was to have made certain that auto companies reduced carbon monoxide and hydrocarbon emissions by 90 percent. These were challenging goals that ultimately proved too difficult to reach on schedule. Delays and postponements were common. Many observers point to those problems when asked why Congress often shies away from supplying many details in the legislation it passes.[12]

While Congress finds it difficult to control or limit bureaucratic power through legislation, it has other tools with which to accomplish these ends. Each year Congress reviews the budget requests of federal agencies and can use that opportunity to scrutinize agency operations. Almost every congressional committee has jurisdiction over a group of federal agencies, and they sometimes exercise their oversight responsibilities by holding public hearings on agency operations. Individual members of Congress often intercede with specific agencies on behalf of their constituents. Members of Congress can also order the General Accounting Office (GAO) to conduct an audit or investigation of any federal program. Finally, the role of the U.S. Senate in confirming political appointments provides that chamber with a unique opportunity to review bureaucratic actions.

The courts also play a role in limiting the power of the federal bureaucracy. Until 1937 the judiciary had often agreed to hear cases challenging the authority given to federal agencies by Congress. Today the courts are much less likely to entertain such cases. Nevertheless, they pay considerable attention to complaints that a federal agency has exceeded its authority or acted in an arbitrary or unreasonable way when carrying out its duties.

A major concern of federal judges is that federal administrators follow the due process of law. The Internal Revenue Service, for example, may seize an individual's property for nonpayment of income taxes—but not until it notifies the taxpayer and provides an opportunity for a formal hearing. If the IRS fails to take these steps, the taxpayer may sue the agency. The prospect of being challenged in court has proven an effective means of control.

Competition among federal agencies is another source of limits on bureaucratic power. Many agencies have competitors in the federal government—agencies that vie for the same set of authorizations or appropriations. The different branches of the armed forces, for instance, compete with each other for a bigger slice of the defense budget. Although such competition may seem inefficient, it does impose restraints on the power of the military bureaucracies by having each keep an eye on the activities of the other.

A strong sense of professionalism and responsibility among public sector employees can also act as a brake on bureaucratic power, especially when someone within an agency exposes inappropriate, unethical, or questionable activities. Ernest Fitzgerald, a civilian analyst at the Defense Department, went public with his concerns about major cost overruns on the purchase of the C5-A transport plane by the Air Force. His complaints led to an investigation of those cost overruns and several new management policies. People like Fitzgerald, who risk their careers to halt bureaucratic misconduct, are called whistle-blowers. Whistle-blowers usually pay a high price for their honesty and candor. In many instances, blowing the whistle in an agency can make one an outcast in the organization and end one's career.[13] Today whistle-blowers have some protection under federal personnel laws, and at least one agency (the National Aeronautics and Space Administration) has arranged for a special telephone number that whistle blowers can call for action. Each agency also has an inspector general's office that can investigate complaints or suspicious behavior.

An alert press corps can also restrain bureaucratic power by investigating leads that might uncover major problems. The Freedom of Information Act and other public disclosure laws restrain bureaucratic power as well. Citizen lobbies such as Common Cause and Ralph Nader's Public Citizen perform much the same function at times.

Troubled skies Airline deregulation in 1978 and an air traffic controllers' strike that ended when President Reagan fired the striking employees thrust the activities of the Federal Aviation Administration into the public limelight. Plagued with a shortage of air traffic controllers (like those shown here) and an abundance of passenger complaints, the FAA struggled to restore confidence in the nation's air transportation system.

Although it is impossible to guarantee that bureaucratic power will not be misused or abused, the mechanisms for limiting that power exist. In the face of all these potential and actual restraints, bureaucratic power in the federal government has a good chance of being controlled.

Subgovernments and Bureaucratic Power

In the United States, bureaucratic power is not exercised in a vacuum. Typically, bureaucracies interact with other actors on the American political stage: the heads of specific agencies, the leaders of interest groups with a special interest in the work of the agency, and members of Congress who preside over relevant committees and subcommittees. Analysts call these alliances **policy subgovernments** because the actors effectively exercise authority in a narrowly defined policy area.

In their most extreme forms, often called *cozy triangles*, subgovernments can be powerful arrangements (see Chapter 8, on interest groups). Cozy triangles come into being when bureaucrats, lobbyists, and members of congressional committees work together regularly to establish policy in their area of common interest. Crucial to the success of any cozy triangle arrangement is keeping it out of public view and limiting the number of participants.

For years one of the best-known cozy triangles—the tobacco subgovernment—generated policies related to tobacco products. There were three sets of actors in the tobacco subgovernment: members of Congress from tobacco-growing states (like North Carolina, South Carolina, and Kentucky) who sat on the agriculture and appropriations committees; lobbyists representing tobacco growers and cigarette-manufacturing companies; and bureaucracies from tobacco-related programs at the Department of Agriculture. These actors would meet regularly to work out policies and programs related to tobacco products. For many years the result was subsidies for tobacco farmers and other programs quite favorable to tobacco.

In 1964 the cozy world of the tobacco subgovernment blew wide open. That year the surgeon general issued a report linking cigarette smoking to lung cancer, heart disease, and emphysema. The report was followed by a Federal Trade Commission proposal that cigarette packages and advertising contain health warnings. The cozy triangle no longer had the low visibility that made it so effective before the surgeon general's announcement. Nevertheless, the tobacco subgovernment remains intact today, although its members can no longer easily set public policies related to tobacco. In fact, they fight a constant battle to maintain their subsidy and marketing programs.[14]

At the opposite extreme from cozy triangles are subgovernments organized as **issue networks.** Issue networks involve a large number of participants with different degrees of interest in and commitment to the policies and problem concerns that bring them together. An issue network is an open and at times highly visible subgovernment. Those who take part in it may come and go constantly, and often there is neither the time nor the leadership to develop shared attitudes toward policy. Bureaucrats also play a role in issue network subgovernments, but that role often depends on their grasp of the issues and their willingness to dive into the open policy-making process.[15]

Environmental policy making is a classic example of an issue network in action. Highly visible since the mid-1960s, the problem of environmental protection has attracted a multitude of actors, including dozens of members of Congress, hundreds of interest groups with varying points of view, and a host of media and academic observers. In the middle of this issue network sits the Environmental Protection Agency, which was created in 1970 to coordinate the implementation of federal environmental policy. The EPA quite successfully maintained a leading role in the environmental issue network during the 1970s. Beginning in 1981, however, the agency's situation changed as it experienced a crisis.

The Reagan administration came to office intent on changing the direction of environmental policy through deregulation and reform. It planned to use the EPA to implement these changes by instituting new agency policies or radically altering the method used by established programs. The administration's strategy virtually ignored the environmental issue network. Incensed at the EPA's positions, environmental interest groups formed alliances to defeat EPA initiatives in a variety of program areas. Furthermore, a coalition of conservationists in and out of Congress began to press for major changes in the Reagan approach. In 1983 the administration acknowledged defeat by replacing the controversial head of the EPA, Ann Gorsuch Burford, with William Ruckelshaus, who had been the first administrator of the agency under Richard Nixon.[16] Ruckelshaus spent two years re-establishing EPA's credibility in the environmental issue network.

Both the tobacco cozy triangle and environmental protection issue network may be extreme examples of subgovernmental politics in the United States. Nevertheless, they are representative of the situations in which most federal bureaucracies find themselves. Whatever power federal bureaucrats and bureaucracies have is qualified and tempered by the subgovernmental arrangements in which they must operate.

Protecting the environment Created in 1970, the Environmental Protection Agency became in the early 1980s a source of conflict between the Reagan administration and environmentalists. Disagreeing with many of the existing environmental regulations, the administration sought to restrict the agency's actions, including those dealing with hazardous waste dumps. Pictured here is an EPA worker disposing of a hazardous chemical.

Control Without Efficiency

The argument that it is necessary to improve the efficiency of the government bureaucracy in order to control it is inherent in the myth of bureaucratic incompetence. We have seen, however, that there are many other forces in our political system that place limits on bureaucratic power. Those forces range from bureaucratic self-restraint to the countervailing power of the president, the Congress, and the courts. Even more impressive are the limits to bureaucratic power implied in the politics of subgovernment policy-making arenas. Taken together, these forces seem to provide sufficient control over bureaucratic power.

CONCLUSION: Expectations and Performance

The popularity of the myth of bureaucratic incompetence makes it a difficult one to challenge. It is impossible to deny that the federal bureaucracy is inefficient and wasteful when compared with just about any major private corporation. It thus seems altogether reasonable that those individuals who support the myth would call for reforms that would radically change the way in which federal agencies operate.

Nevertheless, in this chapter we have discussed how the size and complexity of the federal bureaucracy may make such reforms impossible to carry out. We have noted that, as currently constituted, the federal bureaucracy may be unmanageable. Furthermore, we have seen that the urge for a smaller and more manageable bureaucracy has not had much influence on the proliferation of government agencies. Lastly, we saw how our political system is capable of effectively controlling bureaucratic power without relying on the massive reforms of government advocated by those who adhere to the myth of bureaucratic incompetence.

The principal problem with the myth of bureaucratic incompetence is that it is based on a far too narrow view of what the American people expect from the federal government. The American people are citizens as well as consumers, and as citizens they expect more from government than merely the lowest-costing, most efficiently managed public services. If we were to focus our attention exclusively on efficiency and effectiveness, then there is much to criticize about the way the federal bureaucracy operates. However, Americans place high value on fairness, compassion, democratic rule, constitutional guarantees, and other standards that often conflict with efficiency and effectiveness. They are likely to put a greater priority on making certain that their children are receiving a good education than on keeping the federal funding of education to a minimum. They will be more interested in stopping the spread of AIDS than in saving a few tax dollars by closing a federally funded research facility. There is more to the expectations of the American public than calls for businesslike management of the federal bureaucracy.

Expectations are important for bureaucrats, for federal workers spend most of their time trying to live up to the expectations of others. If we are going to criticize the performance of those bureaucrats—if we are going to accuse them of being incompetent—then we must be certain that they are trying to live up to the expectations we have set for them. The myth of bureaucratic incompetence assumes that federal bureaucrats are (or should be) striving to achieve businesslike efficiency in their work. The reality is that federal bureaucrats are continually attempting to live up to a range of expectations as varied and diverse as programs they administer.

★ ★ ★
SUMMARY

1. The federal bureaucracy comprises diverse groups of people who occupy a variety of white-collar and blue-collar positions. They are organized under several personnel systems, including political appointees, the general civil service, executive service systems, career systems, and wage systems.

2. Much of what federal bureaucrats do is hidden from public view. Nevertheless, they play important roles in the policy-making process—roles that go beyond merely administering government programs.

3. Organizationally, federal bureaucrats work in hundreds of agencies, including the Executive Office of the President, cabinet departments, independent executive branch agencies, regulatory commissions, government corporations, and other types of agencies.

4. The federal bureaucracy has grown in size and changed in nature over the past two centuries, mostly because of increasing demands by the public and changing conditions in American society.

5. Bureaucracies need power to function in the American political system. They derive that power from a variety of sources, such as external support, expertise, bureaucratic discretion, and longevity.

6. There are many limits to bureaucratic power. These limits come from the legal and political controls exercised by the presidency, Congress, the courts, and various agencies.

7. Bureaucratic power is not exercised in a vacuum. It is characterized by subgovernmental politics in which bureaucracies join in alliances with other actors in the policy-making system to formulate and implement public programs.

8. When we judge the performance of federal bureaucracies, we must be clear about the criteria we are applying. Those who contend that the federal bureaucracy is incompetent and inefficient are using only measures of private sector performance to assess government administration. There are, however, other criteria and expectations that federal bureaucrats must live up to, and some of those are in direct conflict with the standards of businesslike performance.

★ ★ ★

KEY TERMS

bureaucracy
political appointees
general civil service
career service
wage systems

policy subgovernments
cozy triangle
issue network
patronage

★ ★ ★

SUGGESTED READINGS

- Fried, Robert C. *Performance in American Bureaucracy.* Boston: Little, Brown, 1976. An introduction to the study of American bureaucracies which focuses on alternative criteria for evaluating administration performance.

- Goodsell, Charles T. *The Case for Bureaucracy: A Public Administration Polemic,* 2nd ed. Chatham, NJ: Chatham House, 1985. A unique defense of bureaucracies that counters major criticisms of public administration with empirical evidence.

- Hummel, Ralph P. *The Bureaucratic Experience,* 3rd ed. New York: St. Martin's Press, 1987. A widely read critique of the impact that bureaucratization is having on American society and culture.

- Kaufman, Herbert. *Red Tape: Its Origins, Uses, and Abuses.* Washington, DC: Brookings Institution, 1977. A short, readable exploration of bureaucratic red tape and its sources. It finds that much of bureaucratic red tape is of our own making.

- Rourke, Francis E. *Bureaucracy, Politics, and Public Policy,* 3rd ed. Boston: Little, Brown, 1984. A classic introduction to bureaucratic power and its role in the policy-making process.

13

C H A P T E R

Courts, Judges, and the Law

On a sunny afternoon in 1975 fifty thousand St. Louis football fans watched their hometown Cardinals stage a dramatic comeback against the favored Washington Redskins. With twenty-five seconds to go in the game and the Cardinals trailing by a single touchdown, Jim Hart, the Cardinal quarterback, lofted a desperate pass to his receiver, Mel Gray. About a yard deep in the end zone, Gray jumped up and caught the ball. Before his feet touched the ground, however, he collided with a Redskin defender. As the two players fell to the Astroturf, the ball flew out of Gray's hands and landed a few feet away. Downfield, one official signaled touchdown, but at the same time a second official signaled incomplete pass. With the fans screaming touchdown, the officials huddled in a corner of the field. Finally, Referee Frank Silvia signaled touchdown—a call that tied the game. In overtime, the Cardinals kicked a game-winning field goal.

For most Redskin fans it was a disappointing loss, but a few were so angered by the touchdown call that they went to federal court to try to have the disputed call overturned.[1] They lost when the suit was dismissed.

In taking their case to court, the fans demonstrated a basic American belief: that the courts can solve almost any kind of problem. In large measure, the uniqueness of the American political system stems from the role played by the courts. No other nation on earth grants so much authority and political power to the judiciary; nor are people of other nations quite as willing to entrust their fate to courts as are Americans. Yet for all their faith in courts, most citizens know very little about the legal system. They may be familiar with the local traffic court or entertained by Judge Wampler's version of small claims court. Nevertheless, when pressed to elaborate on what courts do and why they do it, people fall back on some vague notions about the law.

Thus the image of the courts is shrouded in symbolism and myth. Pomp and circumstance surround even the lowliest of courts. Only in a courtroom will you find a black-robed individual looking down from a raised platform. No other public official is allowed such trappings. In fact, a mayor or senator bedecked in a black robe would seem a pompous fool. Yet when a judge puts on those same robes, no one laughs or even thinks it odd. Instead the robes evoke respect. So it is with the myths that surround the American courts. If they were attributed to any other political institution, they would seem preposterous.

Perhaps the most widespread of the illusions surrounding the courts is that they are above politics. In contrast to the compromise and partisanship of the political world, the myth of the nonpolitical courts represents the judiciary as operating with the certainty and objectivity that comes with the application of a body of specialized knowledge. Members of Congress may act out of self-interest; judges simply apply the law. It is the fate of courts to be characterized as the defenders of the rule of law as opposed to the rule of ordinary men and women.

Breaking the barriers Thurgood Marshall (center), an attorney for the National Association for the Advancement of Colored People (NAACP), celebrates the Supreme Court's 1954 decision declaring segregated public schools to be unconstitutional. In 1967, Marshall further advanced the cause of racial equality by becoming the first black appointed to the U.S. Supreme Court.

As comforting as this myth may be, it distorts reality. In the pages that follow, you will see that even the act of creating the federal courts was fraught with political conflict. Similarly, the process of selecting judges is not only mired in political controversy, but those chosen are often active participants in politics.

The idea that courts have special powers also gives rise to the myth of finality, which assumes that once a court—especially the Supreme Court—has spoken, the decision is implemented. This tendency to view court decisions as an end point in the political process makes courts seem more powerful than they actually are. Final authority does not rest with the Supreme Court, nor should it in a representative democracy. Court orders are not self-executing. Courts cannot compel anyone to comply with decisions. Their orders become effective only with the aid of others—aid that is not always provided.

We will begin our discussion of the role of courts in American society by distinguishing the various sources of law. Then we will look at the structure of the court system and the way that judges are appointed and removed. We will conclude with an examination of the workings of the Supreme Court and the question of compliance.

★ ★ ★
THE ORIGINS AND TYPES OF AMERICAN LAW

As you may recall from Chapter 2, on the Constitution, the oldest source of law applied by U.S. courts is common, or judge-made, law, which dates from medieval England. Although common law is often referred to as "unwritten law," this is somewhat inaccurate, because in applying the common law, judges look to previously published decisions (precedents) for guidance. A comparatively modern and increasingly important source of law is statutory law, which originates from specifically designated law-making bodies (for example, Congress and state legislatures).

The distinction between civil and criminal law is also important in understanding the legal process. **Civil law** involves a conflict between private persons and/or organizations. Typical of the cases arising under civil law are those involving disputes over contracts, claims for damages resulting from a personal injury, and divorce cases. In a civil case, the person bringing the suit is called the plaintiff, and the person being sued is the defendant.

Criminal law, on the other hand, entails offenses against the public order and provides for a specified punishment. Acts in violation of criminal law are specifically detailed in governmental statutes. The party demanding legal action (the federal, state, or other government) is called the prosecution. Most of these cases arise in state courts, although there is a growing body of federal criminal law dealing with such issues as kidnapping, tax evasion, and the sale of narcotics.

★ ★ ★
THE STRUCTURE OF THE COURT SYSTEMS

When most people think about courts, the U.S. Supreme Court immediately comes to mind. As the highest court in the land, the Supreme Court symbolizes the American judiciary. Yet the Supreme Court is only one of more than eighteen thousand American courts, most of which are the creations of the various states. Each state, as well as the Commonwealth of Puerto Rico, has its own independent court system. Since most crimes and civil disputes involve state laws, these are the courts that most affect the average citizen. For example, the motorist accused of speeding will be brought before a court in the state in which the violation occurred.

THE FEDERAL COURT SYSTEM ★ 355

Obviously, among fifty-one court systems there is bound to be a great deal of variability; in fact, no two systems are exactly alike. Nevertheless, two types of courts can be found in all systems.

Trial courts, the lowest level of a court system, are the "courts of first instance," possessing **original jurisdiction** (the power to be the first court to hear a case). These courts take evidence, listen to witnesses, and decide what is true and what is not. Trial courts handle both criminal and civil matters.

Trial court decisions may be made by a single judge (a procedure known as a bench trial) or by a jury composed of citizens selected from the community. The Constitution provides for jury trials in all criminal cases and in civil cases where the value contested exceeds twenty dollars. Most state constitutions contain similar provisions for jury trials. Nevertheless, jury trials tend to be the exception rather than the rule. The desire for quick decisions encourages many defendants to waive the time-consuming jury selection process in favor of the faster decision by a judge. Parties to particularly complicated civil litigation may also assume that members of a jury are less capable of following the detailed arguments than a judge. In criminal cases, a high percentage of defendants enter into plea-bargaining agreements, in which the accused, with the consent of the prosecutor, pleads guilty to a lesser crime and so avoids a trial.

In contrast, **appellate courts** are charged with the responsibility of reconsidering decisions made by trial courts at the request of the losing party. The appellate review is designed to ensure that there is no error in judicial procedures or interpretations of the law. Since appellate courts simply review the written record of lower courts, they do not use juries.

★ ★ ★
THE FEDERAL COURT SYSTEM

On paper, the federal court structure appears to be a relatively simple and eminently rational arrangement. After all, the system is composed of a single Supreme Court, several intermediate appellate and trial courts, and a limited number of specialized trial courts (see Figure 13.1). Each level seems to have its place in the judicial hierarchy. But looks can be deceiving. Behind the judicial system's facade of orderliness is a history of intense political struggle that contradicts the myth of the nonpolitical courts.

Lower Courts

Article III of the Constitution creates only one court, the Supreme Court, leaving to Congress the power to create such "inferior courts" as it deems necessary. This peculiar approach to court structure was the direct result of

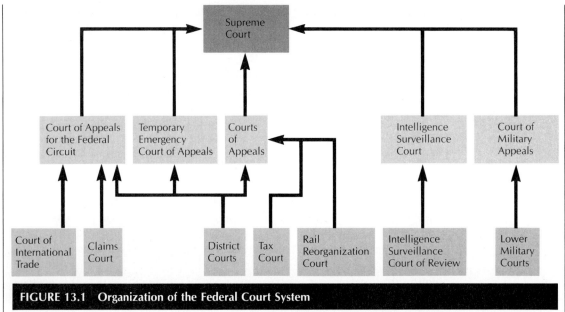

FIGURE 13.1 Organization of the Federal Court System

The lines and arrows show the routes of cases through appeals and Supreme Court grants of hearings.

Source: Lawrence Baum, *American Courts: Process and Policy* (Boston: Houghton Mifflin, 1986), p. 25.

the bitter struggle between the Federalists and the Antifederalists at the Constitutional Convention. The Antifederalists, in order to protect the power of the states, wanted a system in which all cases, even those involving the federal government, would be heard by the state courts. The Federalists argued for a national court system, which would establish the supremacy of the central government and limit the biases of the local courts.[2] Unable to reach agreement, the delegates finally compromised by creating the Supreme Court and leaving to Congress responsibility for filling in the details of the system.

The organization of federal courts remains a divisive political issue, however. For example, it took twenty years of struggle between conservative white southerners and civil rights groups to create a court of appeals for the eleventh **circuit,** or judicial territory. In the 1960s southerners proposed moving conservative southern judges from one circuit to another, creating a Deep South court. Convinced that such restructuring would weaken civil rights enforcement, civil rights groups, principally the National Association for the Advancement of Colored People (NAACP), managed to block the reorganization. In 1980 civil rights groups and liberal members of Congress finally agreed to split an old circuit into two new southern circuits. The

NAACP withdrew its opposition only after the appointment of some black judges to the circuits—demonstrating that even the apparently technical questions of court structure are matters of sharp political conflict.

U.S. district courts. As trial courts of general jurisdiction for the federal system, district courts hear trials in all federal criminal and civil cases. The district courts also hear what are known as diversity cases: suits between parties from different states where the amount in controversy exceeds ten thousand dollars. In addition to their trial duties, the district courts are also responsible for the naturalization of aliens, the approval of passports, and the granting of parole to federal prisoners.

The Judiciary Act of 1789, the first Senate bill introduced in the First Congress, created a national judiciary that included the district courts. Although these courts resulted from the Federalist impulse to establish a strong national judiciary, they were also shaped by the Federalists' need to compromise with the Antifederalists. Thus the Federalist forces attained their goal of a national court system, but the Antifederalists insisted on district boundaries identical to state borders—a situation that remains to this day. By requiring district court and state boundaries to be the same, the Antifederalists achieved a decentralized structure committed to local political values.

Currently, ninety-four U.S. district courts are distributed in the fifty states, the District of Columbia, and the four territories. Twenty-four states contain more than one district, while the remaining states and territories have one district court each.

District court cases are usually heard by a single judge, who presides over both civil and criminal trials. The district courts have a total of 576 judicial positions, but the number of judgeships assigned to each district varies from one to twenty-seven. The state of Rhode Island, for example, constitutes a single judicial district that is staffed by one judge. In contrast, the Southern District of New York, which includes Manhattan and the Bronx, has twenty-seven judges assigned to it.

To most Americans, the district courts may seem like the least important of the federal courts. If the Supreme Court is not more important, certainly it is more noticeable. Yet district courts hear almost 200,000 cases each year, and fewer than 10 percent of them are appealed to a higher court. Of those that are appealed, only a few are reversed. The simple fact is that for most litigants the district court decision is the final decision.

Courts of appeals. Courts of appeals, or circuit courts, as they are sometimes called, serve as the major appellate courts for the federal system. They review all cases—civil and criminal—appealed from the district courts. Moreover, on occasion these courts review decisions of the independent regulatory agencies and departments. For example, decisions of the Federal

Communications Commission (FCC) involving the renewal of radio and television licenses can be appealed only to the District of Columbia Circuit.

There are twelve U.S. courts of appeals, one for the District of Columbia and eleven others covering regional groupings of states (see Figure 13.2). Although the circuits include more than one state, no state is in more than one circuit. A thirteenth court of appeals, the U.S. Court of Appeals for the Federal Circuit, is an appellate court charged with hearing patent cases.

The 12 courts of appeals of general jurisdiction have, as of 1985, 156 authorized judgeships. But as in the district courts, these judges are unevenly distributed among the circuits. Individual circuits have anywhere from six to twenty-eight judges assigned to them. The number is determined by Congress and is supposed to reflect the workload of the circuit. Ordinarily, the courts of appeals hear cases in panels of three judges, and these panels vary in membership from case to case.

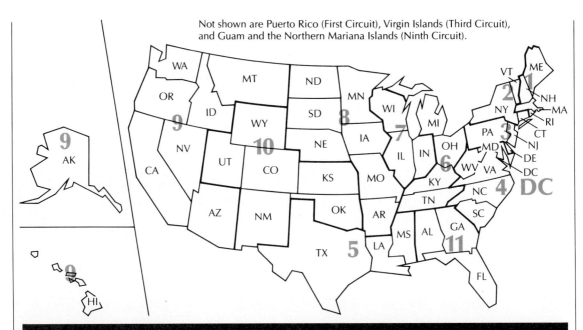

Not shown are Puerto Rico (First Circuit), Virgin Islands (Third Circuit), and Guam and the Northern Mariana Islands (Ninth Circuit).

FIGURE 13.2 United States Circuit Courts of Appeals

At the base of the federal court system are ninety-four district (or trial) courts. Each state has at least one district court and larger states have more. Judgments from district courts can be appealed to one of twelve circuit courts of appeals. Only a fraction of the cases decided in district courts ever come before the appeals courts, and only a tiny fraction of these are reviewed by the Supreme Court.

The Supreme Court

The Constitution is remarkably vague even with regard to the Supreme Court. Take a few moments to compare Article I to Article III. Notice how detailed Article I is concerning the make-up and duties of Congress and how such details are lacking in Article III about the Court.

How many justices serve on the Supreme Court? The answer is nine, but you will not discover that from reading the Constitution. The Constitution does not designate a size for the Court; that is up to Congress. Since 1869 the Court has been staffed by a chief justice and eight associate justices. Until 1869, however, Congress made frequent changes in the size of the Court. Often these changes were thinly disguised efforts to serve partisan political purposes. During the Civil War, for instance, Congress created a tenth seat on the Supreme Court, assuring President Abraham Lincoln a solid majority on the Court.

According to the Constitution, the Supreme Court has both original and appellate jurisdiction (see Background 13.1). Original jurisdiction, as stated earlier in the chapter, means that a court is empowered to make the first decision in a particular kind of dispute; it is the court of first instance. Article III limits the Court's original jurisdiction to cases involving foreign ambassadors and those involving a conflict between two or more states. Suits under original jurisdiction account for a very small portion of the Supreme Court's workload: about 150 such cases since 1789.

The chief labor of the Supreme Court is appellate. For much of the nation's history, the Court was mandated by Congress to hear all cases that came to it. Complaints by the justices that the workload was unmanageable led Congress to pass the Judiciary Act of 1925. Under the provisions of this act, the Court has tremendous latitude in selecting cases it wants to hear.

Of the nearly five thousand cases brought annually to the Supreme Court, approximately 90 percent come by way of a **writ of certiorari**—a request that the Supreme Court order the lower court to send up the record of the case. Cases are accepted for review by means of the rule of four, that is, if four justices vote to consider the case. In more than 95 percent of the writs of certiorari, appeal is denied, generally without explanation. The Court simply notes that certiorari is denied and that the decision of the lower court stands. Cases can also come to the Court by **appeal,** which states that the litigants have some right under the law to have their cases reviewed. In practice, appeals are treated in the same discretionary way as certiorari.

Because the Court receives many more petitions each year than it can possibly process, the freedom to accept a limited number of cases is essential to its effective operation. But efficient management is only one benefit of the screening process. There are political advantages too. By carefully selecting cases for review, the justices can and do advance their policy preferences.

Moreover, the ability to deny review to cases without explanation can be used by the Court to avoid particularly controversial political issues. Thus, the Supreme Court avoided ruling on the constitutionality of the undeclared war in Vietnam by refusing to grant certiorari to cases raising the issue.

Specialized Courts

In addition to the federal courts that we have discussed, Congress has also created a few specialized courts of limited jurisdiction. They include the U.S. Claims Court, created to litigate disputes involving government contracts. Other special courts include the U.S. Court of Military Appeals, the U.S. Court of International Trade, and the U.S. Tax Court. Staffed by judges with expertise in the particular area, these courts reduce the workload of the general courts.

State Court Systems

All states have one appellate court that serves as the highest tribunal. Such courts are not, however, always identifiable by title. For example, in the state of New York the highest court is called the court of appeals, while the trial courts are designated as the supreme courts. Whatever their name, nearly every state possesses one court that reviews the decisions of all other courts. Additionally, slightly over half the states also make use of an intermediate appellate court to hear appeals from the trial court decisions. Such courts permit losers to appeal without overburdening the highest court.

The most numerous state courts, the trial courts, are divided into two types: those with limited jurisdiction and those with general jurisdiction. Trial courts of **limited jurisdiction** are empowered to hear only a narrowly defined class of cases. These specialized courts often process a large number of routine cases involving minor issues. Among the most common are traffic court and small claims court.

On the other hand, trial courts of **general jurisdiction** have authority over a broader class of issues. Ordinarily, such courts hear all civil cases involving nontrivial monetary value and all cases involving serious criminal matters. Although the courts of general jurisdiction are not as specialized as the courts of limited jurisdiction, it is not unusual to find general jurisdiction courts divided into criminal and civil courts, especially in metropolitan areas with heavy case loads.

Interactions Among Court Systems

The existence of so many court systems obviously complicates the interactions among them. Often the litigants (parties involved in a suit) can choose from among several different courts. Indeed, it is common for the plaintiff (the

Removal of a judge Former Chief Justice Rose Bird of the California Supreme Court concedes defeat in her 1986 effort to retain her seat on the high court. Appointed by former Governor Jerry Brown, Bird had long been a target of California conservatives, who mounted an expensive media campaign against her. Under California law, justices are appointed by the governor but must periodically appear before the voters, who can decide yes or no on retention. Bird was the first woman ever appointed to the California Supreme Court and the first California justice to be voted out of office.

party bringing suit) to shop around for a court, hoping to find one favorable to his or her side.

This complexity is heightened by the fact that both state and federal courts may have jurisdiction over the same issues—a situation known as concurrent jurisdiction. Congress has, for example, granted to the federal district courts the right to hear the so-called diversity cases—cases involving citizens of different states contesting a sum greater than ten thousand dollars. In doing so, however, Congress did not deny the state courts the right to hear such cases. It merely added an additional forum for resolving such disputes.

Although the complex network of multiple court systems provides the opportunity to shop around for a favorable court, once the case has been tried, appeals must be made within the same court system. Occasionally, decisions of a state's highest court are successfully appealed to the U.S. Supreme Court, but this can occur only when the state's highest court has rendered a decision interpreting provisions of the U.S. Constitution, a treaty,

BACKGROUND 13.1

The Supreme Court and Judicial Review

Judicial review is the power of the courts to declare an act of a legislature constitutional or unconstitutional, voiding those laws that fall into the latter category. Nowhere in the Constitution is the U.S. Supreme Court specifically granted such authority. Instead judicial review was inferred by the Court in the 1803 case of *Marbury* v. *Madison.*

Following the election of 1800, which saw Thomas Jefferson and his fellow partisans win control of the White House and both chambers of Congress, the incumbent president, John Adams, and the Federalist party attempted to maintain a foothold in the government by filling the judiciary with Federalists. First, John Marshall, secretary of state to Adams, was named the new chief justice of the Supreme Court. Congress then created fifty-eight additional judgeships to be filled by loyal Federalists. (Because these appointments came in the last days of the Adams administration they became known as the "midnight appointments.")

So great was the haste that the Adams administration failed to deliver the commissions of four newly appointed justices of the peace for the District of Columbia. Undelivered, the four commissions were returned to the secretary of state's office, where James Madison, the new secretary of state, found them. On orders of President Jefferson, Madison refused to deliver the commissions, prompting William Marbury, one of the four whose papers were withheld, to bring suit in the Supreme Court. Marbury requested that the Court issue a writ of *mandamus* (an order to a government official to carry out a duty of his or her office) compelling Madison to deliver the commission. The case was filed with the Supreme Court directly because a congressional statute, the Judiciary Act of 1789, empowered the Supreme Court to issue such writs as an act of original jurisdiction.

Marbury's suit placed the Court in a difficult and politically charged situation. Congress had already served warning on the Court by cancelling the 1802 term of the Court, requiring that Marbury's case be put off until 1803. The Court was faced with two choices, neither of which seemed appealing. The justices could have issued the writ and ordered Madison to deliver the commission, but that would have been to no avail. Madison would most certainly have defied the writ, making the Court look powerless. On the other hand, the Court could have refused to issue the writ, but that too would have amounted to an admission of impotence.

Chief Justice Marshall, however, devised a third alternative. After writing an opinion that attacked the administration for neglecting constitutional duties, the Court ruled that it could not issue the writ. According to Marshall, Madison clearly breached his sworn duties, but the Court could not constitutionally issue the writ of mandamus. The Court was powerless in this instance, Marshall argued, because the provision of the Judiciary Act of 1789 that granted original jurisdiction to issue such writs was unconstitutional. Article III of the Constitution specifies the circumstances under which the Court possesses original jurisdiction, but the issuance of writs of mandamus is not included. Therefore, argued Marshall, the Judiciary Act of 1789, by adding such writs to the Court's original jurisdiction, was actually an attempt to alter the Constitution by simple statute rather than the prescribed method of amendment. Since Congress may not do this, Marshall concluded that the act was null and void and the Court was without power to grant Marbury a writ of mandamus.

As a political document, Marshall's decision was a masterpiece. By arguing that Madison was obligated to deliver the commission, Marshall attacked the Jefferson administration. Yet by refusing to issue the writ he avoided a confrontation with the president that the Court was sure to lose. More important, Marshall created for the Court the power of judicial review and insulated that power from attack. After all, Jefferson had benefited from its use. If the Court lacked the power of judicial review, then the writ would have to be issued. The only loser in the case was Marbury, who was sacrificed to Marshall's larger political design.

The political brilliance of Marshall's opinion is unquestionable, but the legal reasoning employed remains to this day a subject of debate. Unlike in the traditional legal opinion, no precedent (previous cases) was cited by Marshall to support his position. Instead he simply stated that: (1) the Constitution is superior to any law; (2) the Judiciary Act of 1789 contradicted the Constitution; and (3) that therefore the Judiciary Act of 1789 must be unconstitutional. As an exercise in logic, the conclusion seems inescapable.

To many critics, however, Marshall's logic misses the point. Why is it the job of the Court, composed as it is of life-tenured appointees, to decide whether an act conflicts with the Constitution? Why, ask Marshall's critics, should this power not belong to elected officials? It is true,

as Marshall claimed, that judges take an oath to support the Constitution, but so too do the president and members of Congress. Are they not equally capable of determining the constitutionality of an act?

Although judicial review has become an element of American politics, its use remains controversial. Those judges and legal scholars who find Marshall's reasoning unconvincing advocate *judicial restraint*—the limited and infrequent use of judicial review. Practitioners of judicial restraint argue that the frequent use of judicial review substitutes the judgment of unelected officials for that of elected representatives and is therefore undemocratic. Opposing judicial restraint are those judges and legal scholars known as *judicial activists*, who believe that the Court has a right, and even an obligation, to exercise judicial review, usually in defense of political minorities.

For a complete account of the Marbury decision, from which much of this discussion has been drawn, see Craig R. Ducat, *Modes of Constitutional Interpretation* (St. Paul, Minn.: West, 1978), pp. 1–41.

or a federal law. Decisions of a court in one state may never be appealed to a court of another state. Nor is it possible to appeal a federal court decision to a state court.

★ ★ ★

RECRUITING AND REMOVING JUDGES

In contrast to nations like Italy, the United States does not have a career judiciary; there is no special training required for judges. In fact, the U.S. Constitution does not even require legal training as a qualification for service on the Supreme Court. All 102 justices who have served on the Court have been lawyers, but this is a political necessity, not a constitutional one.

There is an old saying in American politics that a judge is a lawyer who knew a senator or governor. Though something of an overstatement, the saying serves as a warning that beyond the formal requirements of constitutions and statutes lies a selection process that is highly political. The myth of the nonpolitical courts suggests that judicial selections are or should be based on merit. The reality is that the choices are always political.

Federal Judges

According to Article II of the Constitution, the president shall nominate and with the "advice and consent of the Senate" appoint justices of the Supreme Court. The president proposes a candidate to the Senate; if a majority of the Senate approves, the nominee takes office. This same formal method is used to appoint judges to the courts of appeals and district courts. But the constitutional requirements do not do justice to the political complexity of the selection process. Nor do the constitutional requirements describe the informal methods that have evolved.

Appointment to the district courts. The president has the power to make nominations to the district courts—a power shared with others. Most administrations establish guidelines detailing the qualities the president expects in a nominee and then leave the search for candidates to the Justice Department. In the Reagan administration, for instance, the Justice Department's Office of Legal Policy is chiefly responsible for nominations to the federal district court. To ensure that the nominees share the president's political philosophy, attorneys in the Office of Legal Policy reportedly subject judicial candidates to extensive interviews, said to last six or more hours.

Individual senators are also very important in the selection of district court judges. In nominating candidates for the district courts, the executive branch must always be mindful of the power of individual senators. Under the terms of the unwritten rule of senatorial courtesy, the Senate as a whole will reject the nomination of any candidate opposed by a senator of the president's party from the nominee's state. In recent years senatorial courtesy has been exercised at the committee stage by use of the "blue slip." When it receives a nomination to a federal court, the Senate Judiciary Committee notifies the senators by means of a blue slip. The failure by a senator of the president's party and from the nominee's state to return the blue slip kills the appointment. The committee would simply refuse to take any action until the nomination was withdrawn.

Rather than provoke confrontations with the Senate, presidents have as a rule accepted advice from appropriate senators. Often this translates into formal nomination by the president but informal nomination by a senator. In fact, the prominence of senatorial courtesy led one former assistant attorney general to remark, "the Constitution is backwards. Article II, Section

2, should read: 'the Senators shall nominate, and by and with the consent of the President, shall appoint.' "[3]

Appointment to the courts of appeals.

In making appointments to the courts of appeals, the president and the Justice Department have a freer hand than they do in the case of district courts. Because the circuits contain more than one state, no senator can unambiguously claim senatorial courtesy. Since it is generally assumed that each state in a circuit should have at least one judge on that circuit's appellate bench, the president is constrained by having to maintain the proper balance of state representation.

Attempting to take advantage of this freedom, President Jimmy Carter established by executive order the U.S. Circuit Nominating Commissions—one for each circuit. His announced goal was to create a selection system that elevated merit above political considerations. Judges were supposed to be chosen by the president from lists of three to five candidates presented by the commissions. Despite the emphasis on merit, the judges chosen in the Carter years were overwhelmingly members of the president's party, just as had been true under other presidents. President Ronald Reagan also made a public commitment to select judges on the basis of merit, but not to the nominating commissions, which he abolished in 1981.

Appointment to the Supreme Court.

The Supreme Court is a national institution with no special ties to states or regions. Thus the president need not worry about individual senators exercising senatorial courtesy, although senators from the nominee's state are asked to serve as sponsors. The Senate is not irrelevant to the nomination process, however. Quite the contrary, the Senate has considered itself free to reject candidates for a variety of reasons. Reagan's nomination of Judge Robert Bork, for instance, failed in the Senate because of widespread opposition to his restrictive views on the right to privacy and equal rights for women.

In the nineteenth century the Senate was more likely than it is today to disapprove a presidential nomination on purely partisan grounds. Two of the most recent nominations to fail in the Senate, those of Judges Clement Haynsworth and G. Harrold Carswell, were opposed by Senate liberals for ideological reasons, but both candidates possessed other serious disadvantages. Haynsworth came under attack for purchasing stock in a company that had been a party in a case before him; he bought the stock after the decision had been made but before it was announced. Carswell was criticized for lacking the professional qualifications expected of a Supreme Court justice. Carswell's fate was probably sealed when one of his defenders, Republican Senator Roman Hruska from Nebraska, argued that "there are a lot of mediocre judges and people and lawyers. They are entitled to a little representation, aren't they, and a little chance?"[4]

Because justices of the Supreme Court occupy such a visible position in

Facing the Senate Appointment to the Supreme Court requires nomination by the president and confirmation by the Senate. Here Associate Justice William Rehnquist appears before the Senate Judiciary Committee confirmation hearings. Despite objections from some liberal senators, Rehnquist was confirmed, in 1986, as the nation's sixteenth chief justice.

the American system of government, presidents are particularly sensitive to the type of individuals they select. Most presidents are quite careful to choose justices whose ideological views seem to be in harmony with the administration's. If fate provides enough vacancies, presidential appointments can reshape the judiciary until it reflects the administration. More important, since Supreme Court justices are appointed for life, the president's philosophical positions may be reflected in the court long after the administration has left office.

Of course, presidents are not always successful in predicting what a candidate will do once in office. Perhaps the most famous example of a president frustrated by his own appointment is seen in Theodore Roosevelt's assessment of Justice Oliver Wendell Holmes. Before forwarding the Holmes nomination to the Senate, Roosevelt had assured himself that the candidate shared his views on the antitrust statutes. When Holmes immediately voted against the president's view in an antitrust case, Roosevelt quipped that he could "make a judge with a stronger backbone out of a banana."[5]

President Dwight D. Eisenhower came to regret his appointment of Earl Warren as the chief justice. Eisenhower had made the appointment expecting Warren to express the president's own middle-of-the-road political views. Instead, the Warren Court (1953–1969) became known as the most liberal court in U.S. history. Warren's unexpected devotion to liberalism prompted Eisenhower to refer to the appointment as "the biggest damned-fool mistake I ever made."[6]

Nominations to the Supreme Court also give presidents a chance to recognize important constituent groups, especially social groups that have been unrepresented. President Lyndon Johnson broke the Supreme Court's color barrier by appointing Thurgood Marshall, the first black justice. President Reagan appointed Sandra Day O'Connor as the first woman to serve on the Court. Obviously, the appointment of a single minority member to the Court is unlikely to have a great substantive impact on decisions, but representation for those groups traditionally excluded from the process has great symbolic value.

Who Becomes a Federal Judge?

No recruitment system is ever neutral. Any system will favor certain skills and opportunities and downplay others. The process of selecting Supreme Court justices favors individuals from socially advantaged families. As an observer has noted, "The typical Supreme Court Justice has generally been white, Protestant (with a penchant for a high social status denomination), usually of ethnic stock originating in the British Isles, and born in comfortable circumstances in an urban or small-town environment."[7] What is more, almost two-thirds of the justices came from politically active families. Finally, those appointed to the Court were by and large politically active themselves, with the vast majority having held a previous political office.

When we examine the judiciary in the lower federal courts, we see a similar, although less pronounced, pattern of upper- and middle-class appointees. Compared to Supreme Court justices, judges on the courts of appeals, for instance, are slightly less likely to come from politically active families and more likely to be educated at less prestigious law schools. These courts also manifest a greater gender and racial diversity than does the High Court. This diversity peaked under Carter, who appointed more women and minorities to the federal court than any other president. The situation was made possible by the fact that Carter had more vacancies to fill than any previous president.

Since appointments are for life, the federal courts are an especially rich source of political patronage, and presidents are under some pressure to reward the party faithful by such appointments. Although presidents occasionally nominate a member of the opposition party, most have selected at least 90 percent of the appointees from their own party. Staffing the courts with partisans assures a party a foothold in the government even when the party is out of favor with the voters. Aside from patronage, relying on members of their own party allows presidents to choose judges who most likely share their political outlook. Thus the bias toward fellow party members serves two goals, both of which quite clearly contradict the myth of nonpolitical courts.

Removing Judges

In the early days of the Republic, one of the most important problems facing the federal courts was attracting and retaining judges. As strange as it may seem, President Washington had problems filling positions on the Supreme Court. John Rutledge, for example, one of Washington's first appointees, resigned before the Court ever met to become the chief justice of the South Carolina supreme court—apparently a more attractive position. As the prestige of the federal courts increased, recruitment problems diminished, although attracting and retaining lower court judges is sometimes difficult because the salaries are low when compared with what members of the judiciary would get if they were in private law practice.

The prestige and power of a judgeship occasionally create the need to remove an ill or incompetent judge who refuses to retire. This problem is particularly thorny in the federal courts because the only constitutional means for removing judges is the impeachment process, which requires evidence of "Treason, Bribery, or other high Crimes and Misdemeanors."

Over the years there have been few impeachment trials. In 1986, however, Congress, in its first such trial in fifty years, did impeach and convict U.S. District Court Judge Harry E. Claiborne of Nevada. Claiborne had previously been convicted of evading the payment of more than ninety thousand dollars in income taxes. At the time of his impeachment trial, he was serving a two-year sentence in federal prison but continuing to draw his salary as a federal judge.

Even if impeachment were easier, it would probably not be considered appropriate in cases where a judge suffers from illness or senility. A case in point is that of Utah District Court Judge Willis Ritter. Ritter first drew national attention when he ordered court officials to arrest noisy plumbers who were making repairs near his courtroom.[8] He also engaged in such eccentric behavior as hissing throughout an attorney's presentation to the court. While this behavior is clearly odd, it does not seem to fit the definition of an impeachable offense—"Treason, Bribery, or other high Crimes and Misdemeanors."

Lacking an effective means of removing judges, Congress has turned to providing pension programs as an incentive. Under a 1954 act of Congress, judges can opt for the status of senior judge. Senior judges receive a pension equal to full pay, and they may participate, where needed, in as many cases as they choose. This option allows a judge to enjoy a reduced workload without completely retiring. Senior judges have become essential for the operation of many of the more overworked lower federal courts. Since judges do not have to accept senior status, Congress has also provided a mechanism for denying case assignments to sitting judges on the lower federal courts.[9] The judge retains the post and the salary but receives no work.

★ ★ ★
THE SUPREME COURT AT WORK

The Supreme Court term begins the first Monday in October and runs until the end of June or early in July, depending on the workload. The term of the Court is designated by the year it begins, even though very few decisions will actually be handed down in October, November, and December of that year. Throughout the term, the Court alternates between two weeks of open court, called sessions, and two weeks of recess, the time when the justices read petitions and write opinions.

Oral Argument

During the weeks that the court is in session, the justices meet Monday through Wednesday to hear oral arguments. These sessions begin at 10:00 A.M. and last until about 3:00 P.M., with a one-hour break for lunch. Ordinary cases are allotted one hour for arguments, and the time is evenly divided between the parties. If the case is especially important or involves multiple parties raising a variety of issues, the Court may permit longer presentations.

The attorneys presenting oral arguments are reminded of their time limitations by two lights on the lectern. When the white light appears, they know that they have five minutes left. The flash of the red light signals that their time is up, and they must cease unless the chief justice grants an extension. Most often the parties are strictly held to their allotted time. Chief Justice Hughes (1930–1941) was so rigid in enforcing the time limit that he is said to have stopped an attorney in the middle of the word *if.*

Because all parties have prepared written **briefs** (written documents containing a summary of the issues, the laws applying to the case, and arguments supporting counsel's position), the Court discourages attorneys from reading prepared statements. Generally, the justices expect the attorneys to discuss the case and not to deliver a lecture. Often the attorneys spend their allotted time answering questions posed by the justices. For their part, the justices often use the questions as a means of debating with their colleagues. On one occasion, as Justice Felix Frankfurter repeatedly questioned a nervous attorney, Justice William Douglas repeatedly responded with answers helpful to the attorney. Finally, a frustrated Frankfurter, directing his remarks to the attorney, said, "I thought you were arguing this case." The attorney responded, "I am, but I can use all the help I can get."[10]

The value of oral argument has long been debated by observers, but the Court's reluctance to decide cases solely on the basis of the written briefs suggests that the justices themselves continue to find merit in the process.

The Supreme Court, 1986 Term: The Rehnquist Court
Chief Justice William H. Rehnquist (sitting on table) with the associate justices. From left, John Paul Stevens, Sandra Day O'Connor, Antonin Scalia, William H. Rehnquist, William J. Brennan Jr., Thurgood Marshall, Byron R. White, Lewis F. Powell Jr., and Harry A. Blackmun. Justice Powell retired from the court in June 1987, to be replaced in February 1988 by Judge Anthony M. Kennedy.

Conference Work

Though oral argument may be dramatic, the crucial work of the Court is done in conference. Twice a week, when the Court is in session, the justices gather in the conference room to discuss and decide cases. No one else is admitted—not even secretaries or law clerks to help the justices. If a justice needs anything from outside the room, the junior justice (least senior in terms of service, not the youngest) must go to the door and summon a messenger. In the past the junior justice was even responsible for pouring

Advice and consent
Judge Robert Bork (left),
the first of President
Reagan's Supreme
Court nominees to re-
place retiring Justice
Lewis Powell, consults
with Senate judiciary
committee member
Strom Thurmond, Re-
publican from South
Carolina, prior to com-
mittee hearings. After
twelve days of conten-
tious and highly publi-
cized hearings, includ-
ing thirty hours of
testimony by the nomi-
nee, the committee
recommended that the
full Senate reject the
nomination of Judge
Bork. The Senate's ac-
ceptance of the com-
mittee recommendation
forced President Rea-
gan to submit another
nomination.

the coffee, a practice rumored to have ended with the appointment of Justice
Sandra O'Connor.

Generally, the justices first decide which petitions should be accepted.
Before the conference, the chief justice, with the aid of law clerks, prepares
and circulates to the other justices a "discuss" list: a list of cases that the
chief justice thinks worthy of discussion. Any case not on the list will be
automatically denied review unless another justice requests that it be added
to the list. Apparently, as many as 70 percent of the requests for review are
denied without any discussion.[11]

Cases that make the list are not automatically accepted for review,
however. Instead, each case is considered and voted upon by the justices.
Only the cases that receive four votes (the rule of four) are accepted and

scheduled for further action, and the number of such cases is usually quite small.

After deciding which cases to accept for review, the Court moves on to the cases being argued that week. The chief justice begins the discussion of each case by outlining and commenting on the main issues. Each justice in order of seniority then comments on the case. If the votes of the justices are not clear from the discussion, the chief justice calls for a formal vote. Most questions, however, require no vote since the justices' positions will be clear from their initial comments.

After the vote, the chief justice, if he is in the majority, assigns the writing of the opinion. If the chief justice is not in the majority, then the majority's most senior justice makes the assignment. The assignment of an opinion writer is important because it will determine the grounds for the Court's decision and even, perhaps, the size of the majority. The justice who assigns the writing of the opinion may decide to write the opinion him- or herself, or give the task to the member of the majority closest to his or her views. It has long been rumored that former Chief Justice Burger frequently let his turn in the discussion of important cases pass so that he could remain free to join the majority at the end and therefore assign the opinion writer. This practice reportedly became so common that Justice Potter Stewart is said to have drawn a tombstone for the former chief justice with the words, "I'll Pass for The Moment."[12]

Writing and Announcing the Opinion

Once the writing of the opinion has been assigned, the justice given this task begins work on a draft that expresses his or her own ideas and also takes into account opinions expressed by others in the conference. At the same time other justices may be drafting separate **concurring opinions** (opinions that agree with the conclusion but not the reasoning of the majority) or **dissenting opinions** (opinions that disagree with the majority conclusion). No one is assigned to write a dissenting opinion, although the members of the minority may agree informally on one justice.

As the drafts are completed, they are circulated so that all justices can see and have an opportunity to comment on them. As justices suggest changes in wording and reasoning, negotiations begin. The justice who has drafted the majority opinion, as well as the justices working on the concurring and dissenting opinions, may have to make changes in order to satisfy the others. Sometimes conflicting views among the justices make this process extremely difficult and time-consuming. More important, the evident need to compromise may produce vague decisions that offer little guidance to lower courts.

Occasionally, the justice assigned to write the majority opinion will change positions and become a dissenter or vice versa. Justice William Brennan described the process when he noted: "I have had to convert more than one of my proposed majority opinions into a dissent before the final opinion was announced. I have also, however, had the more satisfying experience of rewriting a dissent as a majority opinion of the Court."[13]

The opinion-writing stage does not end until all the justices decide which opinion to join. Once they do so, the Court announces the opinion. Throughout much of the Court's history, the justices had read their opinions—concurring and dissenting—publicly. Currently, the opinion writers read only short statements describing the issues and the disposition.

★ ★ ★

THE IMPLEMENTATION OF COURT DECISIONS

The pomp and circumstance surrounding the announcement of a Supreme Court decision lends credibility to the myth of finality. Yet this ceremony seldom settles the matter. Rather than being the final decision, the Court's announcement is only the beginning of a long process of implementation.

Court orders are not self-executing, and the court needs the cooperation of others to carry out the announced policy. It cannot force compliance: it cannot call on an army or police force to carry out its orders, nor can it levy taxes to fund their implementation. Even if a previous decision is not being implemented, the Court cannot act until someone brings suit in a lower court.

Furthermore, unlike the other agencies of government, courts must await cases; they cannot seek them out. Their only recourse is to signal their willingness to consider cases involving particular issues by the language that they use in deciding cases before them.

Compliance by Other Courts

Compliance is not just a matter of getting the parties in the cases to go along with the decision. When the Court overturns the decision of a lower court, it generally sends (remands) the case back to the original trial court for a decision "not inconsistent" with its opinion. But trial courts do not always follow the Supreme Court's wishes.

For instance, lower courts may find it difficult to carry out an ambiguous Supreme Court decision. If multiple concurring and dissenting opinions accompany a decision, the lower court may find it difficult to interpret. In *Furman* v. *Georgia* (1972), for example, five justices ruled that the death

Resisting Supreme Court decisions Opposition to the Supreme Court's decision invalidating segregation in public schools provoked several forms of resistance. Here white students in the late 1950s avoid integrated public schools by attending class in a local church turned private school.

penalty was unconstitutional as applied in that particular case, but they could not agree on the reason. Consequently, each justice wrote a separate opinion. Lower courts cannot interpret such a decision accurately, and in such situations lower court judges find it easy to substitute their own values and beliefs.

Because lower federal and state courts are independent of the High Court, they can—and occasionally do—defy Court rulings. There is little that the Court can do in such cases. The judges of these lower courts are sworn to uphold the U.S. Constitution but not the opinions of the Supreme Court, and the Court lacks the power to fire even the most disobedient judge. Thus the Supreme Court's power to reverse lower-court decisions is limited both by its inability to police lower courts and by time constraints (it cannot review every lower-court decision).

TRUTH·JUSTICE·EQUALITY·PUBLIC RELATIONS

Drawing by Richter; © 1987 The New Yorker Magazine, Inc.

Being reversed by a higher court is not necessarily the worst thing that can happen to a judge. Sometimes, in fact, a reversal may be welcomed. Judges who are caught between the mandates of the Supreme Court, located in far-off Washington, and the strong contradictory desires of their neighbors may find the displeasure of the High Court easier to bear than the anger of the community. Elected judges may be especially reluctant to enforce Court orders that risk voter ire, even if they personally agree with the High Court.

In the 1950s federal district court judges were deeply embroiled in the school desegregation issue—a conflict of national versus local values. Many communities resisted, often vehemently, Court-ordered desegregation. Those district judges who enforced the *Brown* v. *Board of Education* (1954) decision found themselves cut off from their own communities, as old friends and colleagues fell away. Many were threatened and even physically abused. For example, South Carolina District Court Judge J. Waties Waring retired from the bench and moved to New York after he became the target of death threats prompted by his enforcement of the *Brown* decision.[14]

Congress and the President

Just as the Supreme Court must depend on the so-called inferior courts to implement decisions, so too must it rely on the cooperation of Congress and the president. Both institutions have the power to aid or hinder the implementation of court orders.

The most important power that Congress has is its control of public funds. By providing or withholding the funds necessary to carry out court policy, Congress can significantly affect implementation, as the history of school desegregation amply illustrates. During Lyndon Johnson's administration, Congress authorized the Department of Health, Education and Welfare to withhold federal funds from school systems that refused to desegregate—providing a strong incentive for the local communities to comply with the Supreme Court's 1954 decision. In 1975, however, Congress, disturbed by court-ordered busing, diminished the incentive by prohibiting the withholding of funds from school districts refusing to implement busing.

The actions of individual members of Congress may also advance or impede Court policy. Whether important political leaders defend or attack a Court decision may have much to do with the willingness of others to accept the judgment. Clearly, the cause of school desegregation was not helped when, in 1956, ninety-six members of Congress signed the Southern Manifesto, a document attacking the *Brown* decision. Those who believed that the Supreme Court was wrong could always point to distinguished members of Congress as sharing their view. Furthermore, the support of so many in Congress undoubtedly gave hope that the decision would someday be overturned.

Congress may also use its powers to directly counteract Court decisions. Court decisions interpreting the Constitution may, for example, be overturned by a congressionally initiated constitutional amendment. Although the process is cumbersome and difficult, it has been used on five occasions. Most recently, the Twenty-sixth Amendment, in lowering the voting age to eighteen, overturned the decision in *Oregon* v. *Mitchell* (1970). (In the Mitchell decision, the Court ruled that Congress could by statute lower the voting age to eighteen in national but not state elections.) The Court's decision to strike down prayer in public schools has generated hundreds of proposals for constitutional amendments, including one put forward by the Reagan administration. To date none of these proposals has passed both houses of Congress.

Occasionally, Congress tries to pressure the Court into reversing its decisions. In 1964, for instance, angered by a series of Warren Court decisions that required reapportionment of state legislatures solely on the basis of population, Congress gave the justices a smaller pay raise than other top-level officials. To underscore the point, Republican Representative Robert Dole from Kansas (now Senate minority leader) proposed that the pay increase be contingent on reversal of the decision.[15]

The president and the executive branch can also be vital to the fate of Supreme Court decisions. On the average, a president appoints a new justice every twenty-two months. Thus a two-term president has the potential to reshape the Court, which can then negate a troublesome policy. Certainly, Richard Nixon intended to do just that when, in 1968, he campaigned for the presidency on the promise to appoint justices who would be tough on criminal defendants. Much of Nixon's 1968 presidential campaign was an attack on the liberal Warren Court. His four Court appointments, including a new chief justice (Warren Burger) managed to stem much of the liberal trend set by the Warren Court and reverse some previous liberal decisions.

Similarly, Reagan has attempted to alter several Court decisions through careful selection of nominees. Reagan's appointments of Associate Justices Sandra Day O'Connor and Antonin Scalia, as well as his elevation of William H. Rehnquist to the post of chief justice, were designed to create a Court ideologically compatible with the administration. Conservatives remain hopeful that Reagan's appointments will lead the Court to overturn liberal decisions on such social issues as school prayer and abortion.

As the most visible public official, the president may influence public opinion by his willingness to accept a decision. His silence, on the other hand, may encourage disobedience or delay implementation. Eisenhower's refusal to endorse the *Brown* decision gave support to those who opposed the Court. As the head of the executive branch, the president may also order the Justice Department to prosecute noncompliance vigorously or to make only a token effort.

CONCLUSION: The Courts are Not What They Seem

This brief discussion of the American legal system demonstrates that no matter how much we may wish it to be otherwise the courts are political institutions. As soothing as it may be, the myth of the nonpolitical courts simply does not reflect the American legal process. Although the conflict that produced the basic structure of the federal courts occurred long ago, the potential for political discord still exists, and we should not be blind to this fact. Nor can we ignore the link between partisan politics and the courts inherent in the system of judicial selection. Since judicial positions go to those who demonstrate faithful service to the party, courts are staffed by individuals of considerable political experience.

The myth of finality likewise fails to capture the reality of American courts. The implementation of court decisions requires the participation and cooperation of many in the political system. A simple pronouncement from a court does not suffice.

★ ★ ★
SUMMARY

1. The oldest source of American law is known as common law or judge-made law. A more modern and increasingly important source of law is statutory law.

2. Civil law involves a conflict between private individuals or organizations. Criminal law, on the other hand, concerns wrongs done to the public.

3. The United States actually has fifty-one court systems, one for the federal government and one for each state. Although these systems differ in many respects, all of them contain two basic types of courts: trial and appellate.

4. Article III of the Constitution creates only a Supreme Court and leaves to Congress the authority to create inferior courts.

5. The ninety-four U.S. district courts are the trial courts for the federal system. Approximately 200,000 cases a year are heard by the district courts, and fewer than 10 percent of their decisions are appealed.

6. The twelve U.S. courts of appeals handle most of the appellate work in the federal system. Organized into state groupings known as circuits, the courts of appeals hear all appeals from the federal district courts and some independent regulatory agencies and departments.

7. The U.S. Supreme Court is authorized to act as a court of original jurisdiction in a few narrowly defined instances, but the vast majority of its work is appellate.

8. Cases are appealed to the Supreme Court primarily by either an appeal or a writ of certiorari—with approximately 90 percent of the cases coming by way of certiorari. The Court has great latitude in deciding which of the almost five-thousand such cases it wants to hear. Writs of certiorari, for instance, are accepted by the Court according to the rule of four. Unless at least four justices vote to hear the case, certiorari is denied without explanation.

9. Congress has also created a few specialized courts, such as the U.S. claims court.

10. Although state court systems vary considerably, all have a layer of trial courts and at least one appellate court. Slightly more than half the states also have a level of intermediate courts to hear appeals from the trial courts and lessen the burden of the highest court.

11. The Constitution requires that federal judges be nominated by the president and appointed with the advice and consent of the Senate.

Appointment procedures vary considerably, however, depending on the level of the court involved. The nomination of district court judges often originates with the senator or senators of the president's party from the nominee's state. These senators may exercise senatorial courtesy. Because courts of appeals are organized into circuits that cross state boundaries, no senator is entitled to exercise senatorial courtesy over these appointments.

12. In making appointments to the Supreme Court, the president need not be concerned with senatorial courtesy. Nevertheless, the Senate as a whole can be a serious obstacle to the appointment of the president's nominees. Although the practice is not as common today, the Senate has historically felt free to reject presidential nominations to the Court on purely partisan grounds.

13. The selection of federal judges produces a judiciary largely composed of upper–middle-class white Protestants who prior to becoming judges were politically active.

14. In nominating federal judges, presidents overwhelmingly select members of their own political party.

15. Since federal judges are appointed for life, occasionally the need arises to remove an ill or incompetent judge. Because the Constitution provides for removal only by impeachment, Congress has created the position of senior judges as a means of encouraging judges to retire.

16. The public phase of the Supreme Court's business consists of oral arguments presented before the justices. These are very formalized procedures conducted under tight time constraints.

17. The most important part of the Court's work takes place in its conferences, which are closed to all but the justices themselves. In these conferences, the justices discuss and vote on the cases.

18. Once a vote has been taken on a case, the chief justice, if he is in the majority, or the senior justice in the majority assigns the writing of the opinion. The justice assigned to write the opinion must then circulate drafts of the decision to the other justices. No opinion is final until at least a majority of the court agrees on an opinion.

19. Justices who disagree with the majority opinion are free to write dissenting opinions explaining why they cannot accept the majority decision. Justices who agree with the majority opinion but not its reasoning may write concurring opinions.

20. Lower courts do not necessarily comply with Supreme Court decisions. Often lower courts find the decisions sufficiently ambiguous to make compliance extremely difficult. When Supreme Court decisions conflict

with locally held values, lower-court judges may be reluctant to displease their communities in order to enforce the rulings of the High Court.

21. Congress also possesses a great deal of power to aid or hinder the implementation of Supreme Court decisions. The execution of Supreme Court policies often requires the appropriation of public funds, a function controlled by Congress. Thus congressional willingness to support the Court's position through appropriations is often crucial. Congress can also propose constitutional amendments to overturn Supreme Court decisions.

22. The successful implementation of Supreme Court decisions also requires the cooperation of the president, or at least his acceptance of the policy. A president's willingness to accept a particular Court opinion will serve to influence public opinion. More important, a president may seek to reshape the Court through the appointment process.

★ ★ ★
KEY TERMS

civil law
criminal law
original jurisdiction
appellate courts
circuit courts
writ of certiorari

appeal
limited jurisdiction
general jurisdiction
briefs
concurring opinions
dissenting opinions

★ ★ ★
SUGGESTED READINGS

- Baum, Lawrence. *The Supreme Court.* 2d ed. Washington, D.C.: Congressional Quarterly Press, 1985. A basic description of the workings of the U.S. Supreme Court that includes a complete discussion of the decision-making process used by the Court.

- Carp, Robert A., and Ronald Stidham. *The Federal Courts.* Washington, D.C.: Congressional Quarterly Press, 1985. A complete account of the federal court system, with an emphasis on the federal courts below the U.S. Supreme Court. The authors provide a full account of the working environment of federal judges.

- Glick, Henry R. *Courts, Politics, and Justice.* New York: McGraw-Hill, 1983. A detailed description of the judicial process, with particular attention to state courts.

- Johnson, Charles A., and Bradley C. Canon. *Judicial Policies: Implementation and Impact.* Washington, D.C.: Congressional Quarterly Press, 1984. An examination of how Supreme Court decisions are implemented.

- Woodward, Bob, and Scott Armstrong. *The Brethren: Inside the Supreme Court.* New York: Simon & Schuster, 1979. A breezy, somewhat gossipy account of the personalities and inner workings of the Supreme Court, written by two Washington reporters.

14

CHAPTER

Domestic Policy and Policy Making

MAKING PUBLIC POLICY

    Stages in the Policy-making Process: *Issue identification, agenda setting, policy formulation, policy adoption, policy implementation, policy evaluation*

    Models of Decision Making: *Rational, incremental, elite, pluralist*

ECONOMIC POLICY

    Economic Development Policies

    Economic Regulatory Policies

    Monetary Policies

    Fiscal Policies

    The Continuing Debates over Economic Policies: *Industrial policy, supply-side economics, economic deregulation, Keynesianism, monetarists*

SOCIAL POLICY

    Aiding the Poor: *General assistance, work assistance, categorical assistance*

    Meeting the Needs of the General Public: *Social insurance; social regulation (consumer protection, worker protection)*

    The Debates over Social Policy

CONCLUSION: THE DYNAMIC MYTHS OF AMERICAN PUBLIC POLICY

Responding to pressures from environmental groups, Congress enacted a law in 1977 requiring coal companies to clean up their mining sites. It was a tough law that, if strictly enforced, would prove costly to mine operators. Some members of Congress feared that the policy's cost might put small mine operators out of business. So they excluded from the act's stringent requirements any mine operation that disturbed less than two acres of land.

That small favor, however, soon became a major loophole in the law. Large coal companies, taking a new approach to mining operations, would build a road into a site they had just purchased and contract with smaller companies to do the actual excavation on two-acre plots. When operations were complete, the contractor would abandon the area without reclaiming the site. As a result, open shafts and pits scarred the landscape throughout the Appalachian region, especially in Virginia and Kentucky.

In 1985 a federal judge closed the loophole by ruling that the small contractors were merely agents of the larger firms and therefore the two-acre exemption did not apply. This decision was a triumph for environmentalists, who had brought the suit, and a relief for the Interior Department's Surface Mining Office, which had been criticized for failing to enforce the cleanup law. In 1987 Congress finally repealed the two-acre loophole, and by that summer thousands of abandoned mining sites were being reclaimed under the watchful eye of both the Mining Office and environmental groups.[1]

The story of the coal-mining reclamation policy is not unique. Most of this nation's public policies are the result of political and legal pressures exerted by groups seeking to promote their interests through government action. In fact, we can define **public policies** as actions taken by government officials in response to problems and issues raised through the political system. Public policies range from formal legislation such as the coal-mining reclamation law to executive branch actions like President John F. Kennedy's establishment of the Peace Corps in 1961. Policies also come from the judicial branch as court decisions and orders. Even a decision not to act is a form of policy making.

What do Americans think about the policies of their government? The answer is that Americans view these in seemingly contradictory ways.

On the one hand, many citizens believe that government does too much and should do a great deal less. According to public opinion polls, most Americans favor cuts in government spending. Thus a majority of those surveyed (54 percent) supported a 1985 law that cut federal spending in order to ensure a balanced federal budget by 1991. Only 20 percent disapproved of the law. Yet when asked about increasing federal taxes to pay for current programs and to reduce the nation's growing debt, some three-fourths of those polled objected to such increases. Clearly, then, most Americans want to spend less on public policies or at least not to pay any more for what they now receive.[2]

These findings, though, give only a partial picture. Most Americans are reluctant to approve cutbacks in major social programs. A 1986 poll found a majority opposed to most program cutbacks proposed by Ronald Reagan's administration. When asked if they approved of possible reductions in programs such as social security and Medicare, only 9 percent of those surveyed said yes, while 88 percent said no.

Americans want to have it both ways: to reduce government spending and avoid raising taxes but at the same time not cut back most major programs. What drives people in these contradictory directions? The answer lies in two basic myths about American domestic policy.

First, in recent years Americans have become increasingly attached to the **myth of too much government,** which says that big government has become the major threat to the well-being and future of American society. In 1959 the Gallup Poll found that only 14 percent of Americans believed that big government poses a greater threat to the country than does big labor or big business. By 1967 that figure had climbed to 49 percent, and it has remained at about that level ever since.[3] If one out of every two Americans fears that government has grown too big and powerful, it is not surprising that many Americans want to decrease government spending and taxes.

Second, Americans have also developed a belief in the **myth of too little government.** According to this myth, government does not fulfill its obligations, especially toward the poor, the homeless, the unemployed, and others who need its help. For many Americans the problem is that government is doing too little in some areas while doing too much in others. For example, in a 1985 Gallup Poll, 42 percent of those questioned thought that government was spending too little on social programs while 22 percent believed that too much was being spent on them. The same poll showed that 46 percent of the public saw the defense budget as too large, whereas only 11 percent judged it to be inadequate.

Is American government doing too much or too little? That question is central to much of the ongoing debate among politicians and policy makers. In this chapter you will see how that debate has influenced economic and social policies. First, however, we will look at the way government makes policy in response to public problems and issues.

★ ★ ★

MAKING PUBLIC POLICY

Congress makes policy by enacting laws, presidents by publishing executive orders, the courts by handing down decisions, and bureaucracies by issuing rules and regulations. None of these actions, however, occurs in a vacuum. Each is the product of formal and informal interactions among hundreds of participants inside and outside government.[4]

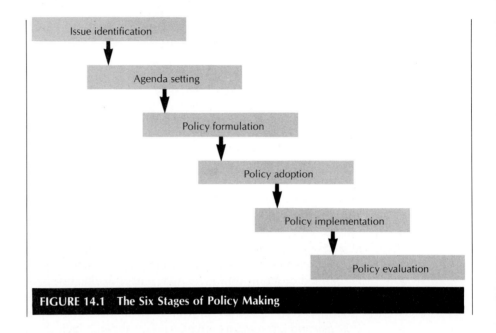

FIGURE 14.1   The Six Stages of Policy Making

Stages in the Policy-making Process

Policy making can be pictured as a six-stage process (see Figure 14.1). In the first stage, **issue identification,** some event, person, or group calls attention to a problem that needs government action. During the early 1980s, for example, the increasing number of deaths attributed to acquired immune deficiency syndrome (AIDS) brought demands for money to fund research into the cause of the deadly disease. Health care professionals, the surgeon general of the United States, and groups representing homosexuals (who were at high risk for the disease) used every opportunity they could to get the attention of policy makers at all levels of American government.[5]

In a second stage, **agenda setting,** the issue or problem is seriously considered by the policy-making institution. Not all the problems identified in the first stage of the process get this far. In mid-November 1953, for instance, a thick cloud of dirty air settled on New York City, causing headaches, itchy eyes, nausea, and other physical ailments. The incident lasted long enough to draw the media's attention, for the clouded atmosphere interfered with football games, astronomical observations, and other outdoor activities. No action followed, however, since the immediate impact of the air pollution was not regarded as serious. Nine years later a review of public health records showed that the incident caused approximately two hundred deaths in the New York area.[6] By the early 1960s environmental pollution was on the agenda of federal policy makers, and problems like New York City's cloud began to get serious attention.

The fact that an issue on the government's agenda gets serious attention does not necessarily mean that a policy will emerge immediately. Someone must develop a proposal or program that can address the issue. This third stage of the policy-making process, **policy formulation,** may take years to complete as policy makers and their staffs deliberate the pros and cons of each issue.

Many policy responses are formulated within government agencies, in Congress, and by groups outside the government, working separately and together. Both the White House and Congress looked to the federal Centers for Disease Control for policy proposals to deal with AIDS. Several proposals for establishing a national health insurance program, for example, have been developed by congressional offices or committees. The push for the deregulation of airlines during the 1970s (see Chapter 12, on the bureaucracy) initially came from the academic community and consumer groups.

The next step, **policy adoption,** includes efforts to obtain enough support so that a proposal can become the government's stated policy. At this point, most policy proposals—particularly congressional legislation—go through a process of bargaining and compromise and emerge significantly changed. When Congress considers tax reform proposals, what may begin as an attempt to close large tax loopholes may wind up creating more or different

A change of policy In the midst of an energy shortage the federal government required states, as a condition for receiving federal funds, to lower highway speed limits. The lower gas prices of 1987 enabled opponents of the 55-miles-per-hour speed limit to lobby successfully for a return to the 65-miles-per-hour limit on rural highways. Defense of the lower speed limits focused not on the fuel savings but rather on the reduction in highway deaths said to result.

loopholes. When members of Congress propose amendments to bills, they can radically change the intent of a bill or give it added meaning. In 1987, for example, a bill funding highway projects included an amendment authorizing states to raise the maximum speed limit on interstate highways to sixty-five miles per hour in rural areas.

Policy adoption is no less complex in the executive branch. Executive orders, vetoes of legislation, and other presidential actions are not made arbitrarily, for the White House cannot operate in a political vacuum. After President Kennedy used an executive order to set up the Peace Corps in 1961, he funded its operation for nearly six months through a special discretionary account. During that period administration officials worked to win congressional support for the program. Although Kennedy was eventually successful, his use of executive orders was questioned by key members of Congress.

Decisions of the Supreme Court are special types of public policies, for they are often rooted in legal doctrines. Nevertheless, even policy adoption in the Supreme Court involves some political give-and-take among its members that has an impact on the resulting policies (see pages 370–373). In recent years we have learned a great deal more about what takes place when the justices of the Supreme Court decide an important case. Conferences involving all the Court's members are held regularly, and the discussions in those closed meetings sometimes focus on the political, as well as the legal, implications of a case.[7]

The policy-adoption stage can last quite a long time. National air pollution laws first authorized the surgeon general to study the problem. Three years later, in 1963, Congress set up a technical committee to monitor air pollution problems and to provide assistance to state and local governments that chose to develop and maintain antipollution programs. In 1965 and 1967 Congress required states and localities to develop air pollution programs and required federal agencies to set emission standards for new automobiles. In 1970 President Richard Nixon created the Environmental Protection Agency (EPA), acknowledging the importance of environmental problems. A few weeks later Congress gave the EPA significant powers to clean America's air. Additional amendments followed during the 1970s, and policy adoption in this area continues today.

Critical to the policy-making process is the stage of **policy implementation**—the carrying out of policy mandates through public programs and actions. Usually, the federal bureaucracy performs this task, although many policies involve the cooperation of state and local officials and individuals outside government. For example, Congress passed an income tax law and created the Internal Revenue Service (IRS) to implement it, but the government still relies on the American people to do most of the paperwork. Washington depends on state and local officials to enforce the national speed limit of 55 or 65 miles per hour. In fact, most domestic policies require the cooperation of private individuals or the intergovernmental relations system (see Chapter 3, on federalism).

The final stage in public policy making often involves **policy evaluation**— looking at government actions and programs to see whether goals have been achieved or to assess a policy's effectiveness and efficiency. Changes in the policy may then be instituted quickly, slowly, or not at all. In the strip-mining situation, Congress took nearly a decade to repeal the two-acre provision despite considerable evidence that the policy was ineffective.

Models of Decision Making

As outlined above, the stages of the policy-making process seem both sequential and logical. What actually takes place during the policy-making process, however, is rarely so neat. During each stage of the process, policy makers must make many decisions about how the issue will be handled or how an adopted policy will be implemented or evaluated. Ideally, these specific policy maker decisions should be made systematically. A policy maker should carefully analyze the issues being addressed, consider all alternative actions that can be taken to address those issues, accurately evaluate those alternatives, and finally select one as the government's policy. This ideal process is called the **rational model of decision making** and it assumes that the policy maker has a clear objective and all the information needed to make a sound and reasoned decision resulting in the selection of the policy alternative that offers the most efficient and effective way to achieve the desired goal.

Few of the conditions required for rationality exist in the real world of public policy. Policy makers rarely have enough information to analyze alternatives. And no matter how much they know, there is always some doubt about the future. This uncertainty affects not only members of Congress and people on the White House staff, but also the advisers in the scientific community and elsewhere.

Furthermore, large groups of decision makers usually have trouble reaching a consensus on goals. There are some exceptions, of course. In May 1961, President Kennedy declared that the aim of U.S. space policy was to land an American on the moon by the end of the decade.[8] With such a clear goal, decision making in the National Aeronautics and Space Administration (NASA) came close to the rational model. But the NASA programs of the 1960s were unique. In most cases, the objectives of public policies are too vague and make the rational model inappropriate.

Is there a model that explains how policy makers really make their decisions? One possibility is the **incremental model of decision making** that sees public policy as a process by which decisions are made at the margins of current policies by adding to or subtracting from those policies that already exist. Each year, for example, the federal government reconsiders the amount of money it will spend on highways and education. Rarely, however, does the White House or Congress start their annual deliberations with a clean slate. Instead, in most cases executive officials and members of Congress begin by assuming that current highway and education programs will remain intact, and the major issues are whether to expand or reduce spending for these programs and, if so, by how much. Sometimes this leads to marginal changes in the policies as well. In recent years, for instance, Congress has made minor modifications to student loan programs that have affected the eligibility for those loans and the interest rates being charged. Thus, under incremental decision making, public policies and programs develop and change from year to year as policy makers make marginal adjustments to budgets and policies.

Other models of decision making trace public policies back to certain groups or classes of people. The **elite model of decision making** holds that public policies are made by a relatively small group of influential leaders who share common goals and points of view. President Dwight D. Eisenhower had this model in mind when, in his 1961 farewell address to the nation, he warned against the emerging influence of the "military-industrial complex."

In contrast, the **pluralist model of decision making** attributes policy outcomes to pressures exerted by different interest groups. Specific policies reflect the relative influence these interests possess at given points in the decision-making process. Thus, while environmentalists might have the upper hand in the Congress, advocates of deregulation might be more influential in the White House or at the EPA. This model assumes that public policies are the product of bargains and compromises among the various interests and policy makers.

The models may differ, but on one issue all observers agree: public policies result from a dynamic process involving a variety of participants and a wide range of factors. One constant feature of the policy-making process seems to be the debate between those who believe strongly in the myth of too much government and those who have adopted the myth of too little government. That debate has an impact on almost all domestic policies, especially in two major areas of concern: economic and social policies.

★ ★ ★

ECONOMIC POLICY

What should government's role be in managing the economy? Those who think government interferes too much in economic matters view most public

A change of leadership for the Federal Reserve President Reagan introduces former Federal Reserve Board Chairman Paul Volcker (center), while the current chairman, Alan Greenspan, looks on. Under Volcker's leadership (1979–1987), the Federal Reserve drastically limited the money supply, thereby driving interest rates to unprecedented highs. Although initially blamed for the high unemployment that followed the rising interest rates, Volcker's reputation rebounded, once it was recognized that his actions had curbed the runaway inflation of the late 1970s.

policies as needlessly restricting the operations of the marketplace and damaging the nation's economic health. Those who fault government for doing too little believe it should be more active in guiding the American economy. They argue that because the private marketplace cannot meet the basic needs of many citizens, the government must step in and correct its imperfections.

Behind this debate is the historical fact that the national government today is significantly engaged in economic policy making. The major types of economic policy are economic development, economic regulation, monetary policies, and fiscal policies.

Economic Development Policies

Government intervention in the marketplace can be traced to colonial times (see Myth and Reality 14.1). The role of the national government in the economy, however, was relatively minor until the last half of the 1800s. Alexander Hamilton, the first secretary of the treasury, and others tried to give the national government a major role in the economy during the presidencies of George Washington and John Adams. Hamilton felt that the young nation's future depended on a strong economy, and he believed the national government should play a major role in shaping that economic future. However, Thomas Jefferson and his successors (especially Andrew Jackson) strongly opposed any form of central controls over the economy. They believed that economic policy matters should be left to local and state governments.

After the Civil War, Congress became much more involved in the nation's economy. It adopted economic development policies intended to protect and promote the growth of American businesses. They passed steadily higher import tariffs—taxes on goods brought into the United States from abroad. These tariffs protected growing industries from foreign competition. Congress also promoted westward expansion by providing land grants to railroads and potential settlers.

Economic Regulatory Policies

In the late 1880s Congress expanded the scope of economic policy to include **regulatory policies,** through which government monitors and controls critical industries and sectors of the economy. The Interstate Commerce Act of 1887 established the first regulatory commission, the Interstate Commerce Commission, and authorized it to regulate prices and standards of service for interstate rail companies.*

During the next fifty years, Congress established other major regulatory agencies. The Food and Drug Administration came into being in 1906 to protect consumers from health-threatening products. The Federal Trade Commission was formed in 1914 to provide safeguards against unfair methods of competition or deceptive practices in the marketplace. In the depths of the Great Depression, Congress created several other agencies. The Federal Communications Commission (FCC) was established to regulate interstate telephone, telegraph, radio, and other telecommunications industries; the Securities and Exchange Commission (SEC) was to oversee the activities of

---

* The act also provided for regulation of grain elevators. Later the Interstate Commerce Commission was given jurisdiction over other forms of interstate transport, such as trucks, water carriers, and buses.

MYTH AND REALITY 14.1

Laissez Faire America

Among the most enduring myths in the area of public policy is that American governments have only recently intervened in the economy. According to this myth of laissez faire America, before the Civil War only a few public policies or programs dealt with the economy, and they did not directly interfere with the free-market system. The term *laissez faire* is applied to an economic policy in which government keeps its hands off the marketplace. According to the myth, until the mid-1800s government activity was limited to establishing law and order, conducting foreign policy, and providing some basic services, such as coining money and delivering the mail. Beyond those activities, the myth holds, government officials allowed the marketplace to operate according to the laws of supply and demand.

The reality behind this myth tells a different story. U.S. governments have played active roles in the economy throughout this nation's history. Colonial governments offered payments (called bounties) to businesses making large investments in the manufacture of certain products or promoting increases in the exportation of locally produced goods. In 1640, for example, Massachusetts offered bounties for the production of wool products. In 1661 Virginia awarded bounties of large quantities of tobacco to shipbuilders and ship owners for every vessel they docked in the colony.

Other forms of business support were available as well. Many colonies provided public instruction to train young men in tanning, silk production, lumbering, and similar trades. Colonial governments even owned and operated businesses and banks. Many of these activities continued long after the Revolution.

During the 1800s state and local governments actively promoted and protected their economies. Tax breaks were provided for the construction of sawmills, textile mills, and other desirable manufacturing plants. Grants-in-aid, low-cost loans, and large parcels of land were offered to companies that promised to build and operate roads, canals, and (eventually) railways. In 1825 Pennsylvania lent $1.8 million to companies involved in building turnpikes—a huge sum of money for that period of our history. By 1850 Maryland had authorized more than $16.5 million in direct aid to such companies while the city of Baltimore had given an additional $13 million.

Federal policy makers did not sit idly by as state and local governments undertook very active economic policy initiatives during the 1800s. Between 1816 and the early 1830s members of Congress from the northeastern states won passage of banking and tariff legislation favorable to their small but growing manufacturing and trade businesses. During the 1830s the power in Congress shifted toward agricultural interests in the South and West. With that shift came lower tariffs and other economic policies favoring farmers and plantation owners. Railroads were important to agrarian America, and between 1850 and 1857 Congress turned over more than 25 million acres of public lands to railroad companies.

For more on economic policy in the United States before the Civil War, see Carl Bridenbaugh, *Cities in the Wilderness: The First Century of Urban Life in America, 1625–1672* (New York: Knopf, 1964); Gerald D. Nash, *State Government and Economic Development: A History of Administrative Policies in California, 1849–1933* (Berkeley, Calif.: Institute of Governmental Studies, 1964), pp. 10–26; and Stuart Bruchey, *The Roots of American Economic Growth, 1607–1861: An Essay in Social Causation* (New York: Harper and Row, 1965).

businesses in the securities and investment markets; and the Federal Power Commission (now called the Federal Energy Regulatory Commission) was to regulate the interstate production and distribution of electric power and natural gas. Reacting to widely publicized episodes of violent confrontations between workers and businesses, Congress also established the National Labor Relations Board (NLRB) to regulate workplace relations between employers and their employees who sought to unionize.

Congress also passed antitrust laws intended to promote greater economic competition. The Sherman Antitrust Act of 1890 made it illegal for businesses to restrain trade or to monopolize a market for some product or service. The Clayton Antitrust Act of 1914 outlawed business practices that might diminish competition or promote monopolies in a market. In 1936 the Clayton Act was amended to prevent corporate mergers that would reduce competition in a sector of the economy.

Monetary Policies

The performance of the American economy has become an important issue in recent decades as policy makers have sought to maintain a healthy economy with stable prices and orderly growth. A key factor in satisfactory economic performance is the supply of money circulating in the economy.

Economists talk of tight and loose money supplies. A **tight money supply** exists when the amount of money circulating in the economy is low relative to demand for money by consumers and investors. Basic economics teaches that when the money supply is tight, interest rates (that is, the cost of using someone else's money) tend to be high, while the cost of most goods and services is likely to fall. A loose money supply exists when the amount of money is high relative to the demand. During a period of loose money supply, interest rates decline and prices of goods and services increase. Thus, economists attribute periods of both high and low interest rates, deflated and inflated prices, and a variety of related economic conditions to the supply of money circulating in the economy.

Monetary policy—the manipulation of the money supply to control the economy—has become a major tool of economic management. The principal mechanisms for making monetary policies are in the hands of the Federal Reserve System, also known as the Fed (see Figure 14.2). The Federal Reserve System, established in 1913, comprises twelve regional banks and a Federal Reserve Board, which is empowered to regulate the circulation of currency in the U.S. economy. When the economy is sluggish—that is, when not enough money is being invested to maintain economic growth or when unemployment is high—policy makers at the Fed can stimulate economic activity by increasing the supply of money. With more money in circulation, people will be likely to make purchases or investments, which, in turn, will

Federal Reserve Banks	Board of Governors	Federal Open Market Committee

Twelve banks representing the nation's twelve Federal Reserve districts. The twelve manage the day-to-day needs of the banking system by maintaining a stable flow of money.

The banks, by districts: 1 Boston, 2 New York, 3 Philadelphia, 4 Cleveland, 5 Richmond, 6 Atlanta, 7 Chicago, 8 St. Louis, 9 Minneapolis, 10 Kansas City, 11 Dallas, 12 San Francisco

What They Do

• Act as lender of last resort to banks, savings associations, and credit unions in trouble
• Keep reserves deposited by depository institutions
• Supply currency and coins to banks
• Destroy worn-out bills, coins
• Operate clearinghouses for checks
• Serve as fiscal agent for the U.S. Treasury
• Conduct domestic and foreign monetary operations through the New York Federal Reserve Bank as agent for the Federal Open Market Committee

Seven members appointed by the president and confirmed by the Senate. Terms are 14 years. The president names one member as chairman for a four-year term. The board is based in Washington, D.C.

What It Does

• Helps carry out policy for regulating the supply of money and credit by—
  Setting reserve requirements for the depository institutions
  Setting the discount rate on the Fed's loans to banks
• Makes margin rules for purchases of securities on credit
• Oversees major banks by regulating the nation's 6,146 bank holding companies
• Inspects and regulates 1,052 state-chartered banks that are members of the reserve system
• Monitors the economy
• Deals with international monetary problems
• Enforces consumer-credit laws
• Supervises Federal Reserve banks

Twelve members: The seven Federal Reserve governors and the president of the New York Federal Reserve Bank plus four of the presidents of the other eleven Federal Reserve banks on a rotating basis.

All twelve bank presidents attend the FOMC meetings, held every five to eight weeks.

What It Does

• Sets overall policy for regulating the supply of money and credit in the country
• Helps carry out that policy by directing the "trading desk" of the Federal Reserve Bank of New York to buy and sell government securities in the open market

FIGURE 14.2 The Long Reach of the Federal Reserve

Source: US News and World Report, © 1986 US News and World Report, reprinted from issue of Jan. 27, 1986.

generate business activity and jobs. If policy makers think that the economy is overheated and generating too much inflation, they can reduce the supply of money and slow down economic activity.

Fiscal Policies

During the Depression, policy makers discovered that changes in how much the government spent and the taxes it collected could influence overall economic performance. The use of these **fiscal policies,** that is, changes in government expenditures and tax rates, became still another way to manage the general condition of the economy. During periods when the economy is sluggish, the federal government can stimulate economic activity through its purchases of goods and services. By reducing taxes, it can put money in the hands of consumers, who can stimulate economic activity through increased purchases and investments. If the economy is overheating, the government can cut spending and raise taxes, which slows down the economy and takes money away from consumers and others who might otherwise spend it (see Background 14.1).

The Continuing Debates over Economic Policies

Although economic development, economic regulation, and monetary and fiscal policies are now widely accepted as useful means of managing the economy, controversy surrounds each. Central to those controversies are the myths of too much and too little government activity.

What kind of economic development?   For much of U.S. history, private business developed behind a wall of high protective tariffs on imported goods and services. From the turn of the century until the 1930s, tariffs slowly increased—taking a big leap with the enactment of the Hawley-Smoot Tariff of 1929. Today Hawley-Smoot is often viewed as a major cause of the Great Depression because it fragmented world trade. Congress has been reluctant to pass protective tariff legislation during the past half century. Most policy makers believe that **free trade** (the abolition of tariffs and other trade barriers) is the best policy to follow.[9]

The free trade policy raised little controversy from the 1940s through the 1970s. During those years the U.S. balance of trade—that is, the difference between the value of what Americans bought and sold overseas—ran a surplus as Americans exported more goods and services than they imported. In the late 1970s, however, the United States began to accumulate an ever-larger trade deficit. By 1987 we were importing nearly $150 billion more in goods and services than we were exporting—the highest trade deficit in the nation's history. Furthermore, many companies were closing their plants here and opening new ones overseas in order to avoid rising labor costs.

BACKGROUND 14.1

Incomes Policies

Although national policy makers rely on monetary and fiscal policies as their main strategies when trying to influence the economy, another set of policy tools—**incomes policies**—has proved useful from time to time. Incomes policies involve government efforts to deal with general economic problems through direct controls over wages, prices, and profits. Such controls are not new. Minimum wage laws have been part of the U.S. economy for nearly half a century. There are also policies dealing with fair trade prices, reasonable rates of return (profits) for regulated public utilities, and other forms of corporate income. Until the early 1960s, however, policies that controlled wage increases or prices throughout the economy were rare and usually limited to periods of war.

The situation changed during the Kennedy administration. In 1962 the White House issued wage and price guidelines that it hoped would help to minimize the pressures of inflation. Although not backed by the force of law, the administration used its influence to convince corporate leaders and union officials to moderate price increases and wage demands. President Johnson maintained the guidelines approach throughout the 1960s.

Incomes policy was even more important during the 1970s, when the threat of inflation became a major concern for many Americans. In 1972, using powers granted by Congress, President Nixon imposed a formal set of wage and price controls. Strictly enforced controls were lifted by the mid-1970s. Wage and price guidelines, however, remained part of U.S. policy until the Reagan administration eliminated them entirely in 1981.

For more information on the use of incomes policies from Kennedy to Reagan, see Herbert Stein, *Presidential Economics: The Making of Economic Policy from Roosevelt to Reagan and Beyond*, rev. ed. (New York: Simon and Schuster, 1985).

Responding to these conditions, some members of Congress advocated raising tariffs or taking other policy measures to protect U.S. industries and jobs from foreign competition. The Reagan administration and other advocates of free trade opposed such proposals, insisting that free and open international markets are the answer to trade deficits. The problem, they contended, was rooted in the barriers to free trade imposed by other countries, especially Japan. Instead of protective tariffs, they suggested diplomatic and other kinds of political pressures to persuade those nations to lower their barriers to the importation of U.S. goods and services.

Tax breaks, too, can promote economic activity in certain industries. For example, the home-building industry has benefited greatly over the past several decades from a provision allowing Americans to deduct their home mortgage interest costs from their personal income taxes. Another well-known but less popular tax break was an oil depletion allowance. Introduced during the 1920s, this tax break absolved owners of oil- or gas-producing properties from paying taxes on more than a fourth of their income. Experts estimate that this tax break saved these property owners as much as $2.5 billion annually. The tax break promoted oil and gas exploration, but many critics thought its benefits were excessive and much too costly. It took more than fifty years, however, to get the tax break eliminated.

Recently, some analysts have argued that policy makers must develop a comprehensive plan for restructuring the economy. This approach, known as **industrial policy,** would let the United States abandon certain industries in which labor costs are too high for successful competition with other nations. At the same time, it would rescue other industries and make them competitive in the world market. Most advocates of industrial policy also call for investments in new high-technology and service industries.

By contrast, advocates of **supply-side economics** believe in giving more attention to policies that promote increased production of goods. Thus supply-siders have supported cutting taxes to help stimulate investment, lifting regulations in the marketplace, and eliminating other government restraints on private business initiatives. Supply-siders claim that past government intervention in the economy relied too much on consumer demand to stimulate economic growth and imposed too many obstacles to private investment. Only through policies that increase suppliers' incentives will jobs be created and the economy grow.

How much regulation? As early as the 1950s critics argued that the major economic regulatory agencies seemed to be serving the interests of those they regulated rather than public interest.[10] In addition, studies conducted in the 1960s and 1970s showed that consumers often paid a higher price for goods and services produced by a regulated industry than they would have if the industry were unregulated. The call for economic deregulation eventually led to legislation in 1978 that phased out the Civil Aeronautics Board.

At the same time, Congress and the commissions lowered restrictions on natural gas producers, banks, trucking companies, interstate buses, and railroads. The Securities and Exchange Commission deregulated stockbroker commissions. The Federal Communications Commission permitted ownership of television and radio stations by local newspaper companies. Agencies charged with enforcing antitrust policies (the Federal Trade Commission and the Antitrust Division of the Department of Justice) relaxed their criteria for approving corporate mergers.[11]

By the early 1980s some observers argued that economic deregulation had gone too far too fast. An increase in the number of bank failures, the elimination of airline and bus service to many communities, a wave of corporate buyouts and mergers, and other events led some to call for reregulation. Regulatory reform, they felt, had "turned out to be an exercise in national self-deception."[12]

How should the economy be managed? The debate has raged between those who believe the government should be using monetary and fiscal tools to manage the overall direction of the economy and those who believe in a much more limited government role. The activists include followers of John Maynard Keynes (pronounced "canes"), a British economist. His theory of deficit spending during periods when the economy is sluggish provided the rationale for fiscal policies from the 1930s to the 1960s. The **Keynesian** approach is reflected in the Employment Act of 1946, which made national government officials responsible for assuring maximum production, high employment, and increased purchasing power in the American economy. The sustained period of relative prosperity from the late 1940s until the late 1960s led many to assume that such government intervention had made the threat of stagnation and major recessions a thing of the past.[13]

The **monetarists,** a group of prominent economists led by Milton Friedman, reject the argument that constant government intervention in the economy can bring either constant prosperity or stability. They believe that the economy kept growing between 1946 and 1970 in spite of government fiscal and monetary policies, not because of them. They argue that government intervention should be limited to maintaining a consistent growth in the nation's money supply in order to control inflation. During the 1970s and early 1980s, when the U.S. economy went through a period of both high inflation and rising unemployment, the country's economic policy makers gave greater attention to the monetarists' argument that government was doing too much.[14]

Thus the conflict between those who see government as doing too little and those who think it is doing too much pervades the economic policy arena. It marks the debates between advocates of protective tariffs and advocates of free trade, between supporters of industrial policies and supporters of supply-side policies, and between followers of Keynes and monetarists. It has become a basic fact of domestic policy life.

★ ★ ★

SOCIAL POLICY

Social policies, like economic policies, have deep roots in American history. America's earliest social policies were based on Elizabethan Poor Laws, which made local communities responsible for taking care of their own needy and sick. Each town selected an overseer for the poor to dispense charity to the needy and to provide able-bodied men with work. State governments became involved in aiding the needy during the 1800s. Many states abolished local debtor prisons, instituted child labor laws, mandated public education, and supported creation of institutions to care for the orphaned, insane, blind and deaf, epileptic, destitute, and others in need. These state and local efforts continued to expand into the twentieth century.[15]

Help in buying the American dream For millions of Americans the very high interest rates of the late 1970s and early 1980s made the dream of home-ownership an impossibility. The joyous couple pictured here waited in line for three days to be among the first to receive a state-funded, low-interest home mortgage.

Except for a few small federal grant-in-aid programs to the states described in Chapter 3, on federalism, the federal government did not become actively involved in social policy until the Depression. Many federal programs followed the tradition of state and local efforts to help meet the needs of the poor or to improve their circumstances. Since the 1930s federal social policy has focused on promoting the general welfare through social programs for all Americans, regardless of their income level. Thus, when discussing social policy, we must address two types of government programs: those that provide benefits and services only to the poor and those that help meet the needs of the general public.

Aiding the Poor

Federal policies aimed at helping those in need have taken at least three forms. General assistance programs provide them with cash or other forms of direct aid. Work assistance programs train and employ the able-bodied poor. Categorical assistance offers various types of aid to specific groups of needy individuals.

General assistance.   In the federal government's first act of social policy, Congress voted to lend money to the states during the Depression to help pay for local relief programs. Eventually, this led to even more cooperation among the various levels of government to make certain that the poor and hungry would receive some form of support.[16] General assistance remains primarily a state and local effort, however, although 1.3 million Americans received such assistance in the early 1980s, with aid averaging $127 per person per month for 1984.[17]

The closest the federal government comes to giving general assistance is the Department of Agriculture's food stamp program. Under this program, eligible persons receive stamps redeemable at participating food stores. The amount of stamps allotted to each recipient depends on such factors as income and family size. The program began on an experimental basis in 1961 and expanded gradually until it became the primary source of food assistance for the poor. By 1984 approximately 20.9 million people were receiving $12.1 billion in food stamps.[18]

Work assistance.   In 1933 and 1934 President Franklin D. Roosevelt's public works programs gave jobs to some of the millions of unemployed. These first examples of federal work assistance policies were dismantled by the start of World War II. Not until the early 1960s was a similar program re-established at the federal level.

In 1962 Congress passed the Manpower Training and Development Act to provide for skill training and retraining for the unemployed or underemployed. In response to Lyndon B. Johnson's War on Poverty in 1964, Congress passed still more work relief programs. Programs were initiated to provide intensive training for poor youths. Work-study programs were established for students from low-income homes to help them attend college. In addition, a variety of programs provided tax incentives for businesses that hired and trained the poor.

Most of the War on Poverty programs were discontinued or transferred to state and local governments under the Nixon administration. In 1973, however, Congress passed the Comprehensive Employment and Training Act (CETA), which provided federal funds for public-sector jobs at the local level and effectively turned over job-training programs to state and local governments. A decade later Congress replaced CETA with the Job Training Partnership Act (JTPA), which eliminated public employment programs for the poor and relied on the private industry to play a major role in the federal work assistance effort. In both cases, Washington provided a significant amount of the needed funding, although the JTPA program represented a significant cutback in federal government involvement.

Categorical assistance. The main focus of social policy for the needy, **categorical assistance,** targets aid to specific groups of low-income or disadvantaged Americans. Such targeted programs are not new. Veterans, for example, have been receiving federal assistance since the first pension for soldiers in 1789. The Social Security Act of 1935, however, provided for the first significant use of such aid.

Categorical aid provided under the Social Security Act has greatly expanded since the 1930s, both in the amount of assistance given and in the number of individuals covered. When the aid to dependent children (ADC) program was established in the late 1930s, it covered 300,000 dependent children. By 1984 the ADC program had been modified to provide aid to families with dependent children (becoming AFDC), and recipients numbered 10.9 million, including 6.8 million children (or one child out of every nine). By the mid-1980s the U.S. government paid more than $14 billion in benefits through AFDC, with the federal government contributing 55 cents of every dollar spent.[19]

Aid to the needy aged and the blind has also changed over the fifty years since passage of the Social Security Act. In 1972 the federal government established the Supplemental Security Income (SSI) program to provide monthly benefits for the aged, blind, and disabled regardless of the level of assistance they receive from state governments. In 1986 that basic aid was $336 per month for individuals and $504 per month for qualified couples. Approximately 3.8 million Americans received some form of SSI assistance in 1985.[20]

Another important categorical assistance program is Medicaid, established in 1965 as part of several major amendments to the Social Security Act. The federal government had been helping low-income families pay for medical costs since 1950. Medicaid, however, was the first program designed to pay for specific services offered to qualified recipients by participating states. By 1984 federal and state governments were paying more than $36 billion to suppliers of medical services for over 21 million Americans.[21]

Other federal programs that aid lower-income Americans include public housing programs and housing assistance programs, run by the Department of Housing and Urban Development; educational programs such as Head Start and Upward Bound, implemented by the Department of Education; and child nutrition programs, funded through the Department of Health and Human Services. These and other efforts have been a key part of the federal government's social policy over the past fifty years. Such programs have emerged incrementally during that period, each being developed with little

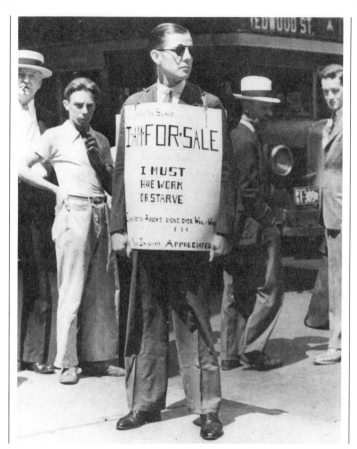

Looking for work During the depths of the Depression in the 1930s about one-fourth of the American workforce was unemployed, while millions more were working only part-time. Pictured here is a Baltimore resident in search of a job, any job.

or no concern for how it fitted in with other federal social policies. Each was a response to some perceived need—a response to criticisms that the government was not doing enough for the poor and disadvantaged. At the same time, each program was shaped by the fear that government might be doing too much for the needy—that by giving them aid it might be taking away their incentive to work. In short, the myths of too little and too much government probably contributed a great deal to the incremental nature of federal social policies.

Meeting the Needs of the General Public

More recently, many social policies have addressed the needs of all Americans regardless of level of income. We will focus on two programs: social insurance and social regulation.

© 1983, Washington Post Writers Group, reprinted with permission.

Social insurance.   Although most people should be saving for that rainy day when they cannot count on their paychecks, few actually set aside enough income to deal with such crises. Social insurance programs are intended to cover income losses due to long-term illnesses, unemployment, retirement, and other interruptions. Funds come from special taxes (often called contributions, although they are usually involuntary) levied on both employers and employees and placed in a special trust. Once a person has made a minimum number of payments into that fund, he or she is entitled to participate in the program's benefits.[22] Among major industrialized nations, the United States was one of the last to adopt such a plan, when unemployment insurance and retirement benefits were built into the Social Security Act of 1935. Under social security, employees and employers contribute a certain portion of employees' earnings to trust funds administered by the Social Security Administration (SSA). The SSA is supposed to use those funds to pay unemployment claims or monthly pension checks when a worker retires. At the outset, the system assured most American workers that they were at least minimally covered when temporarily unemployed or when they retired.

Over the years social insurance programs have grown considerably. In addition to unemployment and old-age pension insurance, social security now applies to the disabled and the survivors (widows/widowers and children) of deceased contributors. The number of Americans covered by social security's general social insurance programs has expanded. In 1940 social security covered only 20 percent of the U.S. work force. By 1985 the old-age, survivors, and disability programs covered 90 percent of the working population. An even greater portion, 97 percent, was protected by unemployment insurance.

With passage of Medicare in 1965, the federal government also began providing health insurance for the elderly and disabled. The basic Medicare program provided insurance for hospitalization, as well as extended care and home-health services. It also contained a voluntary supplementary medical insurance program to help offset the costs of physicians' fees, lab tests, medical supplies and appliances, and related payments. By 1984 more than 30 million Americans were enrolled in the basic hospital insurance program, while 20.3 million paid an additional monthly premium to take part in the supplementary health insurance program.[23]

Despite steady increases in the number of participants who contribute, social insurance programs under social security—especially old-age pensions and Medicare—remain critically underfunded for the future. The federal government spent more than $242 billion through the old-age, survivors, disability, and health insurance programs in 1984. More than 36 million Americans—one out of every six—received some form of regular assistance through the program that year. Even more important, the U.S. population is getting older, and so the financial strains on the program grow each year. To help alleviate this situation, Congress made several modifications in eligibility and other program requirements during the early 1980s. For example, in 1983 Congress increased the retirement age for eligible beneficiaries from the current sixty-five to sixty-seven by the year 2027. In addition, those choosing to retire before the age of sixty-five will have a cut of 20 to 30 percent in their benefits. All this is being done in an attempt to keep the program solvent in the future.[24]

Social regulation. Protecting citizens from the major social hazards and problems associated with life in a highly industrialized economic system has also become a policy focus.[25]

The first federal social regulation programs emerged in the early 1900s as a response to problems of adulterated food and the deceptive advertising of drugs. Stirred to action by research conducted at the Department of Agriculture and investigations by muckraking journalists, Congress passed the Pure Food and Drug Act of 1906 and the Meat Inspection Act of 1907. These laws established federal agencies to deal with questions related to the safety and quality of food and drug products sold in the American marketplace, and over the years those laws have been modified to meet new problems and demands. Other forms of social regulation have followed similar patterns.

The Food and Drug Administration (FDA) regulates a wide range of consumer products, including drugs, cosmetics, medical devices, and food (except for meat and poultry) to assure their safety, purity, and effectiveness. In the case of drugs and medical devices, FDA approval is needed before a product can be marketed. The FDA investigates complaints about the safety or purity of food and cosmetics. If a product is found to be unsafe or adulterated, the FDA can order its removal from the marketplace. Overseeing the processing of meat and related products is the responsibility of the Food Safety and Inspection Service of the Department of Agriculture.

The government also looks out for the traveler and the purchaser of consumer products. The Federal Trade Commission tries to keep businesses from deceiving consumers with false advertising. During Jimmy Carter's presidency, regulatory agencies strove to keep business in line and protect the consumer. Their activity has abated since Reagan's election. At one point, in fact, the Federal Trade Commission had to shut down because Congress refused to approve its budget.

With **worker protection** programs, the federal government has also extended its reach into the workplace, especially in the areas of discrimination, worker rights, and occupational safety and health. Equal employment opportunity programs prohibit workplace discrimination on the basis of race, sex, religion, national origin, or handicapped status. In addition, the federal government requires companies doing business with it to undertake affirmative action, aimed at improving employment and promotion opportunities for minorities, women, the handicapped, and other groups that have traditionally suffered from workplace discrimination. Although these antidiscrimination programs have been in place for nearly two decades, they remain extremely controversial and are constantly being challenged in the courts.

The best-known occupational safety and health program was established in 1970, under the Occupational Safety and Health Act. The primary goal of this legislation is "to assure so far as possible every working man and woman in the Nation safe and healthy work conditions." The act created the Occupation Safety and Health Administration (OSHA) to implement this policy through regulations and on-site inspections. OSHA's regulations and enforcement programs have been controversial from the start. Many critics found its early regulations to be both trivial and costly. By 1986, however, OSHA had issued standards that would eliminate or minimize worker exposure to a variety of highly suspect materials such as asbestos, vinyl chloride, arsenic, benzene, lead, ethylene oxide, and cotton dust. The agency also set workplace standards for construction sites, grain elevators, and chemical plants where hazardous materials were handled. While still subject to criticisms, OSHA remains an important part of federal policies dealing with worker protection.

Besides OSHA, several other agencies are involved in workplace safety and health regulation. For example, agencies such as the Mine Health and Safety Administration and the Nuclear Regulatory Commission have jurisdiction over workplace conditions in specific industries. Overall, these agencies and programs represent a federal policy commitment to protecting the general population of workers from workplace hazards.

The Debates over Social Policy

Like economic policies, social policies have stirred debate between those who see the federal government as doing too much and those who find it doing too little. Social policies intended to help the needy illustrate the point especially well. Some critics of government activity in this area believe that private sector charities rather than federal programs should aid those requiring support. Others argue that social programs for the poor should be the responsibility of local communities. Still others contend that current policies make recipients of federal support increasingly dependent on government programs, that the cycle of dependency is never broken, and that the situation of those in need may in fact worsen.[26]

On the other hand, those who fault the federal government for not doing enough urge a variety of remedial actions. Some favor a guaranteed income or negative income tax program, for such an approach, in their view, might finally break the cycle of poverty in which many Americans find themselves. Under these programs, low-income families would receive a direct cash grant

Bureaucrats protest federal budget cuts Members of the National Federation of Federal Employees picket the White House to protest budget cuts. Although concerned with loss of funds for recipients of federal aid, those pictured here are also angered by the reduction in jobs and benefits for federal employees.

or an income tax refund equal to the difference between what they earn and an income that would put them above the poverty line. Others propose reviving the War on Poverty, started in the 1960s by the Johnson administration, and once again investing in job-training, educational, and other programs that help the poor get ahead.

As for regulation, many critics accuse the government of interfering too much in the workings of the open marketplace. They consider the laws of supply and demand to be the best means of protecting consumers and workers and worry about the costs of social regulatory policy. As one critic put it, "the public does not get a 'free lunch' by imposing public requirements on private industries. Although the costs of government regulation are not borne by the taxpayer directly, they do show up in higher prices of the goods and services that consumers buy."[27]

Those who support social regulations, however, complain that the rules are too few or that they are not enforced stringently enough. Consequently, consumer advocates such as Ralph Nader and Michael Pertschuk have been calling for a revival of the consumer protection movement that achieved so much in the 1960s and 1970s. On worker protection issues, some advocates of a comprehensive industrial policy for the United States have urged legislation that would establish a higher minimum wage, protect the jobs of workers from unannounced plant closings, and increase worker participation in corporate decisions.[28]

CONCLUSION: The Dynamic Myths of American Public Policy

We have touched on only two of the major domestic policy arenas in which the federal government is involved today. In addition to economic and social policies, the federal government has been extremely active in many other areas, including efforts to support public education, construct new highways, promote the conservation of our natural resources, deal with energy shortages, and clean up and protect our environment. While each of those policy arenas has its own distinctive characteristics, all share the two fundamental popular myths we have discussed in this chapter: the myths of too much and too little government activity.

These myths are dynamic forces in the policy-making process. They offer members of the general public, as well as policy makers, numerous opportunities to "mouth off" about the action or inaction of public officials. They also help shape the policies and programs that emerge from the policy-making process. Any decision maker will take into account the real or potential criticisms of those who argue that the policy proposal goes too far or not far enough. Similarly, officials who implement the policy may try to strike some balance between those who believe the policy is being enforced too stringently and those who feel it is not being enforced strictly enough. Even policy evaluations, whether formal or informal, are likely to weigh the policy's achievements against charges that the government is doing too much or too little. As we will see in Chapter 15, similar forces exert pressure on foreign and defense policies.

SUMMARY

1. There are two major myths associated with American public policy: one reflects a widely held belief that government does too much when it gets involved in domestic matters, and the other holds that government gets involved too little.

2. The policy-making process in the United States is difficult to summarize because so many different policies emerge from so many different institutions. However, the overall process can be described in six stages: issue identification, agenda setting, policy formulation, policy adoption, policy implementation, and policy evaluation.

3. Within each one of those stages, the method of decision making varies. Students of public policy making have developed several models of decision making to describe what takes place. Ideally, decisions would be made rationally, but in reality it is more likely that decisions are made incrementally—that is, through additions and substractions from current policies and programs. Other models focus on the role played by elites in the policy-making process. According to the elite model, decisions are made by a relatively small group of influential leaders who share a common perspective and common goals. Finally, many students of public policy have adopted a pluralist model, which holds that decisions are made as the result of pressures from a diverse population of interest groups.

4. In the economic policy area, the federal government has focused its attention on economic development, economic regulation, monetary policies, and fiscal policies. In each of these endeavors, the government's efforts have been shaped by the pressures created by the two myths of "too much" and "too little" government intervention.

5. Social policy covers government action providing aid to low-income Americans and promoting the general welfare of all Americans. As with economic policies, each of these government undertakings has been criticized for being both too much and too little.

6. No area of American domestic public policy escapes the pressures generated by the two myths. This is not necessarily bad, since policy debates and discussions invigorate the policy-making system. In addition, policies are often shaped and implemented in response to real or potential criticisms that government tends to do too much or too little.

★ ★ ★
KEY TERMS

public policies
myth of too much government
myth of too little government
issue identification
agenda setting
policy formulation
policy adoption
policy implementation
policy evaluation
national model of decision
  making
incremental model of decision
  making
elite model of decision making

pluralist model of decision making
regulatory policies
money supply
monetary policy
fiscal policies
free trade
industrial policy
supply-side economics
Keynesians
monetarists
categorical assistance
worker protection
income policies

★ ★ ★
SUGGESTED READINGS

- Dye, Thomas R. *Understanding Public Policy*, 6th ed. Englewood Cliffs, N.J.: Prentice-Hall, 1987. An introductory book on policy analysis that uses different models to explain the development of a wide range of policies, such as civil rights, defense, health care, education, and taxes.

- Kelman, Steven. *Making Public Policy: A Hopeful View of American Government*. New York: Basic Books, 1987. An upbeat analysis of public policy making which focuses on the accomplishments of the process rather than its failures.

- Meier, Kenneth J. *Regulation: Politics, Bureaucracy, and Economics*. New York: St. Martin's, 1985. A survey of the wide range of government regulatory policies with particular attention given to the administrative agencies responsible for their implementation and enforcement.

- Murray, Charles. *Losing Ground: American Social Policy, 1950–1980.* New York: Basic Books, 1984. A critical analysis of social policies of the post–World War II era, which argues that those policies have made the situation of the poor worse rather than better.
- Schwarz, John E. *America's Hidden Success: A Reassessment of Twenty Years of Public Policy.* New York: Norton, 1983. In contrast to the Murray book, this analysis of the Great Society programs of the 1960s argues that antipoverty and environmental protection policies of that period have accomplished much more than is generally thought.
- Shultz, George P., and Kenneth W. Dam. *Economic Policy Beyond the Headlines.* New York: Norton, 1977. An "insider's" view of economic policy making from two people who played a major role in that field during the Nixon and Ford administrations. Both Shultz and Dam were also active in the foreign policy area under the Reagan administration.

15

CHAPTER

Foreign and Defense Policy

At the end of March each year, members of the movie industry gather in Hollywood, California, to give the Academy Awards— a ritual watched by millions of Americans and millions more overseas. On March 30, 1987, Oliver Stone accepted his Academy Award as best director for his film about the Vietnam War, *Platoon*. Under ordinary circumstances, that would have been a moment of pride and happiness for Stone. Instead, he somberly began his acceptance speech by interpreting the reasons for being given the award. By honoring this film about what the war was like for those who fought it, he said, ". . . you are saying . . . that for the first time you really understand what happened over there. And I think what you're saying is that it should never ever in our lifetimes happen again."

Stone is more than a Hollywood director and screenwriter. He is also a Vietnam veteran who experienced many of the events portrayed in *Platoon*. The film was released in 1986, more than a decade after the last U.S. troops left Saigon as the war in Vietnam ended. Nevertheless, more than ten years later the Vietnam War was still dividing Americans. At least 47,318 U.S. service personnel had died in Vietnam. More than 300,000 had been wounded. Many veterans still bear the psychological and physical scars of that war.

Those scars were also left on the nation. Throughout the 1960s and early 1970s bitterness grew between those who supported and those who opposed American military presence in Southeast Asia. The Vietnam War made U.S. foreign and defense policies a real and immediate concern to many Americans. That concern translated into debates, demonstrations, and sometimes violent confrontations.

American foreign and defense policies have always provoked criticism and debate between those advocating greater U.S. involvement in world events and those arguing for less involvement. Faced with these contradictory pressures, policy makers have tended to move cautiously in pursuing America's interests in world affairs. In the view of Henry Kissinger, the secretary of state under President Richard M. Nixon, such caution made America fail in Vietnam. American policy makers, Kissinger believed, "trapped themselves between their convictions and their inhibitions, making a commitment large enough to hazard our global position but then executing it with so much hesitation as to defeat their purpose."[1]

Americans are often of two minds about the actions of their government in international affairs. On one hand, most Americans favor an active role in the international arena. Public opinion polls over the past four decades indicate that most Americans believe involvement in international affairs is "best for the future" of their country. (See Table 15.1.) Most believe the United States should take part in world affairs from a position of military strength. When asked about the military power of the United States relative to the Soviet Union, an overwhelming majority answered that the United States should be at least as strong as the Soviet Union, if not stronger.[2]

TABLE 15.1 U.S. Involvement in World Affairs

In different polls ranging over thirty years, American citizens were asked the following question: "Do you think it will be best for the future of the country if we take an active part in world affairs?"

Year	Percent Responding		
	"Better if we take an active part"	"Better if we stay out"	"Not sure"
1982	53	35	12
1978	59	29	12
1974	66	24	10
1956	71	25	4
1947	68	25	7

Source: John E. Rielly, ed., *American Public Opinion and U.S. Foreign Policy, 1983* (Chicago, Ill.: The Chicago Council on Foreign Relations, 1983), p. 11; based on data from polls conducted by the National Opinion Research Center (1947 and 1956), Louis Harris and Associates (1974), and the Gallup Organization (1978 and 1982).

On the other hand, Americans shrink from supporting foreign policy ventures that are risky, costly, or controversial. For example, in the early 1980s the American public became more and more concerned about international terrorism. As the number and viciousness of airline hijackings and bombings increased, more Americans favored military action against terrorists and their supporters. Early in 1986 nearly 70 percent of those polled endorsed such actions. Yet that support dropped to 41 percent when another polling organization asked if Americans would still favor such actions at the risk of starting a larger conflict. "When the risks are spelled out," notes one public opinion expert, "Americans become much more cautious."[3] Americans are also reluctant to support morally questionable foreign policy actions. When asked whether they would back efforts to kill the leader of a nation that aided terrorists, only 21 percent voiced approval.[4]

Defense costs, too, arouse mixed feelings. While supporting a strong defense, many Americans balk at increasing military spending. A clear majority of those polled about military expenditures between 1960 and 1982 thought the United States was spending the right amount or too much for defense. Polls taken in 1981 and 1982 showed that Americans preferred major reductions in defense spending to significant cuts in spending for domestic programs.

The American tendency to both support and question foreign and defense policies at the same time is partly explained by two popular myths that resemble the myths discussed in Chapter 14, on domestic policies. Many

Americans adhere to the myth of too little government activity in foreign affairs and defense policies. In their view, the United States should do more to combat communism and terrorism, or to promote human rights, or to strengthen America's position in the world economy. But many Americans embrace a second myth—that the government is doing too much when it comes to foreign and defense policies. They see the national government as overly involved in world events and too willing to interfere in other nations' internal affairs. Many also feel that our government spends too much money on defense.

In this chapter, we will consider the sources of those two myths and show how they influence both foreign and defense policy makers and policies.

★ ★ ★
FROM ISOLATIONISM TO WORLD LEADERSHIP

Historically, Americans have shied away from too much involvement in world affairs. During the 1800s policy makers followed the basic principles advocated by George Washington. Washington believed that the U.S. government should seek commercial and trade relations with other countries while avoiding political alliances and maintaining a strong defense against foreign threats. These views led to the adoption of two popular policies, which prevailed throughout much of the 1800s: isolationism and unilateralism.

1800–1914: Isolationism, Unilateralism, and Expansionism

During the nineteenth century American leaders pursued policies that deliberately isolated the United States from the intrigues and entanglements of world politics. Under isolationism, policy makers maintained American neutrality and avoided direct involvement in European affairs.

Isolationism marked American foreign and defense policies until World War I. But we should not conclude that the United States did not take part in world affairs at all during the 1800s. Our nation maintained an army and navy, engaged in diplomatic relations, and even took military actions to protect its neutrality and assert its interests in the international arena. What characterized these actions was a second tenet of U.S. foreign policy: unilateralism. Under unilateralism, Americans "went it alone" in world affairs and avoided political or military alliances.

Isolationism and unilateralism stamped the policies of the United States toward its Latin American and Caribbean neighbors. In 1823 President James Monroe announced that America would keep out of the affairs of European nations so long as those countries, in turn, did not blatantly interfere in the Western Hemisphere. But the Monroe Doctrine did not stop the United States from pursuing its own territorial expansion during the 1830s and 1840s.

Expansionism was another major factor in American policies during the 1800s; the drive to expand U.S. boundaries from the Atlantic to the Pacific often influenced foreign affairs. During that period the United States purchased the Louisiana Territory from France, Alaska from Russia, and portions of the Southwest from Mexico. Territorial expansion also played a role in American wars with Mexico (1846–1848), with a number of native American tribes in the West, and with Spain (1898). An important turning point, the Spanish-American War, brought the United States its first colonial possessions: Puerto Rico, Cuba, Guam, and the Philippines. Spain gave them up as part of the settlement of the conflict. Furthermore, during the 1890s and early 1900s, American presidents intervened politically and militarily in Nicaragua, Panama, the Dominican Republic, Haiti, and other Central American and Caribbean nations.

1914–1960: America Emerges as World Leader

The major challenges to American isolationism came between 1914 and 1917 as pressures mounted for the United States to enter World War I. In 1916 isolationist pressures remained so strong that President Woodrow Wilson ran for re-election using the slogan "He kept us out of war!" In 1917, however, publication of a secret German note proposing a military alliance with Mexico and the sinking of American ships by German submarines generated public support for joining the war on the side of Great Britain and its allies.

Wilson believed that the United States could no longer barricade itself behind isolationism once the war ended. He played a major role in writing the treaty to end the war and helped design the League of Nations and the World Court. When Wilson returned home from Paris, however, he was criticized for his internationalist policies. Although he campaigned for ratification of the peace treaty throughout the United States, isolationism remained powerful and Congress refused to ratify.

Isolationism persisted through the 1920s and 1930s. Many Americans blamed their economic problems and the Great Depression on too much contact with Europe. Even when the rise of militarism in Europe and the Pacific grew threatening, many Americans opposed involvement in another international war. It took the Japanese attack on Pearl Harbor to launch the United States into that conflict.

World War II and its aftermath convinced many Americans that the United States must play a major role in world affairs. The United States emerged from that war as the world's industrial and military giant, and, as the world entered the nuclear age, Americans began to realize just how vulnerable they were to events in the international arena. Isolationism became a less popular position among both policy makers and the general public.

At first America's leaders were hopeful about the prospects for an era of peace. The wartime alliance among the Big Three powers—the United States,

Arranging for peace at Yalta Allied leaders Winston Churchill, Franklin Roosevelt, and Joseph Stalin are pictued in 1945 at Yalta where, in anticipation of the German surrender, they met to discuss peace arrangements. Critics charge that the Yalta agreements surrendered eastern Europe to Stalin and showed the president to be weak and incompetent, but Roosevelt's defenders argue that the concessions were necessary and realistic.

Great Britain, and the Soviet Union—was peaceful and seemed likely to last. The United States played a major role in creating the United Nations to promote world cooperation and peace. By 1946, however, the international scene changed. The Soviet Union tightened its political hold over Eastern Europe, North Korea, and other occupied areas. It also challenged Britain's influence in Greece, Turkey, and the Middle East. At first the United States tried to mediate between its two former allies but before long decided to openly support the British.

Events came to a head in early 1947, when the British realized they could no longer afford to meet their commitments to Greece or Turkey. Within several weeks President Harry S. Truman called for a policy that supported the efforts of "free peoples who are resisting attempted subjugations by armed minorities or by outside pressures." He advocated providing economic and financial aid to countries whose political and economic stability was threatened. This general policy marked the beginning of the Cold War.

The Cold War is a term applied to the international situation between 1947 and the late 1960s, characterized by hostile yet, for the most part, peaceful relations between a Western alliance led by the United States and an Eastern alliance led by the USSR. During the Cold War, U.S. policy makers

BACKGROUND 15.1

Close Encounters in a Bipolar World

Although the United States and the Soviet Union managed to avoid direct confrontations during the Cold War, the two superpowers had a number of close encounters, especially in Berlin and Cuba.

In 1947, for example, the Soviet Union established a ground-based blockade around those parts of Berlin occupied by the United States, Great Britain, and France. The blockade was in response to Allied plans to consolidate and revive the economy of West Germany and West Berlin. For 324 days the Allies flew supplies to the isolated 2.5 million West Berliners. The Soviet Union did not challenge the airlift, and by the time the blockade was lifted the Allies were flying more than 13,000 tons of food and fuel into the city each day.

In 1961 the USSR demanded that the Allies negotiate their withdrawal from the city. President John F. Kennedy responded that the survival of West Berlin was not negotiable. The Soviets responded, in turn, by constructing a wall around the city that physically isolated it as an island within East Germany. Only a ground and air corridor through East Germany linked West Berlin to its support in West Germany. As in the case of the blockade, the Allies, led by the United States, held fast and demonstrated their resolve not to abandon their commitments to West Berlin and the containment foreign policy in general.

Perhaps the hottest encounter between the United States and USSR came in October 1962, when Kennedy demanded that the Soviets dismantle the offensive missile sites they had placed in Cuba and halt the shipment of additional missiles to that Caribbean island. The world stood on the brink of war for thirteen days as Kennedy and Soviet Premier Nikita Khrushchev bargained back and forth. Kennedy ordered a blockade of Cuba and the U.S. Navy was told to make certain that no ships carrying additional missiles would sail into Cuban ports. One ship was boarded while other Soviet vessels turned back rather than confront the blockade. In the meantime, the American and Soviet leaders exchanged heated messages. Finally, on October 28, 1962, the crisis ended when the Soviet Union agreed to dismantle the Cuban missile sites in return for Kennedy's assurances that the United States was in the process of removing some of its missiles from Turkey and Italy.

tended to perceive the world as **bipolar:** they saw nations as being allied with either of the two "poles," represented by the United States and the Soviet Union.

Cold War battles raged primarily on the level of ideology: the democracy of the West against the totalitarianism of the East, the capitalism of the West against the communism of the East, and so on. Sometimes the Cold War became hot and bloody, but these conflicts were typically limited in scope. The Korean War (1950–1952), for example, pitted the United States and its allies against North Korean and Chinese troops. In addition, on several occasions the world held its breath as the two major powers confronted each other in crisis situations (see Background 15.1).

Throughout the Cold War, the United States followed a policy called **containment.** According to proponents of containment, the Soviets did not seek immediate victories. Instead they exercised patience, caution, and flexibility in pursuit of expansionist goals. Only through a policy of "long-term, patient, but firm and vigilant containment" would U.S. efforts succeed in countering the USSR's unrelenting commitment to conquer the capitalist world.[5]

Containment led to significant changes in American foreign and defense policies. In 1949 President Truman signed a treaty establishing the North Atlantic Treaty Organization (NATO), thus formally ending a longstanding commitment of American policy makers to unilateralism. NATO was a response to the perceived threat of communist expansion in Europe. It closely tied American security to political conditions in Europe by guaranteeing the maintenance of Western European governments. It committed the United States to ongoing military collaboration with the armed services of other NATO member nations. Most important, the establishment of NATO signified a break with policies of the past and reflected American determination to halt communist expansion.[6]

The policy of containment took on military dimensions in 1950, when Truman authorized the use of American forces in South Korea after that country was invaded by North Korean troops. Under his successor, Dwight D. Eisenhower, however, the United States avoided direct military actions while getting more involved in formal alliances with other nations. By 1960 our country was committed to the defense of nations in almost every region of the world, especially those bordering on Soviet bloc states.

1960s to the Present: Policies in a Changing World

By the early 1960s international conditions were rapidly changing. Third World nations emerged as important actors in world affairs. Poor, less industrialized countries such as India, Kenya, and Indonesia sought aid from the industrialized world while avoiding excessive dependence on either the United States or the Soviet Union. Furthermore, both the American and the Soviet alliances experienced growing dissent. In NATO, France developed a more independent foreign and defense policy. In the East, policy disagreements between the Soviet Union and the People's Republic of China weakened that alliance, as did the desire of some Eastern European countries (for example, Albania, Yugoslavia, and Rumania) to conduct their own foreign policy.

By the 1970s economic strength had become just as important as political and military power, and American policy makers realized just how dependent they were on the very nations they previously dominated. The oil-rich countries of the Middle East, for example, imposed an oil embargo in 1973 to protest Western support of Israel. Even after the embargo was lifted, the oil-exporting nations cooperated to keep the price of oil high. In the Pacific,

Japan, Taiwan, Singapore, and Korea emerged as major economic competitors for American businesses in both world and domestic markets.[7]

The failure of the containment policy in Vietnam and the negative reaction of the American people to that war effort also led to major changes in U.S. foreign policy—changes that are still shaping America's role in world affairs. Richard Nixon's administration established a policy of **détente**—or relaxation of tensions—reflecting a more cooperative approach to dealing with Soviet bloc nations while enhancing U.S. security arrangements with its allies. It was a period of negotiations with the Soviets, bringing an end to direct American involvement in the Vietnam conflict, establishing diplomatic relations with the People's Republic of China, strengthening NATO and other alliances, and providing indirect assistance to nations threatened by communist takeovers.[8]

When the Soviet Union sent troops into Afghanistan in 1979, President Jimmy Carter ended the era of détente with the USSR by imposing a grain embargo, canceling cultural exchange programs, and withdrawing U.S. teams

Shattering the foreign policy consensus American involvement in the Vietnam War deeply divided Americans at home and led Congress to enact limitations on the president's war-making powers.

from the 1980 Olympic Games, scheduled for Moscow. Carter also pursued more formal relations with China, helped negotiate a peace agreement between Israel and Egypt, concluded a treaty to give Panama control over the Panama Canal, and took other actions that helped adjust U.S. foreign and defense policies to the changing international scene of the 1970s. Events in Iran, however, had the most impact on the Carter administration. In 1979 Iranian revolutionaries seized the U.S. embassy in Teheran and took more than a hundred Americans hostage. The hostage crisis lasted more than a year, ending on the day President Ronald Reagan was sworn into office in 1981.

The Reagan administration stressed military superiority over the Soviet Union and the need to strengthen America's leadership in the Western world. It supported stepped-up military spending and increased American involvement in the Middle East, Latin America, and other international "hot spots."[9] In many respects, Reagan's policies resembled the containment policies of the Cold War, but the realities of a changing world posed major challenges to such an approach.

★ ★ ★
MAKING FOREIGN AND DEFENSE POLICY

U.S. foreign and defense policy making resembles in many ways the stages described in Chapter 14 for domestic policies. In foreign and defense policy making, however, the president and his advisers play even more important roles in the overall process than they play in making domestic policies.

The President and the White House

The president's role in foreign and military affairs is rooted in constitutional provisions giving him the power to make treaties, appoint ambassadors, receive diplomatic representatives from other nations, and serve as commander in chief of the armed forces. Thus, while Congress shares some of the responsibility for shaping, funding, and implementing our foreign and defense policies, the "lion's share" of the power in these policy arenas belongs to the president of the United States.[10]

Formulating and implementing foreign and defense policies is a complex affair today, and the president must increasingly rely on special advisers. The National Security Act of 1947 authorized the president to establish a National Security Council, comprising the president, the vice president, the secretaries of defense and state, and other officials the president wishes to invite, such as the secretary of commerce, the director of the Central

Serious talk in Venice Leaders of the major noncommunist industrial countries—Japan, Britain, the United States, Italy, France, Germany, and Canada—gathered at the 1987 Economic Summit in Venice. Concerned about the potential for a world-wide recession, the leaders sought agreements that would boost global economic growth.

Intelligence Agency (CIA), or the chairman of the Joint Chiefs of Staff. The National Security Council's primary functions are to advise the president on national security issues and to coordinate the implementation of policy. The council was not intended to be a decision-making body, but its members are often called on for their opinions and advice. In 1975, for example, President Gerald Ford sought the council's advice on how to respond to the Cambodian seizure of an American merchant ship. Similarly, in 1980 Carter asked for the council's reaction to plans for freeing the hostages being held in Iran.

The National Security Council staff also plays an important role in shaping U.S. foreign and military policies. Typically, the staff consists of experts who monitor the world situation for the White House, prepare analyses and policy options for the president's consideration, and oversee the coordination of foreign and defense policies.

The council staff is headed by the special assistant to the president for national security affairs, also called the national security adviser. Under some presidents, the national security adviser strongly influences foreign and defense policies. In the Nixon administration, for instance, the national security adviser, Henry Kissinger, played a central role in negotiating agreements with the Soviets, as well as in efforts to end the Vietnam War and open relations with the People's Republic of China. Eventually, Nixon appointed Kissinger to serve simultaneously as secretary of state and national security adviser.

The Foreign and Defense Bureaucracies

The president relies on several agencies to help formulate and implement foreign and defense policies—especially the Departments of State and Defense and the Central Intelligence Agency.

The Department of State is the oldest agency associated with the conduct of foreign affairs. Its personnel conduct the day-to-day operations of American foreign relations. They operate our embassies, look after U.S. interests abroad, conduct formal negotiations between the United States and other nations, and provide advice and assistance to the president and other foreign policy makers. At the heart of the State Department is the Foreign Service, consisting of approximately thirty-five hundred people with expertise and training in foreign diplomacy.

The Defense Department (also called the Pentagon, after its five-sided office complex) is the agency most closely linked to military policy making. Actually, it comprises three subordinate agencies—the Departments of the Navy, Army, and Air Force—which are responsible for managing their respective branches of the armed services. The civilian leadership of the Defense Department strives to integrate the policies and programs of the different military branches. In this task they are assisted by the Joint Chiefs of Staff, a group of high-ranking military officers representing the navy, army, air force, and marines. The Joint Chiefs of Staff also advise the president and the National Security Council when requested.

No foreign or defense policy making can take place without information provided through intelligence-gathering agencies. These agencies obtain much of the needed information from newspapers, magazines, public documents, and other openly available material. When seeking more detailed or hard-to-get information, policy makers often rely on the U.S. Central Intelligence Agency (CIA). With a staff of fifteen thousand, the CIA can both gather needed intelligence and provide analyses of the data. The CIA has also conducted covert, or secret, operations. In 1961, for example, the CIA supplied and trained the anti-Castro troops who took part in the ill-fated invasion of Cuba. More recently, CIA operatives have helped pro-U.S. forces in Central America.

The CIA is not the only U.S. intelligence agency. The National Security Agency, a highly secretive unit located just outside Washington, uses sophisticated technologies to obtain intelligence. The Defense Department operates its own intelligence-gathering units to collect needed information

TABLE 15.2 Agencies Involved in U.S. Foreign Policy

It is not just the Departments of State and Defense that are charged with the making of U.S. foreign and defense policy. Listed below are some important agencies that are responsible for vital, specific aspects of foreign policy.

Agency	Function
Arms Control and Disarmament Agency	Conducts negotiations with the Soviet Union on arms limitations.
United States Information Agency	Coordinates educational, cultural, and media programs to provide a positive image of the United States in foreign nations.
Agency for International Development	Coordinates economic aid programs to Third World nations.
Office of the Special Representative for Trade Negotiations	Supervises and coordinates U.S. trade agreements with foreign nations.

for military purposes. Similarly, there are other agencies that assist in the formulation and implementation of U.S. policies (see Table 15.2).

The Congressional Role in Policy Making

Congress can rely on several mechanisms when seeking to influence foreign and defense policies.[11] The Senate can affect presidential policies through its power to ratify treaties negotiated by the White House. For example, Carter had difficulty obtaining Senate support for two controversial treaties. The Panama Canal Treaty barely gained enough votes, but a strategic arms limitation treaty with the Soviet Union (SALT II) was not ratified.

The Senate can also express its displeasure with White House policies indirectly, by delaying or rejecting confirmation of a presidential appointment to a high-level post in the foreign policy bureaucracy or to an ambassadorship. In 1981, for example, Reagan withdrew the name of his nominee for assistant secretary of state for humanitarian affairs when it became clear that the nomination lacked sufficient support in the Senate and would not be confirmed.

Both the House and the Senate can influence foreign and defense policies through direct legislation. In 1973, for example, Congress passed the War Powers Resolution, limiting the president's power to commit U.S. troops overseas without congressional authorization. The resolution's provisions were first implemented in 1983, when Reagan ordered American troops to Grenada and successfully sought authorization to keep those forces on the island nation for six months.*

Congressional control of the nation's purse strings provides an additional source of influence over foreign and defense policies. In 1983, for instance, congressional opponents of Reagan's policies toward Nicaragua imposed a $24-million limit on funding to support military efforts aimed at overthrowing that nation's government. In 1984 Congress forbade the use of any funds for that purpose. The decision was eventually reversed in 1986, when Congress appropriated $100 million for support to Nicaraguan rebels.†

When considering legislation or appropriations, members of Congress have an opportunity to question key foreign or defense policy makers. Each year the secretaries of state and defense, the director of the CIA, and other agency chiefs or their assistants appear before congressional committees and subcommittees to answer questions that can cover a broad range of policy concerns. Congress also uses its investigative power to influence foreign and defense policies. Thus in 1987 both houses of Congress selected special committees to investigate the charges that members of Reagan's National Security Council staff had violated a 1985 congressional action that prohibited the U.S. government from assisting rebel forces fighting the government of Nicaragua. The right to conduct these and similar investigations gives Congress leverage in shaping U.S. foreign and defense policies.

The Mass Media and Attentive Publics

The media influences foreign and defense policy making in several ways. In their increasing search for stories to stir the interest of their readers and listeners, news reporters constantly monitor American involvement in world affairs. News reports from Vietnam, for example, greatly affected public attitudes toward that war.

The main audience for media coverage of foreign and defense policies is not the mass public, but the segments of the public that are normally more interested in, as well as informed on, relevant issues. Called **attentive publics,** this group makes up less than one-fifth of the American public and yet plays an important role in the shaping of U.S. policies. Much of what the general

---

* The original act also included provisions that allowed Congress to order the troops home immediately by passing a concurrent resolution in both houses. This type of "legislative veto" was declared unconstitutional by the U.S. Supreme Court in June 1983.

† These particular congressional restrictions eventually led members of the Reagan administration to develop alternative—and legally questionable—means for funding the rebel forces. The resulting scandal became known as the Iran-Contra Affair.

public (see below) knows and thinks about foreign and defense policies comes from contacts with these attentive members of the public.

An important characteristic of these attentive publics is that many of them join and support organizations and groups with specific positions on U.S. foreign and defense policies. While these interest groups do not play a formal role in deciding national security policy, they are often highly influential in identifying key issues and setting policy agendas (see Chapter 8, on interest groups). In 1975, for instance, several organizations representing the American Jewish community pressed for legislation that would prohibit U.S. corporations from cooperating in an economic boycott of Israel being promoted by Arab countries. When members of Congress introduced antiboycott proposals, the Ford Administration and various business groups opposed them. After months of debate, representatives from both the Jewish and business interest groups met to formulate a compromise; it was finally passed by Congress in 1977 and signed into law by President Carter.[12]

The activity of interest groups in the foreign and defense policy arenas is extremely diverse. Groups such as the influential Council on Foreign Relations work to increase citizen awareness of foreign and defense policy issues. Others promote a specific ideological perspective, such as defeating international communism or establishing a world government. Still others advocate a particular goal, such as support for the United Nations or a nuclear test ban treaty. Many more promote their own community or business interests. Greek-American organizations, for example, lobby actively for U.S. policies that favor Greece and give less support to its long-time foe, Turkey. Trade associations representing almost every sector of the U.S. economy—from farmers seeking international markets for their surplus crops and computer chip manufacturers seeking protection from Japanese imports to defense contractors wanting Congress to fund a new weapons system—are also frequently involved in the foreign policy-making process. There are even lobbyists representing foreign governments and seeking favorable policies from the White House and Congress.

The Role of Public Opinion

Students of public opinion often note that the general American public does not show a deep or enduring interest in foreign and defense policies. For most Americans, domestic policy concerns and personal affairs overshadow interest in world affairs. Most look to the president and other policy makers for leadership in these matters.[13] When it is aroused, the mass public's interest in foreign and defense policies usually focuses on some immediate threat or foreign policy crisis.[14]

For example, few Americans, until the Arab oil embargo of 1973, knew how heavily the United States relied on imported oil. Nor could most

Protesting racism abroad Although public opinion does not often play a direct role in forming American foreign policy, some issues arouse specific sectors of the public. Pictured here are anti-apartheid demonstrators protesting U.S. relations with the white South African government.

Americans point to Vietnam on a world map until thousands of American troops were sent to that Southeast Asian country in the early 1960s. When the general public does pay attention to a national security issue, its responses are often highly volatile and based on scant information.

The volatility of public opinion poses a dilemma for policy makers. To gain public support in foreign and defense affairs, they must often oversell the challenges being faced or the need for the administration's programs. Examples abound. Presidential trips abroad and summit meetings with leaders of other nations become media events that dominate the news for weeks. Each year the Pentagon issues reports showing the growing threat of Soviet military superiority. The dramatization of such events helps rouse the public out of its normal passivity in matters of foreign affairs and defense.[15]

Some analysts believe that the mass public's main influence on policy derives from its attitude, or "mood," regarding U.S. involvement in world affairs. According to this "mood theory," the general public has very little direct impact on specific foreign and defense matters. But its perceived willingness to accept certain views, tactics, and programs carries considerable weight in policy decisions.[16]

Historically, the public's mood has fluctuated between a willingness to accept greater U.S. involvement in world affairs and a contrary urge to withdraw from the international scene. When the public mood favors involvement, policy makers find it easier to engage in diplomacy or military ventures. When the public mood favors withdrawal, policy makers are reluctant to sign treaties, increase foreign aid, or commit U.S. troops abroad. Carter faced such a public mood during his term in office. After the Vietnam War, most Americans were leery of new diplomatic initiatives or military ventures on foreign soil. By 1981 Reagan found the American public more willing to support increasing U.S. commitments abroad. The Reagan administration responded by calling for increased defense spending and a greater commitment in Central America.[17]

The public mood is just one of many factors that have helped shape U.S. foreign and defense policies over the past two centuries. Still other factors are the diplomatic tools and the military capabilities available to our foreign and defense policy makers.

★ ★ ★

DIPLOMATIC TOOLS

Like all nations, the United States uses several diplomatic tools in its relationships with other countries. One of the most common is **formal recognition** of another nation. For the United States, formal recognition means that the president publicly accepts and acknowledges the sovereignty of another nation and receives its ambassador in Washington as that country's official representative. Granting or withdrawing formal recognition can have great bearing on foreign policy. For example, in 1948 Truman formally recognized Israel within hours of receiving word that the new nation had been formed. Since controversy and violence accompanied Israel's birth, diplomatic recognition by the United States was critically important and helped establish a close relationship between the two countries.

In contrast, when the United States fails to recognize a nation or breaks off formal diplomatic relations, it clearly signals its views on that country's leadership. American policy makers have shrunk from extending recognition to communist countries. Although the Russian Revolution took place in 1917, the United States did not establish formal relations with the Soviet Union until 1933. Similarly, nearly thirty years passed before the United States and the People's Republic of China agreed to exchange ambassadors in 1978.

Breaking off diplomatic relations is an extreme step in international affairs and is usually a response to some dramatic event. The United States ended its formal recognition of Cuba in 1961, when Fidel Castro seized American property without compensation and entered into a close relationship with the Soviet Union. In 1979 Carter broke off formal ties with Iran after the American embassy was seized and its employees taken hostage. In most other cases, however, the United States has maintained formal relations with a country even if it objected to that country's policies. Reagan, for example, did not sever American ties with the Nicaraguan government during the 1980s even though his administration openly supported rebel groups (the contras) seeking to overthrow that nation's leadership. Similarly, the United States maintains its relations with South Africa despite public condemnation of that country's apartheid policies.

Foreign aid is another major diplomatic tool. It usually takes the form of a grant of money or supplies to another nation, although it can also be a low-interest loan. As a tool of U.S. foreign policy, the best-known example of foreign aid was the Marshall plan. Proposed in 1947 by the then Secretary of State George C. Marshall, the plan provided financial aid and low-cost loans to help America's allies rebuild and strengthen their economies after World War II.

As Third World nations emerged in the 1960s and 1970s, the United States provided an increasing amount of direct and indirect assistance for economic development in these poor nations. Foreign aid was also used to support and reward friendly governments threatened by internal rebellions or hostile neighbors. Most such aid was intended to strengthen the military capabilities of recipient governments. Reagan, for example, supported sending billions of dollars of military aid to El Salvador and other Central American nations as "security assistance," to help them withstand what the Reagan administration saw as the spread of Soviet influence in the region. Very little of that assistance was devoted to building schools and highways or promoting effective health care and birth control programs.[18]

A third major tool of diplomacy, **treaties** are legally binding pacts by which two or more nations formalize an agreement reached through negotiation. Some treaties form the basis of international or regional organizations, for example, the United Nations Charter. Others establish standards of behavior among the nations that sign them. In 1986, for instance, the United States signed an international treaty outlawing genocide, or the mass murder of a group of people, such as occurred in Hitler's Germany during World War II. Other agreements address the treatment of prisoners of war and refugees. Treaties can also reflect solutions to disputes or problems arising between two or more nations. The United States and the Soviet Union, for example, have signed a number of treaties since 1960 dealing with issues such as the proliferation of nuclear weapons, the use of nuclear weapons in outer space, the testing of nuclear weapons in the atmosphere, and arms limitations. The best-known use of treaties, however, relates to agreements about defense issues, such as NATO.

Covert actions can also have a considerable impact. As the phrase implies, covert actions involve activities intentionally hidden from public view. Sometimes covert actions are justified on grounds that the operation cannot be successfully conducted in full public view. At other times they are justified in order to protect the lives of those involved. Nevertheless, the secrecy surrounding covert actions frequently raises questions about their legality. They range from gathering intelligence through bugging devices to paying an informant or planning the overthrow or assassination of another nation's leaders. The CIA, for example, played a major role in such activities as the 1961 Bay of Pigs invasion of Cuba that sought to overthrow Castro, the training of a hundred thousand Laotian troops that fought in the Vietnam War, the funding of striking truckers in Chile to destablilize that country's government in the early 1970s, and the training and funding of Nicaraguan rebel forces.

Aside from the moral and legal questions, covert activities pose a difficult dilemma for American policy makers. In 1987, for example, a special presidential commission appointed by Reagan to study the covert actions of the National Security Council staff concluded that such operations greatly burden policy making in a free society. Disclosure of some covert operations might jeopardize their effectiveness and embarrass government officials. Yet democratic and free societies traditionally thrive on openness and access to information.[19]

A hero to some . . . Former National Security Council official Lieutenant Colonel Oliver North testifies before a congressional committee investigating the sale of arms to Iran and the diversion of profits from those sales to contras in Nicaragua. Nationally televised, North's testimony detailed secret activities of government officials seeking to evade a congressional ban on military aid to the contras.

★ ★ ★

MILITARY AND DEFENSE STRATEGIES

Differing views of U.S. military and defense policies have given rise to a debate involving many complicated questions. Two issues dominate. One has to do with the amount of money that should be spent on defense. It is at the heart of the "guns-or-butter" debate and reflects disagreements between those who believe in higher defense expenditures and those who think additional funds would be better spent on consumer goods and social services.

The second issue is how to allocate the dollars to be spent on defense. To put it another way, the question is what kind of defense would provide the most effective military protection for this country at the least cost. In its most extreme form, the debate on this issue pits those who support a nuclear strategy for defense against those who favor improving the preparedness of conventional (nonnuclear) forces.

Guns or Butter

As noted above, the key question in the guns-or-butter debate is how much of our nation's resources should go for defense. Before the Cold War, peacetime military spending in the United States remained relatively low compared with that in European nations. Our military expenditures consumed only a small portion of our economic resources—usually about 1 percent of the gross national product (GNP).

All this changed in the late 1940s. By 1950 the United States was a world power, and its leadership of the Western alliance made a large and costly military establishment necessary. That same year the Cold War became even more costly when the United States sent troops to help South Korea repel an attack by North Korea. The defense budget more than tripled, from $12.2 billion in 1950 to about $43 billion just five years later. During the 1960s, defense spending climbed to more than $80 billion and consumed over 9 percent of the nation's GNP.

After American forces withdrew from Vietnam in the early 1970s, defense expenditures continued to grow, though at a slower rate. When Reagan took office in 1981, military spending had reached the $157.5-billion mark, but that represented only 5.5 percent of the nation's GNP (see Table 15.3). Within four years, however, Reagan administration policies had increased defense expenditures to nearly $238 billion.

Those who support more spending for defense argue that the United States needs a strong military capability in the face of a constant Soviet military buildup. They point out that in 1982 the Soviet Union spent an estimated $952 per capita on its military; that same year the United States

TABLE 15.3 Federal Spending for Defense, 1960–1986

After a long period of relative stability or only moderate increases in defense spending, the defense budget has risen steeply under President Reagan. The drop in defense spending, however, as a percentage of both the federal budget and the GNP is a consequence of increased funding for social services.

Year	Total Defense Spending (in billions of dollars)	Spending as a Percentage of	
		Federal Budget	Gross National Product
1960	48.1	52.2	9.7
1963	54.8	48.0	9.2
1966	58.1	43.2	8.0
1969	82.5	44.9	9.1
1972	79.2	34.3	7.0
1975	86.5	26.7	4.8
1978	104.5	23.3	5.0
1981	157.5	24.0	5.5
1984	227.4	26.7	6.4
1985	252.7	26.7	6.4
1986 (est.)	265.8	27.1	6.3

Source: Statistical Abstract of the United States, 1987. Washington, D.C.: U.S., Bureau of the Census, 1986 Table 537.

spent only $846 per capita. According to the U.S. Arms Control and Disarmament Agency, more than 15 percent of the Soviet Union's GNP was devoted to military expenditures—more than twice the figure for the United States. If we are going to be able to catch up to the Soviets, they argue, we must be willing to make as great an effort as they do.

Countering this argument are analysts who claim that Americans neither need to spend more on defense nor can they afford to. Former Secretary of State Cyrus Vance contended that "America's military strength is formidable. I know of no responsible military official who would exchange our strategic position for that of any other nation."[20] Furthermore, the money for increased defense spending would have to come from one of three sources: higher taxes, greater government debt, or funds that would otherwise be spent on nondefense programs. Raising taxes would mean leaving the taxpayer with less money for consumer items and for investing in the U.S. economy. Funding higher military expenditures through greater government debt, or what is called deficit financing—that is, by having the government borrow the money it needs—would add to a huge public debt that many observers believe has already caused major economic problems.

In its effort to increase defense spending, the Reagan administration adopted the third approach: increasing the funds for military expenditures by reducing federal spending for economic, social, and other domestic programs. Reagan advocated higher defense spending while simultaneously fighting any tax increase and struggling to hold the federal deficit in check. Reducing expenditures for domestic programs was not easy. Many of the most costly programs, like social security and highway construction funds, had powerful backing in Congress. Opponents of cuts in nondefense programs also argued that such expenditures help assure the continued economic and social strength of the American system. In their view, our priorities for government spending should be at home.

The guns-or-butter controversy is a longstanding debate that arises whenever the White House submits its budget recommendations to Congress. Sometimes the president favors higher defense spending; at other times, members of Congress seek such increases. The debate reflects the basic conflict between those who believe the United States is doing too much in the area of defense and those who are convinced it is doing too little.

Nuclear or Conventional Strategies

The first and only use of nuclear weapons in time of war occurred in 1945, when the United States dropped atomic bombs on the Japanese cities of Hiroshima and Nagasaki. Nevertheless, the new weapon changed the nature of war and military strategy. A special report prepared in 1950 by the National Security Council staff underscored this change. It argued for a **deterrence strategy** based on the buildup of nuclear and conventional (nonnuclear) forces so that any potential enemy would hesitate to attack the United States or its allies. Almost all U.S. defense strategy since that time has been rooted in the deterrence approach.

At first, the Council's appeal for a strategy based on both nuclear and conventional forces was ignored. During the 1950s the principal defense strategy emphasized nuclear weapons. Called **massive retaliation,** this strategy required stockpiling nuclear weapons and warning the Soviet Union and its allies that any confrontation with the United States and its allies could wipe out Moscow and other major cities.

Massive retaliation was a very risky and controversial strategy. By spending so much on nuclear weapons, the policy makers had let conventional forces deteriorate. By 1960 many felt that the United States had lost its capacity to respond effectively to small, localized conflicts. Thus during the 1960s the emphasis shifted to a strategy of **flexible response,** which called for the buildup of America's nonnuclear, limited-war capabilities. Advocates of this strategy believed that strengthened conventional troops would make deterrence more credible, for the United States could counter enemy aggression with the right amount of force.

The enormous buildup of the Soviet nuclear arsenal during the 1950s and 1960s focused attention on the dangers of massive retaliation as a policy. Given the development of intercontinental ballistic missiles (ICBMs), multiple independently targeted re-entry vehicles (MIRVs), and other delivery technology, the Soviet Union could also devastate American cities. A new strategy emerged based on **mutual assured destruction (MAD):** each of the nuclear powers would hold the other in check by maintaining the ability to annihilate the other in any major confrontation.

Throughout the 1970s American policy makers stressed the need for keeping our nuclear-weapons force at a level roughly equivalent to that of the Soviet force. In other words, nuclear equality rather than nuclear superiority would suffice. We would be safe if our enemies knew that we could retaliate effectively when attacked. As for nonnuclear forces, during the 1970s our defense strategy shifted to improving conventional weapon systems and training all-volunteer armed forces. Most military leaders, however, became reluctant to have U.S. forces engaged in any type of long-term, land-based operation that might lead to the kind of war we fought in Vietnam.

During the 1980s the United States concentrated on strengthening both its nuclear and its nonnuclear forces. On the nuclear side, Reagan called for maintaining a weapons force to provide a margin of safety over the Soviets. As for conventional warfare, the Reagan administration sought more spending on new, more sophisticated nonnuclear weapons. Perhaps the most significant development in our strategic defense policy under Reagan was the adoption of the **strategic defense initiative (SDI),** also known as Star Wars. Officially proposed in 1983, SDI called for the development of a system of satellites and earth-based stations that "could intercept and destroy strategic ballistic missiles before they reached our own soil or that of our allies. . . ." Critics of SDI believed it to be unfeasible and feared that it would militarize outer space. In spite of these criticisms, the Reagan administration made SDI a top priority in its defense budget.

CONCLUSION: The Shaping of Foreign and Defense Policy

U.S. foreign and defense policies have moved completely away from the isolationism and unilateralism that characterized most of this nation's history. Since World War II, the international emphasis of American policies has been clear even to the most casual observer. Between 1948 and 1951 the United States became the clear leader of the West in its relations with the Soviet bloc. Yet despite this new willingness on the part of the United States to engage in world affairs, the isolationist legacy of the past remains a strong force in shaping our international involvements. It was evident in 1953 when

MYTH AND REALITY 15.1

The Domino Theory

The myths of too little and too much government activity in world affairs were not the only ones to play an important role in shaping U.S. foreign and defense policies. In 1954 John Foster Dulles, President Dwight D. Eisenhower's secretary of state, spoke of what would occur if Southeast Asia fell into the hands of the communists. "You have a row of dominoes set up," he told a meeting of reporters, "and you knock over the first one, and what will happen to the last one is certainly that it will go over very quickly." Dulles believed that Southeast Asia was the first domino, and once it fell it would not be long before Australia, New Zealand, Japan, and the Philippines followed. Soon the United States itself would be threatened. And so the myth of the domino theory was born.

The domino theory had a profound effect on American thinking throughout the 1950s and 1960s. It was widely assumed that the United States must defend Southeast Asia, and Vietnam in particular, if it was to save its Pacific-basin allies and itself. Not only presidents and their advisers expressed this view, but the mass media as well. In 1968 *Time* magazine editorialized that if the communist North Vietnamese were to overrun South Vietnam, "the fall of all of Southeast Asia would only be a matter of time."

South Vietnam eventually did fall—in 1975—but with few of the consequences predicted by the domino theory. Southeast Asia, like other regions in the world, is composed of both communist and noncommunist nations. The Pacific-basin allies of the United States have not been threatened by major communist insurgencies, and the West Coast of the United States remains safe from the threat of invasion.

Yet the myth of the domino theory lives on in the policies of the Reagan administration. Today, however, the dominoes are set up a bit closer to home, in Central America. Reagan and others have frequently argued that Nicaragua poses a major threat to the stability of Honduras, El Salvador, Costa Rica, and other countries in that region. Once those nations fall, Mexico would be next. It follows that the next domino would be the United States.

For more information see William Manchester, *The Glory and the Dream: A Narrative History of America, 1932–1972* (Boston: Little, Brown, 1974), especially p. 837.

public opinion polls indicated that most Americans wanted an end to the Korean conflict. It was evident in the opinion polls and public demonstrations that called for a pullout of U.S. forces from Vietnam in the early 1970s. It was evident in the lack of popular support for President Reagan's policy of supplying arms to the Nicaraguan rebels in the 1980s.

The myths discussed at the start of this chapter play a crucial role in our policies. The myth that the United States is doing too little in world affairs has been fed by the realities of international relations over the past four decades. It has generated demands for American involvement in almost every corner of the world. That myth resulted in arms being shipped to the Middle East, in aid being given to Nicaraguan rebels, and in more spending for new tanks and bombers. The opposite myth, that the United States is doing too much in world affairs, has deep roots in the nation's past, and such failures of our foreign and defense policies as the Vietnam War have increased its influence (see Myth and Reality 15.1).

Together these contrasting myths have helped to shape and direct foreign and defense policies. Few policy decisions are made in a vacuum. Policy makers realize that adherents of both myths are constantly exerting pressure. Whether the issue at hand is formulating U.S. policies toward South Africa or South Korea, sending the American fleet into the Persian Gulf or American troops to Central America, breaking off diplomatic relations with Nicaragua, or resuming trade with Cuba, U.S. policy makers must deal with the impact of the myths of too little and too much government activity in foreign affairs and defense.

★ ★ ★

SUMMARY

1. Historically, U.S. foreign and defense policies were guided by principles of isolationism and unilateralism established by George Washington and other early presidents.

2. The isolationist policies of the United States were challenged in the 1880s and 1890s, but not until World War II did American policy makers and the American people accept the nation's role as an international leader. U.S. involvement was a response to the perceived threat of Soviet expansionism and took the form of a policy of containment. The end to unilateralism came with the Cold War, as the United States entered into formal alliances with the nations of Western Europe to form NATO. Other alliances followed.

3. In more recent years the United States has adapted its foreign and defense policies to changes in world affairs. Among the most important changes have been the emergence of Third World nations and an end to the bipolar world situation, as countries such as France and the People's Republic of China broke from their respective alliances.

4. The making of U.S. foreign and defense policies involves a unique set of policy-making institutions, although there are many factors that help determine decisions in each area. The crucial decision makers in foreign and defense matters are part of an inner circle centered in the White House. The moods and attitudes of the general public also influence the decisions made in both arenas.

5. U.S. policy makers have a variety of foreign policy tools at their disposal. They include formal recognition, foreign aid, treaties, and covert actions.

6. Two issues have marked American defense policies since the start of the Cold War: how much money to spend on defense and which defensive strategies to rely on. The latter issue has two major aspects—how much the United States should depend on its nuclear forces and how much on its conventional forces.

7. One key to understanding U.S. foreign and defense policies is to see how they are shaped and directed by public pressures on policy makers to do more or less in the international arena.

★ ★ ★
KEY TERMS

bipolar
containment
detente
attentive publics
formal recognition
foreign aid
treaties

covert actions
deterrence strategies
massive retaliation
flexible response
mutual assured destruction (MAD)
strategic defense initiative (SDI)
   (common name, Star Wars)

★ ★ ★
SUGGESTED READINGS

- Baylis, John, Ken Booth, John Garnett, and Phil Williams. *Contemporary Strategy.* 2 vols. 2nd ed. New York: Holmes and Meier, 1987. A comprehensive analysis of modern military strategies that focuses on the United States.

- Congressional Quarterly, *U.S. Foreign Policy: The Reagan Imprint.* Washington, D.C.: Congressional Quarterly, 1986. A region-by-region overview of U.S. foreign policy during the first five years of President Reagan's terms in office.

- Karnow, Stanley. *Vietnam: A History.* New York: Penguin Books, 1983. A history of U.S. involvement in the Southeast Asian nation, which eventually led to a conflict that changed the direction of U.S. foreign and defense policies in the 1970s and 1980s.

- Kissinger, Henry. *White House Years.* Boston: Little, Brown, 1979. Kissinger, Henry. *Years of Upheaval.* Boston: Little, Brown, 1982. The memoirs and insights of a major U.S. foreign policy maker during the late 1960s and 1970s.

- Reichart, John F., and Steven R. Strum, eds. *American Defense Policy*, 5th ed. Baltimore: Johns Hopkins University Press, 1982. A comprehensive resource for anyone interested in scholarly studies of U.S. defense policy and its relations to foreign policy.
- Yoder, Amos. *The Conduct of American Foreign Policy Since World War II.* New York: Pergamon Press, 1986. A readable, short survey of U.S. foreign policy during the Cold War.

Appendixes

THE DECLARATION OF INDEPENDENCE IN CONGRESS JULY 4, 1776

The unanimous declaration of the thirteen United States of America

When, in the course of human events, it becomes necessary for one people to dissolve the political bonds which have connected them with another, and to assume, among the powers of the earth, the separate and equal station to which the laws of nature and of nature's God entitle them, a decent respect to the opinions of mankind requires that they should declare the causes which impel them to the separation.

We hold these truths to be self-evident: That all men are created equal; that they are endowed by their Creator with certain unalienable rights; that among these are life, liberty, and the pursuit of happiness; that, to secure these rights, governments are instituted among men, deriving their just powers from the consent of the governed; that whenever any form of government becomes destructive of these ends, it is the right of the people to alter or to abolish it, and to institute new government, laying its foundation on such principles, and organizing its powers in such form, as to them shall seem most likely to effect their safety and happiness. Prudence, indeed, will dictate that governments long established should not be changed for light and transient causes; and accordingly all experience hath shown that mankind are more disposed to suffer, while evils are sufferable, than to right themselves by abolishing the forms to which they are accustomed. But when a long train of abuses and usurpations, pursuing invariably the same object, evinces a design to reduce them under absolute despotism, it is their right, it is their duty, to throw off such government, and to provide new guards for their future security. Such has been the patient sufferance of these colonies; and such is now the necessity which constrains them to alter their former systems of government. The history of the present King of Great Britain is a history of repeated injuries and usurpations, all having in direct object the establishment of an absolute tyranny over these states. To prove this, let facts be submitted to a candid world.

He has refused his assent to laws, the most wholesome and necessary for the public good.

He has forbidden his governors to pass laws of immediate and pressing importance, unless suspended in their operation till his assent should be obtained; and, when so suspended, he has utterly neglected to attend to them.

He has refused to pass other laws for the accommodation of large districts of people, unless those people would relinquish the right of representation in the legislature, a right inestimable to them, and formidable to tyrants only.

He has called together legislative bodies at places unusual, uncomfortable, and distant from the depository of their public records, for the sole purpose of fatiguing them into compliance with his measures.

He has dissolved representative houses repeatedly, for opposing, with manly firmness, his invasions on the rights of the people.

He has refused for a long time, after such dissolutions, to cause others to be elected; whereby the legislative powers, incapable of annihilation, have returned to the people at large for their exercise; the state remaining, in the mean time, exposed to all the dangers of invasions from without and convulsions within.

He has endeavored to prevent the population of these states; for that purpose obstructing the laws for naturalization of foreigners; refusing to pass others to encourage their migration hither, and raising the conditions of new appropriations of lands.

He has obstructed the administration of justice, by refusing his assent to laws for establishing judiciary powers.

He has made judges dependent on his will alone, for the tenure of their offices, and the amount and payment of their salaries.

He has erected a multitude of new offices, and sent hither swarms of officers to harass our people and eat out their substance.

He has kept among us, in times of peace, standing armies, without the consent of our legislatures.

He has affected to render the military independent of, and superior to, the civil power.

He has combined with others to subject us to a jurisdiction foreign to our constitution, and unacknowledged by our laws, giving his assent to their acts of pretended legislation:

For quartering large bodies of armed troops among us;

For protecting them, by a mock trial, from punishment for any murders which they should commit on the inhabitants of these states;

For cutting off our trade with all parts of the world;

For imposing taxes on us without our consent;

For depriving us, in many cases, of the benefits of trial by jury;

For transporting us beyond seas, to be tried for pretended offenses;

For abolishing the free system of English laws in a neighboring province, establishing therein an arbitrary government, and enlarging its boundaries, so as to render it at once an example and fit instrument for introducing the same absolute rule into these colonies;

For taking away our charters, abolishing our most valuable laws, and altering fundamentally the forms of our governments;

For suspending our own legislatures, and declaring themselves invested with power to legislate for us in all cases whatsoever.

He has abdicated government here, by declaring us out of his protection and waging war against us.

He has plundered our seas, ravaged our coasts, burned our towns, and destroyed the lives of our people.

He is at this time transporting large armies of foreign mercenaries to complete the works of death, desolation, and tyranny already begun with circumstances of cruelty and perfidy scarcely paralleled in the most barbarous ages, and totally unworthy the head of a civilized nation.

He has constrained our fellow-citizens, taken captive on the high seas, to bear arms against their country, to become the executioners of their friends and brethren, or to fall themselves by their hands.

He has excited domestic insurrection among us, and has endeavored to bring on the inhabitants of our frontiers the merciless Indian savages, whose known rule of warfare is an undistinguished destruction of all ages, sexes, and conditions.

In every stage of these oppressions we have petitioned for redress in the most humble terms; our repeated petitions have been answered only by repeated injury. A prince, whose character is thus marked by every act which may define a tyrant, is unfit to be the ruler of a free people.

Nor have we been wanting in our attentions to our British brethren. We have warned them, from time to time, of attempts by their legislature to extend an unwarrantable jurisdiction over us. We have reminded them of the circumstances of our emigration and settlement here. We have appealed to their native justice and magnanimity; and we have conjured them, by the ties of our common kindred, to disavow these usurpations, which would inevitably interrupt our connections and correspondence. They, too, have been deaf to the voice of justice and of consanguinity. We must, therefore, acquiesce in the necessity which denounces our separation, and hold them, as we hold the rest of mankind, enemies in war, in peace friends.

We, therefore, the representatives of the United States of America, in General Congress assembled, appealing to the Supreme Judge of the world for the rectitude of our intentions, do, in the name and by the authority of the good people of these colonies, solemnly publish and declare, that these United Colonies are, and of right ought to be, FREE AND INDEPENDENT STATES; that they are absolved from all allegiance to the British crown, and that all political connection between them and the state of Great Britain is, and ought to be, totally dissolved; and that, as free and independent states, they have full power to levy war, conclude peace, contract alliances, establish commerce, and do all other acts and things which independent states may of right do. And for the support of this declaration, with a firm reliance on the protection of Divine Providence, we mutually pledge to each other our lives, our fortunes, and our sacred honor.

JOHN HANCOCK
and fifty-five others

THE CONSTITUTION OF THE UNITED STATES OF AMERICA*

Preamble

We the people of the United States, in order to form a more perfect union, establish justice, insure domestic tranquility, provide for the common defense, promote the general welfare, and secure the blessings of liberty to ourselves and our posterity, do ordain and establish this Constitution for the United States of America.

Article I

Section 1 All legislative powers herein granted shall be vested in a Congress of the United States, which shall consist of a Senate and a House of Representatives.

---

* Passages no longer in effect are printed in italic type.

Section 2 The House of Representatives shall be composed of members chosen every second year by the people of the several States, and the electors in each State shall have the qualifications requisite for electors of the most numerous branch of the State Legislature.

No person shall be a Representative who shall not have attained to the age of twenty-five years, and been seven years a citizen of the United States, and who shall not, when elected, be an inhabitant of that State in which he shall be chosen.

Representatives and direct taxes shall be apportioned among the several States which may be included within this Union, according to their respective numbers, *which shall be determined by adding to the whole number of free persons, including those bound to service for a term of years and excluding Indians not taxed, three-fifths of all other persons.* The actual enumeration shall be made within three years after the first meeting of the Congress of the United States, and within every subsequent term of ten years, in such manner as they shall by law direct. The number of Representatives shall not exceed one for every thirty thousand, but each State shall have at least one Representative; *and until such enumeration shall be made, the State of New Hampshire shall be entitled to choose three, Massachusetts eight, Rhode Island and Providence Plantations one, Connecticut five, New York six, New Jersey four, Pennsylvania eight, Delaware one, Maryland six, Virginia ten, North Carolina five, South Carolina five, and Georgia three.*

When vacancies happen in the representation from any State, the Executive authority thereof shall issue writs of election to fill such vacancies.

The House of Representatives shall choose their Speaker and other officers; and shall have the sole power of impeachment.

Section 3 The Senate of the United States shall be composed of two Senators from each State, *chosen by the legislature thereof,* for six years; and each Senator shall have one vote.

Immediately after they shall be assembled in consequence of the first election, they shall be divided as equally as may be into three classes. The seats of the Senators of the first class shall be vacated at the expiration of the second year, of the second class at the expiration of the fourth year, and of the third class at the expiration of the sixth year, so that one-third may be chosen every second year; *and if vacancies happen by resignation or otherwise, during the recess of the legislature of any State, the Executive thereof may make temporary appointments until the next meeting of the legislature, which shall then fill such vacancies.*

No person shall be a Senator who shall not have attained to the age of thirty years, and been nine years a citizen of the United States, and who shall not, when elected, be an inhabitant of that State for which he shall be chosen.

The Vice-President of the United States shall be President of the Senate, but shall have no vote, unless they be equally divided.

The Senate shall choose their other officers, and also a President *pro tempore,* in the absence of the Vice-President, or when he shall exercise the office of President of the United States.

The Senate shall have the sole power to try all impeachments. When sitting for that purpose, they shall be on oath or affirmation. When the President of the United States is tried, the Chief Justice shall preside: and no person shall be convicted without the concurrence of two-thirds of the members present.

Judgement in cases of impeachment shall not extend further than to removal from the office, and disqualification to hold and enjoy any office of honor, trust or profit under the United States: but the party convicted shall nevertheless be liable and subject to indictment, trial, judgment and punishment, according to law.

Section 4 The times, places and manner of holding elections for Senators and Representatives shall be prescribed in each State by the legislature thereof; but the Congress may at any time by law make or alter such regulations, except as to the places of choosing Senators.

The Congress shall assemble at least once in every year, and such meeting *shall be on the first Monday in December, unless they shall by law appoint a different day.*

Section 5 Each house shall be the judge of the elections, returns and qualifications of its own members, and a majority of each shall constitute a quorum to do business; but a smaller number may adjourn

from day to day, and may be authorized to compel the attendance of absent members, in such manner, and under such penalties, as each house may provide.

Each house may determine the rules of its proceedings, punish its members for disorderly behavior, and with the concurrence of two-thirds, expel a member.

Each house shall keep a journal of its proceedings, and from time to time publish the same, excepting such parts as may in their judgment require secrecy; and the yeas and nays of the members of either house on any question shall, at the desire of one-fifth of those present, be entered on the journal.

Neither house, during the session of Congress, shall, without the consent of the other, adjourn for more than three days, nor to any other place than that in which the two houses shall be sitting.

Section 6 The Senators and Representatives shall receive a compensation for their services, to be ascertained by law and paid out of the treasury of the United States. They shall in all cases except treason, felony and breach of the peace, be privileged from arrest during their attendance at the session of their respective houses, and in going to and returning from the same; and for any speech or debate in either house, they shall not be questioned in any other place.

No Senator or Representative shall, during the time for which he was elected, be appointed to any civil office under the authority of the United States, which shall have been created, or the emoluments whereof shall have been increased, during such time; and no person holding any office under the United States shall be a member of either house during his continuance in office.

Section 7 All bills for raising revenue shall originate in the House of Representatives; but the Senate may propose or concur with amendments as on other bills.

Every bill which shall have passed the House of Representatives and the Senate, shall, before it become a law, be presented to the President of the United States; if he approve he shall sign it, but if not he shall return it with objections to that house in which it originated, who shall enter the objections at large on their journal, and proceed to reconsider it. If after such reconsideration two-thirds of that house shall agree to pass the bill, it shall be sent, together with the objections, to the other house, by which it shall likewise be reconsidered, and, if approved by two-thirds of that house, it shall become a law. But in all such cases the votes of both houses shall be determined by yeas and nays, and the names of the persons voting for and against the bill shall be entered on the journal of each house respectively. If any bill shall not be returned by the President within ten days (Sundays excepted) after it shall have been presented to him, the same shall be a law, in like manner as if he had signed it, unless the Congress by their adjournment prevent its return, in which case it shall not be a law.

Every order, resolution, or vote to which the concurrence of the Senate and House of Representatives may be necessary (except on a question of adjournment) shall be presented to the President of the United States; and before the same shall take effect, shall be approved by him, or being disapproved by him, shall be repassed by two-thirds of the Senate and House of Representatives, according to the rules and limitations prescribed in the case of a bill.

Section 8 The Congress shall have power

To lay and collect taxes, duties, imposts, and excises, to pay the debts and provide for the common defense and general welfare of the United States; but all duties, imposts and excises shall be uniform throughout the United States;

To borrow money on the credit of the United States;

To regulate commerce with foreign nations, and among the several States, and with the Indian tribes;

To establish an uniform rule of naturalization, and uniform laws on the subject of bankruptcies throughout the United States;

To coin money, regulate the value thereof, and of foreign coin, and fix the standard of weights and measures;

To provide for the punishment of counterfeiting the securities and current coin of the United States;

To establish post offices and post roads;

To promote the progress of science and useful arts by securing for limited times to authors and inventors the exclusive right to their respective writings and discoveries;

To constitute tribunals inferior to the Supreme Court;

To define and punish piracies and felonies committed on the high seas and offenses against the law of nations;

To declare war, grant letters of marque and reprisal, and make rules concerning captures on land and water;

To raise and support armies, but no appropriation of money to that use shall be for a longer term than two years;

To provide and maintain a navy;

To make rules for the government and regulation of the land and naval forces;

To provide for calling forth the militia to execute the laws of the Union, suppress insurrections, and repel invasions;

To provide for organizing, arming, and disciplining the militia, and for governing such part of them as may be employed in the service of the United States, reserving to the States respectively the appointment of the officers, and the authority of training the militia according to the discipline prescribed by Congress;

To exercise exclusive legislation in all cases whatsoever, over such district (not exceeding ten miles square) as may, by cession of particular States, and the acceptance of Congress, become the seat of government of the United States, and to exercise like authority over all places purchased by the consent of the legislature of the State, in which the same shall be, for erection of forts, magazines, arsenals, dock-yards, and other needful buildings;— and

To make all laws which shall be necessary and proper for carrying into execution the foregoing powers, and all other powers vested by this Constitution in the government of the United States, or in any department or officer thereof.

Section 9 *The migration or importation of such persons as any of the States now existing shall think proper to admit shall not be prohibited by the Congress prior to the year 1808; but a tax or duty may be imposed on such importation, not exceeding $10 for each person.*

The privilege of the writ of habeas corpus shall

not be suspended, unless when in cases of rebellion or invasion the public safety may require it.

No bill of attainer or ex post facto law shall be passed.

No capitation, or other direct, tax shall be laid, unless in proportion to the census or enumeration herein before directed to be taken.

No tax or duty shall be laid on articles exported from any State.

No preference shall be given by any regulation of commerce or revenue to the ports of one State over those of another; nor shall vessels bound to, or from, one State, be obliged to enter, clear, or pay duties in another.

No money shall be drawn from the treasury, but in consequence of appropriations made by law; and a regular statement and account of the receipts and expenditures of all public money shall be published from time to time.

No title of nobility shall be granted by the United States: and no person holding any office of profit or trust under them, shall, without the consent of the Congress, accept of any present, emolument, office, or title, of any kind whatever, from any king, prince, or foreign state.

Section 10 No State shall enter into any treaty, alliance, or confederation; grant letters of marque and reprisal; coin money; emit bills of credit; make anything but gold and silver coin a tender in payment of debts; pass any bill of attainder, ex post facto law, or law impairing the obligation of contracts, or grant any title of nobility.

No State shall, without the consent of Congress, lay any imposts or duties on imports or exports, except what may be absolutely necessary for executing its inspection laws: and the net produce of all duties and imposts, laid by any State on imports or exports, shall be for the use of the treasury of the United States; and all such laws shall be subject to the revision and control of the Congress.

No State shall, without the consent of Congress, lay any duty of tonnage, keep troops or ships of war in time of peace, enter into any agreement or compact with another State, or with a foreign power, or engage in war, unless actually invaded, or in such imminent danger as will not admit of delay.

Article II

Section 1 The executive power shall be vested in a President of the United States of America. He shall hold his office during the term of four years, and, together with the Vice-President, chosen for the same term, be elected as follows:

Each State shall appoint, in such manner as the legislature thereof may direct, a number of electors, equal to the whole number of Senators and Representatives to which the State may be entitled in the Congress; but no Senator or Representative, or person holding an office of trust or profit under the United States, shall be appointed an elector.

The electors shall meet in their respective States, and vote by ballot for two persons, of whom one at least shall not be an inhabitant of the same State with themselves. And they shall make a list of all the persons voted for, and of the number of votes for each; which list they shall sign and certify, and transmit sealed to the seat of government of the United States, directed to the President of the Senate. The President of the Senate shall, in the presence of the Senate and House of Representatives, open all the certificates, and the votes shall then be counted. The person having the greatest number of votes shall be the President, if such number be a majority of the whole number of electors appointed; and if there be more than one who have such majority, and have an equal number of votes, then the House of Representatives shall immediately choose by ballot one of them for President; and if no person have a majority, then from the five highest on the list said house shall in like manner choose the President. But in choosing the President the votes shall be taken by States, the representation from each State having one vote; a quorum for this purpose shall consist of a member or members from two-thirds of the States, and a majority of all the States shall be necessary to a choice. In every case, after the choice of the President, the peson having the greatest number of votes of the electors shall be the Vice-President. But if there should remain two or more who have equal votes, the Senate shall choose from them by ballot the Vice-President.

The Congress may determine the time of choosing the electors and the day on which they shall give their votes; which day shall be the same throughout the United States.

No person except a natural-born citizen, *or a citizen of the United States at the time of the adoption of this Constitution*, shall be eligible to the office of President; neither shall any person be eligible to that office who shall not have attained to the age of thirty-five years, and been fourteen years a resident within the United States.

In cases of the removal of the President from office or of his death, resignation, or inability to discharge the powers and duties of the said office, the same shall devolve on the Vice-President, and the Congress may by law provide for the case of removal, death, resignation, or inability, both of the President and Vice-President, declaring what officer shall then act as President, and such officer shall act accordingly, until the disability be removed, or a President shall be elected.

The President shall, at stated times, receive for his services a compensation, which shall neither be increased nor diminished during the period for which he shall have been elected, and he shall not receive within that period any other emolument from the United States, or any of them.

Before he enter on the execution of his office, he shall take the following oath or affirmation:—"I do solemnly swear (or affirm) that I will faithfully execute the office of the President of the United States, and will to the best of my ability preserve, protect and defend the Constitution of the United States."

Section 2 The President shall be commander in chief of the army and navy of the United States, and of the militia of the several States, when called into the actual service of the United States; he may require the opinion, in writing, of the principal officer in each of the executive departments, upon any subject relating to the duties of their respective offices, and he shall have power to grant reprieves and pardons for offenses against the United States, except in cases of impeachment.

He shall have power, by and with the advice and consent of the Senate, to make treaties, provided two-thirds of the Senators present concur; and he shall nominate, and by and with the advice and consent of the Senate, shall appoint ambassadors, other public ministers and consuls, judges of the Supreme court, and all other officers of the United States, whose appointments are not herein otherwise provided for, and which shall be established

by law: but Congress may by law vest the appointment of such inferior officers, as they think proper, in the President alone, in the courts of law, or in the heads of departments.

The President shall have power to fill up all vacancies that may happen during the recess of the Senate, by granting commissions which shall expire at the end of their next session.

Section 3 He shall from time to time give to the Congress information of the state of the Union, and recommend to their consideration such measures as he shall judge necessary and expedient; he may, on extraordinary occasions, convene both houses, or either of them, and in case of disagreement between them, with respect to the time of adjournment, he may adjourn them to such time as he shall think proper; he shall receive ambassadors and other public ministers; he shall take care that the laws be faithfully executed, and shall commission all the officers of the United States.

Section 4 The President, Vice-President and all civil officers of the United States shall be removed from office on impeachment for, and on conviction of, treason, bribery, or other high crimes and misdemeanors.

Article III

Section 1 The judicial power of the United States shall be vested in one Supreme Court, and in such inferior courts as the Congress may from time to time ordain and establish. The judges, both of the Supreme and inferior courts, shall hold their offices during good behavior, and shall, at stated times, receive for their services a compensation which shall not be diminished during their continuance in office.

Section 2 The judicial power shall extend to all cases, in law and equity, arising under this Constitution, the laws of the United States, and treaties made, or which shall be made, under their authority;—to all cases affecting ambassadors, other public ministers and consuls;—to all cases of admiralty and maritime jurisdiction;—to controversies to which the United States shall be a party;—to controversies between two or more States;—*between a State and citizens of another State;*—between citizens of different States;—between citizens of the same State claiming lands under grants of different States, and between a State, or the citizens thereof, and foreign states, citizens or subjects.

In all cases affecting ambassadors, other public ministers and consuls, and those in which a State shall be party, the Supreme Court shall have original jurisdiction. In all the other cases before mentioned, the Supreme Court shall have appellate jurisdiction, both as to law and fact, with such exceptions, and under such regulations, as the Congress shall make.

The trial of all crimes, except in cases of impeachment, shall be by jury; and such trial shall be held in the state where said crimes shall have been committed; but when not committed within any State, the trial shall be at such place or places as the Congress may by law have directed.

Section 3 Treason against the United States shall consist only in levying war against them, or in adhering to their enemies, giving them aid and comfort. No person shall be convicted of treason unless on the testimony of two witnesses to the same overt act, or on confession in open court.

The Congress shall have power to declare the punishment of treason, but no attainder of treason shall work corruption of blood, or forfeiture except during the life of the person attained.

Article IV

Section 1 Full faith and credit shall be given in each State to the public acts, records, and judicial proceedings of every other State. And the Congress may by general laws prescribe the manner in which such acts, records, and proceedings shall be proved, and the effect thereof.

Section 2 The citizens of each State shall be entitled to all privileges and immunities of citizens in the several States.

A person charged in any State with treason, felony, or other crime, who shall flee from justice, and be found in another State, shall on demand of the executive authority of the State from which he fled, be delivered up, to be removed to the State having jurisdiction of the crime.

No person held to service or labor in one State, under the laws thereof, escaping into another, shall, in consequence of any law or regulation therein, be discharged from such service or labor, but shall be delivered up on claim of the party to whom such service or labor may be due.

Section 3 New States may be admitted by the Congress into this Union; but no new State shall be formed or erected within the jurisdiction of any other State; nor any state be formed by the junction of two or more States, or parts of States, without the consent of the legislatures of the States concerned as well as of the Congress.

The Congress shall have power to dispose of and make all needful rules and regulations respecting the territory or other property belonging to the United States; and nothing in this Constitution shall be so construed as to prejudice any claims of the United States, or of any particular State.

Section 4 The United States shall guarantee to every State in this Union a republican form of government, and shall protect each of them against invasion; and on application of the legislature, or of the executive (when the legislature cannot be convened), against domestic violence.

Article V

The Congress, whenever two-thirds of both houses shall deem it necessary, shall propose amendments to this Constitution, or, on the application of the legislatures of two-thirds of the several States, shall call a convention for proposing amendments, which, in either case, shall be valid to all intents and purposes, as part of this Constitution, when ratified by the legislatures of three-fourths of the several States, or by conventions in three-fourths thereof, as the one or the other mode of ratification may be proposed by the Congress; provided *that no amendments which may be made prior to the year one thousand eight hundred and eight shall in any manner affect the first and fourth clauses in the ninth section of the first article;* and that no State, without its consent, shall be deprived of its equal suffrage in the Senate.

Article VI

All debts contracted and engagements entered into, before the adoption of this Constitution, shall be as valid against the United States under this Constitution, as under the Confederation.

This Constitution, and the laws of the United States which shall be made in pursuance thereof; and all treaties made, or which shall be made, under the authority of the United States, shall be the supreme law of the land; and the judges in every State shall be bound thereby, anything in the Constitution or laws of any State to the contrary notwithstanding.

The Senators and Representatives before mentioned, and the members of the several State legislatures, and all executive and judicial officers, both of the United States and of the several States, shall be bound by oath or affirmation to support this Constitution; but no religious test shall ever be required as a qualification to any office or public trust under the United States.

Article VII

The ratification of the conventions of nine States shall be sufficient for the establishment of this Constitution between the States so ratifying the same.

Done in Convention by the unanimous consent of the States present, the seventeenth day of September in the year of our Lord one thousand seven hundred and eighty-seven and of the Independence of the United States of America the twelfth. In witness whereof we have hereunto subscribed our names.

GEORGE WASHINGTON
and thirty-seven others

Amendments to the Constitution*

Amendment I

Congress shall make no law respecting an establishment of religion, or prohibiting the free exercise

---

* The first ten amendments (the Bill of Rights) were adopted in 1791.

thereof; or abridging the freedom of speech, or of the press; or the right of the people peaceably to assemble, and to petition the government for a redress of grievances.

Amendment II

A well-regulated militia being necessary to the security of a free State, the right of the people to keep and bear arms shall not be infringed.

Amendment III

No soldier shall, in time of peace, be quartered in any house without the consent of the owner, nor in time of war, but in a manner to be prescribed by law.

Amendment IV

The right of the people to be secure in their persons, houses, papers, and effects, against unreasonable searches and seizures, shall not be violated, and no warrants shall issue but upon probable cause, supported by oath or affirmation, and particularly describing the place to be searched, and the persons or things to be seized.

Amendment V

No person shall be held to answer for a capital, or otherwise infamous crime, unless on a presentment or indictment of a grand jury, except in cases arising in the land or naval forces, or in the militia, when in actual service in time of war or public danger; nor shall any person be subject for the same offense to be twice put in jeopardy of life or limb; nor shall be compelled in any criminal case to be a witness against himself, nor be deprived of life, liberty, or property, without due process of law; nor shall private property be taken for public use without just compensation.

Amendment VI

In all criminal prosecutions, the accused shall enjoy the right to a speedy and public trial, by an impartial jury of the State and district wherein the crime shall have been committed, which district shall have been previously ascertained by law, and to be informed of the nature and cause of the accusation; to be confronted with the witnesses against him; to have compulsory process for obtaining witnesses in his favor, and to have the assistance of counsel for his defense.

Amendment VII

In suits at common law, where the value in controversy shall exceed twenty dollars, the right of trial by jury shall be preserved, and no fact tried by a jury shall be otherwise reexamined in any court of the United States, than according to the rules of the common law.

Amendment VIII

Excessive bail shall not be required, nor excessive fines imposed, nor cruel and unusual punishments inflicted.

Amendment IX

The enumeration in the Constitution, of certain rights, shall not be construed to deny or disparage others retained by the people.

Amendment X

The powers not delegated to the United States by the Constitution, nor prohibited by it to the States, are reserved to the states respectively, or to the people.

Amendment XI
[Adopted 1798]

The judicial power of the United States shall not be construed to extend to any suit in law or equity, commenced or prosecuted against one of the United States by citizens of another state, or by citizens or subjects of any foreign state.

Amendment XII
[Adopted 1804]

The electors shall meet in their respective States, and vote by ballot for President and Vice-President, one of whom, at least, shall not be an inhabitant of the same State with themselves; they shall name in their ballots the person voted for as President, and in distinct ballots the person voted for as Vice-President, and they shall make distinct lists of all persons voted for as President, and of all persons voted for as Vice-President, and of the number of votes for each, which lists they shall sign and certify, and transmit sealed to the seat of government of the United States, directed to the President of the Senate;—the President of the Senate shall, in the presence of the Senate and House of Representatives, open all the certificates and the votes shall then be counted;—the person having the greatest number of votes for President shall be the President, if such number be a majority of the whole number of electors appointed; and if no person have such majority, then from the persons having the highest numbers not exceeding three on the list of those voted for as President, the House of Representatives shall choose immediately, by ballot, the President. But in choosing the President, the votes shall be taken by States, the representation from each State having one vote; a quorum for this purpose shall consist of a member or members from two-thirds of the States, and a majority of all the States shall be necessary to a choice. And if the House of Representatives shall not choose a President whenever the right of choice shall devolve upon them, before *the fourth day of March* next following, then the Vice-President shall act as President, as in the case of the death or other constitutional disability of the President.

The person having the greatest number of votes as Vice-President shall be the Vice-President, if such number be a majority of the whole number of electors appointed; and if no person have a majority, then from the two highest numbers on the list the Senate shall choose the Vice-President; a quorum for the purpose shall consist of two-thirds of the whole number of Senators, and a majority of the whole number shall be necessary to a choice. But no person constitutionally ineligible to the office of President shall be eligible to that of Vice-President of the United States.

Amendment XIII
[Adopted 1865]

Section 1 Neither slavery nor involuntary servitude, except as a punishment for crime whereof the party shall have been duly convicted, shall exist within the United States, or any place subject to their jurisdiction.

Section 2 Congress shall have power to enforce this article by appropriate legislation.

Amendment XIV
[Adopted 1868]

Section 1 All persons born or naturalized in the United States, and subject to the jurisdiction thereof, are citizens of the United States and of the State wherein they reside. No State shall make or enforce any law which shall abridge the privileges or immunities of citizens of the United States; nor shall any State deprive any person of life, liberty, or property, without due process of law; nor deny to any person within its jurisdiction the equal protection of the laws.

Section 2 Representatives shall be apportioned among the several States according to their respective numbers, counting the whole number of persons in each State, excluding Indians not taxed. But when the right to vote at any election for the choice of Electors for President and Vice-President of the United States, Representatives in Congress, the executive and judicial officers of a State, or the members of the legislature thereof, is denied to any of the male inhabitants of such State, being twenty-one years of age and citizens of the United States, or in any way abridged, except for participation in rebellion, or other crime, the basis of representation therein shall be reduced in the proportion which the number of such male citizens shall bear to the whole number of male citizens twenty-one years of age in such State.

Section 3 No person shall be a Senator or Representative in Congress, or Elector of President and Vice-President, or hold any office, civil or military, under the United States, or under any State, who, having previously taken an oath, as a member of Congress, or as an officer of the United States, or as a member of any State legislature, or as an executive or judicial officer of any State, to support the Constitution of the United States, shall have engaged in insurrection or rebellion against the same, or given aid or comfort to the enemies thereof. Congress may, by a vote of two-thirds of each house, remove such disability.

Section 4 The validity of the public debt of the United States, authorized by law, including debts incurred for payment of pensions and bounties for services in suppressing insurrection or rebellion, shall not be questioned. But neither the United States nor any State shall assume or pay any debt or obligation incurred in aid of insurrection or rebellion against the United States, or any claim for the loss of emancipation of any slave; but all such debts, obligations, and claims shall be held illegal and void.

Section 5 The Congress shall have power to enforce, by appropriate legislation, the provisions of this article.

Amendment XV
[Adopted 1870]

Section 1 The right of citizens of the United States to vote shall not be denied or abridged by the United States or by any State on account of race, color, or previous condition of servitude.

Section 2 The Congress shall have power to enforce this article by appropriate legislation.

Amendment XVI
[Adopted 1913]

The Congress shall have power to lay and collect taxes on incomes, from whatever source derived, without apportionment among the several States, and without regard to any census or enumeration.

Amendment XVII
[Adopted 1913]

Section 1   The Senate of the United States shall be composed of two Senators from each State, elected by the people thereof, for six years; and each Senator shall have one vote. The electors in each State shall have the qualifications requisite for electors of [voters for] the most numerous branch of the State legislatures.

Section 2   When vacancies happen in the representation of any State in the Senate, the executive authority of such State shall issue writs of election to fill such vacancies: Provided, that the Legislature of any State may empower the executive thereof to make temporary appointments until the people fill the vacancies by election as the Legislature may direct.

Section 3   This amendment shall not be so construed as to affect the election or term of any Senator chosen before it becomes valid as part of the Constitution.

Amendment XVIII
[Adopted 1919, repealed 1933]

Section 1   After one year from the ratification of this article the manufacture, sale or transportation of intoxicating liquors within, the importation thereof into, or the exportation thereof from the United States and all territory subject to the jurisdiction thereof, for beverage purposes, is hereby prohibited.

Section 2   The Congress and the several States shall have concurrent power to enforce this article by appropriate legislation.

Section 3   This article shall be inoperative unless it shall have been ratified as an amendment to the Constitution by the legislatures of the several States, as provided by the Constitution, within seven years from the date of the submission thereof to the States by the Congress.

Amendment XIX
[Adopted 1920]

Section 1   The right of citizens of the United States to vote shall not be denied or abridged by the United States or by any State on account of sex.

Section 2   The Congress shall have power to enforce this article by appropriate legislation.

Amendment XX
[Adopted 1933]

Section 1   The terms of the President and Vice-President shall end at noon on the 20th day of January, and the terms of Senators and Representatives at noon on the 3d day of January, of the years in which such terms would have ended if this article had not been ratified; and the terms of their successors shall then begin.

Section 2   The Congress shall assemble at least once in every year, and such meetings shall begin at noon on the 3d day of January, unless they shall by law appoint a different day.

Section 3   If, at the time fixed for the beginning of the term of the President, the President-elect shall have died, the Vice-President-elect shall become President. If a President shall not have been chosen before the time fixed for the beginning of his term, or if the President-elect shall have failed to qualify, then the Vice-President-elect shall act as President until a President shall have qualified; and the Congress may by law provide for the case wherein neither a President-elect nor a Vice-President-elect shall have qualified, declaring who shall then act as President, or the manner in which one who is to act shall be selected, and such persons shall act accordingly until a President or Vice-President shall have qualified.

Section 4   The Congress may by law provide for the case of the death of any of the persons from whom the House of Representatives may choose a President whenever the right of choice shall have devolved upon them, and for the case of the death of any of the persons from whom the Senate may choose a Vice-President whenever the right of choice shall have devolved upon them.

Section 5   Sections 1 and 2 shall take effect on the 15th day of October following the ratification of this article.

Section 6   This article shall be inoperative unless it shall have been ratified as an amendment to the

Constitution by the Legislatures of three-fourths of the several States within seven years from the date of its submission.

Amendment XXI
[Adopted 1933]

Section 1 The eighteenth article of amendment to the Constitution of the United States is hereby repealed.

Section 2 The transportation or importation into any State, Territory, or Possession of the United States for delivery or use therein of intoxicating liquors, in violation of the laws thereof, is hereby prohibited.

Section 3 This article shall be inoperative unless it shall have been ratified as an amendment to the Constitution by conventions in the several States, as provided in the Constitution, within seven years from the date of submission thereof to the States by the Congress.

Amendment XXII
[Adopted 1951]

Section 1 No person shall be elected to the office of President more than twice, and no person who has held the office of President, or acted as President, for more than two years of a term to which some other person was elected President shall be elected to the office of President more than once. But this article shall not apply to any person holding the office of President when this article was proposed by the Congress, and shall not prevent any person who may be holding the office of President, or acting as President, during the term within which this article becomes operative from holding the office of President or acting as President during the remainder of such term.

Section 2 This article shall be inoperative unless it shall have been ratified as an amendment to the Constitution by the legislatures of three-fourths of the several States within seven years from the date of its submission to the States by the Congress.

Amendment XXIII
[Adopted 1961]

Section 1 The District constituting the seat of Government of the United States shall appoint in such manner as the Congress may direct:

A number of electors of President and Vice-President equal to the whole number of Senators and Representatives in Congress to which the District would be entitled if it were a State, but in no event more than the least populous State; they shall be in addition to those appointed by the States, but they shall be considered for the purposes of the election of President and Vice-President, to be electors appointed by a State; and they shall meet in the District and perform such duties as provided by the twelfth article of amendment.

Section 2 The Congress shall have the power to enforce this article by appropriate legislation.

Amendment XXIV
[Adopted 1964]

Section 1 The right of citizens of the United States to vote in any primary or other election for President or Vice-President, for electors for President or Vice-President, or for Senator or Representative in Congress, shall not be denied or abridged by the United States or any State by reason of failure to pay any poll tax or other tax.

Section 2 The Congress shall have the power to enforce this article by appropriate legislation.

Amendment XXV
[Adopted 1967]

Section 1 In case of the removal of the President from office or of his death or resignation, the Vice-President shall become President.

Section 2 Whenever there is a vacancy in the office of the Vice-President, the President shall nominate a Vice-President who shall take office upon confirmation by a majority vote of both Houses of Congress.

Section 3 Whenever the President transmits to the President pro tempore of the Senate and the speaker of the House of Representatives his written declaration that he is unable to discharge the powers and duties of his office, and until he transmits to them a written declaration to the contrary, such powers and duties shall be discharged by the Vice-President as Acting President.

Section 4 Whenever the Vice-President and a majority of either the principal officers of the executive departments or of such other body as Congress may by law provide, transmit to the President pro tempore of the Senate and the Speaker of the House of Representatives their written declaration that the President is unable to discharge the powers and duties of his office, the Vice President shall immediately assume the powers and duties of the office as Acting President.

Thereafter, when the President transmits to the President pro tempore of the Senate and the Speaker of the House of Representatives his written declaration that no inability exists, he shall resume the powers and duties of his office unless the Vice-President and a majority of either the principal officers of the executive department(s) or of such other body as Congress may by law provide, transmit within four days to the President pro tempore of the Senate and the Speaker of the House of Representatives their written declaration that the President is unable to discharge the powers and duties of his office. Thereupon Congress shall decide the issue, assembling within forty-eight hours for that purpose if not in session. If the Congress, within twenty-one days after receipt of the latter written declaration, or, if Congress is not in session, within twenty-one days after Congress is required to assemble, determines by two-thirds vote of both Houses that the President is unable to discharge the powers and duties of his office, the Vice-President shall continue to discharge the same as Acting President; otherwise, the President shall resume the powers and duties of his office.

Amendment XXVI
[Adopted 1971]

Section 1 The right of citizens of the United States, who are eighteen years of age or older, to vote shall not be denied or abridged by the United States or by any State on account of age.

Section 2 The Congress shall have power to enforce this article by appropriate legislation.

★ ★ ★

FEDERALIST NO. 10   1787

To the People of the State of New York: Among the numerous advantages promised by a well-constructed union, none deserves to be more accurately developed than its tendency to break and control the violence of faction. The friend of popular governments, never finds himself so much alarmed for their character and fate, as when he contemplates their propensity to this dangerous vice. He will not fail, therefore, to set a due value on any plan which, without violating the principles to which he is attached, provides a proper cure for it. The instability, injustice, and confusion introduced into the public councils, have, in truth, been the mortal diseases under which popular governments have everywhere perished; as they continue to be the favourite and fruitful topics from which the adversaries to liberty derive their most specious declamations. The valuable improvements made by the American constitutions on the popular models, both ancient and modern, cannot certainly be too much admired; but it would be an unwarrantable partiality, to contend that they have as effectually obviated the danger on this side, as was wished and expected. Complaints are everywhere heard from our most considerate and virtuous citizens, equally the friends of public and private faith, and of public and personal liberty, that our governments are too unstable; that the public good is disregarded in the conflicts of rival parties; and that measures are too often decided, not according to the rules of justice, and the rights of the minor party, but by the superior force of an interested and overbearing majority. However anxiously we may wish that these complaints had no foundation, the evidence of known facts will not permit us to deny that they are in some degree true. It will be found, indeed, on a candid review of our situation, that some of the distresses under which we labour have been erroneously charged on the operation of our governments; but it will be found, at the same time, that other causes will not alone account for many of our heaviest misfortunes; and, particularly, for that prevailing and increasing distrust of public engagements, and alarm for private rights, which are echoed from one end of the continent to the other. These must be chiefly, if not wholly, effects of the unsteadiness and injustice, with which a factious spirit has tainted our public administrations.

By a faction, I understand a number of citizens, whether amounting to a majority or minority of the whole, who are united and actuated by some common impulse of passion, or of interest, adverse to the rights of other citizens, or to the permanent and aggregate interests of the community.

There are two methods of curing the mischiefs of faction: The one, by removing its causes; the other, by controlling its effects.

There are again two methods of removing the causes of faction: The one, by destroying the liberty which is essential to its existence; the other, by giving to every citizen the same opinions, the same passions, and the same interests.

It could never be more truly said, than of the first remedy, that it was worse than the disease. Liberty is to faction what air is to fire, an aliment without which it instantly expires. But it could not be a less folly to abolish liberty, which is essential to political life, because it nourishes faction, than it would be to wish the annihilation of air, which is essential to animal life, because it imparts to fire its destructive agency.

The second expedient is as impracticable, as the first would be unwise. As long as the reason of man continues fallible, and he is at liberty to exercise it, different opinions will be formed. As long as the connection subsists between his reason and his self-love, his opinions and his passions will have a reciprocal influence on each other; and the former will be objects to which the latter will attach themselves. The diversity in the faculties of men, from which the rights of property originate, is not less an insuperable obstacle to an uniformity of interests. The protection of these faculties is the first object

of government. From the protection of different and unequal faculties of acquiring property, the possession of different degrees and kinds of property immediately results; and from the influence of these on the sentiments and views of the respective proprietors, ensues a division of the society into different interests and parties.

The latent causes of action are thus sown in the nature of man; and we see them everywhere brought into different degrees of activity, according to the different circumstances of civil society. A zeal for different opinions concerning religion, concerning government, and many other points, as well as of speculation as of practice; an attachment to different leaders ambitiously contending for preeminence and power; or to persons of other descriptions whose fortunes have been interesting to the human passions, have, in turn, divided mankind into parties, inflamed them with mutual animosity, and rendered them much more disposed to vex and oppress each other, than to cooperate for their common good. So strong is this propensity of mankind, to fall into mutual animosities, that where no substantial occasion presents itself, the most frivolous and fanciful distinctions have been sufficient to kindle their unfriendly passions and excite their most violent conflicts. But the most common and durable source of factions, has been the various and unequal distribution of property. Those who hold, and those who are without property, have ever formed distinct interests in society. Those who are creditors, and those who are debtors, fall under a like discrimination. A landed interest, a manufacturing interest, a mercantile interest, a moneyed interest, with many lesser interests, grow up of necessity in civilized nations, and divide them into different classes, actuated by different sentiments and views. The regulation of these various and interfering interests forms the principal task of modern legislation, and involves the spirit of the party and faction in the necessary and ordinary operations of the government.

No man is allowed to be a judge in his own cause; because his interest will certainly bias his judgment, and, not improbably, corrupt his integrity. With equal, nay, with greater reason, a body of men are unfit to be both judges and parties at the same time; yet what are many of the most important acts of legislation, but so many judicial determinations, not indeed concerning the right of single persons, but concerning the rights of large bodies of citizens? And what are the different classes of legislators, but advocates and parties to the causes which they determine? Is a law proposed concerning private debts? It is a question to which the creditors are parties on one side, and the debtors on the other. Justice ought to hold the balance between them. Yet the parties are, and must be, themselves the judges; and the most numerous party, or, in other words, the most powerful faction, must be expected to prevail. Shall domestic manufactures be encouraged, and in what degree, by restrictions on foreign manufactures? are questions which would be differently decided by the landed and the manufacturing classes; and probably by neither with a sole regard to justice and the public good. The apportionment of taxes, on the various descriptions of property, is an act which seems to require the most exact impartiality; yet there is, perhaps, no legislative act, in which greater opportunity and temptation are given to a predominant party to trample on the rules of justice. Every shilling, with which they overburden the inferior number, is a shilling saved to their own pockets.

It is in vain to say, that enlightened statesmen will be able to adjust these clashing interests, and render them all subservient to the public good. Enlightened statesmen will not always be at the helm: nor, in many cases, can such an adjustment be made at all, without taking into view indirect and remote considerations, which will rarely prevail over the immediate interest which one party may find in disregarding the rights of another, or the good of the whole.

The inference to which we are brought is, that the *causes* of faction cannot be removed; and that relief is only to be sought in the means of controlling its *effects*.

If a faction consists of less than a majority, relief is supplied by the republican principle, which enables the majority to defeat its sinister views, by regular vote. It may clog the administration, it may convulse the society; but it will be unable to execute and mask its violence under the forms of the constitution. When a majority is included in a faction, the form of popular government, on the other hand, enables it to sacrifice to its ruling passion or interest, both the public good and the rights of other citizens. To secure the public good, and private rights, against the danger of such a faction, and at the same time to preserve the spirit and the form of popular government, is then the great object to which our inquiries are directed. Let me add, that it is the great desideratum, by which alone this form of government can be rescued from the opprobrium under which it has so long laboured, and be recommended to the esteem and adoption of mankind.

By what means is this object attainable? Evidently by one of two only. Either the existence of the same passion or interest in a majority, at the same time, must be prevented; or the majority, having such coexistent passion or interest, must be rendered, by their number and local situation, unable to concert and carry into effect schemes of oppression. If the impulse and the opportunity be suffered to coincide, we well know that neither moral nor religious motives can be relied on as an adequate control. They are not found to be such on the injustice and violence of individuals, and lose their efficacy in proportion to the number combined together; that is, in proportion as their efficacy becomes needful.

From this view of the subject, it may be concluded, that a pure democracy, by which I mean a society consisting of a small number of citizens, who assemble and administer the government in person, can admit of no cure for the mischiefs of faction. A common passion or interest will, in almost every case, be felt by a majority of the whole; a communication and concert, results from the form of government itself; and there is nothing to check the inducements to sacrifice the weaker party, or an obnoxious individual. Hence, it is, that such democracies have ever been spectacles of turbulence and contention; have ever been found incompatible with personal security, or the rights of property; and have in general been as short in their lives, as they have been violent in their deaths. Theoretic politicians, who have patronized this species of government, have erroneously supposed, that by reducing mankind to a perfect equality in their political rights, they would, at the same time, be perfectly equalized and assimilated in their possessions, their opinions, and their passions.

A republic, by which I mean a government in which the scheme of representation takes place, opens a different prospect, and promises the cure for which we are seeking. Let us examine the points in which it varies from pure democracy, and we shall comprehend both the nature of the cure and the efficacy which it must derive from the union.

The two great points of difference, between a democracy and a republic, are, first, the delegation of the government, in the latter, to a small number of citizens, elected by the rest; secondly, the greatest number of citizens, and greater sphere of country, over which the latter may be extended.

The effect of the first difference is, on the one hand, to refine and enlarge the public views, by passing them through the medium of a chosen body of citizens, whose wisdom may best discern the true interest of their country, and whose patriotism and love of justice, will be least likely to sacrifice it to temporary or partial considerations. Under such a regulation, it may well happen, that the public voice, pronounced by the representatives of the people, will be more consonant to the public good, than if pronounced by the people themselves, convened for the purpose. On the other hand the effect may be inverted. Men of factious tempers, of local prejudices, or of sinister designs, may by intrigue, by corruption, or by other means, first obtain the suffrages, and then betray the interest of the people. The question resulting is, whether small or extensive republics are most favourable to the election of proper guardians of the public weal; and it is clearly decided in favour of the latter by two obvious considerations.

In the first place, it is to be remarked that, however small the republic may be, the representatives must be raised to a certain number, in order to guard against the cabals of a few; and that however large it may be, they must be limited to a certain number, in order to guard against the confusion of a multitude. Hence, the number of representatives in the two cases not being in proportion to that of the constituents, and being proportionally greatest in the small republic, it follows, that if the proportion of fit characters be not less in the large than in the small republic, the former will present a greater option, and consequently a greater probability of a fit choice.

In the next place, as each representative will be chosen by a greater number of citizens in the large than in the small republic, it will be more difficult for unworthy candidates to practise with success the vicious arts, by which elections are too often carried; and the suffrages of the people being more free, will be more likely to centre in men who possess the most attractive merit, and the most diffusive and established characters.

It must be confessed, that in this, as in most other cases, there is a mean, on both sides of which inconveniences will be found to lie. By enlarging too much the number of electors, you render the representatives too little acquainted with all their local circumstances and lesser interests; as by reducing it too much, you render him unduly attached to these, and too little fit to comprehend and pursue great and national objects. The federal constitution forms a happy combination in this respect; the great and aggregate interests being referred to the national, the local and particular to the state legislatures.

The other point of difference is, the greater number of citizens, and extent of territory, which may be brought within the compass of republican, than of democratic government; and it is this circumstance principally which renders factious combinations less to be dreaded in the former, than in the latter. The smaller the society, the fewer probably will be the distinct parties and interests composing it; the fewer the distinct parties and interests, the more frequently will a majority be found of the same party; and the smaller the number of individuals composing a majority, and the smaller the compass within which they are placed, the more easily will they concert and execute their plans of oppression. Extend the sphere, and you take in a greater variety of parties and interests; you make it less probable that a majority of the whole will have a common motive to invade the rights of other citizens; or if such a common motive exists, it will be more difficult for all who feel it to discover their own strength, and to act in unison with each other. Besides other impediments, it may be remarked, that where there is a consciousness of unjust or dishonourable purposes, communication is always checked by distrust, in proportion to the number whose concurrence is necessary.

Hence, it clearly appears, that the same advantage, which a republic has over a democracy, in controlling the effects of faction, is enjoyed by a large over a small republic,—is enjoyed by the union over the states composing it. Does this advantage consist in the substitution of representatives, whose enlightened views and virtuous sentiments render them superior to local prejudices, and to schemes of injustice? It will not be denied that the representation of the union will be most likely to possess these requisite endowments. Does it consist in the greater security afforded by a greater variety of parties, against the event of any one party being able to outnumber and oppress the rest? In an equal degree does the increased variety of parties, comprised within the union, increase the security? Does it, in fine, consist in the greater obstacles opposed to the concert and accomplishment of the secret wishes of an unjust and interested majority? Here, again, the extent of the union gives it the most palpable advantage.

The influence of factious leaders may kindle a flame within their particular states, but will be unable to spread a general conflagration through the other states; a religious sect may degenerate into a political faction in a part of the confederacy; but the variety of sects dispersed over the entire face of it, must secure the national councils against any danger from that source: a rage for paper money, for an abolition of debts, for an equal division of property, or for any other improper or wicked project, will be less apt to pervade the whole body of the union than a particular member of it; in the same proportion as such a malady is more likely to taint a particular county or district, than an entire state.

In the extent and proper structure of the union, therefore, we behold a republican remedy for the diseases most incident to republican government. And according to the degree of pleasure and pride we feel in being republicans, ought to be our zeal in cherishing the spirit, and supporting the character of federalists.

JAMES MADISON

★ ★ ★

FEDERALIST NO. 51   1788

To the People of the State of New York: To what expedient then shall we finally resort for maintaining in practice the necessary partition of power among the several departments, as laid down in the constitution? The only answer that can be given is, that as all these exterior provisions are found to be inadequate, the defect must be supplied, by so contriving the interior structure of the government, as that its several constituent parts may, by their mutual relations, be the means of keeping each other in their proper places. Without presuming to undertake a full development of this important idea, I will hazard a few general observations, which may perhaps place it in a clearer light, and enable us to form a more correct judgment of the principles and structure of the government planned by the convention.

In order to lay a due foundation for that separate and distinct exercise of the different powers of government, which to a certain extent, is admitted on all hands to be essential to the preservation of liberty, it is evident that each department should have a will of its own; and consequently should be so constituted, that the members of each should have as little agency as possible in the appointment of the members of the others. Were this principle rigorously adhered to, it would require that all the appointments for the supreme executive, legislative, and judiciary magistracies, should be drawn from the same fountain of authority, the people, through channels, having no communication whatever with one another. Perhaps such a plan of constructing the several departments would be less difficult in practice than it may in contemplation appear. Some difficulties however, and some additional expense, would attend the execution of it. Some deviations therefore from the principle must be admitted. In the constitution of the judiciary department in particular, it might be inexpedient to insist rigorously on the principle; first, because peculiar qualifications being essential in the members, the primary consideration ought to be to select that mode of choice, which best secures these qualifications; secondly, because the permanent tenure by which the appointments are held in that department, must soon destroy all sense of dependence on the authority conferring them.

It is equally evident that the members of each department should be as little dependent as possible on those of the others, for the emoluments annexed to their offices. Were the executive magistrate, or the judges, not independent of the legislature in this particular, their independence in every other would be merely nominal.

But the great security against a gradual concentration of the several powers in the same department, consists in giving to those who administer each department, the necessary constitutional means, and personal motives, to resist encroachments of the others. The provision for defense must in this, as in all other cases, be made commensurate to the danger of attack. Ambition must be made to counteract ambition. The interest of the man must be connected with the constitutional rights of the place. It may be a reflection on human nature, that such devices should be necessary to control the abuses of government. But what is government itself but the greatest of all reflections on human nature? If men were angels, no government would be necessary. If angels were to govern men, neither external nor internal controls on government would be necessary. In framing a government which is to be administered by men over men, the great difficulty lies in this: You must first enable the government to control the governed; and in the next place, oblige it to control itself. A dependence on the people is no doubt the primary control on the government; but experience has taught mankind the necessity of auxiliary precautions.

This policy of supplying by opposite and rival interests, the defect of better motives, might be traced through the whole system of human affairs, private as well as public. We see it particularly displayed in all the subordinate distributions of power; where the constant aim is to divide and arrange the several offices in such a manner as that each may be a check on the other; that the private interest of every individual, may be a sentinel over the public rights. These inventions of prudence cannot be less requisite in the distribution of the supreme powers of the state.

But it is not possible to give to each department an equal power of self defense. In republican government the legislative authority, necessarily, predominates. The remedy for this inconveniency is, to divide the legislature into different branches; and to render them by different modes of election, and different principles of action, as little connected with each other, as the nature of their common functions, and their common dependence on the society, will admit. It may even be necessary to guard against dangerous encroachments by still further precautions. As the weight of the legislative authority requires that it should be thus divided, the weakness of the executive may require, on the other hand, that it should be fortified. An absolute negative, on the legislature, appears at first view to be the natural defense with which the executive magistrate should be armed. But perhaps it would be neither altogether safe, nor alone sufficient. On ordinary occasions, it might not be exerted with the requisite firmness; and on extraordinary occasions, it might be perfidiously abused. May not this defect of an absolute negative be supplied, by some qualified connection between this weaker department, and the weaker branch of the stronger department, by which the latter may be led to support the constitutional rights of the former, without being too much detached from the rights of its own department?

If the principles on which these observations are founded be just, as I persuade myself they are, and they be applied as a criterion, to the several state constitutions, and to the federal constitution, it will be found, that if the latter does not perfectly correspond with them, the former are infinitely less able to bear such a test.

There are moreover two considerations particularly applicable to the federal system of America, which place that system in a very interesting point of view.

First. In a single republic, all the power surrendered by the people, is submitted to the administration of a single government; and usurpations are guarded against by a division of the government into distinct and separate departments. In the compound republic of America, the power surrendered by the people, is first divided between two distinct governments, and then the portion allotted to each, subdivided among distinct and separate departments. Hence a double security arises to the rights of the people. The different governments will control each other; at the same time that each will be controlled by itself.

Second. It is of great importance in a republic, not only to guard the society against the oppression of its rulers; but to guard one part of the society against the injustice of the other part. Different interests necessarily exist in different classes of citizens. If a majority be united by a common interest, the rights of the minority will be insecure. There are but two methods of providing against this evil: The one by creating a will in the community independent of the majority, that is, of the society itself; the other by comprehending in the society so many separate descriptions of citizens, as will render an unjust combination of a majority of the whole, very improbable, if not impracticable. The first method prevails in all governments possessing an hereditary or self appointed authority. This at best is but a precarious security; because a power independent of the society may as well espouse the unjust views of the major, as the rightful interests, of the minor party, and may possibly be turned against both parties. The second method will be exemplified in the federal republic of the United States. While all authority in it will be derived from and dependent on the society, the society itself will be broken into so many parts, interests and classes of citizens, that the rights of individuals or of the minority, will be in little danger from interested combinations of the majority. In a free government, the security for civil rights must be the same as for religious rights. It consists in the one case in the multiplicity of interests, and in the other in the multiplicity of sects. The degree of security in both cases will depend on the number of interests and sects; and this may be presumed to depend on the extent of country and number of people comprehended under the same government. This view of the subject must particularly recommend a proper federal system to all the sincere and considerate friends of republican government: Since it shows that in exact proportion as the territory of the union may be formed into more circumscribed confederacies or states, oppressive combinations of a majority will be facilitated; the best security under the re-

publican form, for the rights of every class of citizens, will be diminished; and consequently, the stability and independence of some member of the government, the only other security, must be proportionally increased. Justice is the end of government. It is the end of civil society. It ever has been, and ever will be pursued, until it be obtained, or until liberty be lost in the pursuit. In a society under the forms of which the stronger faction can readily unite and oppress the weaker, anarchy may as truly be said to reign, as in a state of nature where the weaker individual is not secured against the violence of the stronger: And as in the latter state even the stronger individuals are prompted by the uncertainty of their condition, to submit to a government which may protect the weak as well as themselves: So in the former state, will the more powerful factions or parties be gradually induced by a like motive, to which for a government which will protect all parties, the weaker as well as the more powerful. It can be little doubted, that if the state of Rhode Island was separated from the confederacy, and left to itself, the insecurity of rights under the popular form of government within such narrow limits, would be displayed by such reiterated oppressions of factious majorities, that some power altogether independent of the people would soon be called for by the voice of the very factions whose misrule had proved the necessity of it. In the extended republic of the United States, and among the great variety of interests, parties and sects which it embraces, a coalition of a majority of the whole society could seldom take place on any other principles than those of justice and the general good; and there being thus less danger to a minor from the will of the major party, there must be less pretext also, to provide for the security of the former, by introducing into the government a will not dependent on the latter; or in other words, a will independent of the society itself. It is no less certain than it is important, notwithstanding the contrary opinions which have been entertained, that the larger the society, provided it lie within a practicable sphere, the more duly capable it will be of self government. And happily for the *republican cause,* the practicable sphere may be carried to a very great extent, by a judicious modification and mixture of the *federal principle.*

JAMES MADISON

PRESIDENTS OF THE UNITED STATES

	Party	Term
1. George Washington (1732–1799)	Federalist	1789–1797
2. John Adams (1735–1826)	Federalist	1797–1801
3. Thomas Jefferson (1743–1826)	Democratic-Republican	1801–1809
4. James Madison (1751–1836)	Democratic-Republican	1809–1817
5. James Monroe (1758–1831)	Democratic-Republican	1817–1825
6. John Quincy Adams (1767–1848)	Democratic-Republican	1825–1829
7. Andrew Jackson (1767–1845)	Democratic	1829–1837
8. Martin Van Buren (1782–1862)	Democratic	1837–1841
9. William Henry Harrison (1773–1841)	Whig	1841
10. John Tyler (1790–1862)	Whig	1841–1845
11. James K. Polk (1795–1849)	Democratic	1845–1849
12. Zachary Taylor (1784–1850)	Whig	1849–1850
13. Millard Fillmore (1800–1874)	Whig	1850–1853
14. Franklin Pierce (1804–1869)	Democratic	1853–1857
15. James Buchanan (1791–1868)	Democratic	1857–1861
16. Abraham Lincoln (1809–1865)	Republican	1861–1865
17. Andrew Johnson (1808–1875)	Union	1865–1869
18. Ulysses S. Grant (1822–1885)	Republican	1869–1877
19. Rutherford B. Hayes (1822–1893)	Republican	1877–1881
20. James A. Garfield (1831–1881)	Republican	1881
21. Chester A. Arthur (1830–1886)	Republican	1881–1885
22. Grover Cleveland (1837–1908)	Democratic	1885–1889
23. Benjamin Harrison (1833–1901)	Republican	1889–1893
24. Grover Cleveland (1837–1908)	Democratic	1893–1897
25. William McKinley (1843–1901)	Republican	1897–1901
26. Theodore Roosevelt (1858–1919)	Republican	1901–1909
27. William Howard Taft (1857–1930)	Republican	1909–1913
28. Woodrow Wilson (1856–1924)	Democratic	1913–1921
29. Warren G. Harding (1865–1923)	Republican	1921–1923
30. Calvin Coolidge (1871–1933)	Republican	1923–1929
31. Herbert Hoover (1874–1964)	Republican	1929–1933
32. Franklin Delano Roosevelt (1882–1945)	Democratic	1933–1945
33. Harry S Truman (1884–1972)	Democratic	1945–1953
34. Dwight D. Eisenhower (1890–1969)	Republican	1953–1961
35. John F. Kennedy (1917–1963)	Democratic	1961–1963
36. Lyndon B. Johnson (1908–1973)	Democratic	1963–1969
37. Richard M. Nixon (b. 1913)	Republican	1969–1974
38. Gerald R. Ford (b. 1913)	Republican	1974–1977
39. Jimmy Carter (b. 1924)	Democratic	1977–1981
40. Ronald Reagan (b. 1911)	Republican	1981–

Glossary

Affirmative action A set of procedures that attempts to correct the effects of past discrimination against minority groups and that can include specific goals and quotas for hiring minority applicants. (4)

Agenda setting The second stage of policy making. The issue or problem is seriously considered by the policy-making institution. (14)

Anarchism The belief that government is unnecessary and that all problems now solved by government can be left to other social institutions. (1)

Appeal A route for cases to reach the Supreme Court. By this route litigants have some right under the law to have their cases reviewed. (13)

Appellate courts Courts of appeal that reconsider the decisions rendered by trial courts, at the request of the losing party seeking to appeal. (13)

Articles of Confederation Ratified in 1781 as the United States' first constitution. They established a loose union of states and a congress with few powers. (2).

Attentive publics Those segments of the public that are normally more interested, as well as informed, about relevant issues. These groups are the main audience for media coverage of foreign and defense policies. (15)

Bad tendency test The principle that the Supreme Court began to prefer, in First Amendment cases, over the clear and present danger test. It allowed the government to punish speech that might cause people to engage in illegal action. *Gitlow* v. *New York* (1925). (4)

Bicameral Refers to a legislature that is divided into two separate houses, such as the U.S. Congress. (10)

The Bill of Rights The first ten amendments to the Constitution, which collectively guarantee the fundamental liberties of citizens from abuse by the national government. (2)

Bipolar The state of the world during the Cold War, with nations being allied either with the United States or the Soviet Union, the two "poles"—this being the perception of many U.S. policy makers. (15)

Block grants Money given to the states by Congress that could be used in broad areas and was not limited to specific purposes like categorical grants. A means introduced in the mid-1960s of giving states greater freedom. (3)

Briefs Documents written by attorneys that contain a summary of the issues, the laws applying to the case, and arguments supporting counsel's position, and which are submitted to the court. (13)

British Bill of Rights An act of Parliament passed in 1689 that established some basic principles of constitutional government. One of several major acts of Parliament that helped to shape the British constitutional tradition. (2)

Bureaucracy Any large, complex organization in which employees have specific job responsibilities and work within a hierarchy. Often used in a negative sense to refer to both government agencies and the people who work in them. (12)

Career service A special personnel system for highly specialized agencies like the Coast Guard and Foreign Service. (12)

Casework Work done by members of Congress to provide constituents with personal services and help them through the maze of federal programs and benefits. (10)

Categorical assistance The main focus of social policy for the needy that targets aid to specific groups of low-income or disadvantaged Americans, such as dependent children and the elderly. (14)

Categorical, or conditional, grants Money given to the states and localities by Congress that was to be used for limited purposes under specific rules. (3)

Caucus A forum closed to the public until the Progressive Era; the contemporary caucuses are local party meetings open to all who live in the precinct and in which citizens discuss and then vote for delegates to district and state conventions. (7)

Charter A British legal institution that originated during the Middle Ages and forms part of the British constitution. Specifically, a formal agreement that describes the rights and duties of both the landowner and those bound to him. (2)

Checks and balances The principle that lets the executive and legislative branches share some responsibilities and gives each branch some control over the other's activities. The major support for checks and balances comes from the Constitution's distribution of powers. (2)

Circuit courts The Federal Courts of Appeal that rank above the district courts and serve as the major appellate courts for the federal system. They review all cases, both civil and criminal, and the decisions of independent regulatory agencies and departments. (13)

Civil law Law involving conflicts between private persons and/or organizations and which typically includes disputes over contracts, claims for damages, and divorce cases. (13)

Civil liberties Freedoms, most of which are spelled out in the Bill of Rights, that protect individuals from excessive or arbitrary government interference. (4)

Civil rights Rights that guarantee protection of individuals by the government against discrimination or unreasonable treatment by other individuals or groups. (4)

Clear and present danger test The proposition proclaimed by the Supreme Court in *Schenk* v. *U.S.* (1919) that the government had the right to punish speech if it could be shown to present a grave and immediate danger to its interests. (4)

Closed primary A primary election that allows voters to obtain only a ballot of the party for which they are registered. (7)

Cloture The rule for ending debate in the Senate that requires a vote of at least sixty senators to cut off discussion. (10)

Coalition building The bringing together of diverse interest groups in a common lobbying effort. (8)

Common law Constituting one-third of the British constitution, it is also called judge-made law. It represents the collection of legal doctrines that grew out of the many cases heard, beginning in medieval times, by judges appointed by the British Crown. (2)

Communism A doctrine that advocates a centrally directed economic and political system. Its goals are to abolish private property and establish a classless society through class struggle. (1)

Concurring opinions Opinions written by Supreme Court justices that agree with the conclusion but not with the reasoning of the majority opinion. (13)

Confederal system A government in which formal authority rests with the political subdivisions, which join together in an agreement that permits some powers to be exercised at the national level. The Articles of Confederation established such a system. (3)

Conference committees Temporary joint committees that are formed to reconcile differences between House and Senate versions of a bill. Such committees often play a critical role in shaping legislation. (10)

Connecticut Compromise The plan for government that the Constitutional Convention (1787) adopted after being faced with the conflict between the Virginia and New Jersey plans. The compromise called for a bicameral congress and also provided for separate executive and judicial branches of government. (2)

Conservatism A set of beliefs tending to favor individual liberty and to resist any change that might curb this freedom, even if such change would benefit the majority. Most conservatives seek to restrict the scope of government activity. (1)

Containment The foreign policy, pursued by the United States throughout the Cold War, that called for preventing the Soviet Union from making further expansionist moves in its effort to conquer the capitalist world. (15)

Cooperative federalism The form of cooperation between state and national government that began during the Great Depression. The national government began to take on new responsibilities, while state and local officials accepted it as an ally, not an enemy. (3)

Covert actions Activities intentionally hidden from public view that range from gathering intelligence to assassinating foreign leaders, and that may be of questionable legality. (15)

Cozy triangle An informal network of interest groups, congressional committee members, and staff that exchange information and provide mutual assistance. (8)

Criminal law Covers offenses against the public order and provides for a specified punishment. Most criminal law cases arise in state courts. (13)

Dealignment A period in which the public disassociates itself from either party and splits its votes between the parties. (6)

Decentralized A term used to describe the Republican and Democratic parties, meaning that decision-making power is dispersed, the party is regulated at the state level, and no single individual controls the system. (6)

Declaration of Independence The document declaring the colonies to be a free and independent nation that was adopted by the Second Continental Congress on July 2, 1776. The Declaration also articulated the fundamental principles under which the new nation would be governed. (2)

Delegated powers The powers the constitution gives the Congress that are specifically named in Section 8 of Article I. (2)

Democracy A system of government, in the American sense, derived from belief in government based on the consent and will of the majority. (1)

Democratic socialism A theory of government that advocates more substantial governmental intervention in the economy than does liberalism. Its major goals are limiting private ownership and bringing workers into the government. (1)

Détente The relaxation of tensions between nations became the name for President Nixon's policy of taking a more cooperative approach in dealing with Soviet bloc nations while enhancing U.S. security arrangements with its allies. (15)

Deterrence strategy The policy of building and maintaining large stockpiles of nuclear and conventional forces to make any potential enemy hesitate in attacking the United States or its allies. (15)

Dissenting opinions Legal opinions written by Supreme Court justices that disagree with the majority conclusion. (13)

Dual federalism The viewpoint that emerged from the conflict between state- and nation-centered federalism. It saw the national and state governments as equal partners, with each responsible for distinct policy functions and each barred from interfering with the other's work. (13)

Electoral coalitions Groups of loyal supporters who agree with the party's stand on most issues and vote for its candidates for office. (6)

Electoral college The system set up by the Constitution that provides for the people to elect a number of electors in each state equal to the number of U.S. senators and representatives for that state. The presidential candidate winning the majority vote in a state receives all of its electoral college votes. (7)

Elite model of decision making A model which

holds that public policies are made by a relatively small group of influential leaders who share common goals and points of view. (14)

Equal-time provision   A Federal Communications Commission rule that requires a broadcaster who permits one candidate to campaign on the station to allow equal time at identical rates to all other candidates for the same office. (7)

Exclusionary rule   The principle that evidence, no matter how incriminating, cannot be used to convict someone if it is gathered illegally. Established by the Supreme Court in *Mapp* v. *Ohio* (1961). (4)

Executive agreements   Agreements with other nations made by the president without the Senate's consent. They have all the legal force of treaties, but unlike treaties, they are not binding on succeeding presidents. (10)

Executive order   A rule or regulation that has the effect of law. (10)

Executive privilege   The traditional right, claimed by presidents since Washington, to withhold information from Congress. (10)

Fairness doctrine   A Federal Communications Commission rule that required broadcasts to provide reasonable time for reply to opposing interests in matters of controversial issue. After 1987, no longer in effect. (9)

Federal system   A system for national government in which some powers are exercised at a national level, other powers are reserved to the states, and still others shared by the two. This system solved the conflicts between the states and national government that plagued the constitutional convention. (2)

Filibuster   A prolonged debate held in the Senate that is intended to kill a bill by preventing a vote. (10)

Fiscal policy   The management of government expenditures and tax rates in order to control the economy. Policy makers raise or lower government spending and taxes to execute fiscal policy. (14)

Flexible response   The military strategy adopted by the United States during the 1960s that shifted emphasis from solely nuclear weapons to increasing U.S. ability to engage in limited, conventional wars, in order to make deterrence more credible. (15)

Foreign aid   Assistance provided by the United States to another country. This usually takes the form of a grant of money or supplies, but it can also be a low-interest loan. (15)

Formal recognition   The act whereby the president publicly accepts and acknowledges the sovereignty and government of another nation and receives its ambassador in Washington as that country's official representative. (15)

Franking privilege   The power of members of Congress to send out mail free of charge; this allows incumbents to cultivate a favorable image among constituents. (10)

Free riders   Those who benefit from the actions of interest groups without expending effort or money for the groups. (8)

Free trade   An international economic policy that calls for the abolition of tariffs and other barriers so that goods and services may be exchanged freely among nations. (14)

General civil service   The corps of federal civilian workers ranging from weather forecasters to financial analysts who usually obtain their jobs through some form of competitive merit system. (12)

General jurisdiction   The power of trial courts to hear cases from a broad class of issues, ordinarily including all civil cases involving nontrivial monetary value and all cases involving serious criminal matters. (13)

General revenue sharing   A small but innovative grant-in-aid program that had no significant conditions attached to it. State and local governments received funds according to a formula based on population and related factors. (3)

Gerrymandering   The practice by the party controlling the state legislature of drawing congressional district boundaries to maximize the number of seats it can win. (10)

Government   Those institutions and officials who execute and enforce public programs. In the United States, it consists of the executive, legislative, and judicial branches of federal, state, and local governmental systems. (4)

Grant-in-aid programs   Federal appropriations that

are given to states to fund state policies and programs. The Morrill Act (1862) was the first instance of such a program. (3)

Grassroots pressure Lobbying by rank-and-file members of an interest group, who use such tactics as letter writing and public protests to influence government. (8)

Home style The way in which incumbent members of Congress present themselves to their constituents in an attempt to win the voter's trust. (10)

Ideology A set of strongly held beliefs about social processes and institutions. (1)

Impeachment The power of Congress to remove the president from office if found guilty of "high crimes and misdemeanors," and to remove judges from the courts if charged with a major crime. (2)

Implied powers Those powers given to the Congress by Article I of the Constitution that are not specifically named but are provided for by the "necessary and proper" clause. (2)

Impoundment When a President withholds funds for a bill that have been appropriated by Congress. Used by a president in place of an item veto—a power so far denied the president. (10) See *item veto*.

Incremental model of decision making A more realistic model of decision making that sees public policy as a process, making decisions at the margins of current policies by adding to or subtracting from current policies. (14)

Incumbent A candidate who holds the contested office at the time of the election. (7)

Industrial policy A comprehensive plan for restructuring the nation's economy. Some economists claim this policy must be developed by the federal government. (14)

Interest group Any organized group of individuals who share one or more common goals and seek to influence government decision making. (8)

Intergovernmental lobby Individuals and groups that have a special interest in the policies and programs implemented through the growing intergovernmental relations systems. These lobbyists represent private, consumer, and business groups. (3)

Intergovernmental relations The new style of federalism that emerged by the 1960s, which recognized the interdependence of Washington and state and local governments. The various levels of government share functions, and each level is able to influence the others. (4)

Issue identification The first of six stages in policy making, in which some event, person, or group calls attention to a problem that needs government action. (14)

Issue networks Subgovernments that (unlike cozy triangles) involve a large number of participants with different degrees of in. (12) See *cozy triangle*.

Item veto The power to veto portions of a bill but leave the rest intact for signing. The president does not possess this specialized veto power. (10)

Joint committees Congressional committees composed of an equal number of members from both houses that are usually of a permanent nature. (10)

Judicial review The power of the courts to declare acts of Congress to be in conflict with the Constitution. This power makes the courts part of the system of checks and balances. (2)

Legislative veto A device in a bill that allowed Congress or a congressional committee to veto the actions of an executive agency or the president in an area covered by the bill. Was declared unconstitutional by the Supreme Court in 1985. (10)

Libel The use of print or picture to harm someone's reputation. An offense that is punishable by criminal law and subject to civil prosecution for damages. (4)

Liberalism A set of beliefs which holds that government must ensure an adequate standard of living for every citizen. Liberals usually favor government intervention in the economy and high levels of government activity. (1)

Libertarianism The belief that government should do no more than what is minimally necessary to maintain law and order, protect basic individual rights, and provide for national defense in order to allow the greatest possible freedom for the individual. (1)

Limited jurisdiction The power of certain trial courts that are allowed to hear only a narrowly defined class of cases. (13)

Lobbying Named after the public rooms in which it first took place, lobbying is the act of trying to influence government decision makers. (8)

Magna Carta A document signed by King John in 1215 that reaffirmed the long-standing rights and duties of the English nobility and defined the limits placed on the king. It stands for the principle that everyone including the king must obey the law. (2)

Majority leader The second-ranking party position in the House (and the first in the Senate). The majority leader schedules floor actions on bills and guides the party's legislative program through the House. (10)

Mark up session A meeting of a congressional subcommittee to vote on amendments to and decide the precise language of a bill before sending the bill to the full committee for further debate and mark up. (10)

Massive retaliation The military strategy favored by the United States during the 1950s, according to which the United States warned the Soviet Union and its allies that any military confrontation would produce a complete nuclear attack on Moscow and other Russian cities. (15)

Minority leader The head of the minority party in the Senate. Also the leader of the minority party in the House who represents its interests by consulting with the speaker and majority leader over the scheduling of bills and rules for floor action. (10)

Monetarists A group of economists led by Milton Friedman who reject the argument that constant government intervention in the economy can bring either sustained prosperity or stability. (14)

Monetary policy The manipulation of the money supply to control the economy. The Federal Reserve System, or "Fed," is the principal mechanism for making monetary policy. (14)

Mutual assured destruction (MAD) The strategy that evolved in the 1970s whereby each of the nuclear powers would hold the other in check by maintaining the ability to annihilate the other in any major, nuclear confrontation. (15)

Myths In the political sense are widely held popular attitudes about politics and government that give a distorted view of reality. A myth is a partial truth, a shorthand way of thinking, or an oversimplification about the role and activities of government and the people who run it—for example, the myth of the courts above politics. (1)

The myth of too little government The American belief that government does not fulfill its obligations, especially toward the poor, the homeless, the unemployed, and others who need its help. The liberal side of the debate. (14)

The myth of too much government The American belief that says that big government has become the major threat to the well-being and future of American society. The conservative side of the debate. (14)

National supremacy The principle that makes the Constitution and those laws and treaties passed under it the "supreme law of the land." The supremacy clause of Article VI guarantees this principle. (2)

Nation-centered federalism The view that the authority of the national government goes beyond the responsibilities listed in Article I, Section 8 of the Constitution. Based on the "necessary and proper" clause and the principle of national supremacy. (3)

New Jersey Plan The proposal of the New Jersey delegation to the Constitutional Convention in 1787. It was favored by smaller states against the Virginia Plan, because it called for a strengthened congress with the ability to force reluctant states to cooperate with the national government. (2)

Nonpartisan primary A primary in which candidates are listed on a ballot with no party identification. (7)

Open primary A primary election in which any qualified voter may participate, regardless of party affiliation. The voter chooses one party ballot at the polling place. (7)

Opportunity structure The political ladder of local, state, and federal offices that brings greater prestige and power as one moves toward the presidency at the very top. (7)

Original jurisdiction The authority to hear a case before any other court does. (13)

Partisan primary A primary in which candidates run for their own party's nomination. (7)

Party identification The tendency of people to think of themselves as Democrats, Republicans, or independents. Children tend to adopt the party identification of their parents. (5)

Party-in-the-electorate Includes anyone who identifies with a particular party, tends to vote for that party's candidates, and may even contribute to its campaigns. (6)

Party-in-government The individuals who have been elected or appointed to a governmental office under a party label. Plays a major role in organizing government and in setting policy. (6)

Party-as-organization With few members, it primarily consists of state and county chairpersons and ward and precinct captains who work for the party throughout the year, recruiting candidates and participating in fund-raising activities. (6)

Party realignments A major shift by voters from one party to another that occurs when one party becomes dominant in the political system, controlling the presidency and Congress, as well as many state legislatures. (6)

Party whips Members of Congress who support the party leaders in the House and Senate by communicating the party positions to the membership and keeping the leaders informed of members' views. (10)

Patronage The providing of services, jobs, or contracts in return for political support that party committee members supervise and use to court voters. (6)

Platforms Statements of goals for the party and specific policy agendas that are taken seriously by the party's candidates but are not binding. (6)

Pluralist model of decision making A theory that attributes policy outcomes to pressures exerted by different interest groups. (14)

Pocket veto An action whereby the president fails to sign a bill during the last ten days of a term and thus effectively kills the bill. (10)

Policy adoption The fourth step in policy making, which is usually a fight to gain government support for a policy that demands much bargaining and compromise. (14)

Policy evaluation The final stage in the policy making process. Looking at government actions and programs to see whether goals have been achieved or to assess a policy's effectiveness and efficiency. (14)

Policy formulation The third stage in policy making, in which policy makers and their staffs deliberate the pros and cons of each issue in a process that may take years to complete. (14)

Policy implementation The carrying out of policy mandates through public programs and actions. The fifth stage in the policy making process. (14)

Policy subgovernments Those alliances in which bureaucrats interact with other actors, such as the heads of specific agencies, the leaders of interest groups, and members of Congress on relevant committees. These alliances effectively exercise authority in a narrow policy area. (12)

Political action committees (PACS) Organizations that interest groups set up solely for the purpose of contributing money to the campaigns of candidates who sympathize with their aims. Because federal laws prohibit interest groups from donating money to political campaigns. (6)

Political appointees Government officials who occupy the approximately 2,000 most strategically important positions in the government and who are appointed by the president, although their formal appointments must be confirmed by the Senate. (12)

Political efficacy The perception of one's ability to have an impact on the political system. (5)

Political machines Centrally controlled and tightly structured organizations that used rewards such as jobs and lucrative contracts to recruit and retain many of its supporters. The machines ran America's big cities in the late nineteenth and early twentieth centuries. (6)

Political participation Defined by one scholar as "those activities of citizens that attempt to influence the structure of government, the selection of government authorities, or the policies of government." Can cover a broad range of involvement both active and passive. (5)

Political parties In the United States, coalitions of people organized formally to recruit, nominate, and elect individuals to office and to use elected office to achieve shared political goals. (6)

Political public opinion The collective preferences expressed by people on political issues, policies, and individuals. (5)

Political socialization The process by which individuals acquire political values and knowledge about politics. It is strongly influenced by people with whom the individual has contact from early childhood through adulthood. (5)

Politics The activities involved in influencing or controlling government for the purpose of formulating or guiding public policy. (1)

Popular sovereignty The concept that the best form of government is one that reflects the general will of the people, which is the sum total of those interests that all citizens have in common. First described by writer Jean-Jacques Rousseau around the time of the American Revolution. (2)

Pork barrel legislation Legislation that appropriates funds for local projects in an area that a member of Congress represents. (10)

Precinct The bottom of the typical, local party structure—a voting district generally covering an area of several blocks. (6)

Preferred freedoms test The principle that some freedoms—free speech among them—are so fundamental to a democracy that they merit special protection. The test was instituted by the Warren Court of the 1960s and practically banned all government restrictions on speech. (4)

Primary An election in which party members select candidates to run for office under the party banner. (6,7)

Prior restraint The blocking by the government of a publication before it can be made available to the public. The Supreme Court has repeatedly struck down laws imposing prior restraint on newspapers. (9)

Progressive movement A reform movement that grew up around the turn of the century and set out to clean up the corruption of machine politics in the big cities. (6)

Proportional representation The electoral system used by many European nations whereby legislative seats are assigned to party candidates in proportion to the percentage of the vote that the party receives in the election. (6)

Pseudo events Events staged by politicians, such as speeches, rallies, and personal appearances that are staged simply to win maximum media coverage. (7)

Public interest groups Citizen activist groups that try to represent what they deem to be the interests of the public at large. (8)

Public opinion The distribution of individual preferences on any given issue or question. (5)

Public policies Actions taken by government officials in response to problems and issues raised through the political system. (14)

Public sector interest groups A new lobby emerging recently that represents the interests of elected officials and other major government actors involved in the intergovernmental relations system. For example, the National Governors Association. (3)

Random sampling A method by which pollsters choose interviewees, based on the idea that the opinions of individuals selected by chance will be representative of the opinions of the population at large. (5)

Rational model of decision making The ideal process whereby a policy maker has a clear objective and all the information needed to make a sound and reasoned decision, resulting in the selection of the best way to achieve the desired goal. (14)

Regulatory policies Economic policies through which government monitors and controls critical industries and sectors of the economy. (14)

Representative democracy A government in which decisions are made by elected or appointed officials. The people do not rule directly, but govern indirectly through the officials they elect. (1)

Republic   A constitutional form of government in which decisions are made democratically by elected or appointed officials. (1)

Republicanism   A doctrine of government in which decisions are made by elected or appointed officials who are answerable to the people; decisions are not made directly by the people themselves. (2)

Reserved powers   The powers that the Constitution provides for the states, although it does not list them specifically. These include all powers not expressly given to the national government or denied to the states. (2)

Retrospective voting   The process by which individuals base their vote for candidates on the candidates' or parties' past record of performance. (2)

Riders   Provisions that Congress knows the president opposes but that Congress attaches to bills that the president otherwise desires. (10)

Rule of law   The idea that no individual stands above the law and, further, that rulers, like those they rule, are answerable to the law. One of the most important legacies of the framers of the Constitution. (2)

Run-off primary   An electoral contest that is held between the top two vote-getters to determine the party's candidate in a general election. Held in the ten southern states where a majority of the vote is needed to win the primary. (7)

Search warrant   A written grant of permission to conduct a search that is issued by a neutral magistrate to police authorities. Police must describe what they expect to find and must show "probable cause." (4)

Select or special committees   Temporary committees established by the House or Senate to study particular problems. (10)

Selective incorporation   The Supreme Court's practice of making applicable to the states only those portions of the Bill of Rights that a majority of justices felt to be fundamental to a democratic society. (4)

Seniority system   A tradition through which the member of the majority party with the longest continuous service on a committee automatically becomes its chair. (10)

Separation of powers   The division of the powers to make, execute, and judge the law among the three branches of American government: Congress, the presidency, and the courts. This principle was adopted by the framers to avoid tyranny and factionalism in the government. (2)

Shays' rebellion   A rebellion by small farmers in western Massachusetts led by Daniel Shays in 1786. It convinced the nation's leaders that major changes had to be made in the American constitutional system. (2)

Single-issue group   A citizen activist group that seeks to lobby Congress on a narrow range of issues. (8)

Single-member plurality electoral system   The system of election used in the United States in all national and state elections and in most local elections. Officials are elected from districts that are served by only one legislator and a candidate must win a plurality—the most votes. (6)

Slander   Injury by spoken word, which like libel, is outside First Amendment protection and punishable by criminal law and civil prosecution. (4)

Speaker of the House   The only House position created by the Constitution to be chosen by a vote of the majority party and who is the presiding officer of the House, the leader of its majority party, and second in line to succeed the president. (10)

Stamp Act   The first tax levied directly on the American colonists by the British Parliament in 1765. Was repealed within several months after causing the colonists to protest against "taxation without representation." (2)

Standing committees   Permanently established committees that consider proposed legislation in specified policy areas and decide whether to recommend passage by the larger body. (10)

State-centered federalism   The view that states could overrule national laws. Was first expressed in the Virginia and Kentucky Resolutions in 1798. (3)

Strategic Defense Initiative (SDI)   The plan proposed in 1983 by the Reagan administration to develop a system of space satellites and earth-based stations that could intercept and destroy strategic ballistic missiles and so protect the United States from a Soviet nuclear attack. (15)

Supply-side economics An economic policy that advocates increasing the production of goods by cutting taxes to help stimulate investment, lifting regulations in the marketplace, and eliminating other government restraints on private business initiatives. (14)

Tight money supply An economic condition that exists when the amount of money circulating in the economy is low relative to the demand for money by consumers and investors. (14)

Treaties Legally binding pacts by which two or more nations formalize an agreement reached through negotiation. (15)

Unitary system A government, such as Great Britain's, in which constitutional authority rests entirely in the hands of a national government. Political subdivisions created by the central government perform much of the day-to-day work in governing. (3)

Veto An important check on the power of Congress. It is the president's power to reject legislation passed by Congress. The veto can be overruled, however, by a two-thirds vote of both chambers of Congress. (2)

Virginia Plan The proposal of the Virginia delegation to the Constitutional Convention in 1787. It was favored by large states because it called for a unicameral congress in which each state's representation would be based on its population relative to other states. (2)

Wage system The group of over a million federal workers who perform blue-collar and related jobs and are largely represented by unions or other associations with limited bargaining rights. (12)

War Powers Resolution Provides that the president can send troops into hostile territory for a period not to exceed sixty days and, if within that time Congress does not approve the actions or if by resolution it votes to withdraw the troops, they must be removed. (10)

Wards City council districts that are the level of party organization below that of the city-wide level. (6)

Worker protection Federal programs that protect the worker in areas of discrimination, worker rights, and occupational safety and health. (14)

Writ of certiorari A request that the Supreme Court order the lower court to send up the record of a case. (13)

References

Chapter 1 / Myth and Reality in American Politics / pp. 1–13

1. Mary Beth Norton et al., *A People and a Nation*, 2nd ed. (Boston: Houghton Mifflin Company, 1986), p. 241.

Chapter 2 / Constitutional Foundations / pp. 14–41

1. Martin Diamond, *The Founding of the Democratic Republic* (Itasca, Ill.: F.E. Peacock, 1981), p. 15.
2. See C. Herman Pritchett, *The American Constitution*, 3rd ed. (New York: McGraw-Hill, 1977), pp. 4–7.
3. These comments were communicated to the French foreign ministry by the French ambassador to the United States in 1788. See Saul K. Padover, *The Living Constitution* (New York: Mentor Books, 1953), pp. 51ff.
4. Quoted in Padover, *The Living Constitution*, p. 21.
5. See Seymour Martin Lipset and William Schneider, *The Confidence Gap: Business, Labor, and Government in the Public Mind* (New York: The Free Press, 1983), pp. 15–29.
6. Samuel P. Huntington, *American Politics: The Politics of Disharmony* (Cambridge, Mass.: Harvard University Press, 1981), p. 30.
7. Theodore H. White, "The American Idea," *The New York Times Magazine*, July 6, 1986, p. 13.
8. See Michael Kammen, *A Machine that Would Go of Itself: The Constitution in American Culture* (New York: Alfred A. Knopf, 1987).
9. Charles Howard McIlwain, *The American Revolution: A Constitutional Interpretation* (Ithaca, N.Y.: Cornell University Press, 1958), p. 5.
10. A classic exposition on the development of the British constitutional system is found in Walter Bagehot, *The English Constitution* (London: Oxford University Press, 1928); his views on the use of charters are presented on pp. 247–249.
11. See the reference to Bonham's Case and common law tradition in Charles Rembar, *The Law of the Land: The Evolution of Our Legal System* (New York: Simon and Schuster, 1980), pp. 43–47, 286–287.
12. Compare with Thomas L. Pangle, "The Constitution's Human Vision," *The Public Interest*, 86 (Winter 1987), 79–81.13.
13. See Lawrence J. R. Herson, *The Politics of Ideas: Political Theory and American Public Policy* (Homewood, Ill.: The Dorsey Press, 1984), pp. 28–29.
14. See Abraham I. Katsh, "Hebraic Foundations of American Democracy," in *The Hebrew Impact on Western Civilization*, ed. Dagobert D. Runes (Secaucus, N.J.: The Citadel Press, 1951), especially pp. 39–52.
15. For more on Hobbes's contribution to the work of the framers, see Walter Berns, "The new pursuit of happiness," *The Public Interest*, 86 (Winter 1987), pp. 68–69.
16. See Diamond, *The Founding of the Democratic Republic*, pp. 3–6. For a controversial interpretation of the Declaration, see Garry Wills, *Inventing America: Jefferson's Declaration of Independence* (New York: Vintage Books, 1978).
17. See "Federalist No. 51," in *The Federalist Papers*, ed. Clinton Rossiter (New York: Mentor Books, 1961), pp. 320–325.
18. "Federalist No. 44," *The Federalist Papers*, p. 287.

Chapter 3 / American Federalism / pp. 42–67

1. Frances Frank Marcus, "Mountain of Trouble in Gypsum Hills," *The New York Times*, December 7, 1986, Section 1, p. 13.
2. Alexis de Tocqueville, *Democracy in America*, ed. J.P. Mayer (Garden City, N.Y.: Doubleday Anchor, 1969), p. 386.

3. Tocqueville, *Democracy in America*, p. 394.
4. See Elizabeth Hastings and Philip Hastings, eds., *Index to International Public Opinion* (Westport, Conn.: Greenwood Press, 1983), p. 132. Also Advisory Commission on Intergovernmental Relations, *Changing Public Attitudes on Governments and Taxes, 1982* (Washington, D.C.: ACIR, 1982), p. 6.
5. Terry Sanford, *Storm Over the States* (New York: McGraw-Hill, 1967), p. 35.
6. James A. Stever, quoted in Advisory Commission on Intergovernmental Relations, *The Question of State Government Capability* (Washington, D.C.: ACIR, 1985), p. 2; hereafter cited as ACIR, *State Government Capability*. For a similar view, see Mel Dubnick and Alan Gitelson, "Nationalizing State Policies," in *The Nationalization of State Government*, ed. Jerome J. Hanus (Lexington, Mass.: Lexington Books, 1981), pp. 39–74.
7. "Can States Act Without Federal Permission," *The New York Times*, November 16, 1986, Section E, p. 5.
8. For a detailed survey of the concept of federalism, see S. Rufus Davis, *The Federal Principle: A Journey Through Time in Quest of Meaning* (Berkeley, Calif.: University of California Press, 1978).
9. For a general overview of the conflicting theories of federalism, see Richard H. Leach, *American Federalism* (New York: Norton, 1970), Ch. 1. Also see William H. Riker, *Federalism: Origin, Operation, Significance* (Boston, Mass.: Little, Brown, 1964).
10. From the Supreme Court in *Tarbel's Case*, quoted in Deil S. Wright, *Understanding Intergovernmental Relations*, 2nd ed. (Monterey, Calif.: Brooks/Cole, 1982), p. 31.
11. *Hammer* v. *Dagenhart* (1918).
12. See David B. Walker, *Toward a Functioning Federalism* (Cambridge, Mass.: Winthrop, 1981), pp. 60–62.
13. See Walker, *Federalism*, pp. 65–67. Also see Wright, *Intergovernmental Relations*, pp. 49–56.
14. Roscoe C. Martin, *The Cities and the Federal System* (New York: Atherton Press, 1965), Chs. 4 and 5. Also see Advisory Commission on Intergovernmental Relations, *Public Assistance: The Growth of a Federal Function* (Washington, D.C.: ACIR, 1980), pp. 24–25.15.
15. See Kenneth T. Palmer, "The Evolution of Grant Policies," in *The Changing Politics of Federal Grants*, eds. Lawrence D. Brown, James W. Fossett, and Kenneth T. Palmer (Washington, D.C.: The Brookings Institution, 1984).
16. See Advisory Commission on Intergovernmental Relations, *Regulatory Federalism: Policy, Process, Impact and Reform* (Washington, D.C.: ACIR, 1984).
17. See George E. Peterson, "Federalism and the States: An Experiment in Decentralization," in *The Reagan Record: An Assessment of America's Changing Domestic Priorities*, eds. John L. Palmer and Isabel V. Sawhill (Cambridge, Mass.: Ballinger, 1984), p. 228.
18. Peterson, "Federalism and the States," pp. 229–230.
19. Robert Pear, "Study Urges Fight For States' Power," *The New York Times*, November 9, 1986, pp. 1, 20.
20. See Morris P. Fiorina, *Congress: Keystone of the Washington Establishment* (New Haven, Conn.: Yale University Press, 1977), p. 48.
21. David E. Satterfield III, representative from Richmond, Virginia, quoted in Rochelle I. Stanfield, "Federal Aid—Taking the Good with the Bad," *National Journal*, July 8, 1978, p. 1076.
22. See Ann O'M. Bowman and Richard C. Kearney, *The Resurgence of the States* (Englewood Cliffs, N.J.: Prentice-Hall, 1986), p. 136.
23. Bowman and Kearney, *The Resurgence of the States*, pp. 25–27.
24. See ACIR, *The Question of State Government Capability*.
25. Luther H. Gulick, quoted in ACIR, *The Question of State Government Capability*, p. 1.
26. See Ira Sharkansky, *The Maligned States: Policy Accomplishments, Problems, and Opportunities* (New York: McGraw-Hill, 1972).
27. See ACIR, *The Question of State Capability*.
28. For an interesting view of how Americans have viewed their local governments, see Anwar Syed, *The Political Theory of American Local Government* (New York: Random House, 1966).
29. See Donald H. Haider, *When Governments Come to Washington: Governors, Mayors, and Intergovernmental Lobbying* (New York: The Free Press, 1974).

Chapter 4 / The Heritage of Rights and Liberties / pp. 68–103

1. See David Hamlin, *The Nazi-Skokie Conflict* (Boston: Beacon, 1980).
2. 32 U.S. (7 Pet.) 243.
3. See his concurring opinion in *Adamson* v. *California* 332 U.S. 67, 1947.
4. 302 U.S. 319.
5. *Milk Wagon Drivers Union* v. *Meadowmoor Dairies* 312 U.S. 287, 1941.
6. 249 U.S. 47.
7. 415 U.S. 566.
8. *United States* v. *O'Brien* 391 U.S. 367, 1968.
9. *Clark* v. *Community for Creative Non-Violence*, 1984.
10. 283 U.S. 697.
11. 403 U.S. 713.
12. *New York Times* v. *Sullivan* 376 U.S. 254, 1964.
13. 424 U.S. 96.
14. 354 U.S. 476.
15. *Memoirs of a Woman of Pleasure* v. *Massachusetts* 382 U.S. 975, 1966.

16. 413 U.S. 15.
17. C. Herman Pritchett, *Constitutional Civil Liberties*, (Englewood Cliffs, N.J.: Prentice-Hall, 1984), pp. 132–133.
18. *Everson* v. *Board of Education* 330 U.S. 1, 1947.
19. 403 U.S. 602.
20. *Engel* v. *Vitale* 370 U.S. 421, 1962.
21. *School District of Abington Township* v. *Schempp* 374 U.S. 203, 1963.
22. *Marsh* v. *Chambers* 103 S. Ct. 3330, 1983.
23. *Lynch* v. *Donnelly* 104 S. Ct. 1355, 1984.
24. *Reynolds* v. *United States* 98 U.S. 145, 1879.
25. *Braunfeld* v. *Brown* 366 U.S. 599, 1961.
26. *Jacobson* v. *Massachusetts* 197 U.S. 11, 1905.
27. *Wisconsin* v. *Yoder* 406 U.S. 215, 1972.
28. *Adderly* v. *Florida* 385 U.S. 39, 1966.
29. *Greer* v. *Spock* 424 U.S. 828, 1976.
30. *Grayned* v. *City of Rockford* 408 U.S. 104, 1972.
31. 287 U.S. 45, 1932.
32. 372 U.S. 335, 1963.
33. *Argersinger* v. *Hamlin* 407 U.S. 25, 1972.
34. 378 U.S. 478.
35. 384 U.S. 436, 1966.
36. *New York* v. *Quarles*, 1984.
37. *Schneckloth* v. *Bustamonte* 412 U.S. 218, 1973.
38. 367 U.S. 643.
39. *Nix* v. *Williams* 467 U.S. 431, 1984.
40. *United States* v. *Leon* 468 U.S. 897, 1984.
41. *Olmstead* v. *United States* 277 U.S. 438, 1928.
42. *Katz* v. *United States* 389 U.S. 347, 1967.
43. 370 U.S. 660.
44. 408 U.S. 238.
45. 428 U.S. 280.
46. Charles Warren and Louis Brandeis, "The Right of Privacy," vol. 4 *Harvard Law Review* 193 (1980).
47. 381 U.S. 479.
48. 410 U.S. 113.

49. 478 U.S.
50. C. Vann Woodward, *The Strange Career of Jim Crow* (New York: Oxford University Press, 1966).
51. 163 U.S. 537, 1896.
52. Paul Oberst, "The Strange Career of *Plessy* v. *Ferguson*," vol. 15 *Arizona Law Review*, 389 (1973).
53. *Cumming* v. *Richmond County Board of Education* 175 U.S. 528, 1899.
54. *Missouri ex. rel. Gaines* v. *Canada* 305 U.S. 337, 1938.
55. *Sweatt* v. *Painter* 339 U.S. 629, 1950.
56. 347 U.S. 483.
57. *Alexander* v. *Holmes County Board of Education* 396 U.S. 19, 1969.
58. *Milliken* v. *Bradley* 418 U.S. 717, 1974.
59. See Pritchett, *Constitutional Liberties*, p. 345.
60. 335 U.S. 464.
61. 368 U.S. 62, 1961.
62. *Craig* v. *Boren* 429 U.S. 190, 1976.
63. *Kahn* v. *Shevin* 416 U.S. 351, 1974.
64. *General Electric Co.* v. *Gilbert* 429 U.S. 125, 1976.
65. 438 U.S. 265, 1978.

Chapter 5 / Public Opinion and Political Participation / pp. 104–131

1. Barry Sussman, "In Pollsters We Trust," *The Washington Post National Weekly Edition*, August 25, 1986, p. 37.
2. An examination of one popular high school textbook reinforces this conclusion. The index of the book lists two topics for discussion under the subject "participation in government": participation as a distinguishing characteristic between dictatorships and democracy and participation as it relates to low voting turnout in the United States. William A. McClenaghan, *Magruder's American Government* (Boston: Allyn and Bacon, 1979), pp. 21–22, 221–225, and as listed in the index, p. 812.

3. W.H. Hartley and W.S. Vincent, *American Civics*, 4th ed. (New York: Harcourt Brace Jovanovitch, 1983), p. 221.
4. *National Journal*, June 7, 1986, p. 1398; *The Washington Post National Weekly Edition*, February 9, 1987, p. 37.
5. V.O. Key Jr., *Public Opinion and American Democracy* (New York: Knopf, 1961).
6. Harry Holloway with John George, *Public Opinion: Coalitions, Elites, and Masses*, 2nd. ed. (New York: St. Martin's Press, 1986), p. 71.
7. Bernard Hennessy, *Public Opinion*, 5th ed. (Monterey, Calif.: Brooks/Cole, 1985), p. 199, and Holloway, *Public Opinion*, p. 72.
8. Hennessy, *Public Opinion*, p. 200.
9. See John L. Sullivan et al., *Political Tolerance and American Democracy* (Chicago: University of Chicago Press, 1982); and Herbert McClosky and Alida Brill, *Dimensions of Tolerance: What Americans Believe About Civil Liberties* (New York: Russell Sage Foundation, 1983).
10. M. Margaret Conway, Mikel L. Wyckoff, Eleanor Feldbaum, and David Ahern, "The News Media in Children's Political Socialization," *Public Opinion Quarterly*, 45 (1981), 164–178; M. Margaret Conway, David Ahern, and Mikel L. Wyckoff, "The Mass Media and Changes in Adolescents' Political Knowledge During an Election Cycle," *Political Behavior*, 3 (1981), 69–80.
11. *American National Election Study, 1984*, Center for Political Studies, University of Michigan, Ann Arbor.
12. Leo Bogart, *Silent Politics: Polls and the Awareness of Public Opinion* (New York: John Wiley & Sons, 1972), p. 18.
13. *Public Opinion* (April/May, 1985), 8.
14. *American National Election Studies Data Sourcebook, 1952–1984*. Center for Political Studies, University of Michigan, Ann Arbor.
15. *The New York Times/CBS News*

Poll, January Survey, January 19–23, 1986.
16. Ibid.
17. Survey by Civil Service, Inc., March 5–18, 1981.
18. Linda S. Lichter, *Public Opinion* (August/September 1985), 42.
19. See Daniel Yankelovich, "The Status of Resentment in America," *Social Research* (Winter 1975).
20. E. J. Dionne Jr., "Government Trust: Less in West Europe than U.S.," *The New York Times*, February 16, 1986, p. 1.
21. David S. Broder, *The Washington Post National Weekly Edition*, February 9, 1987, p. 37.
22. *American National Election Study, 1984.*
23. Harry Holloway, "Gender and Opinion: An Exploration of Differences," paper delivered at the Annual Meeting of the Southern Political Science Association, Atlanta, Ga., November 6–8, 1980.
24. On the issue of the Equal Rights Amendment, see *The New York Times Women's Survey*, November 11–20, 1983; on the ERA and the issue of abortion, see *Gallup Report* (July 1981).
25. Evans Witt, "What the Republicans Have Learned about Women," *Public Opinion* (October/November 1985), 51.
26. See, for example, Celinda Lake, *Power, Equity, and Policy Dimensions of the Women's Vote in 1984*, paper presented at the Annual Meeting of the American Political Science Association, Washington, D.C., August 1986.
27. Terry W. Hartle and John Taylor, *Public Opinion* (August/September 1985), 51.
28. Ibid., p. 53.
29. Ibid., p. 51.
30. Ibid., p. 52.
31. See Lichter, pp. 41–44, 58.
32. Juan Williams and Kenneth E. John, "Blacks and Whites Are Agreeing on Key Issues Facing the Nation," *The Washington Post National Weekly Edition*, October 27, 1986, p. 37.
33. Paul R. Abramson, John H.

Aldrich, and David W. Rohde, *Change and Continuity in the 1984 Elections* (Washington, D.C.: Congressional Quarterly Press, 1986), p. 213.
34. Williams and John, "Blacks and Whites Are Agreeing," p. 37.
35. Adam Clymer, "Poll Studies Hispanic Party Loyalties," *The New York Times*, July 18, 1986, p. 1.
36. Hennessy, *Public Opinion*, p. 181.
37. For a comprehensive review of research on religion and political attitudes, see Hennessy, *Public Opinion*, pp. 180–87, and Holloway and George, *Public Opinion*, ch. 5.
38. Hennessy, *Public Opinion*, p. 184.
39. Ibid., pp. 180–187.
40. M. Margaret Conway, *Political Participation in the United States* (Washington, D.C.: Congressional Quarterly Press, 1985), p. 2.
41. Sidney Verba and Norman H. Nie, *Participation in America: Political Democracy and Social Equality* (New York: Harper and Row, 1972), pp. 95–101.
42. Data were collected by the American National Election Study, 1984.
43. *The Gallup Report* (May 1986), 14–15.
44. *The Gallup Report* (January/February 1986), 45.
45. Sandra Baxter and Marjorie Lansing, *Women and Politics*, rev. ed. (Ann Arbor, Mich.: University of Michigan Press, 1983), ch. 2. For an excellent discussion and review of group participation patterns, see Conway, *Political Participation*.
46. Nancy McGlen and Karen O'Conner, *Women's Rights: The Struggle for Equality in the Nineteenth and Twentieth Centuries* (New York: Praeger, 1983), p. 110, table 4.5.
47. Paul R. Abramson and William H. Claggett, "Race-Related Differences in Self-reported and Validated Turnout," *Journal of Politics* 46 (1984), 719–738.

48. Luis Caban, director of the National Puerto Rican–Hispanic Voter Registration Project. See *Congressional Quarterly Weekly Report*, July 5, 1986, p. 1538.

Chapter 6 / Political Parties / pp. 132–161

1. See Richard J. Trilling, *Party Image and Electoral Behavior* (New York: John Wiley & Sons, 1976), pp. 221–222; and William H. Flanigan and Nancy H. Zingale, *Political Behavior of the American Electorate*, 6th ed. (Boston: Allyn and Bacon, 1987), p. 136.
2. See Jeff Fishel, ed., *Parties and Elections in an Anti-Party Age* (Bloomington, Ind.: Indiana University Press, 1978); and Merle Black and George Rabinowitz, "American Electoral Change: 1952–1972," in *The Party Symbol: Readings on Political Parties*, ed. William Crotty. (San Francisco: W.H. Freeman, 1980).
3. Martin P. Wattenberg, "The Decline of Political Partisanship in the United States: Negativity or Neutrality?," *The American Political Science Review*, 75 (December 1981), 950.
4. Larry J. Sabato, *PAC Power: Inside the World of Political Action Committees* (New York: Norton, 1984), p. 163.
5. National Election Studies, University of Michigan's Survey Research Center/Center for Political Studies.
6. Alan R. Gitelson, M. Margaret Conway, and Frank B. Feigert, *American Political Parties: Stability and Change* (Boston: Houghton Mifflin Company, 1984), p. 4.
7. For one of the most comprehensive studies of comparative party organizations, see Kenneth Janda, *Political Parties: A Cross-National Survey* (New York: Free Press, 1980); also see Kenneth Janda, "A Comparative Analysis of Party Organizations: The United States, Europe, and the World," in *The*

Party Symbol, Readings on Political Parties, ed. William Gatty, pp. 339–358; and Kay Lawson, *The Comparative Study of Political Parties* (New York: St. Martin's, 1976).

8. Frank J. Sorauf, *Party Politics in America,* 5th ed. (Boston: Little, Brown, 1984), p. 8.

9. See Martin P. Wattenberg, *The Decline of American Political Parties: 1952–1984* (Cambridge, Mass.: Harvard University Press, 1986).

10. Gitelson, Conway, and Feigert, *American Political Parties,* p. 131.

11. For one of the classic defenses of the role of parties, see E.E. Schattschneider, *Party Government* (New York: Rinehart, 1942). For an equally compelling argument in support of parties by a leading proponent of the view that parties are in decline, see Walter Dean Burnham, "The Changing Shape of the American Political Universe," in *Controversies in American Voting Behavior,* eds. Richard G. Niemi and Herbert F. Weisberg (San Francisco: W. H. Freeman, 1976), pp. 451–483.

12. Allan D. Monroe, "American Party Platforms and Public Opinion," *American Journal of Political Science* 27 (February 1983), 27–42; and Gerald M. Pomper with Susan M. Lederman, *Elections in America: Control and Influences in Democratic Politics,* 2nd ed. (New York: Longman, 1980).

13. Op. cit., pp. 173–176.

14. *Congressional Quarterly Weekly Report,* January 11, 1986, pp. 86–91.

15. James MacGregor Burns, *The Deadlock of Democracy: Four-Party Politics in America* (Englewood Cliffs, N.J.: Prentice-Hall, 1963), p. 27.

16. Woodrow Wilson, *Constitutional Government in the United States* (New York: Columbia University Press, 1961), pp. 206, 217.

17. Three excellent discussions of the development of American parties are William N. Cham-

bers, *Political Parties in a New Nation* (New York: Oxford University Press, 1963); William N. Chambers and Walter D. Burnham, eds., *The American Party System* (New York: Oxford University Press, 1967); and Everett C. Ladd Jr., *American Political Parties* (New York: Norton, 1970).

18. See Robert P. Formisano, "Federalists and Republicans: Parties, Yes—System, No," in *The Evolution of American Electoral Systems,* ed. Paul Kleppner (Westport, Conn.: Greenwood Press, 1981), p. 35; and Formisano, "Deferential-Participant Politics: The Early Republic's Political Culture, 1789–1840," *American Political Science Review* 58 (June 1984), 473–487.

19. For a concise review of the splits within the Democratic-Republican party, see Burns, *The Deadlock of Democracy,* ch. 3.

20. For the most comprehensive discussion of the realignment process, see Walter Dean Burnham, *Critical Elections and the Mainspring of American Politics* (New York: Norton, 1970).

21. For a review of the several theories that we will be discussing in this section, see Frank J. Sorauf, *Party Politics in America,* 5th ed. (Boston: Little, Brown, 1984), pp. 39–43.

22. Two proponents of the institutionalist explanation for the two-party system are E.E. Schattschneider, *Party Government* (New York: Rinehart, 1942); and Maurice Duverger, *Political Parties* (New York: Wiley, 1954).

23. V. O. Key, *Politics, Parties and Pressure Groups,* 5th ed. (New York: Crowell, 1964); and Louis Hartz, *The Liberal Tradition in America* (New York: Harcourt, Brace & World, 1955).

24. The American "Know-Nothings" party, an anti-immigrant organization, received its nickname because of its original goal of keeping its purposes secret, responding to all questions

with the words "I know nothing." See Mary Beth Norton et al., *A People and A Nation: A History of the United States,* 2nd ed. (Boston: Houghton Mifflin Company, 1986), p. 365.

25. For a revealing review of state laws that restrict participation by third parties in the electoral process, see Jim McClellan, "Two-Party Monopoly: Democrats and Republicans Pass Go, Collect Millions," in *American Government 85/86,* ed. Bruce Stinebrickner (Guilford, Conn.: Dushkin, 1985), pp. 183–186.

26. Gitelson, Conway, and Feigert, *American Politial Parties,* p. 82.

27. For comprehensive reviews of party reform over the past two decades, see William Crotty, *Political Reform and the American Experiment* (New York: Thomas Y. Crowell, 1977); Crotty, *Party Reform* (New York: Longman, 1983); and Charles Longley, "National Party Renewal," in *Party Renewal in America,* ed. Gerald M. Pomper (New York: Praeger, 1980), pp. 69–86.

28. See Burnham, *Critical Elections;* William Crotty, *American Parties in Decline* (Boston: Little, Brown, 1984); and Martin P. Wattenberg, *The Decline of American Political Parties* (Cambridge, Mass.: Harvard University Press, 1984).

29. *The Gallup Report* (December 1985), 15.

30. See Gitelson, Conway, and Feigert, *American Political Parties,* ch. 15, for a discussion of the transformation of political parties.

Chapter 7 / Campaigns and Elections / pp. 162–195

1. Stephen A. Salmore and Barbara G. Salmore, *Candidates, Parties, and Campaigns: Electoral Politics in America* (Washington, D.C.: Congressional Quarterly Press, 1985), p. 28. See also Wayne C. Williams, *William Jennings Bryan* (New York: Putnam, 1936), p. 162.

2. Francis T. Russell, *The Shadow-*

ing of Blooming Grove (New York: McGraw-Hill, 1968), p. 125. See also Salmore and Salmore, *Candidates, Parties, and Campaigns*, p. 28.

3. Salmore and Salmore, *Candidates, Parties, and Campaigns*, p. 29.

4. *American National Election Study, 1984,* Center for Political Studies of the Institute for Social Research, University of Michigan, Ann Arbor, Mich.

5. "Attitudes Toward Campaign Financing," survey conducted by Civic Service, Inc., February 1985, p. 6. Special mailing, Civil Service, Inc.

6. See Joseph A. Schlesinger, *Ambition and Politics: Political Careers in the United States* (Chicago: Rand McNally, 1966); Gordon Black, "A Theory of Political Ambition: Career Choices and the Role of Structural Incentives," *American Political Science Review* 66 (March 1972), 144–159; and Robert McClure and Linda Fowler, *Political Ambition: Unseen Candidates for Congress* (New Haven, Conn: Yale University Press, 1988).

7. Schlesinger, *Ambition and Politics,* pp. 16–20.

8. M.I. Ostrogorski, *Democracy and the Organization of Political Parties* (New York: Macmillan, 1902), XI, 4. For the curious and those with a cast-iron stomach, the drink flip is a hot mixture of beer, cider, sugar, egg, and nutmeg—an excellent eye opener.

9. For a concise discussion of the presidential nomination process, see William Crotty and John S. Jackson III, *Presidential Primaries and Nominations* (Washington, D.C.: Congressional Quarterly Press, 1985).

10. *Federal Election Commission Report,* June 4, 1986.

11. Barbara Farah, "Delegate Polls: 1944–1984," *Public Opinions* (August/September 1984), 44.

12. *Congressional Quarterly Weekly Report,* February 11, 1984, p. 252, and June 16, 1984, p. 1443.

13. Austin Ranney, *Participation in American Presidential Nominations* (Washington, D.C.: American Enterprise Institute, 1977).

14. George Thayer, *Who Shakes the Money Tree?* (New York: Simon & Schuster, 1973), p. 150.

15. *Elections '86* (Washington, D.C.: Congressional Quarterly Press, 1986), p. 38.

16. *Federal Election Commission Record* (October 1985), 5 and 7.

17. For a discussion on the impact of spending by challengers in congressional races, see Paul R. Abramson, John H. Aldrich, and David W. Rhode, *Change and Continuity in the 1980 Elections,* rev. ed. (Washington, D.C.: Congressional Quarterly Press, 1983), p. 201.

18. Gary C. Jacobson, "Money in the 1980 and 1982 Congressional Elections," in *Money and Politics in the United States: Financing Elections in the 1980s,* ed. Michael J. Malbin (Chatham, N.J.: Chatham House Publishers, 1984), p. 65.

19. Alan R. Gitelson, M. Margaret Conway, and Frank B. Feigert, *American Political Parties: Stability and Change* (Boston: Houghton Mifflin Company, 1984), p. 242.

20. Barry Sussman, "Do Pre-Election Polls Influence People to Switch Their Votes?," *The Washington Post National Weekly Edition,* June 10, 1985, p. 37.

21. For the most comprehensive study of campaign consultants, see Larry J. Sabato, *The Rise of Political Consultants: New Ways of Winning Elections* (New York: Basic Books, 1981).

22. Marchette Chute, *The First Liberty: A History of the Right to Vote in America, 1619–1850* (New York: Dutton, 1969), p. 223; for a brief but concise review of the early development of the electorate, see Bruce Campbell, *The American Electorate: Attitudes and Action* (New York: Holt, Rinehart and Winston, 1979), ch. 2.

23. Campbell, *The American Electorate,* pp. 12–13.

24. See Raymond E. Wolfinger and Steven J. Rosenstone, *Who Votes?* (New Haven, Conn.: Yale University Press, 1980).

25. Ibid., p. 18.

26. Ibid.

27. In one recent public opinion poll, close to 50 percent of the respondents disagreed with the statement that "the members of Congress are honest, decent human beings." See *Attitudes Toward Campaign Financing,* p. 7.

28. See Abramson and Aldrich, "The Decline of Electoral Participation in America," pp. 502–521; and, Richard A. Brody, "The Puzzle of Participation in America," in *The New American Political System,* ed. Anthony King (Washington, D.C.: American Enterprise Institute, 1978).

29. Paul R. Abramson, John H. Aldrich, and David W. Rohde, *Change and Continuity in the 1984 Elections* (Washington, D.C.: Congressional Quarterly Press, 1986), p. 176.

30. *The New York Times/CBS News Poll,* September Survey, September 28-October 1, 1986.

31. Sidney Lens, "What Socialists Can Do in 1984," *The Nation,* July 21–28, 1984, pp. 41–42.

32. *American National Election Study, 1984.*

33. *The New York Times/CBS News Poll,* September 28-October 1, 1986.

34. For the most comprehensive discussion of retrospective voting, see Morris P. Fiorina, *Retrospective Voting in American National Elections* (New Haven, Conn.: Yale University Press, 1981).

35. See Adam Clymer, "Displeasure with Carter Turned Many to Reagan," *The New York Times,* November 9, 1980, p. 28; John Stacks, "New Beginnings; Old Anxieties," *Time,* February 2, 1981, p. 22; and Barry Sussman, "Americans Have Moved Away From Reagan on Key Issues," *Washington Post National Weekly Edition,* January 7, 1985, p. 37.

36. See Gerald M. Pomper with Susan S. Lederman, *Elections in America: Control and Influence in*

Democratic Politics, 2nd ed. (New York: Longman, 1985).

Chapter 8 / Interest Groups / pp. 196–225

1. This story is adapted from Francis X. Clines, "Like a Wallflower at the Lobbyists' Waltz," *The New York Times,* December 11, 1985, p. 30.
2. American National Election Study, Center for Political Studies, University of Michigan, 1984.
3. "Attitudes Toward Campaign Financing," Civic Service, Inc., February 1985.
4. See Jeffrey M. Berry. *The Interest Group Society* (Boston: Little, Brown, 1984); Carol Greenwald, *Group Power: Lobbying and Public Policy* (New York: Praeger, 1977); Kay Lehman Schlozman and John T. Tierney, *Organized Interests and American Democracy* (New York: Harper & Row, 1986); and Allan J. Cigler and Burdett A. Loomis, *Interest Group Politics,* 2nd ed. (Washington, D.C.: Congressional Quarterly Press, 1986).
5. Alan R. Gitelson, M. Margaret Conway, and Frank B. Feigert, *American Political Parties: Stability and Change* (Boston: Houghton Mifflin Company, 1984), pp. 333–335.
6. Schlozman and Tierney, *Organized Interests and American Democracy,* p. 50.
7. *Congressional Quarterly Weekly Report,* March 16, 1985, p. 505.
8. For an excellent discussion of public interest groups, see Jeffrey M. Berry, *Lobbying for the People* (Princeton, N.J.: Princeton University Press, 1977).
9. These categories are drawn, in part, from an excellent study on interest group politics, Schlozman and Tierney, *Organized Interests and American Democracy,* pp. 45–49.
10. Berry, *The Interest Group Society,* p. 29. See also Charles Mc-

Carry, *Citizen Nader* (New York: Saturday Review Press, 1972).
11. *Congressional Quarterly Weekly Report* (September 6, 1980), p. 2627.
12. Schlozman and Tierney, *Organized Interests and American Democracy,* pp. 45–46.
13. Robert H. Salisbury, "Interest Groups: Toward a New Understanding," in *Interest Group Politics,* eds. Allan J. Cigler and Burdett A. Loomis (Washington, D.C.: Congressional Quarterly Press, 1983), p. 364.
14. Ibid., p. 364.
15. Burt Solomon, "How Washington Works," *National Journal,* June 14, 1986, p. 1430.
16. Berry, *The Interest Group Society,* p. 96.
17. See Mancur Olson, *The Logic of Collective Action* (Cambridge, Mass.: Harvard University Press, 1965).
18. For an excellent explanation of the free-rider problem, see Olson, *The Logic of Collective Action.* See also E. E. Schattschneider, *The Semisovereign People* (New York: Holt, Rinehart and Winston, 1960).
19. Schlozman and Tierney, *Organized Interests and American Democracy,* pp. 103–106.
20. Ibid., p. 106.
21. Ibid., pp. 150–51.
22. *Guide to Current American Government,* Spring 1983 (Washington, D.C.: Congressional Quarterly Press), p. 48.
23. Primaries, run-off primaries, and general elections are treated as separate elections. For a comprehensive review of the Federal Election Campaign Act and related information on campaign financing by PACs, see *Federal Election Campaign Laws,* compiled by the Federal Election Commission, January 1980; and Herbert E. Alexander and Brian A. Haggerty, *The Federal Election Campaign Act* (Los Angeles: Citizens' Research Foundation, 1981). For a fascinating exposé of PAC spending in

congressional campaigns, see Elizabeth Drew, "Politics and Money," Parts I and II, *The New Yorker,* December 6 and 13, 1982.
24. Federal Election Commission press release, December 1, 1985.
25. *The Washington Post National Weekly Edition,* June 24, 1985, p. 13.
26. Schlozman and Tierney, *Organized Interests and American Democracy,* p. 233.
27. Ibid., p. 150.
28. See John R. Wright, "PACs, Contributions, and Roll Calls: An Organizational Perspective," *The American Political Science Review,* 79 (June 1985), 400–414.
29. Larry Sabato, *PAC Power: Inside the World of Political Action Committees* (New York: Norton, 1985), p. 8.
30. See Walter V. Robinson, "The Common Roots of Mondale Delegates," *Boston Globe,* July 9, 1984, p. 7. See also Schlozman and Tierney, *Organized Interests and American Democracy,* pp. 206–209.
31. Burdett A. Loomis, "Coalitions of Interests: Building Bridges in the Balkanized State," in Cigler and Burdett *Interest Group Politics,* p. 258.
32. Gitelson, Conway, and Feigert, *American Political Parties,* p. 339.
33. See Allan J. Cigler and John Mark Hansen, "Group Formation Through Protest: The American Agricultural Movement," in *Interest Group Politics,* eds. Cigler and Loomis, pp. 84–109.
34. Berry, *The Interest Group Society,* p. 151. Also see John W. Kingdon, *Congressmen's Voting Decisions,* 2nd ed. (New York: Harper & Row, 1981).
35. Karen O'Connor, *Women's Organizations' Use of the Courts* (Lexington, Mass.: Lexington Books, 1980), p. 118.
36. For a more detailed, and supporting view of the cozy triangle, see Hugh Heclo, "Issue Networks and the Executive Es-

tablishment," in *The New American Political System*, ed. Anthony King (Washington, D.C.: American Enterprise Institute, 1978), p. 8.

Chapter 9 / Media and Politics / pp. 226–251

1. Quoted in David Halberstam, *The Powers That Be* (New York: Dell, 1979), pp. 15–16.
2. Quoted in Robert Metz, *CBS: Reflections in a Bloodshot Eye* (New York: Signet, 1975), p. 352.
3. Halberstam, *The Powers That Be*, p. 716.
4. Roan Conrad, "TV News and the 1976 Election: A Dialogue," *The Wilson Quarterly* (Spring 1977), 84.
5. Ronald Berkman and Laura W. Kitch, *Politics in the Media Age* (New York: McGraw-Hill, 1986), p. 21.
6. Phillip Knightley, *The First Casualty* (New York: Harcourt Brace and Jovanovich, 1975), p. 56.
7. Quoted in Berkman and Kitch, *Politics in the Media Age*, p. 25.
8. Doris A. Graber, *Mass Media and American Politics* (Washington, D.C.: Congressional Quarterly Press, 1984), p. 45.
9. Kathleen Hall Jamieson and Karlyn Kohrs Campbell, *The Interplay of Influence* (Belmont, Calif.: Wadsworth, 1983), p. 10.
10. Ibid., p. 16.
11. Graber, *Mass Media and American Politics*, pp. 77–79.
12. Herbert J. Gans, *Deciding What's News: A Study of CBS Evening News, NBC Nightly News, Newsweek and Time* (New York: Vintage, 1980), p. 9.
13. Stephen Hess, *The Washington Reporters* (Washington, D.C.: The Brookings Institution, 1981), pp. 16–19.
14. G. Cleveland Wilhoit, David H. Weaver, and Richard G. Gray, *The American Journalist* (Bloomington, Ind.: Indiana University Press, 1985).

15. Hess, *The Washington Reporters*, pp. 70–71.
16. Ibid., pp. 67–69.
17. William Schneider and I. A. Lewis, "Views on the News," *Public Opinion* (August/September 1985), 6–8.
18. Graber, *Mass Media and American Politics*, pp. 58–59.
19. Paul Lazarfeld, Bernard Berelson, and H. Gaudet, *The People's Choice* (New York: Columbia University Press, 1948).
20. Thomas E. Patterson, *The Mass Media Election: How Americans Choose Their President* (New York: Praeger, 1980), pp. 86–91.
21. Benjamin I. Page, Robert Y. Shapiro, and Glenn R. Dempsey, "What Moves Public Opinion," *American Political Science Review*, 81 (March 1987), 23–43.
22. Austin Ranney, *Channels of Power, The Impact of Television on American Politics* (New York: Basic Books, 1983), p. 17.
23. Shanto Iyengar, Mark D. Peters, and Donald R. Kinder, "Experimental Demonstrations of the 'Not-So-Minimal' Consequences of Television News Programs," *American Political Science Review*, 76 (December 1982), 848–858.
24. Timothy Crouse, *The Boys on the Bus* (New York: Ballantine, 1972), 176–177
25. Thomas E. Patterson and Robert D. McClure, *The Unseeing Eye: The Myth of Television Power in National Elections* (New York: Putnam, 1976), p. 41.
26. Graber, *Mass Media and American Politics*, pp. 200–202
27. Quoted in Leon V. Sigal, *Reporters and Officials: The Organization and Politics of Newsmaking* (Lexington, Mass.: Heath, 1973), p. 135.
28. David Wise, *The Politics of Lying: Government Deception, Secrecy, and Power* (New York: Vintage, 1973), p. 460.
29. Michael Baruch Grossman and Martha Joynt Kumar, *Portraying the President: The White House and the Media* (Baltimore: Johns

Hopkins University Press, 1981), p. 116.
30. Charles Peters, "Why the White House Press Didn't Get the Watergate Story," *The Washington Monthly*, 4 (July/August 1973), 6.
31. Quoted in Joseph C. Spear, *Presidents and the Press: The Nixon Legacy* (Cambridge, Mass.: The MIT Press, 1984), pp. 10–11.
32. Quoted in Spear, *Presidents and the Press: The Nixon Legacy*, p. 292.
33. Quoted in Graber, *Mass Media and American Politics*, p. 237.
34. Hess, *The Washington Reporters*, pp. 98–99.
35. Stephen Hess, *The Ultimate Insiders: U.S. Senators in the National Media* (Washington, D.C.: The Brookings Institution, 1986), p. 30.
36. Quoted in David M. O'Brien, *Storm Center: The Supreme Court in American Politics* (New York: Norton, 1986), p. 281.

Chapter 10 / Congress / pp. 252–283

1. Quoted in Albert R. Hunt, "In Defense of a Messy Congress," *The Washingtonian* (September 1982), p. 180.
2. "The Age of Inefficiency," *Newsweek*, August 4, 1986, p. 4.
3. Richard F. Fenno Jr., *Home Style: House Members in Their Districts* (Boston: Little, Brown, 1978), p. 168.
4. Roger H. Davidson and Walter J. Oleszek, *Congress and Its Members* (Washington, D.C.: Congressional Quarterly Press, 1981), pp. 102–103.
5. Cited in Barbara Hinckley, *Congressional Elections* (Washington, D.C.: Congressional Quarterly Press, 1981), p. 89.
6. Albert D. Cover, "One Good Term Deserves Another: The Advantage of Incumbency in Congressional Elections," *American Journal of Political Science* 21 (August 1977), 523–541.

7. *Wesberry* v. *Sanders* 376 U.S. 1, 1964.
8. See "Redistricting Procedure Has Few Rules," *Congressional Quarterly Weekly Report*, February 21, 1981, p. 354.
9. Gary C. Jacobson, *The Politics of Congressional Elections*, 2d ed. (Boston: Little, Brown, 1987), p. 13.
10. Morris P. Fiorina, *Congress: Keystone of the Washington Establishment* (New Haven: Yale University Press, 1977), pp. 17–19.
11. Jim Wright, *You and Your Congressman* (New York: Coward, McCann and Geoghegan, 1972), p. 22.
12. David R. Mayhew, *Congress: The Electoral Connection* (New Haven: Yale University Press, 1974), p. 37.
13. Ibid., p. 61.
14. Fenno, *Home Style*.
15. Jacobson, *The Politics of Congressional Elections*, p. 50.
16. Quoted in Davidson and Oleszek, *Congress and Its Members*, p. 69.
17. *McCulloch* v. *Maryland*, 17 U.S. (4 Wheat.) 316, 1819.
18. For a detailed account of the budget process, see Allen Schick, *Congress and Money* (Washington, D.C.: The Urban Institute, 1980). See also James P. Pfiffner, *The President, the Budget, and Congress: Impoundment and the 1974 Budget Act* (Boulder, Colo.: Westview Press, 1979).
19. Hanna Pitkin, *The Concept of Representation* (Berkeley, Calif.: University of California Press, 1969), p. 209.
20. Roger H. Davidson, *The Role of the Congressman* (New York: Pegasus, 1969), p. 117.
21. Quoted in George B. Gallaway, *History of the House of Representatives* (New York: Crowell, 1969), p. 215.
22. Morris P. Fiorina, "The Case of the Vanishing Marginals: The Bureaucracy Did It," *American Political Science Review* 71 (March 1977), 180.
23. Fenno, *Home Style*, p. 240.

24. Quoted in Barbara Hinckley, *Stability and Change in Congress* (New York: Harper & Row, 1983), p. 243.
25. *Immigration and Naturalization Service* v. *Chadha* 103 S. Ct. 2764, 1983.
26. For a general discussion of the legislative veto and its alternatives, see Joseph Cooper, "The Legislative Veto in the 1980s," in *Congress Reconsidered*, 3rd ed., eds. Lawrence C. Dodd and Bruce I. Oppenheimer (Washington, D.C.: Congressional Quarterly Press, 1985), pp. 364–389.
27. Paul F. Boller, *Presidential Anecdotes* (New York: Penguin, 1981), p. 18.
28. See Steven S. Smith and Christopher J. Deering, *Committees in Congress* (Washington, D.C.: Congressional Quarterly Press, 1984), pp. 7–34.
29. *How Congress Works*, (Washington, D.C.: Congressional Quarterly Inc., 1983), p. 82.
30. Richard F. Fenno Jr., *Congressman in Committees*, (Boston: Little, Brown, 1973).
31. Quoted in *Origins and Development of Congress* (Washington, D.C.: Congressional Quarterly Inc., 1982) p. 135.
32. Quoted in Davidson and Oleszek, *Congress and Its Members*, p. 216.
33. See Mark F. Ferber, "The Formation of the Democratic Study Group," in *Congressional Behavior*, ed. Nelson Polsby (New York: Random House, 1971).
34. Burdett A. Loomis, "Congressional Caucuses and the Politics of Representations," in *Congress Reconsidered*, 2d. ed., eds. Lawrence C. Dodd and Bruce I. Oppenheimer (Washington, D.C.: Congressional Quarterly Press, 1981), pp. 204–220.
35. Quoted in Davidson and Oleszek, *Congress and Its Members*, p. 352.
36. Ibid., p. 266.
37. Quoted in *Origins and Development of Congress*, p. 122.
38. For an excellent discussion of

House and Senate rules, see Walter J. Oleszek, *Congressional Procedures and the Policy Process* (Washington, D.C.: Congressional Quarterly Press, 1978).
39. Quoted in William J. Keefe and Morris S. Ogul, *The American Legislative Process: Congress and the States* (Englewood Cliffs, N.J.: Prentice-Hall, 1981), pp. 259–260.
40. Woodrow Wilson, *Congressional Government*, rev. ed. (New York: Meridian Books, 1956), p. 210.
41. Quoted in Bernard Asbell, *The Senate Nobody Knows* (Baltimore, Md.: The Johns Hopkins University Press, 1978).

Chapter 11 / The Presidency / pp. 284–317

1. Thomas E. Cronin, *The State of the Presidency* (Boston: Little, Brown, 1980).
2. Louis W. Koenig, *The Chief Executive*, 3rd. ed. (New York: Harcourt Brace Jovanovich, 1975).
3. Michael Nelson, "Evaluating the Presidency," in *The Presidency and the Political System*, ed. Michael Nelson (Washington, D.C.: Congressional Quarterly Press, 1984), pp. 5–28.
4. Quoted in Koenig, *The Chief Executive*, p. 8.
5. Quoted in Edward S. Corwin, *The President: Office and Powers* (New York: New York University Press, 1957), p. 22.
6. Paul F. Boller Jr., *Presidential Anecdotes* (New York: Penguin Books, 1981), p. 86.
7. Nelson, "Evaluating the Presidency," pp. 5–28.
8. Marcus Cunliffe, "A Defective Institution?" *Commentary* (February 1968), 28.
9. Arthur M. Schlesinger, *The Imperial Presidency* (Boston: Houghton Mifflin, 1973).
10. Thomas Franck, ed., *The Tethered Presidency* (New York: New York University Press, 1981).
11. Charles Funderburk, *Presidents and Politics: The Limits of Power*

(Monterey, Calif.: Brooks/Cole, 1982), p. 7.

12. Michael Novak, *Choosing Our King* (New York: Macmillan, 1974).

13. Mary Klein, ed., *Viewpoints on the Presidency: The Power and the Glory* (Minneapolis: Winston Press, 1974), pp. 18–19.

14. *Humphrey's Executor v. United States* (295 U.S. 602, 1935).

15. Quoted in Louis Fisher, *The Politics of Shared Power: Congress and the Executive* (Washington: Congressional Quarterly Press, 1981), p. 9.

16. Richard M. Pious, *The American Presidency* (Basic Books, 1979), p. 340.

17. Quoted in Robert E. Diclerico, *The American Presidency* (Englewood Cliffs, N.J.: Prentice-Hall, 1983), p. 51.

18. Corwin, *The President: Office and Powers*, p. 189.

19. Quoted in Harold M. Barger, *The Impossible Presidency: Illusions and Realities of Executive Power* (Glenview, Ill.: Scott, Foresman, 1984), p. 237.

20. Quoted in Pious, *The American Presidency*, p. 395.

21. Richard Neustadt, "The Presidency and Legislation: Planning the President's Program," *The American Political Science Review*, 49 (1955), 1015.

22. Clinton Rossiter *The American Presidency* (New York: Harcourt, Brace, 1960).

23. For a complete account of the growth of presidential staffing see Stephen Hess, *Organizing the Presidency* (Washington, D.C.: The Brookings Institution, 1976).

24. Cronin, *The State of the Presidency*, pp. 276–278.

25. For the history of such clearance procedures, see Richard E. Neustadt, "Presidency and Legislation: the Growth of Central Clearance," *American Political Science Review*, 48 (1954), 150–158.

26. George Edwards and Stephen Wayne, *Presidential Leadership: Politics and Policy Making* (New York: St. Martin's, 1985), p. 189.

27. Barbara Hinckley, *Problems of the Presidency: A Text with Readings* (Glenview, Ill.: Scott, Foresman, 1985), p. 101.

28. Quoted in Hinckley, *Problems of the Presidency*, p. 105.

29. Quoted in Richard E. Neustadt, *Presidential Power: The Politics of Leadership from FDR to Carter* (New York: John Wiley, 1980), p. 9.

30. Neustadt, *Presidential Power*, chapter 3.

31. Quoted in Doris Kearnes, *Lyndon Johnson and the American Dream* (New York: Harper and Row, 1976), p. 226.

32. Quoted in Pious, *The American Presidency*, p. 189.

33. George Edwards, *Presidential Influence in Congress* (San Francisco: W. H. Freeman, 1980), p. 89.

34. Neustadt, *Presidential Power*, p. 67.

35. For a discussion of the strategy of going public, see Samuel Kernell, *Going Public: New Strategies of Presidential Leadership* (Washington, D.C.: Congressional Quarterly Press, 1986).

Chapter 12 / Bureaucracy / pp. 318–349

1. See John J. Fialka, "Battle of the Barons," in *The Culture of Bureaucracy*, eds. Charles Peters and Michael Nelson (New York: Holt, Rinehart and Winston, 1979), pp. 88–90.

2. J. Peter Grace, *War on Waste: President's Private Sector Survey on Cost Control* (New York: Macmillan, 1984), p. 3.

3. The rest were employed in the legislative (approximately 39,000) and judicial (16,000) branches. Civilian employment does not include figures from the Central Intelligence Agency and other intelligence-gathering organizations. All figures are from the *Statistical Abstract of the United States*, an annual publication of the U.S. Bureau of the Census that can be found at any public library.

4. See the "Profile of the 'Typical' Federal Employee," in *Federal Civilian Workforce Statistics: Employment and Trends as of May 1986*, U.S. Office of Personnel Management (Washington, D.C.: U.S. Government Printing Office, 1986), Section II.

5. Herbert Kaufman, *Red Tape: Its Origins, Uses, and Abuses* (Washington, D.C.: The Brookings Institution, 1977), 2.

6. See David A. Stockman, *The Triumph of Politics: How the Reagan Revolution Failed* (New York: Harper and Row, 1986).

7. Norton E. Long, "Power and Administration," *Public Administration Review*, 9 (Autumn 1949), 257–264.

8. See Francis E. Rourke, *Bureaucracy, Politics, and Public Policy*, 3rd ed. (Boston: Little, Brown, 1984).

9. Stockman, *The Triumph of Politics*, pp. 278, 296–297.

10. See Richard P. Nathan, *The Administrative Presidency* (New York: John Wiley, 1983), pp. 74–76.

11. Quoted in James L. Sunquist, *The Decline and Resurgence of Congress* (Washington, D.C.: The Brookings Institution, 1981), p. 320.

12. See Alfred A. Marcus, *Promise and Performance: Choosing and Implementing an Environmental Policy* (Westport, Conn.: Greenwood Press, 1980).

13. See Taylor Branch, "Courage Without Esteem: Profiles in Whistle-Blowing," in *The Culture of Bureaucracy*, pp. 217–238.

14. See A. Lee Fritschler, *Smoking and Politics: Policymaking and the Federal Bureaucracy*, 3rd ed. (Englewood Cliffs, N.J.: Prentice-Hall, 1983).

15. Hugh Heclo, "Issue Networks and the Executive Establishment," in *The New American Political System*, ed. Anthony King (Washington, D.C.: American

Enterprise Institute for Public Policy Research, 1978), ch. 3.
16. See Norman J. Vig and Michael E. Kraft, eds., *Environmental Policy in the 1980s* (Washington, D.C.: CQ Press, 1984).

Chapter 13 / Courts, Judges, and the Law / pp. 350–381

1. Jethrow K. Lieberman, *The Litigious Society* (New York: Basic Books, 1981).
2. Richard J. Richardson and Kenneth N. Vines, *The Politics of Federal Courts: Lower Courts in the United States* (Boston: Little, Brown, 1970).
3. Quoted in Howard Ball, *Courts and Politics: The Federal Judicial System* (Englewood Cliffs, N.J.: Prentice-Hall, 1980), p. 176.
4. "CQ on the Floor," *Congressional Quarterly Weekly Report*, March 20, 1970, p. 776.
5. Quoted in Stephen Wasby, *The Supreme Court in the Federal Judicial System*, 2d ed. (New York: Holt, Rinehart and Winston, 1984), p. 89.
6. "The Supreme Court: Justice and the Law," Washington, D.C.: Congressional Quarterly, 1981, p. 163.
7. John Schmidauser, *Judges and Justices: The Federal Appellate Judiciary* (Boston: Little, Brown, 1979), p. 96.
8. Sheldon Goldman and Thomas P. Jahnige, *The Federal Courts as a Political System* (New York: Harper and Row, 1985), p. 250.
9. See Stephen Wasby, *The Supreme Court in the Federal System* (New York: Holt, Rinehart and Winston, 1984), pp. 72–74.
10. Henry J. Abraham, *The Judicial Process* (New York: Oxford University Press, 1980), p. 203.
11. Doris Marie Provine, *Case Selection in the United States Supreme Court* (Chicago: University of Chicago Press, 1980).
12. Bob Woodward and Scott Armstrong, *The Brethren: Inside the Supreme Court* (New York: Avon Books, 1979), p. 490.
13. William J. Brennan, "Inside View of the High Court," *New York Times* Magazine, October 6, 1963, p. 22.
14. See Jack Peltason, *Fifty-eight Lonely Men: Southern Federal Judges and School Desegregation* (Urbana: University of Illinois Press, 1971)
15. Cited in David M. O'Brien, *Storm Center: The Supreme Court in American Politics* (New York: Norton, 1986), p. 312.

Chapter 14 / Domestic Policy and Policy Making / pp. 382–411

1. Robert E. Taylor, "Coal Firms Start to Cooperate with Small-Mine Cleanup Bid," *Wall Street Journal,* December 30, 1986, p. 17; also Ben A. Franklin, "Mine Law: The Scars and Gains," *The New York Times,* June 7, 1987, p. 13.
2. These figures come from Gallup Polls taken between January 1983 and January 1986.
3. See *Washington Post National Weekly Edition,* July 8, 1985, p. 38.
4. See Charles O. Jones, *An Introduction to the Study of Public Policy,* 2nd ed. (North Scituate, Mass.: Duxbury Press, 1977); also Charles S. Bullock III, James E. Anderson, and David W. Brady, *Public Policy in the Eighties* (Monterey, Calif.: Brooks/Cole, 1983), especially ch. 1.
5. See Steven V. Roberts, "AIDS Alert: Politicians Awaken to the Threat of a Global Epidemic," *The New York Times,* June 7, 1987, Section 4, p. 1.
6. See Matthew A. Crenson, *The Un-Politics of Air Pollution: A Study of Non-Decisionmaking in the Cities* (Baltimore, Md.: Johns Hopkins University Press, 1971), pp. 1–2.
7. See Bob Woodward and Scott Armstrong, *The Brethren: Inside The Supreme Court* (New York: Simon and Schuster, 1979).
8. See John M. Logsdon, *The Decision to Go to the Moon: Project Apollo and the National Interest* (Chicago, Ill.: University of Chicago Press, 1970).
9. See I.M. Destler, *American Trade Politics: System Under Stress* (Washington, D.C.: Institute for International Economics, 1986).
10. See Louis M. Kohlmeier Jr., *The Regulators: Watchdog Agencies and the Public Interest* (New York: Harper and Row, 1969).
11. See George C. Eads and Michael Fix, eds., *The Reagan Regulatory Strategy: An Assessment* (Washington, D.C.: The Urban Institute, 1984); also Roger C. Noll and Bruce M. Owen, eds., *The Political Economy of Deregulation: Interest Groups and the Regulatory Process* (Washington, D.C.: American Enterprise Institute for Public Policy Research, 1983).
12. Susan J. Tolchin and Martin Tolchin, *Dismantling America: The Rush to Deregulate* (Boston, Mass.: Houghton Mifflin Company, 1983).
13. Arthur M. Okun, *The Political Economy of Prosperity* (Washington, D.C.: Norton, 1970), p. 37; also see Herbert Stein, *Presidential Economics: The Making of Economic Policy From Roosevelt to Reagan and Beyond,* rev. ed. (New York: Simon and Schuster, 1985).
14. See Alan S. Blinder, *Economic Policy and the Great Stagflation,* student ed. (New York: Academic Press, 1981).
15. See Sidney Fine, *Laissez Faire and the General-Welfare State: A Study in Conflict in American Thought, 1865–1901* (Ann Arbor, Mich.: Ann Arbor Paperbacks, 1969), pp. 22–23, 360–361; also see Clarke A. Chambers, *Seedtime of Reform: American Social Service and Social Action, 1918–1933* (Ann Arbor, Mich.: Ann Arbor Paperbacks, 1963), and Robert Morris, *Social Policy of the*

American Welfare State: An Introduction to Policy Analysis, 2nd ed. (New York: Longman, 1985).

16. Patterson, *America's Struggle Against Poverty, 1900–1980* (Cambridge, Mass.: Harvard University Press, 1981), pp. 57–59.
17. Sar A. Levitan, *Programs in Aid of the Poor,* 5th ed. (Baltimore, Md.: Johns Hopkins University Press, 1985), pp. 41–42.
18. Levitan, *Programs in Aid of the Poor,* pp. 77–78; also see James E. Anderson, David W. Brady, and Charles Bullock III, *Public Policy and Politics in America* (North Scituate, Mass.: Duxbury Press, 1978), pp. 144–146.
19. Patterson, *America's Struggle Against Poverty,* pp. 67–71; also Levitan, *Programs in Aid of the Poor,* pp. 31–39.
20. Levitan, *Programs in Aid of the Poor,* pp. 39–41.
21. See Frank J. Thompson, *Health Policy and the Bureaucracy: Politics and Implementation* (Cambridge, Mass.: The MIT Press, 1981), pp. 111–115; also see Levitan, *Programs in Aid of the Poor,* pp. 63–64.
22. For a general survey of social insurance programs, see Arnold J. Heidenheimer, Hugh Heclo, and Carolyn Teich Adams, *Comparative Public Policy: The Politics of Social Choice in Europe and America,* 2nd ed. (New York: St. Martin's Press, 1983), ch. 7.
23. Thompson, *Health Policy and the Bureaucracy,* pp. 155–160; also Levitan, *Programs in Aid of the Poor,* pp. 62–63.
24. On the politics of dealing with that crisis, see Paul Light, *Artful Work: The Politics of Social Security Reform* (New York: Random House, 1985).
25. Much of the discussion in this section relies on Kenneth J. Meier, *Regulation: Politics, Bureaucracy, and Economics* (New York: St. Martin's Press, 1985).
26. See George Gilder, *Wealth and Poverty* (New York: Basic Books,

1981); also Charles Murray, *Losing Ground: American Social Policy, 1950–1980* (New York: Basic Books, 1984).
27. Murray L. Weidenbaum, *Business, Government, and the Public,* 2nd ed. (Englewood Cliffs, N.J.: Prentice-Hall, 1981), p. 27.
28. See Michael Pertschuk, *Revolt Against Regulation: The Rise and Pause of the Consumer Movement* (Berkeley, Calif.: University of California Press, 1982); also Barry Bluestone and Bennett Harrison, *The Deindustrialization of America: Plant Closing, Community Abandonment, and the Dismantling of Basic Industry* (New York: Basic Books, 1982).

Chapter 15 / Foreign and Defense Policy / pp. 412–439

1. Henry Kissinger, *Years of Upheaval* (Boston Little, Brown, 1982), p. 82.
2. See John E. Rielly, ed., *American Public Opinion and U.S. Foreign Policy, 1983* (Chicago, Ill.: The Chicago Council on Foreign Relations, 1983).
3. William Schneider, "Wanted: A Low-Risk Foreign Policy," *National Journal* (April 19, 1986), 962–963.
4. See "Opinion Roundup: The Public Assesses The Reagan Record on Foreign Policy," *Public Opinion* (Summer 1986), 27.
5. The policy of containment is most closely associated with George F. Kennan, an American diplomat and scholar who was very influential in shaping United States strategies during the Cold War. See his *American Diplomacy, 1900–1950* (New York: Mentor Books, 1951).
6. See Stephen E. Ambrose, *Rise to Globalism: American Foreign Policy since 1938* (Baltimore: Penguin Books, 1971), pp. 174–175.
7. See Richard Rosecrance, *The Rise of the Trading State: Commerce and Conquest in the Modern World* (New York: Basic Books,

1986); also Roy Hofheinz Jr. and Kent E. Calder, *The Eastasia Edge* (New York: Basic Books, 1982).
8. Kissinger, *Years of Upheaval,* pp. 235–246, 339.
9. See Congressional Quarterly, *U.S. Foreign Policy: The Reagan Imprint* (Washington, D.C.: Congressional Quarterly, 1986).
10. See Edward S. Corwin, *The President: Office and Powers, 1787–1857* (New York: New York University Press, 1957), ch. 5.
11. See David D. Newsom, "The Executive Branch in Foreign Policy," in *The President, The Congress, and Foreign Policy,* ed. Edmund S. Muskie, Kenneth Rush, and Kenneth W. Thompson (Lanham, Md.: The University Press of America, 1986), pp. 113–115.
12. See Harold H. Saunders, "The Middle East, 1973–84: Hidden Agendas," in *The President, The Congress, and Foreign Policy,* ed. Muskie et al., ch. 7.
13. John Spanier and Eric M. Uslaner, *How American Foreign Policy Is Made* (New York: Praeger, 1974), p. 92.
14. See Gabriel A. Almond, *The American People and Foreign Policy* (New York: Praeger, 1960).
15. See Theodore J. Lowi, *The Personal President: Power Invested, Promise Unfulfilled* (Ithaca, N.Y.: Cornell University Press, 1985), pp. 170–173.
16. The mood theory concept was originally articulated by Frank L. Klingberg. See Jack E. Holmes, *The Mood/Interest Theory of American Foreign Policy* (Lexington, Ky.: The University Press of Kentucky, 1985).
17. Bruce Russett and Donald R. DeLuca, " 'Don't Tread on Me,' Public Opinion and Foreign Policy in the Eighties," *Political Science Quarterly,* 96, No. 3 (Fall 1981), 381–387; also Congressional Quarterly, *U.S. Foreign Policy: The Reagan Imprint.*
18. In his 1985 State of the Union

address, Reagan equated this aid with defense rather than diplomacy. He argued that "dollar for dollar, our security assistance contributes as much to global security as our own defense budget." See Congressional Quarterly, *U.S. Foreign Policy: The Reagan Imprint*.

19. John Tower et al., *The Tower Commission Report: The Full Text of the President's Special Review Board* (New York: Bantam/Times Books, 1987), p. 15.

20. Quoted in Christopher A. Kojm, *The ABCs of Defense: America's Military in the 1980s* (New York: The Foreign Policy Association, 1981), p. 3.

Index to References

Abraham, Henry J., Ch. 13 n. 10
Abramson, Paul R., Ch. 5 n. 33, 47;
  Ch. 7 n. 17, 28, 29
Adams, Carolyn Teich, Ch. 14 n. 22
Ahern, David, Ch. 5 n. 10
Aldrich, John H., Ch. 5 n. 33; Ch. 7
  n. 17, 28, 29
Alexander, Herbert E., Ch. 8 n. 23
Almond, Gabriel A., Ch. 15 n. 14
Ambrose, Stephen E., Ch. 15 n. 6
Anderson, James E., Ch. 14 n. 4
Armstrong, Scott, Ch. 13 n. 12; Ch.
  14 n. 7
Asbell, Bernard, Ch. 10 n. 41

Bagehot, Walter, Ch. 2 n. 10
Ball, Howard, Ch. 13 n. 3
Barger, Harold M., Ch. 11 n. 19
Baxter, Sandra, Ch. 5 n. 45
Berelson, Bernard, Ch. 9 n. 19
Berkman, Ronald, Ch. 9 n. 5, 7
Berns, Walter, Ch. 2 n. 15
Berry, Jeffrey M., Ch. 8 n. 4, 8, 10,
  16, 34
Black, Gordon, Ch. 7 n. 6
Black, Merle, Ch. 6 n. 2
Blinder, Alan S., Ch. 14 n. 14
Bluestone, Barry, Ch. 14 n. 28
Bogart, Leo, Ch. 5 n. 12
Boller, Paul F., Ch. 10 n. 27; Ch. 11
  n. 6
Bowman, Ann O'M., Ch. 3 n. 22,
  23
Brady, David W., Ch. 14 n. 4
Branch, Taylor, Ch. 12 n. 13
Brandeis, Louis, Ch. 4 n. 46
Brennan, William J., Ch. 13 n. 13
Brill, Alida, Ch. 5 n. 9

Broder, David S., Ch. 5 n. 21
Brody, Richard A., Ch. 7 n. 28
Brown, Lawrence D., Ch. 3 n. 15
Bullock, Charles S., III, Ch. 14 n. 4
Burnham, Walter Dean, Ch. 6 n. 11,
  17, 20, 28
Burns, James MacGregor, Ch. 6 n.
  15, 19

Caban, Luis, Ch. 5 n. 48
Calder, Kent E., Ch. 15 n. 7
Campbell, Bruce, Ch. 7 n. 22, 23
Campbell, Karlyn Kohrs, Ch. 9 n. 9,
  10
Chambers, Clarke A., Ch. 14 n. 15
Chambers, William N., Ch. 6 n. 17
Chute, Marchette, Ch. 7 n. 22
Cigler, Allan J., Ch. 8 n. 4, 13, 14,
  31, 33
Claggett, William H., Ch. 5 n. 47
Clines, Francis X., Ch. 8 n. 1
Clymer, Adam, Ch. 5 n. 35; Ch. 7
  n. 35
Conrad, Roan, Ch. 9 n. 4
Conway, M. Margaret, Ch. 5 n. 10,
  40, 45; Ch. 6 n. 6, 10, 26, 30; Ch.
  7 n. 19; Ch. 8 n. 5, 32
Cooper, Joseph, Ch. 10 n. 26
Corwin, Edward S., Ch. 11 n. 5, 18;
  Ch. 15 n. 10
Cover, Albert D., Ch. 10 n. 6
Crenson, Matthew A., Ch. 14 n. 6
Cronin, Thomas E., Ch. 11 n. 1,
  24
Crotty, William, Ch. 6 n. 2, 7, 27,
  28; Ch. 7 n. 9
Crouse, Timothy, Ch. 9 n. 24
Cunliffe, Marcus, Ch. 11 n. 8

Davidson, Roger H., Ch. 10 n. 4,
  16, 20, 32, 35, 36
Davis, S. Rufus, Ch. 3 n. 8
Deering, Christopher J., Ch. 10 n.
  28
DeLuca, Donald R., Ch. 15 n. 17
Dempsey, Glenn R., Ch. 9 n. 21
Destler, I.M., Ch. 14 n. 9
Diamond, Martin, Ch. 2 n. 1, 16
Diclerico, Robert E., Ch. 11 n. 17
Dionne, E.J., Jr., Ch. 5 n. 20
Dodd, Lawrence C., Ch. 10 n. 26,
  34
Drew, Elizabeth, Ch. 8 n. 23
Dubnick, Mel, Ch. 3 n. 6
Duverger, Maurice, Ch. 6 n. 22

Eads, George C., Ch. 14 n. 11
Edwards, George, Ch. 11 n. 26, 33

Farah, Barbara, Ch. 7 n. 11
Feigert, Frank B., Ch. 6 n. 6, 10, 26,
  30; Ch. 8 n. 5, 32
Feldbaum, Eleanor, Ch. 5 n. 10
Fenno, Richard F., Jr., Ch. 10 n. 3,
  14, 23, 30
Ferber, Mark F., Ch. 10 n. 33
Fialka, John J., Ch. 12 n. 1
Fine, Sidney, Ch. 14 n. 15
Fiorina, Morris P., Ch. 3 n. 20; Ch.
  7 n. 34; Ch. 10 n. 10, 22
Fishel, Jeff, Ch. 6 n. 2
Fisher, Louis, Ch. 11 n. 15
Fix, Michael, Ch. 14 n. 11
Flanigan, William H., Ch. 6 n. 1
Formisano, Robert P., Ch. 6 n. 18
Fossett, James W., Ch. 3 n. 15
Fowler, Linda, Ch. 7 n. 6

Index

Illustration Credits (continued from copyright page)

Chapter 3: **Opener, page 42,** © Jerry Howard 1981/Positive Images; **48,** © Marty Brown/ Gamma-Liaison; **49,** © Zigy Kaluzny/Gamma Liaison; **53,** AP/Wide World Photos; **57,** AP/Wide World Photos; **63,** AP/Wide World Photos.

Chapter 4: **Opener, page 68,** AP/Wide World Photos; **71,** Alan Tannenbaum/Sygma; **82,** UPI/Bettmann Newsphotos; **85,** © Gilles Peress/Magnum Photos; , **86,** Brown Brothers; **88,** AP/ Wide World Photos; **94,** © Bruce Davidson/Magnum Photos; **95,** Paul Conklin.

Chapter 5: **Opener, page 104,** © Hazel Hankin/Stock, Boston; **107,** Paul Conklin; **111,** © Mark Reinstein/Click/Chicago; **116,** Susan May Tell/Sygma; **123,** © Mark Reinstein 1986/Click/ Chicago.

Chapter 6: **Opener, page 132,** Patricia Ann Schwab/Stock, Boston; **136,** © Mark Reinstein/ Click/Chicago; **139,** Paul Conklin; **147,** UPI/Bettmann Newsphotos; **157,** UPI/Bettmann Newsphotos; **158,** R. Taylor/Sygma.

Chapter 7: **Opener, page 162,** Michael Hayman/Stock, Boston; **166,** © Halstead/Gamma Liaison; **167,** R. Taylor/Sygma; **169,** AP/Wide World Photos; **171,** O. Franken/Sygma; **186,** Jean-Louis Atlan/Sygma; **189,** AP/Wide World Photos.

Chapter 8: **Opener, page 196,** Jim Moore/Gamma Liaison; **202,** © Lionel Delevingne/Stock, Boston; **205,** Diana Walker/Gamma Liaison; **207,** José R. Lopez/NYT Pictures; **215,** Paul Conklin; **220,** UPI/Bettmann Newsphotos; **223,** AP/Wide World Photos.

Chapter 9: **Opener, page 226,** Paul Conklin; **231,** UPI/Bettmann Newsphotos; **235,** AP/Wide World Photos (reprinted with permission of the *Miami Herald*); **240,** © 1987/Click/Chicago; **241,** © Eli Reed/Magnum Photos; **245,** AP/Wide World Photos; **248,** AP/Wide World Photos.

Chapter 10: **Opener, page 252,** Mike Mazzaschi/Stock, Boston; **255,** AP/Wide World Photos; **259,** © Michael Evans/Sygma; **260,** courtesy of Rare Books and Manuscripts Division, The New York Public Library, Astor, Lenox and Tilden Foundations; **264,** AP/Wide World Photos; **268,** © J. L. Atlan/Sygma; **272,** Paul Conklin; **279,** Paul Conklin. Source for Figure 10.1, page 275: K, Janda, J. Berry, and J. Goldman, *The Challenge of Democracy* (Boston: Houghton Mifflin, 1987), page 352. Copyright © 1987 by Houghton Mifflin Company. Used by permission.

Chapter 11: **Opener, page 284,** Llewellyn/Uniphoto; **287,** The Bettmann Archive; **292,** AP/ Wide World Photos; **293,** © Gilles Peress/Magnum Photos; **296,** UPI/Bettmann Newsphotos; **301,** UPI/Bettmann Newsphotos; **306,** AP/Wide World Photos; **311,** © David Hume Kennerly 1978/Contact Press Images.

Chapter 12: **Opener, page 318,** © Daemmrich/Uniphoto; **327,** AP/Wide World Photos; **335,** AP/Wide World Photos; **339,** UPI/Bettmann Newsphotos; **344,** © Steiner/Sygma; **346,** © O. Franken/Sygma.

Chapter 13: **Opener, page 350,** © Tommy Noonan/Uniphoto; **353,** AP/Wide World Photos; **363,** AP/Wide World Photos; **366,** AP/Wide World Photos; **370,** Supreme Court Historical Society; **371,** José R. Lopez/NYT Pictures; **374,** AP/Wide World Photos.

Chapter 14: **Opener, page 382,** © Bryce Flynn/Stock, Boston; **387,** © Paul S. Howell/Gamma Liaison; **391,** AP/Wide World Photos; **400,** AP/Wide World Photos; **403,** AP/Wide World Photos; **407,** AP/Wide World Photos.

Chapter 15: **Opener, page 412,** © 1986 Chris Cross/Uniphoto; **418,** Brown Brothers; **421,** McCullin/Magnum; **431,** Brad Markel/Gamma Liaison; **428,** J. L. Atlan/Sygma; **431,** Brad Markel/ Gamma Liaison.